Digital Technologies in Designing and Technology Education Tasks

MATHEMATICS EDUCATION IN THE DIGITAL ERA
Volume 8

More information about this series at http://www.springer.com/series/10170

Allen Leung · Anna Baccaglini-Frank
Editors

Digital Technologies in Designing Mathematics Education Tasks

Potential and Pitfalls

 Springer

Editors
Allen Leung
Department of Education Studies
Hong Kong Baptist University
Kowloon Tong
Hong Kong SAR
China

Anna Baccaglini-Frank
Department of Mathematics
"G. Castelnuovo"
"Sapienza" University of Rome
Rome
Italy

ISSN 2211-8136   ISSN 2211-8144   (electronic)
Mathematics Education in the Digital Era
ISBN 978-3-319-82820-6   ISBN 978-3-319-43423-0   (eBook)
DOI 10.1007/978-3-319-43423-0

Contents

Introduction

This book is about the role and potential of using digital technology in designing teaching and learning tasks in the mathematics classroom. Digital technology has opened up different new educational spaces for the mathematics classroom in the past few decades and, as technology is constantly evolving, novel ideas and approaches are brewing to enrich these spaces with diverse didactical flavors. A key issue is always how technology can, or cannot, play epistemic and pedagogic roles in the mathematics classroom. The main purpose of this book is to explore mathematics task design when digital technology is part of the teaching and learning environment. What features of the technology used can be capitalized upon to design tasks that transform learners' experiential knowledge, gained from using the technology, into conceptual mathematical knowledge? When do digital environments actually bring an essential (educationally speaking) new dimension to classroom activities? What are some pragmatic and semiotic values of the technology used? These are some of the concerns addressed in the book by expert scholars in this area of research in mathematics education.

Task Design in Mathematics Education and the Growing Interest for Task Design with Digital Technology

More than a decade ago Sierpinska (2003) identified task design as a core research area in mathematics education. She commented that research reports rarely gave sufficient details about tasks for them to be used by someone else in the same way. At the time, few studies justified task choice or identified what features of a task were essential and what features were irrelevant. A growing body of research grounded within different theories, such as the Adaptive Control of Thought learning theory (e.g., Anderson and Schunn 2000), the Theory of Variation applied to teaching and learning (e.g., Runesson 2005), or learning from worked-out examples (e.g., Renkl 2005), suggested that seemingly minor differences in tasks can have significant effects on learning. A growing scientific interest in task design is shown by the hosting, in 2008, of a Topic Study Group (TSG) by the International Congress on Mathematics Education (ICME) entitled *Research and development in task design and analysis* (http://tsg.icme11.org/tsg/show/35) where participants were given the opportunity to experience various tasks, and compare and critique design principles. A number of issues started to emerge. For example, Schoenfeld (2009) advised on the utility of having more communication between designers and researchers, in order to bridge educational research and design. A volume of the *Handbook of Mathematics Teacher Education* was devoted to issues regarding the relationship between teacher education and task design (Tirosh and Wood 2009). A particular issue treated in this context is the role and use of tasks for teacher education purposes, which has recently received particular attention also in a triple special issue of the *Journal of Mathematics Teacher Education* (volume 10, 46) edited by Mason, Watson and Zaslavsky, and in a book edited by Zaslavsky and Sullivan (2011).

The interest in task design in mathematics education has grown more and more, culminating in specific conferences entirely devoted to the topic, including ICMI Study 22. This study "was initiated to produce an up-to-date summary of relevant research about task design in mathematics education and to develop new insights and new areas of relevant knowledge and study." (Watson and Ohtani 2015, p. 3) In the study, task design was described as follows.

> The design and use of tasks for pedagogic purposes is at the core of mathematics education (Artigue and Perrin-Glorian 1991). Tasks generate activity which affords opportunity to encounter mathematical concepts, ideas, strategies, and also to use and develop mathematical thinking and modes of enquiry. Teaching includes the selection, modification, design, sequencing, installation, observation and evaluation of tasks. This work is often undertaken by using a textbook and/or other resources designed by outsiders. (Margolinas 2013, p. 12)

Growing attention has been devoted to tasks that specifically make use of digital technology in the mathematics classroom, since the use of tools and manipulatives in the classroom has been a common pedagogical practice. Drjvers (2012) argued that there are three key factors decisive and crucial to promote or hinder the successful integration of digital technology in mathematics education: the role of the teacher, the educational context, and design. Design is intended not only as the design of the digital technology involved but also as the design of corresponding tasks and activities, and as the design of lessons and teaching in general. Moreover, the scholar argues that emphasis should also be put on the priority of pedagogical and didactical considerations as main guidelines and design heuristics over technology's limitations and properties related to its affordances and constraints.

The design of tasks that make use of digital technology was also discussed in one of the theme chapters in the ICMI Study 22 book (Watson and Ohtani 2015), *Designing Mathematics Tasks: The Role of Tools*, where a tool-based task in the mathematics classroom was described as follows.

Tools are broadly interpreted as physical or virtual artifacts that have potential to enhance mathematical understanding. A *tool-based task* is seen as a teacher/researcher design aiming to be a thing to do or act on in order for students to activate an interactive tool-based environment where teacher, students, and resources mutually enrich each other in producing mathematical experiences. In this connection, this type of task design rests heavily on a complex relationship between tool mediation, teaching and learning, and mathematical knowledge. (Leung and Bolite-Frant 2015, p. 192)

In that chapter, five tool-based mathematics task design heuristics are proposed to serve as guiding posts to conceptualize mathematics task design in which physical concrete and/or digital tools play central roles in pedagogical activities. This book builds on the existing research on task design in the context of digital technology, exploring some of its potential and pitfalls.

Roles and Potential of Digital Technology in Mathematics Education

This book explores theories and practices of designing mathematics education tasks within what we will call *Dynamic and Interactive Mathematics Learning Environments (DIMLEs)*, coined by Karadag et al. (2011). Rather than showing "how" tasks can be designed using a chosen digital tool, the emphasis of the discussion is on the role and potential of digital pedagogical environments in designing and implementing tasks for the mathematics classroom. Design is seen as the creation of a plan to construct something. It usually starts with some assumptions from which a plan is devised or conjured to achieve some given intended purposes. Different pedagogical or theoretical orientations (the assumptions) and different choices of tools frame pedagogical task design differently. A theme of great interest, which can be studied by contrasting and comparing such framing choices, and which is explored within the chapters of this book, is how different types of task design converge or diverge with respect to the nature and acquisition of mathematical knowledge.

If a *role* is considered a function assumed or a part played by a person or thing in a particular situation, and *potential* considered what is possible in terms of gaining knowledge, the role played by a DIMLE in the mathematics classroom can be multifaceted, and multiple tools can be orchestrated to foster mathematical experiences for the learners. The role of the DIMLE and of tools within it depends on how tasks involving their use are designed and implemented. Meaningful tasks in a DIMLE should capitalize on the affordances, encouraging learners to engage in purposeful and, possibly, non-prescriptive mathematical activities. A challenge in digital task design is to conceive tasks that can extend and amplify pedagogical features present in non-digital environments. For example, an affordance of many DIMLEs is to provide different types of feedback; this can be exploited to establish connections or forms of communication between the learners, the teachers and mathematical knowledge. The potential of a DIMLE can be interpreted with respect to different pedagogical intentions: a *procedural pedagogical intention* that focuses on routine practices for using certain features of the DIMLE, or on establishing algorithmic procedures to generate (desired) results; a *conceptual pedagogical intention* that enables learners to engage in exploring and conceptualizing mathematics. A DIMLE designed with potential to bring about specific the mathematical knowledge may still fail to do so, because whether a DIMLE provides potential or pitfalls for the learners is also very closely related to choices made by the teacher. Indeed, the teacher's pedagogical orientation and mathematical beliefs are key factors in determining how s/he designs and implements tasks developed within the DIMLE. Knowledge/meaning gaps may exist between digital-based mathematical discourses and the intended mathematical content. Potential can become a pitfall or vice versa depending on the ways in which the teacher handles this gap. Inappropriate expectations of the teacher pertaining to a digital tool's potential may turn the digital tool into a pitfall for the learners. Thus, the role and potential of using digital technologies in designing mathematics education tasks are intertwined in a dynamic epistemic complex where mathematical knowledge, pedagogy, and skills are meshed together.

This book, focusing on task design within DIMLEs, expands and extends the discussion of the task design theme *Tools and Representations* in ICMI Study 22 (Margolinas 2013; Watson and Ohtani 2015). In the next section, an overview of the structure and the chapters of the book are presented to summarize how the above ideas are threaded together.

Specific Contents of the Book

The chapters in this book explore task design in DIMLEs from multiple perspectives. The authors of each chapter, who are expert scholars in this area of research in mathematics education, employ diverse theoretical dispositions and DIMLEs with different degrees of sophistication in expounding their ideas. The purpose of this book is not to compare and say which DIMLEs are "more conducive" to mathematical learning, whatever that might mean. Whether a (digital) tool is pedagogically significant depends on how the tool is being designed for use in the classroom and how the teachers and students can or cannot actually use it to create meaningful mathematical discourses. The focus of the book is mainly on searching for and ascertaining viable digital tool-based task design approaches for students to engage meaningfully in mathematical experiences. Concerns for the interested readers may lie in the pitfall or potential of tool-based pedagogy and in the "ontological connection" between tools and mathematical knowledge. These issues are addressed, enriching current research literature on task design and on the use of technology in mathematics education, and outlining new research scenarios. The book is divided into four parts that, more specifically, address: (1) theories used to frame and guide digital task design in general; (2) specific kinds of tasks designed for a same type of DIMLE, dynamic geometry environments; (3) design features of five specific

DIMLEs, emphasizing how these features come into play in tasks designed within them; (4) additional issues in digital task design, such as how "variation" principles can be integrated into a digital intervention, how the notions of "feedback" and "discrepancy" can help gain insight into potential and pitfalls of using virtual realizations of physical artifacts, how task design can authentically reflect on the role of digital technologies in solving problems situated in the work place or in daily life.

Part I is mainly about theories. Chapter "Exploring Techno-Pedagogic Task Design in the Mathematics Classroom" explores the idea of techno-pedagogic design in the mathematics classroom. The concept of Mathematics Digital Boundary Object is introduced to stress the role and function of digital technology as a translator and discourse generator between different participants in the mathematics classroom. Task design follows an epistemic nested sequence (Leung 2011) where students' routine algorithmic actions progressively evolve into tool-based situated discourses. The teacher's knowledge plays a critical role in anticipating knowledge/meaning gaps between digital-based mathematical discourses and the intended mathematical content. Chapter "Revisiting Theory for the Design of Tasks: Special Considerations for Digital Environments" discusses Brousseau's notions of 'modes of production' to describe the different types of dialectic interactions between students and the milieu, and of 'ontogenic, didactical and epistemological obstacles' to guide the design of tasks in digital environments (Brousseau 1997). The distinction between 'actual reality' and 'virtual reality' is expounded using Noss, Healy and Hoyles' (1997) terminologies 'pragmatic/empirical' and 'mathematical/systematic'. A digital graphing environment is used as a context to illustrate these theoretical constructs. Chapter "Task Design Potential of Using an Interactive Whiteboard for Implementing Inquiry-Based Learning in Mathematics" makes use of Chevallard's Anthropological Theory of Didactic (Chevallard 1992) which is based on the postulate that a student learns by autonomous adaptation or confrontation in interaction with a milieu. It further frames inquiry-based learning within a milieu through three consecutive processes: mesogenesis, topogenesis, and chronogenesis (Chevallard 2011). As an example, the Interactive White Board is chosen as the milieu for the discussion. Chapter "Designing Technology that Enables Task Design" addresses the question of how technology has been designed to enable task design through interviews with four developers of DIMLEs, carried out with the aim of fostering mathematical learning. Questions ranged from more general ones concerning the purposes and challenges faced in designing the environments to more specific aspects concerning task design, such as the management of processes of instrumental genesis and how feedback is provided. Crucial design aspects of the DIMLEs to be conserved and further developed are disclosed in the interviews. Such aspects include maintaining an appropriate balance between flexibility and constraint as well as addressing issues such as the way in which the environment responds to students' actions.

Part II discusses the design of three different kinds of tasks in a particular type of DIMLE, Dynamic Geometry Environments (DGEs): tasks for geometry assessment, tasks fostering indirect argumentation in Euclidean geometry and tasks in which a real artifact is modeled. Chapter "Designing Assessment Tasks in a Dynamic Geometry Environment" explores designing assessment tasks in DGEs, taking into account how feedback provided by the DGE involves a new dynamic of action/interaction during assessment. This chapter draws on previous work on task design in DGEs (in particular by Laborde 2001) to suggest a framework for identifying and designing different types of assessment tasks according to the specific goals of the teacher. These types of tasks are exemplified using tasks designed for the iPad-based multi-touch Sketchpad Explorer. The DGE assessment tasks presented evaluate different kinds of competencies including digital tools as a main and essential component of the problem-solving process. The authors argue that in order for technology to be a valid part of formal assessment, tasks should assess not only what students know in mathematics, but also what students can do with the technology, like make and test conjectures and, more broadly, students' technological competencies. Chapter "Designing Non-constructability Tasks in a Dynamic Geometry Environment" discusses about the potential offered by specific tasks designed in a DGE leading to production of indirect arguments and proof by contradiction. The main objective is to elaborate on the potentials of designing problems of non-constructability in a DGE with respect to fostering processes of indirect argumentation. The crux of this type of task design is to elicit cognitive conflict through a visual anomaly that to be explained leads students to resort to Euclidean geometry. Using the idea of figural concept (Fischbein 1993) as a "harmony" between a figural and conceptual component, an anomaly can be thought of as a break between the two components (figural and conceptual). It may be possible to restore the harmony within the figural concept by dragging to make a certain configuration vanish or degenerate, or by re-interpreting the figure obtained, rectifying the anomaly. Chapter "The Planimeter as a Real and Virtual Instrument that Mediates an Infinitesimal Approach to Area" focuses on task design involving the digital realization of a model of a specific artifact: the planimeter. The planimeter is a professional tool used for measuring areas of flat regular or irregular shapes. In a teaching experiment, a concrete planimeter and a virtual model built through the DIMLE GeoGebra are used to mediate an infinitesimal approach to area. The planimeter virtualization is displayed to introduce new mathematical knowledge through the construction and the exploration of real situations with the employment of technological tools. The notions of semiotic mediation and didactic cycle by Bartolini Bussi and Mariotti (2008) are used as theoretical framing ingredients in the design of the planimeter tasks.

Part III introduces design features of five specific DIMLEs, providing analyses of examples of tasks designed within each of them. Chapter "Engagement with Interactive Diagrams: The Role Played by Resources and Constraints" establishes theoretical foundations of digital task design for student–textbook–teacher interactions, in particular for analyzing how the designed features of the Interactive Diagrams (IDs) function in actual interaction processes. A semiotic framework is proposed characterized by three types of IDs' functions that address a variety of learning and teaching settings: presentational, orientational, and organizational. The chapter summarizes major design decisions about resources and constraints of interactive texts according to various semiotic functions and the role of the designed constraints and resources of the IDs in processes of engagement with interactive texts. Students' engagements with different types of ID are presented to elaborate the theoretical discussion. Chapter "Everybody Counts: Designing Tasks for *TouchCounts*" introduces the open-ended multi-touch app called Touch Counts (Sinclair and Jackiw 2011) which provides unconventional engagement with the introductory concept of a number and number operations for young children. This chapter describes a series of tasks that have been specifically designed to take advantage of the affordances of TouchCounts. These tasks are analyzed in terms of their novel potential for supporting the development of number, as well as the different functions they draw on in terms of how children are invited to count, operate, and attend to both the ordinal and the cardinal dimensions of number. A guiding feature in the task design is to allow feedback obtained through direct manipulation to serve as evaluation feedback. The authors present and analyze a series of tasks designed and implemented for these two sub-environments in TouchCounts, one for enumerating and the other for operating. The analyses highlight the pragmatic/epistemic values of the tasks, suggesting that the pragmatic value of a task is almost always equivalent to the completion of the task itself, while the epistemic value of each task usually depends strongly on the children's execution of certain bodily actions. Chapter "Designing Innovative Learning Activities to Face Difficulties in Algebra of Dyscalculic Students: Exploiting the Functionalities of *AlNuSet*" presents the DIMLE AlNuSet (Algebra of Numerical Sets), a dynamic algebra environment, designed for students of lower and upper secondary school. Its main function is to afford semiotic multi-representations for algebraic notions such as variable, unknown, algebraic expression, equation, and solution of an equation. The task design focused upon within the chapter deals with how tasks within AlNuSet can be used to promote meaning making in students with low achievement in mathematics, or even diagnosed with Developmental Dyscalculia (DD), including adult learners. The author reports on a case study with a 26-year old DD student. This case study shows that AlNuSet tasks can indeed support the construction of algebraic notions using especially the visual non-verbal and kinaesthetic channels of access to information. Furthermore, the discussion shows how dynamicity is key in the task design, as it fosters students' construction of algebraic meanings and their perception of relations between expressions, also compensating for weak memorization skills when solving algebraic tasks. Chapter "What Can You Infer from This Example? Applications of Online, Rich-Media Tasks for Enhancing Pre-service Teachers' Knowledge of the Roles of Examples in Proving" introduces the online interactive digital platform LessonSketch. The chapter reports and elaborates on the LessonSketch design of a rich-media task "What can you infer from this example?" that addressed pre-service teachers' content and pedagogical knowledge of the status of examples in proving. The focus is on the theoretical and empirical considerations that guided the task design aimed at providing rich learning opportunities for the pre-service teachers to enhance their content and pedagogical knowledge of the interplay between examples and proving, and address some of the challenges involved in the task implementation. The task involves multiple aspects of the environment and use of data collected from actual students represented through scenarios of non-descript cartoon characters. Buchbinder and Zaslavsky's (2009) framework for describing the status of examples in proving is used as the theoretical basis for task design; moreover, the authors present an emergent framework for designing tasks in digital environments for pre-service teachers. Such framework proposes a systematic approach to combining theoretical grounds, empirically tested design features and advanced technological tools through the process of design-research with the aim of creating instructional tasks that address prospective teachers' content and pedagogical knowledge for engaging students in proving.

Part IV collects chapters that discuss a variety of issues in digital task design for mathematics education. Chapter "Supporting Variation in Task Design Through the Use of Technology" describes a digital intervention aimed at fostering algebraic expertise that was built on three principles: crises, feedback, and fading. The principles are retrospectively scrutinized through the Theory of Variation, concluding that the principles share several elements with the patterns of variation: contrast, generalization, separation, and fusion (Marton et al. 2004). The integration of these principles into a digital intervention suggests that technology has affordances with respect to task design with variation. The principles are demonstrated by discussing a sequence of tasks involving quadratic formulas designed in a DIMLE called *Digital Mathematical Environment* (DME, http://www.fi.uu.nl/dwo/en). Chapter "Feedback and Discrepancies of a Physical Toolkit and a Digital Toolkit: Opportunities and Pitfalls for Mediating the Concept of Rotational Symmetry" presents analyses of excerpts of lessons from a lesson study where tool-based tasks were designed to teach the concept of rotational symmetry in Grade 5. The instrumentational approach and the theory of semiotic mediation are used as the theoretical frameworks to analyze and compare the excerpts of a lesson using a tailor-made physical tool and of a lesson using PowerPoint (a digital tool). The discussion focuses on the opportunities and pitfalls that these two tools, given the same tasks assigned, offer and on how the tasks could have and did (or could not or did not) exploit the semiotic potential of the tool used to solve them. In particular, the notions of feedback and discrepancy are theorized and hypothesized in the context of designing and implementing tool-based mathematics tasks. Chapter "Designing for Mathematical Applications and Modelling Tasks in Technology Rich Environments" touches on the important issue of how task design can authentically reflect on the role of digital technologies in solving problems situated in the work place or in daily life. The chapter draws on data sourced from a research and development project that investigated the use of digital technologies in teaching and learning mathematical modeling and applications. Six principles for designing effective modeling tasks are identified; and the instantiation of these principles within classroom practice is illustrated through a classroom vignette. The chapter further reflects on the research needed to further develop understanding of the role of technology in designing mathematical modeling tasks. Chapter "Designing Interactive Dynamic Technology Activities to Support the Development of Conceptual Understanding" discusses how DIMLEs can foster task design for active and transformative learning to support the development of conceptual understanding in mathematics. The author argues how digital task design should follow the experiential learning cycle: concrete experience, reflective observation, abstract conceptualization, and active experimentation in order to create opportunities for students to engage in mathematical discussions. The Building Concepts software is used as a DIMLE illustrating task design rationales for different fundamental mathematical concepts such as fractions, ratios, proportional relations, expressions, and equations. Design guidelines and principles for building concepts activities are proposed and supported with a number of examples. Chapter "Tensions in the Design of Mathematical Technological Environments: Tools and Tasks for the Teaching of Linear Functions" begins by describing a longitudinal study and its theoretical framework that resulted in a rubric to inform the design of tasks that privilege the exploration of mathematical variants and invariants. This rubric is then used as a construct for the post-priori analysis of two tasks introducing the concept of linear functions through the use of different technologies. Conclusions are drawn highlighting subtle tensions that relate to the mathematical knowledge at stake and to the design principles of the underlying technology and task.

Allen Leung
Anna Baccaglini-Frank

References

Anderson, J. R., & Schunn, C. D. (2000). Implications of the ACT-R learning theory: No magic bullets. In R. Glaser (Ed.), *Advances in instructional psychology: Educational design and cognitive science* (Vol. 5, pp. 1–34). Mahwah, NJ: Lawrence Erlbaum Associates.

Artigue, M., & Perrin-Glorian, M.-J. (1991). Didactic engineering, research and development tool: some theoretical problems linked to this duality. *For the Learning of Mathematics, 11*(1), 3–17.

Bartolini Bussi, M. G., & Mariotti, M. A. (2008). Semiotic mediation in the mathematics classroom. In L. English, M. Bartolini Bussi, G. Jones, R. Lesh & D. Tirosh (Eds.), *Handbook of international research in mathematics education* (pp. 746–783). Lea, USA: Routledge.

Brousseau, G. (1997). *Theory of didactical situations in mathematics: didactique des mathematiques, 1970–1990.* Dordrecht: Kluwer Academic Publishers.

Buchbinder, O., & Zaslavsky, O. (2009). A framework for understanding the status of examples in establishing the validity of mathematical statements. In M. Tzekaki, M. Kaldrimidou & C. Sakonidis (Eds.). *Proceedings of the 33rd conference of the international group for the psychology of mathematics education.* (Vol. 2, pp. 225–232). Thessaloniki, Greece.

Chevallard, Y. (1992). Fundamental concepts in didactics: Perspectives provid-ed by an anthropological approach. *Recherches en Didactique des Mathématiques, special issue,* 131–167.

Chevallard, Y. (2011). La notion d'ingénierie didactique, un concept à réfon-der. Questionnement et éléments de réponse à partir de la TAD. In C. Margolinas, M. Abboud-Blanchard, L. Bueno-Ravel, N. Douek, A. Fluckiger, N. Douek, F. Vandebrouck & F. Wozniak (Eds.), *En amont et en aval des ingénieries didactiques* (pp. 81–108). Grenoble: La pensée sauvage.

Drjvers, P. (2012) *Digital technology in mathematics education: why it works (or doesn't). Plenary talk at the ICME-12*, Seoul, 8 July–15 July 2012, http://www.icme12.org/upload/submission/2017_F.pdf

Fischbein, E. (1993). The theory of figural concepts, *Educational Studies in Mathematics, 24,* 139–162.

Karadag, Z., Martinovic, D., & Freiman, V. (2011). Dynamic and Interactive Mathematics Learning Environments (DIMLE). In L. R. Wiest & T. Lamberg (Eds.), *The Proceedings of the 33rd annual meeting of the North American chapter of the international group for the psychology of mathematics education*. Reno, Nevada.

Laborde, C. (2001). Integration of Technology in the Design of Geometry Tasks with Cabri-Geometry. *International Journal of Computers for Mathematical Learning, 6*(3) (pp. 283–317).

Leung, A. (2011). An epistemic model of task design in dynamic geometry environment. *ZDM - The International Journal on Mathematics Education, 43,* 325–336

Leung, A. & Bolite-Frant, J. (2015). Designing mathematics tasks: The role of tools. In Anne Watson & Minoru Ohtani (Eds.). *Task design in mathematics education: The 22nd ICMI study (New ICMI study series)* (pp. 191–225). New York: Springer.

Margolinas, C. (Ed.) (2013). *Proceedings of ICMI Study 22 Task design in mathematics education.* Oxford, UK. Retrieved July 2013 from http://hal.archives-ouvertes.fr/hal-0083405

Marton, F., Runesson, U., & Tsui, A. B. M. (2004). The space of learning. In F. Marton & A. B. M. Tsui (Eds.), *Classroom discourse and the space of learning* (pp. 3–40). New Jersey: Lawrence Erlbaum Associates, INC Publishers.

Noss, R., Healy, L., & Hoyles, C. (1997). The Construction of Mathematical Meanings: Connecting the Visual with the Symbolic. Symbolic'. *Educational studies in mathematics, 33*(2), 203–233.

Renkl, A. (2005). The worked-out-example principle in multimedia learning. In R. Mayer (Ed.), *The Cambridge handbook of multimedia learning,* (pp. 229–246). Cambridge, UK: Cambridge University Press.

Runesson, U. (2005). Beyond discourse and interaction. Variation: a critical aspect for teaching and learning mathematics. *The Cambridge Journal of Education, 35*(1), 69–87.

Schoenfeld, A. H. (2009) Bridging the Cultures of Educational Research and Design. *Educational Designer*, 1(2). Retrieved from http://www.educationaldesigner.org/ed/volume1/issue2/article5

Sierpinska, A. (2003). Research in Mathematics Education: Through a Keyhole. In E. Simmt & B. Davis (Eds.), *Proceedings of the annual meeting of Canadian mathematics education study group*. Acadia University.

Sinclair, N. & Jackiw, N. (2011). *TouchCounts* [software application for the iPad].

Tirosh, D., & Wood, T. (Eds.). (2009). *The international handbook of mathematics teacher education* (Vol. 2). Rotterdam: Sense publishers.

Watson, A. & Ohtani, M. (Eds.) (2015). *Task design in mathematics education: The 22nd ICMI study (New ICMI study series).* New York: Springer.

Zaslavsky, O., & Sullivan, P. (Eds.). (2011). *Constructing knowledge for teaching secondary mathematics task to enhance prospective and practicing teacher learning.* New-York: Springer.

Part I
Theoretical Considerations

Exploring Techno-Pedagogic Task Design in the Mathematics Classroom

Allen Leung

Suppose every instrument could by command or by anticipation of need execute its function on its own; suppose (like the carvings of Daedalus or the figurines of Hephaestus which, the poet says, could take on a life of their own) that spindles could weave of their own accord, and plectra strike the strings of zithers by themselves; then craftsmen would have no need of hand-work, and masters have no need of slaves

—Aristotle

Abstract This chapter explores task design in Dynamic and Interactive Mathematics Learning Environments. Teacher knowledge and pedagogical digital tool are discussed under the ideas of Mathematics Digital Task Design Knowledge and Mathematical Digital Boundary Object. Leung's (*ZDM-The International Journal on Mathematics Education, 43*, 325–336, 2011) techno-pedagogic task design is revisited and refined with respect to these two ideas. A GeoGebra applet on exploring the meaning of convergent sequence is used to illustrated features of techno-pedagogic task design.

Keywords Task design · Digital-based task · Boundary object · Teacher knowledge

1 Introduction

Aristotle, who was a realist, probably was dreaming of the day of automata when human designs and controls machines to take over all manual labor. And indeed, since Aristotle, the developments of human civilization have been successfully flourishing in this direction. When human society is gearing toward a technocratic orientation, we might ask the question to what extent technology can replace knowledge? What kind of role does human "handiworks" play in knowledge formation? What are worthy to know? In mathematics education, when the classroom is immersed in a technology-rich teaching and learning environment, what kind of

A. Leung (✉)
Department of Education Studies, Hong Kong Baptist University, Kowloon Tong
Hong Kong, SAR, China
e-mail: aylleung@hkbu.edu.hk

© Springer International Publishing Switzerland 2017
A. Leung and A. Baccaglini-Frank (eds.), *Digital Technologies in Designing Mathematics Education Tasks*, Mathematics Education in the Digital Era 8,
DOI 10.1007/978-3-319-43423-0_1

3

mathematics do we want our students to learn, and how do teachers make use of technology to design the teaching of "worthy" mathematics?

Design teaching and learning tasks in the mathematics classroom is a major pedagogical activity. Generally speaking a mathematics teaching/learning task asks students to do something mathematical in the classroom and this doing should lead students to experience, in the broadest sense, mathematics. In particular, a *tool-based task* can be described as follows:

> A teacher/researcher design aiming to be a thing to do or act on in order for students to activate an interactive tool-based environment where teacher, students, and resources mutually enrich each other in producing mathematical experiences (Leung and Bolite-Frant 2015, p. 192).

The word "design" carries a meaning of accomplishing goals in a particular environment satisfying a set of requirements or subject to a set of constraints; it is a strategic approach (roadmap) towards achieving a certain expectation. Design necessarily creates boundary; a structure or framework on which meaning and knowledge can grow. Mathematics task design can be thought of as designing activities situated in pedagogical environments that provide boundaries within which students engage in doing mathematics leading to construction of mathematical knowledge. A boundary differentiates and thus creates a contrasting experience which may lead to discernment of differences and invariants. Tool (technology), along with their usages in the context of teaching and learning, is a means to create pedagogical boundaries. For example, in older days abacus-like tools were used as an instrument for calculation. Embedded in a Chinese abacus is a manual-driven structure (finger movement patterns constrained on a set of beads in a preset frame) under which arithmetic operations can be performed. This preset boundary enables creation of mnemonic chant formulas synchronizing with finger motions to move the beads and perform calculations. For abacus-based arithmetic, the mnemonic chant formulas for moving the abacus beads form a situated system of mathematical abstraction. Designing teaching and learning tasks based on these mnemonic chant formulas in order to explore their relationships with traditional arithmetic operations in school curriculum should be fruitful in finding deeper mathematical and pedagogical meaning for number.

What kind of mathematical knowledge can be accessed through the use of tools and technology? Noss and Hoyles (1996), while reflecting on the traditional approach to abstraction where mathematical concepts are "de-contextualized", saw abstraction "as a process of connection rather than ascension" (p. 48) and used *webbing* to refer to

> the presence of a structure that learners can draw up and reconstruct for support – in ways that they can choose as appropriate for their struggle to construct meaning for some mathematics (p. 108).

With this they introduced the notion of *situated abstraction* to describe "how learners construct mathematical ideas by drawing on the webbing of a particular setting which, in turn, shapes the way the ideas are expressed" (p. 122) Thus a (mathematical) abstract concept can be thought of as a *generalized image* that one can "draw out" from a situated setting. This is the meaning of the Chinese word "抽象 *chōu xiàng*" (which literally means "take out the image") that stands for abstraction. With respect to tools, situated abstraction has been described as

> an orienting framework to describe and explore how interaction with semiotic tools shapes the development of mathematical meanings and in turn is shaped by the conceptions and social context of the students (Hoyles and Noss 2009, p. 131).

In a research on designing for mathematical abstraction in the context of an ICT (Information Communication Technology) environment, Pratt and Noss (2010) explored heuristic in designing for abstraction that required "the intentional blurring of the key mathematical concepts with the tools whose use might foster the construction of that abstraction." (p. 95) Intentional blurring of the boundary between technology and mathematical concepts opens up a pedagogical space in which technology-based task design can flourish. Blurring implies uncertainty and inaccuracy, capitalizing this *discrepancy potential* embedded in an ICT tool is a task design heuristic that can creates learning opportunities conducive to discernment of critical aspects of abstract mathematical concepts. Discrepancy potential of a tool is defined as

> a pedagogical space generated by (i) feedback due to the nature of the tool or design of the task that possibly deviates from the intended mathematical concept or (ii) uncertainty created due to the nature of the tool or design of the task that requires the tool users to make decisions (Leung and Bolite-Frant 2015, p. 212).

These ideas on the potentialities of (digital) tool in the construction of mathematical knowledge set up a background to explore *techno-pedagogic task design* in the mathematics classroom. Leung (2011) gave a description of techno-pedagogic task design as follows:

> Task design that focuses on pedagogical processes in which learners are empowered with amplified abilities to explore, re-construct (or re-invent) and explain mathematical concepts using tools embedded in a technology-rich environment (p. 327).

In this chapter, this description will be explored and refined further in terms of teacher (as task designer) knowledge, an idea of mathematics digital boundary object and a nested epistemic sequence.

2 Teacher (as Task Designer) Knowledge

Teacher knowledge plays a key role in pedagogical task design for the mathematics classroom. This knowledge is a complex construct composing of interactions among different knowledge domains. For examples, Mishra and Koehler (2006, 2009) proposed a theoretical concept that built on Shulman's (1986) idea of Pedagogical Content Knowledge (PCK) by merging a technological knowledge domain with the pedagogical knowledge domain and content knowledge domain.

These three domains 'interplay' at the intersection which Mishra and Koehler termed Technological, Pedagogical And Content Knowledge (TPACK)

> Underlying truly meaningful and deeply skilled teaching with technology, TPACK is different from knowledge of all three concepts individually. Instead, TPACK is the basis of effective teaching with technology, requiring an understanding of the representation of concepts using technologies; pedagogical techniques that use technologies in constructive ways to teach content; knowledge of what makes concepts difficult or easy to learn and how technology can help redress some of the problems that students face; knowledge of students' prior knowledge and theories of epistemology; and knowledge of how technologies can be used to build on existing knowledge to develop new epistemologies or strengthen old ones (Koehler and Mishra 2009, p. 66).

This is a complex interplay where mathematical knowledge, technology and epistemology (pedagogy) fuse together into a fluid state with flexible boundary. The degree of fluidity of this kind of integrated knowledge depends very much on the teachers themselves. Crisan, Lerman, and Winbourne, in their explorative research on the interplays between content knowledge, pedagogy and ICT exhibited by secondary school mathematics teachers in UK, proposed the idea of teacher's own personal ICT pedagogical construct to conceptualise mathematics teachers' incorporation of ICT into their classroom practices:

> Learning to teach with ICT is a process. It demands doing and practice ... the teachers developed their own 'expertise' with ICT, which we call here personal ICT pedagogical construct, consisting of conceptions of how the ICT tools and resources at their disposal benefited their teaching of mathematics and their pupils' understanding and learning of mathematics (Crisan et al. 2007, p. 33).

Tapan (2003) claimed that in order to prepare mathematics teachers for technology-rich classroom, one must take into account all aspects of teaching, specifically, the four types of knowledge: mathematical knowledge, knowledge about the artifact, didactic knowledge of mathematics, and didactic knowledge about the artifact. Teacher must masters the use of technology for a mathematical activity and instruments technology for organizing learning (Laborde 2007). Furthermore, teachers' own learning experience with digital tools is a critical process in the formation of their technology-integrated knowledge. Teachers must experience for themselves, as learners, the potentials and pitfalls of digital tool in the learning of mathematics, thus gain knowledge about how students can learn mathematics in various digital environments.

Thus mathematics teacher as a task designer needs to possess a kind of plastic (personal) knowledge that is an integration of many knowledge dimensions. Figure 1 depicts a knowledge intersection among four broad knowledge domains which suggests an integrated *Mathematics Digital Task Design Knowledge (MDTDK)*.

Teachers as task designers shape their own MDTDK according to their experiences on the four knowledge domains and in particular, on how these domains interact with each other. Different digital artifacts used for different mathematics topics could result in different task designs. Therefore, MDTDK is plastic in the sense that it should not be a rigid knowledge structure and is susceptible to change as the interactions among the four knowledge domains evolve. Furthermore, it

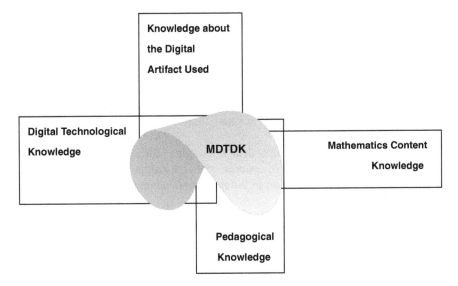

Fig. 1 An integrated plastic Mathematics Digital Task Design Knowledge (MDTDK) that teachers need to possess for digital tool-based mathematics task design

could also be a situated institutional knowledge that is culturally bounded, that is; rather than just a personal knowledge, MDTDK can be shaped by a mathematics community of practice. In this connection, the next section explores the concept of boundary object.

3   Mathematics Digital Boundary Object

Star and Griesemar (1989), while addressing the tension created between divergent viewpoints and the need for generalizable findings in scientific work, proposed the concept of *boundary object* as a means to offer *translations* among the heterogeneous groups of actor (e.g. amateur, professional, institutional) engaged in the scientific inquiry process.

> Boundary objects are objects which are both plastic enough to adapt to local needs and the constraints of several parties employing them, yet robust enough to maintain a common identity across sites. They are weakly structured in common use, and become strongly structured in individual-site use. These objects may be abstract or concrete. They have different meanings in different social worlds but their structure is common enough to more than one world to make them recognizable, a means of translation. The creation and management of boundary objects is a key process in developing and maintaining coherence across intersecting social worlds (Star and Griesemer 1989, p. 393).

A major function of a boundary object is to mediate among different interpretations and viewpoints to reconcile meanings and maintain coherence. In this sense, MDTDK can act like a boundary object for the four knowledge domains.

A digital tool can be regarded as *boundary object* that translates experience and expression between different types of *mathematical worlds*. A mathematical world, for example, can be

1. a social community where the participants engage in mathematical activities (for example, a class of students, a group of teachers), or
2. a body of conventionally established or/and institutionalized mathematical knowledge (for example, formal axiomatic Euclidean geometry, a mathematics curriculum), or
3. a body of experiential mathematical knowledge (for example, mathematical knowledge based on the use of concrete physical manipulatives like an abacus, mathematical usage/application in different contexts, mathematical practices in workplace), etc.

Digital tool has the potential to create "virtually real" objects and representations that could open up multi-interpretations of mathematical knowledge. In particular, it can act as a regulatory balance between the pragmatic and epistemic dimensions in mathematical knowledge acquisition: learning the mathematics while using the digital tool.

> *Mathematics Digital Boundary Object (MDBO)* is a digital artifact that can bridge between different mathematical worlds making use of the virtual immediate reality created by the artifact.

"Bridge" here refers to the digital artifact's actual potential to create a (transitory and temporal) situated discourse through which the inhabitants of different mathematical worlds can communicate. Of course, a MDBO can create its own mathematical world. Some examples of type of MDBO are: calculating and measuring digital tools, Dynamic Geometrical Environment (DGE), digital library or museum, Computer Algebra System (CAS), interactive applets for specific mathematics topics, digital sensory enhancement or extension apparatus, digital tools that affords creation of alternative mathematical experiences. Task design using digital tool to teach and learn mathematics can be thought of as *the designing of pedagogical paths (trajectories) to create MDBO-based situated discourses that can reconcile meanings and maintain coherence between mathematical worlds.*

3.1 Features of MDBO

What characterize and what are some pedagogical features of a MDBO? As a boundary object, MDBO's primary function is to mediate and to translate. In Leung and Bolite-Frant (2015), five task design heuristics for tool-based mathematics task design were discussed: strategic feedback and mediation, instrumental/pragmatic-semiotic/epistemic continuum, boundary between mathematical and pedagogical fidelity, discrepancy potential and multiplicity (pp. 219–221). These heuristics are different aspects in tool-based mediation processes for mathematic teaching and learning. Therefore, from the perspective of task design, MDBO should support these heuristics.

Feedback is a key opening up mediation processes. MDBO should act like a communication device that makes possible interactive feedbacks and mediation between different mathematical worlds (e.g. the learners and the body of mathematical knowledge to be learnt). For example, a learner using DGE can dynamically visualize his/her mental images of geometrical objects such that s/he can reason the correctness (mediate by dynamic feedback tool like dragging) of the mental images with respect to the Euclidean world embedded in DGE.

MDBO can be designed or used strategically to allow shifting of attention between mathematical skill and concept, and between pedagogy and mathematical content. As a boundary object, MDBO possesses a "duality" (a blurring of the boundary between different domains) that allows passages to connect different knowledge domains with a minimal losing of the fidelity of each domain. As a MDBO, a robust square constructed in DGE is a figural concept (cf. Fischbein 1993) that possesses a dual nature where visual perceptions harmonized with logical constraints, and construction skills are cognate with rigorous mathematical definitions. DGE as a MDBO is an interpreter between the phenomenal geometrical world and the axiomatic geometrical world. Knowledge gap exists in interpretation. In tool-based mathematics task design, this knowledge gap can be seen as a discrepancy potential. As a medium that negotiates between mathematical worlds, MDBO should allow pedagogical opportunities for open interpretations on how to relate phenomena in the two worlds. The existence of knowledge gap due to the nature of design of a particular MDBO provides such opportunities where learners need to make mathematical sense out of uncertain experiences produced by a MDBO. Soft construction in DGE is an example where discrepancy potential of a dragging tool (dragging in this case) can be used to bring about geometrical conjecture formation. A learner drags and traces a movable point of a DGE figure to maintain a given condition and in doing so a wriggling uncertain trajectory of the point is being traced out. The learner makes sense of the geometry of the trajectory and proposes a conjecture about the figure and the given condition.

Simultaneity and co-variation play key role in learning and discernment (cf. Marton 2015). As a boundary object that translate mathematical meaning, if a MDBO supports multi-representations, then meaning can be deepened in a multi-facet way. In a Dynamic and Interactive Mathematics Learning Environments like GeoGebra, multi-windows (e.g. 2-D DGE, 3-D DGE, Spreadsheet) can be presented together on the same screen. The same mathematical idea is represented in each window and elements in these windows can be constructed to co-vary together while a variable is taking different values in certain window. This kind of multiplicity offers mathematical idea/concept diverse communicable expressions/translations that are amiable to different mathematical worlds.

3.2   An Example of MDBO

In Cheng and Leung (2015), a dynamic applet created in GeoGebra was designed to study student exploration of the concept of the limit of a sequence. It can be conceived as a MDBO that mediates between two mathematical worlds: the world where students engage in explorative activity on developing (personal) understanding the concept of the limit of a sequence and the formal mathematical world with a rigorous $\varepsilon - N$ definition of a sequence approaching to the limit L:

$$\forall \varepsilon > 0, \exists N \in \mathbb{N} \text{ such that for all } n > N, \quad |a_n - L| < \varepsilon$$

A dynamic (ε, N) ruler was designed in this MDBO to facilitate formation of situated discourses which bridge between students' perceptions on how N and ε can be related and the rigid (ε, N) relationship stated in the definition.

Figure 2 is a snapshot of the applet for the sequence $a_n = \text{Exp}(-0.05)(1 + \sin n)$. The (ε, N) ruler is a draggable rectangular strip that opens "ad infinitum" to the right rigidly attached to a point L. L can be dragged freely, hence the whole (ε, N) ruler, to anywhere on the sketch and the width of the ruler is controlled by an ε-slider. The horizontal dotted half-line starts from L and continues to the right splits the open-ended ruler into two equal halves. The dotted line perpendicular to the x-axis through L is attached to the ruler and its intersection with the x-axis is denoted

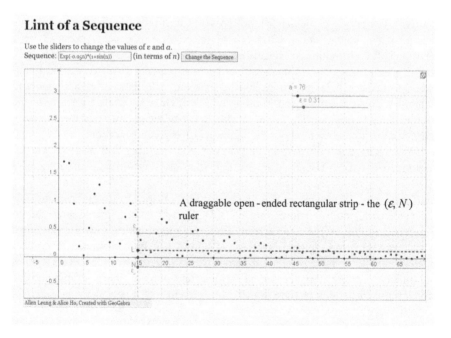

Fig. 2 A snapshot of the GeoGebra dynamic applet (henceforth it will be called the Applet) for the sequence $a_n = \text{Exp}(-0.05n)(1 + \sin n)$

by N. An a-slider controls the number of sequence terms to appear in the applet. Press, hold (the Shift button), scroll and drag activate the zoom mode, the moving of the whole applet and the scaling of the x, y-axes.

The (ε, N) ruler is a visual interpretation of the inequality $|a_n - \mathrm{L}| < \varepsilon$. The dynamic width of the ruler is determined by choices of ε, the left vertical end of the ruler marks the location (existence) of possible N's, and the right open end of the ruler captures the meaning of "for all n > N". Students are free to choose the ε value, and to locate N by moving the ruler. Thus the dependency between ε and N was not embedded in the dynamism by design intention, rather the (ε, N) dependency should be a critical discernment that students need to be aware of under properly guided task design. There are at least two possible operational procedures to guide the use of the (ε, N) ruler:

P1   Choose an ε, then move the strip (hence the N value) so that all the sequence points to the right of N fall inside the strip.
P2   Move the strip (hence the N value) to a desired position, then choose an ε so that all the sequence points to the right of N all fall inside the strip.

A critical discernment is that when the sequence under studied converges, both P1 and P2 work for any ε and N always; but when the sequence diverges, P1 and P2 might or might not work for any ε and N. The pedagogical content of the applet thus lies on building up enough epistemic experience (via situated discourses) for students to contrast the behaviours of different sequence types using the (ε, N) ruler, hence to decide whether P1 or P2 would ascertain convergence which gives hint to the ε and N dependency (ibid., pp. 191–192). How the features described in the Sect. 3 of this MDBO can be manifested would depend on how tasks are being designed to guide student to explore the meaning of the convergence (or divergence) of sequence. In the next section, a possible task design for this MDBO will be discussed. The design rationale behind this applet was to instrument feedback, uncertainty, simultaneous attention and co-variation that are conducive to discernment to bring about an epistemic connection between skill and concept.

4   A Nested Epistemic Task Design Sequence

As mentioned in the Introduction, Leung (2011) gave a description of techno-pedagogic task design. The technology-rich environment mentioned in the description refers to a teaching and learning environment where teachers and students can access to (different) technological resources (e.g. digital tools, Internet, concrete pedagogical tools, etc.) that can amplified students' abilities to experience, explore, (re)construct, (re)invent and explain mathematical ideas/concepts. With the use of an appropriately chosen tool, learning happens as a process where routine algorithmic actions using the tool can be evolved or transformed into internalized cognitive activities. In this connection, Leung proposed a nested sequence of

Fig. 3 A modified
diagrammatic representation
of the nested epistemic
sequence presented in Leung
(2011) for task design in a
digital environment. The
progressive *greyscale*
represents the consecutive
gradual inclusion and
deepening in meaning of the
previous mode

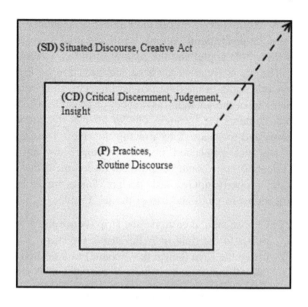

epistemic modes to guide tool-based task design (ibid.). It consisted of three nested modes in a cognitive expansion order: Establishing Practices (P), Critical Discernment (CD) and Establishing Situated Discourses (SD). Each mode progressively expands and merges into the next one as the learner's cognitive ability is cumulatively strengthened with respect to using the tool to do mathematics. Figure 3 is a modified diagrammatic representation of the nested sequence presented in Leung (2011). The ideas of routine discourse in P, judgement and insight in CD and creative act in SD are added in this new version. These modes are signposts to mark learning with tools as an expanding progression in which creativity can be born out of well-developed routine practices using a chosen tool. The epistemic potential of the tool is triggered by task design which embeds learning opportunities requiring mathematical judgement, reasoning and insight.

4.1 A Design Example

For illustration, the GeoGebra applet presented in Sect. 3.2 is used as the Dynamic and Interactive Mathematics Learning Environment. This applet was designed to empower learners with amplified abilities to explore, construct (invent) and explain the meaning of sequence convergence. The nested sequence of epistemic modes could frame a task design sequence using the following design guide.

Establishing Practices (P). Start with simple convergent sequences and ask students to practice the following:

1. Drag the (ε, N) ruler to different positions and change the two sliders' values in order to "trap" the "tail" of the sequence inside the (ε, N) ruler
2. Zoom in and out to observe different parts of the sequence and discuss how the sequence behave with respect to the (ε, N) ruler as a is getting larger and larger
3. Discuss the meaning of L, N and make guesses on their values
4. Discuss possible relationships among the values ε, N, L and a
5. Device possible procedures on how to use the (ε, N) ruler to verify that a sequence converges

These activities aim to develop in the student operational routines to use the applet and to cultivate a visual dynamic sense of sequence convergence that depends on various inter-related parameters.

Critical Discernment (CD). Give students different types of divergent sequences (without telling students that they diverge) and ask students to explore the following:

6. Try the procedures devised in 5 above on these sequences and discuss how effective these procedures are to determine the behaviours of these sequences
7. Refine the (ε, N) ruler procedures to cater for all types of sequences

These more cognitive oriented activities aim to create disturbances (or uncertainty) to the operational routines developed in (P) thus forcing students to re-exam their procedures and to discover critical aspects (relations between ε and N) of the concept of convergent sequences

Situated Discourses (SD). Use the sequences in (P) and (CD), ask students to engage in a tool-based discourse:

8. Use the (ε, N) ruler to discuss necessarily and sufficient conditions for a sequence to converge to a limit L
9. Write down a (ε, N) ruler-based definition for sequence convergence

This is where students engage in mathematical discourse based on the use of the applet. Students should develop mathematical definitions, conjectures and arguments to explain the phenomena they produced in the applet.

With respect to other theoretical orientations, this design can be regarded as an instrumental genesis process (cf. Trouche 2005) of the (ε, N) ruler where a tool is transformed into a personal cognitive instrument, or as a semiotic mediation process (cf. Bartolini and Mariotti 2008) where the (ε, N) ruler acts as a semiotic sign (artifact) that mediates between different types of mathematical meaning.

4.2 Knowledge Gap

There could be a knowledge gap between the student produced tool-based discourses and the formal mathematics discourse (in this case the rigorous $\varepsilon - N$ definition of a sequence converges to the limit L). That is, the student produced definitions of sequence convergence may look different, even incorrect, from the teacher expected definition. The existence of this knowledge/meaning gap has important pedagogical significant in task design. In particular, the "width" of this gap can be seen as a measure on how "effective" was the tool-based task designed and implemented. Teacher engaging with students in a didactical discourse to "narrow" this gap should be part of the intended pedagogical process in the task design. This knowledge gap can also be thought of as a "boundary" produced by the MDBO (the applet); that is, *a boundary produced by a boundary object*. The applet translates experience/expression between student's perceptual mathematical world and the world of formal abstract mathematics. In any translation, there are gap and discrepancy as there are aspects in the two worlds that cannot be translated "perfectly". This knowledge/meaning gap opens up opportunities or pitfalls where the MDBO can be a medium conducive for learning or an obstacle preventing learning to progress. Teachers should be sensitive to the existence of this gap while designing and implementing MDBO tasks. As mentioned, the student-produce discourses may contain unexpected "disturbances" which contribute to this gap. This is where teachers' MDTDK play a significant role to open up didactical discussion to treat the cognitive conflicts produced by this gap.

5   Techno-Pedagogic Task Design Revisited

To summarize the above discussion, the techno-pedagogic task design proposed in Leung (2011) is revised as follows:

> A *techno-pedagogic task design* is a task design that focuses on pedagogical processes in which learners are empowered by MDBO in a Dynamic and Interactive Mathematics Learning Environment with amplified abilities to explore, re-construct (or re-invent) and explain mathematical concepts. The design could follow an epistemic nested sequence where students' routine algorithmic actions using the MDBO progressively evolve or transform into tool-based situated discourses. Teacher's MDTDK plays a significant role in the task design (1) to anticipate a knowledge/meaning gap between the MDBO-based mathematical discourse and the intended mathematical content (2) to open up didactical discourse with students bridging the gap between the student-produced tool-based discourse and the intended mathematical content.

Aristotle's dream of automaton does not verse well in this type of digital-based epistemology. The Master (Teacher) is a key participant in the process of students' knowledge acquisition. In this respect, a (mathematical) digital tool can also be thought of as a boundary object between the teacher and the students, acting as a communicator (or a translator) between the teacher's mathematical world and the student's mathematical world. In this sense, techno-pedagogic task design is a pedagogical design of a digital boundary object and using it to bring about mathematical meaning(s).

5.1 Potential and Pitfall

Any tool-based task design has potential and pitfall. A digital tool's pedagogical potential for one teacher may be is a pitfall for another teacher. Teacher's design and treatment of the gap between the student-produced tool-based discourse and the intended mathematical content determine the pedagogical "value" of MDBO. The degree of plasticity of a teacher's Mathematics Digital Task Design Knowledge (MDTDK) is a key factor to determine this pedagogical value. On the one hand, the more a teacher is willing to blend different knowledge domains, the more likely alternative mathematical discourses (even meanings) will emerge; however, the teacher would then have less control on fixing intended mathematical meaning. On the other hand, a digital tool for a teacher can be designed and used as a powerful medium to support rigid mathematical knowledge. Either ways or any way in between is a teacher's choice.

In brief, techno-pedagogic task design is about designing meaningful entanglements between digital tools and mathematical knowledge. Its potential and pitfall can be interpreted as values relative to the knowledge possessed by the teachers and the students. A key idea in techno-pedagogic task design is participation in mathematical knowledge formation using digital tools strategically as extensions of teachers' and students' sensual and cognitive abilities. It has a materialistic and dynamic orientation towards the nature of mathematical knowledge that could open up alternative mathematics pedagogy.

References

Bartolini Bussi, M. G., & Mariotti, M. A. (2008). Semiotic mediation in the mathematics classroom: Artifacts and signs after a Vygotskian perspective. In L. English (Ed.), *Handbook of international research in mathematics education* (2nd ed., pp. 746–783). New York: Routledge.

Cheng, K., & Leung, A. (2015). A dynamic applet for the exploration of the concept of the limit of a sequence. *International Journal of Mathematics Education in Science and Technology, 46* (2),187–204.

Crisan, C., Lerman, S., & Winbourne, P. (2007). Mathematics and ICT: A framework for conceptualising secondary school mathematics teachers' classroom practices. *Technology, Pedagogy and Education, 16*(1), 21–39.

Fischbein, E. (1993). The theory of figural concepts. *Educational Studies in Mathematics, 24*, 139–162.

Hoyle, C., & Noss, R. (2009). The technological mediation of mathematics and its learning. *Human Development, 52*, 129–147.

Koehler, M. J., & Mishra, P. (2009). What is technological pedagogical content knowledge? *Contemporary Issues in Technology and Teacher Education, 9*(1), 60–70.

Laborde, C. (2007). The role and uses of technologies in mathematics classrooms: Between challenge and modus Vivendi. *Canadian Journal of Science, Mathematics and Technology Education, 7*(1), 68–92.

Leung, A. (2011). An epistemic model of task design in dynamic geometry environment. *ZDM—The International Journal on Mathematics Education, 43*, 325–336.

Leung, A., & Bolite-Frant, J. (2015). Designing mathematics tasks: The role of tools. In A. Watson & M. Ohtani (Eds.), *Task design in mathematics education: The 22nd ICMI study. New ICMI study series* (pp. 191–225). New York: Springer.

Marton, F. (2015). *Necessary conditions of learning*. New York: Routledge.

Mishra, P., & Koehler, M. J. (2006). Technological pedagogical content knowledge: A new framework for teacher knowledge. *Teachers College Record, 108*(6), 1017–1054.

Noss, R., & Hoyle, C. (1996). *Windows on mathematical meanings*. Dordrecht, The Netherlands: Kluwer.

Pratt, D., & Noss, R. (2010). Designing for mathematical abstraction. *International Journal of Computers for Mathematical Larning, 15*, 81–97.

Star, L. S., & Griesemer, J. R. (1989). Institutional ecology, 'translations' and boundary objects: Amateurs and professional in Berkeley's museum of vertebrate zoology, 1907–1930. *Social Studies of Science, 19*(3), 387–420.

Shulman, L. (1986). Those who understand: Knowledge growth in teaching. *Educational Researcher, 15*(2), 4–14.

Tapan, S. (2003, February–March). *Integration of ICT in the teaching of mathematics in situations for treatment of difficulties in proving*. Paper presented to 3rd Conference of the European Society for Research in Mathematics Education (CERME 3), Bellaria, Italy.

Trouche, L. (2005). Instrumental genesis, individual and social aspects. In D. Guin, K. Ruthven, & L. Trouche (Eds.), *The didactical challenge of symbolic calculators: Turning a computational device into a mathematical instrument* (pp. 197–230). New York: Springer.

Revisiting Theory for the Design of Tasks: Special Considerations for Digital Environments

Marie Joubert

Abstract Teachers should and do design tasks for the mathematics classroom, with specific mathematical learning as the objective. Completing the tasks should require students to engage in dialectics of action, formulation and validation (Brousseau in *Theory of didactical situations in mathematics : didactique des mathematiques,* Dordrecht: Kluwer Academic Publishers, 1997) and to move between the pragmatic/empirical field and the mathematical/systematic field (Noss et al. in *Educational Studies in Mathematics, 33*(2), 203–233, 1997). In the classroom, students act within a *milieu*, and where computers are part of this *milieu*, particular considerations with respect to task design include questions about the mathematics the student does and the mathematics the computer does, and the role of feedback from the computer. Whilst taking into account the role of the computer, the design of tasks can also be guided by theoretical constructs related to obstacles of various kinds; ontogenic, didactical and epistemological (Brousseau in *Theory of didactical situations in mathematics : didactique des mathematiques,* Dordrecht: Kluwer Academic Publishers, 1997), and, whereas the first two should be avoided, the third should be encouraged. An example of a task taken from empirical research in an ordinary classroom is used to illustrate some of these ideas, also demonstrating how difficult and complex it is for many teachers to design tasks that use computer software in ways that provoke the sort of student activity that would be likely to lead to mathematical learning. Implications for teacher professional development are discussed.

Keywords Task design · Feedback · Modes of production · Pragmatic/empirical field · Mathematical/systematic field · Digital tools · Epistemological obstacles

M. Joubert (✉)
African Institute for Mathematical Sciences, Cape Town, South Africa
e-mail: marievjoubert@gmail.com

© Springer International Publishing Switzerland 2017
A. Leung and A. Baccaglini-Frank (eds.), *Digital Technologies in Designing Mathematics Education Tasks,* Mathematics Education in the Digital Era 8,
DOI 10.1007/978-3-319-43423-0_2

17

1 Introduction

This chapter outlines a theoretical approach to task design, where a 'task' is taken to mean what the teachers ask the students to do (Christiansen and Walther 1986; Joubert 2007; Monaghan and Trouche 2016). Activity is taken to mean what the students actually do and the focus is on tasks for digital environments. Although digital environments can change classrooms in significant ways, the theoretical approach described here is equally applicable in all mathematics classrooms.

The chapter is underpinned by three key assumptions. The first is that teachers should and do design or redesign tasks for their mathematics classrooms (Hoyles et al. 2013; Watson et al. 2013) and that tasks are adapted and tweaked by teachers to suit each context in which they give the task to students. The second assumption is that teachers want the tasks they set to provoke mathematical learning and have some understanding of the relationship between the task and the intended learning. This may seem obvious, but, as Brousseau (1997) argues, the detail of the intended learning is frequently not sufficiently well understood by teachers and as Watson et al. (2013), state:

> A distinct mathematical contribution can be made in understanding whether and how doing tasks, of whatever kind, enables conceptual learning (p. 10).

The third assumption is that students in mathematics classrooms do no more than is necessary to complete the task (Sierpinska 2004). The implication of these assumptions, taken together, is that teachers should have a clear idea of the sorts of activity their designed tasks will force the students to engage in and the mathematics they will learn by doing so, as well as factors that might hinder or prevent this activity taking place.

Digital technologies have the potential to contribute in significant ways to learning in mathematics, but designing tasks that use digital technologies well is complex and difficult (Joubert 2007; Laborde and Sträßer 2010) at least partly because of the ability of the computer to 'do' some mathematics and to provide mathematically relevant feedback. Importantly, the theoretical underpinnings of good task design are no less relevant when digital technologies are brought into the picture.

The chapter begins with a discussion of students' mathematical activity, out-lining the sorts of activity that might lead to mathematical learning; this is the kind of activity a task for mathematical learning should provoke. It goes on to discuss tools in the mathematics classroom, with a focus on computer software, empha-sising how complex it is to really understand the role and potential of the software. The chapter then turns to the notion of obstacles, suggesting that some obstacles should be avoided because they get in the way of learning and some should be encouraged because they require students to engage in the sorts of activity that might lead to mathematical learning (as discussed previously). Obstacles provide a framework for the analysis of tasks, allowing us to predict likely student activity and hence mathematical learning. The chapter goes on to analyse of a teacher-designed task in which students work on computers. This has two purposes: first it illustrates the ideas outlined in the chapter and second it emphasises the importance of understanding the role and potential of digital technologies within classroom mathematics tasks. Finally the implications are discussed.

2 Students' Activity

Given the assumption that tasks in the mathematics classroom are designed to bring about student activity that might lead to mathematical learning, it seems important to understand how students engage with a task and what mathematical learning might look like. Of course, students come to a task with different backgrounds and the prior learning of students has been shown to be a key ingredient in determining how they react to different situations, as argued in detail by Roschelle (1997).

When students engage in a task, they tend to operate under a 'law of economy' Sierpinska (2004) and they find the easiest and shortest way to complete the task. Hillel (1992) explains that for many students, it is the end rather than the means that is important. and Mavrikis et al. suggest that 'students are inevitably focused on task completion, bypassing any need to mobilize structural reasoning or algebraic generalization' (2013, p. 2). However, as Brousseau (op. cit.) suggests, it is perhaps more likely that valuable and genuine mathematical learning will take place when students are invested in, and committed to, a problem situation. He contrasts this sort of motivation, mathematical motivation, with didactical motivation, where the student aims to solve the problem because this is what they were asked to do.

In completing the task, the students interact with the *milieu*, or the environment. In the case of tasks within digital environments, an important element of the *milieu* will be the device used, such as the computer, smartphone, tablet or graphical calculator. Together with the device, software ranging from networking capability, to generic software such as web browsers and spreadsheet packages, to mathematics-specific software such as computer-algebra systems (CAS) will be used. The interactions between the student and the *milieu* can be conceptualised as a dialogue between the student (or group of students) and the feedback from the *milieu* (Brousseau 1997). The importance of feedback should not be underestimated; as pointed out by Balacheff (1990):

> The pupils' behaviour and the type of control the pupils exert on the solution they produce strongly depend on the feedback given during the situation. If there is no feedback, then the pupils' cognitive activity is different from what it could be in a situation in which the falsity of the solution could have serious consequences (p. 260).

In the context of task design for digital environments, feedback from the *milieu* can be particularly powerful and important (see, for example, Bokhove and Drijvers 2010). Understanding what form the dialogue between the students and the *milieu* might take is crucial.

2.1   The Modes of Production

Brousseau (1997) uses the notion of 'modes of production' to describe the different types of dialectic interactions between students and the *milieu*; he suggests that as they work through a mathematical task, they will engage in all or some of the dialectics of action, formulation and validation. These are explained below.

2.1.1   Dialectic of Action

A dialectic of *action* involves the student constructing an initial solution to the problem straight away, informed by her current knowledge and using strategies that 'are, in a way, propositions confirmed or invalidated by experimentation in a sort of dialogue with the situation' (ibid, p. 9). For example, suppose the mathematical task a student is given requires them to produce a graph, perhaps on a graphing calculator, in a web-based graphing environment or in a specific graphing software package. If the student knows how to do this, and types the equation in, and the graph is produced on a big or small screen, this would be a dialectic of action. There may be an argument that, in some cases, the feedback from the *milieu* seems to have little or no role. However, as Brousseau argues, the student can be seen to be anticipating the results of her choices or strategies, and in this sense the *milieu* provides feedback, which can perhaps be seen as unrequested and as expected; it does not require the student to adapt her strategies. In the example given above, for example, the student would expect a graph to appear on the screen. She does not have to adapt her strategy. On the other hand, feedback may occur from time to time as the student works. For example, students may use a computer-based homework package, such as 'Mathspace' to check answers as they go along, or they may check answers to exercises in the back of the textbook or they could use self-checking methods such as multiplying out factorised functions. Very commonly, the teacher provides feedback either by checking the students' work as she walks around the classroom or by going through answers in a whole-class discussion. In these cases, the dialectical nature of the student interactions is clearer, and the feedback from the *milieu* can be seen as requested and as 'a positive or negative sanction relative to her action' (Brousseau 1997).

Whereas a negative sanction could encourage the students to formulate new strategies, it may also result in students simply trying something different but not using the feedback to inform the guess; this approach is sometimes called a trial and error approach (and is different to a trial and improvement approach which, it is argued below, requires some formulation). However, it is also possible that, although the task presents some mathematical challenges to the student (in other words she does not know exactly what to do and how to do it), she will choose to engage only in dialectics of action, perhaps by inventing easier ways to solve problems or perhaps by adopting a trial and error approach, which can be seen as didactically motivated rather than mathematically motivated (Sutherland 2007). It is possible that *all* dialectics between the student and the *milieu* in a given didactical situation are dialectics of action; if, for example, the student knows what to do and how to do it in order to complete the task. This would mean that, although she completes the task, she does not need to extend her mathematical knowledge or understanding to do so; 'simple familiarity, even active familiarity ... never suffices to provoke a mathematization' (Brousseau 1997, p. 211). To a large extent this can be seen to depend on the demands of the task which in turn depends on the student's previous knowledge and understanding, as argued above.

2.1.2 Dialectic of Formulation

On the other hand, some action dialectics are *necessary* within any didactical situation; and the suggestion is that it is when the action dialectics are motivated by the mathematics rather than the didactics, these actions may lead to a sequence of mathematical dialectical interactions which could include the development of hypotheses, alternative strategies, justifications and proofs, as described below. As suggested above, dialectics of *formulation* occur when students meet a difficulty or problem as they engage in mathematical activity; Brousseau explains that when a solution to a problem is inappropriate, the situation should feed back to the students in some way, perhaps by providing a new situation. The means that the student may become conscious of her strategies and begin to make suggestions. Brousseau includes in this category 'classifying orders, questions etc. ...' (p. 61). He goes on to say that in these communications students do not 'expect to be contradicted or called upon to verify ... information' (p. 61). Formulations necessarily include communication and have an explicit social dimension (Balacheff 1990) such as detailed descriptions and designations of phenomena, statements of properties or relationships, using and developing a language of a formal system. In making these formulations the students construct and acquire explicit models and language, which, as Christiansen and Walther (1986) argue, serves to make the learner conscious of strategies: 'actions become conscious for the learner' (p. 268).

A key activity in mathematics classrooms, and very often seen in classrooms where digital technologies are used, is 'noticing'. In the context of research where digital technologies are used, Martin and Pirie (2003) provide an example. In their research, the teacher gives the students a printed sheet of a number of equations and asks them 'to see what they can notice and find out about the graphs in relation to the printed equations' (p. 176). When the didactical intention is that the student should make some observations, or to notice, it is likely that the students will begin to formulate choices; noticing requires the student to make conscious choices about what to notice, which aspects to attend to, which to suppress (Mason 1989) and how to express and articulate these. Whereas students can notice while remaining in action dialectics, noticing can also lead to conjecturing and engaging more in formulation dialectics.

Feedback has a variety of roles in formulation dialectics and can come from other people or from other elements of the *milieu*. As with action dialectics, the feedback can be immediate or delayed. For example, in the context of Brousseau's example game 'The Race to 20', feedback would be delayed until the effect of the chosen strategy can be seen (whether the student wins or not). Clearly, digital technologies are able to provide unique, usually immediate, feedback and this is discussed later in the chapter.

In the discussion above, the possibility of trial and error cycles of student behaviour was proposed. In these trial and error dialectics, the role of the feedback was seen to be only to inform the student that the strategy she had tried was incorrect. However, depending on the nature of the problem, it is possible that the feedback may also provide some clue for the student about how to improve her strategy and she may formulate a new strategy; this 'trial and improvement' or 'trial and refinement' approach is described by Sutherland (2007). She includes some cautionary remarks about the value of such approaches, arguing that, in some cases, trial and improvement may lead to a correct answer but perhaps not to the intended learning.

2.1.3 Dialectic of Validation

Both action and formulation involve manipulating 'moves in the game' or mathematical objects; validation however involves manipulating 'statements about the moves' (Sierpinska 2000, p. 6). Validation therefore takes place when an interaction intentionally includes an element of proof, theorem or explanation and is treated thus by the interaction partner, which could be the teacher, called the 'interlocutor' by Brousseau: 'this means that the interlocutor must be able to provide feedback...' (Brousseau 1997, p. 16). Brousseau argues that this interaction should be seen as a dialectic; this, he suggests, is due to the presence of the interlocutor. Examples of dialectics of *validation* include justification (perhaps of a procedure, a word, a language or a model), organising theoretical notions, 'axiomization' (ibid, p. 216), and a range of proofs.

Brousseau, while suggesting that all three modes of production are 'expected from students', (ibid, p. 62) argues that it is through situations of validation that genuine mathematical activities take place in the classroom. Romberg and Kaput (1999) echo Brousseau's sentiments in their vision of mathematics worth teaching: "Students will develop the habit of making and evaluating conjectures and of constructing, following and judging valid arguments" (p. 7). Brousseau suggests that situations of validation do not occur very often and are unlikely to occur spontaneously and it is probable that validation will not take place unless it is explicitly called for. "In order to obtain the latter [validation], one must organize a new type of didactical situation." (ibid, p. 13) The implication from Brousseau's 'interlocutor' (above) is that this interlocutor provides feedback. It is in discussion with this interlocutor that the individual develops his or her arguments; it is unlikely that feedback will come from any source in the *milieu* other than classmates or the teacher because of the need to convince someone else. Clearly, the teacher's role is crucial in encouraging students to engage in dialectics of formulation and particularly validation.

2.2 The Pragmatic/Empirical Field and the Mathematical/Systematic Field

It can be that the mathematical activity of the students relates only to the physical or concrete characteristics of the mathematical objects they work with. On the other hand, students may relate their activity to mathematical notions underpinning the objects. For example, on the one hand students may construct a tangent to a circle by rotating a straight line so that it touches the circle, and on the other hand they may use the geometrical property that the tangent is perpendicular to the radius to construct the tangent (Laborde et al. 2004).

A range of mathematics education theorists from a variety of theoretical backgrounds describe these different ways of working in different contexts; for Laborde (1998) the distinction is between 'spatio-graphical' and 'theoretical' and for Sfard (2000) it is between 'actual reality' and 'virtual reality'. While the varying theoretical perspectives imply variations on these ideas, the point for all of them is that it is useful to make the distinction and this chapter uses Noss et al. (1997) terminology 'pragmatic/empirical' and 'mathematical/systematic'. In addition to the perceived need to distinguish between the 'pragmatic/empirical' and 'mathematical/ systematic' fields, there seems to be a consensus that a transition between the two fields is required for mathematical learning to take place (Dörfler 2000; Laborde 1998; Mason 1989; Sfard 2000). Brousseau, for example, describes different types of proofs, including contingent and experimental proofs and proofs by exhaustion. These, he suggests, relate to implicit models students hold and therefore they are likely to take place in the pragmatic/empirical field discussed above and not relate explicitly to theoretical mathematical knowledge. However, for 'mathematization' to take place, according to Brousseau, mathematical proofs which relate to the theoretical mathematics involved in the situation, are required. Similarly, Mariotti (2000) claims that the solution of geometry problems requires continuous moves between the two fields and Laborde (op. cit.) suggests that there is a need for interactions between images and concepts.

The implication, in terms of the relationship between the students' dialectics (particularly of formulation and validation), and student learning is that, where these dialectics remain in the pragmatic/empirical field, mathematical learning will be limited; however, transitions into the mathematical/systematic field are likely to lead to mathematical learning. This discussion about student activity has made frequent reference to the *milieu*. It now turns to a key component of the *milieu*; the tools used in the classroom.

3   Tools (Especially Digital Tools) in the Mathematics Classroom

It can be argued that mathematical activity, like all human activity, is mediated by tools (Vygotsky 1980). In the mathematics classroom, some tools are designed specifically for the teaching and learning of mathematics (Sutherland 2007) such as Dienes blocks or Cuisenaire rods, and can be seen to embody specific mathematical concepts. Other tools, such as matchsticks and mirrors are also frequently used in practical classroom work. These differ from those designed specifically for the teaching and learning of mathematics in that they do not embody mathematical concepts in the same way. The literature suggests that there is often an expectation or belief that these tools will support mathematical learning but that the effective use of tools is more complex and difficult than it first seems (McNeil and Jarvin 2007; Orton and Frobisher 1996; Pimm 1995; Resnick 1984; Sutherland 2007). Pimm (1995), for example, warns that objects cannot offer mathematical experience or understanding in themselves, particularly when the students direct all their attention to manipulating the equipment: 'Pupils may end up *just* manipulating the equipment' (p. 13). McNeil and Jarvin (2007) go further, suggesting that the use of such tools can actually hinder mathematical learning, stating that recent studies "have suggested that manipulatives may not only be ineffective, but also detrimental to learning and performance in some cases" (ibid, p. 312).

The point is that the introduction of all tools into the classroom is a complex issue and their use does not guarantee the desired mathematical learning, and that, as argued convincingly by Sutherland (op. cit.), it is important for teachers to understand the potential and the limitations of the tools and be clear about the role of the tool in the mathematical activity. It can be argued that this is particularly true for computer software, which has an 'intrinsically cognitive character' (Balacheff and Kaput 1996, p. 469) which means first that for some software used in the teaching and learning of mathematics, the software can perform some mathematical processes or 'do the mathematics' (Bokhove and Drijvers 2010; Hoyles and Noss 2003; Sutherland 2007) for the user and second that it can provide mathematically relevant feedback for the user (Bokhove and Drijvers 2011; Granberg and Olsson 2015).

In addition, the feedback is 'quick and essentially unlimited…at 'no cost" (Hillel 1992, p. 205). As argued above, built into the tools specifically designed for teaching and learning mathematics, is a set of epistemological assumptions. In the case of software, these assumptions are likely to be considerably more complex than with non-digital tools, because of the ability of the software to do (some of) the mathematics and to provide feedback.

3.1 Computers Can Do the Mathematics

The ability of software to perform mathematical operations may have the potential to make a significant contribution to the teaching and learning of mathematics. For example, its use can enable mathematical experiences which, for example, allow students to focus on patterns, to construct multiple representations and to interpret representations (Ainley and Pratt 2002; Balacheff and Kaput 1996; Condie and Munro 2007; Ruthven et al. 2004; Sutherland 2007). However, as Love et al. (1995) caution, it is common for students to avoid the mathematical ideas intended to be the focus of study by using the software in unintended ways.

It was argued above that teachers should be clear about the mathematics their students should do as they complete a task that has been set for them. When computers are used, however, working this out can be difficult, because much of the mathematics curriculum is directed towards the learning of techniques, such as finding areas of shapes, making calculations and plotting graphs. Completing the technique is frequently seen as the end point of the task (Love et al. 1995; Schwarz and Hershkowitz 2001). As Hoyles et al. put it, 'digital representations change the epistemological map' (2013, p. 1058). If computers are able to do the 'work' for the students, then what is the work of the students?

Monaghan and Trouche (2016) illustrate this idea. They contrast two tasks. In the first, students are required to sketch a cubic graph: $y = x^3 - x^2 + 2x - 1$. In the second, students are given three graphs of quadratic functions and asked to reflect them in the x-axis. Monaghan and Trouche discuss the fact that, for the first task, using a computer graphing package renders the task trivial but doing the task using pencil and paper would be more difficult; for the second using the same software would probably present a considerable challenge whereas the pencil and paper approach would probably not be difficult.

Working out the intended mathematical processing to be performed by each of the computer and the students relates to what the software is able to do and what opportunities it offers the students in terms of doing mathematics. It is perhaps the relationship between these that is particularly important; as Nevile et al. (1995) suggest, it is important to look 'at the software' in tandem with looking 'through the software' (ibid, p. 157). To understand this relationship, it is perhaps useful to think in terms of the 'epistemological domain of validity' of the software which 'refers to the knowledge and the relation to knowledge which is allowed by a piece of software' (Balacheff and Sutherland 1994, p. 138).

In a well-known example, Balacheff and Sutherland (1994) explain this notion; they compare the software *Logo* and *Cabri* in terms of what epistemological opportunities they offer students engaged in constructing a parallelogram. They point out that the environments differ significantly in terms of the mathematical concepts students need to mobilise in order to make the construction. To create a parallelogram in *Logo*, students need to use knowledge about the equality in length of opposite sides and about the relationship between internal and external angles. In *Cabri*, however, to construct the parallelogram, they need to understand that the parallelogram is completely determined either by one point and two directions or by three points. While it may be necessary for teachers to understand these relationships, it is sometimes very difficult, because of the complexity of much of the software available for use in mathematics classrooms (Bokhove and Drijvers 2010). Sutherland (2007) argues this case convincingly, suggesting that 'many of these tools are so powerful, have so much potential, that it is difficult for teachers to know where to get started' (p. 68). What this means is that, if the potential of the tool is not thoroughly analysed, then it is difficult for teachers to work out what mathematics it does and hence what mathematics they want the students to do.

The ability of software to do the mathematics also opens possibilities for tasks in which students are able to work inductively, from the products of the software's mathematical processing, to develop conjectures and theories. It can perhaps be argued that this is a more natural way to learn than the traditional deductive approaches in classrooms. However, as Goldenberg (1988) suggests, these approaches should be carefully thought out:

> Put simply, a wrong theory is the most likely result of the casual introduction of an inductive learning experience … into a curriculum that is not otherwise designed to make use of the questions such an experience raises (p. 144).

In these cases, an understanding of the way the feedback offered by the environment can support inductive working may also be very important in encouraging students to develop and test their theories. An understanding of feedback is perhaps crucially important in both these situations and more generally when computers are used.

3.2 Feedback

In the example about creating parallelograms in *Logo* and *Cabri* above, Balacheff and Sutherland also compare the feedback from the two environments. In both environments, the students use the computer feedback to make a decision about whether they have constructed what they intended to construct. In both cases, they are able to determine whether they are correct or not by looking at the feedback on the screen. However, the *Cabri* environment offers more; students are able to test the correctness of their parallelogram more thoroughly by making sure that it resists manipulation (dragging).

This highlights the important role played by the feedback and raises questions about the role of feedback in computer based learning environments (see also, for example, Bokhove and Drijvers 2012; Granberg and Olsson 2015; Monaghan and Trouche 2016). The general conception of computer feedback seems to be that it is beneficial in teaching and learning mathematics (e.g. Becta 2004). Feedback provides opportunities 'to quickly test ideas, to observe invariants … and, generally, to be bolder about making generalisations' (Hillel 1992, p. 205). Further, there is evidence (e.g. Hillel 1992) that with the quick availability of feedback, students are likely to engage with problems for longer, and with more persistence. However, there is also considerable evidence to suggest that the effect of feedback needs careful analysis. Säljö (1999), in his discussion about feedback, suggests that 'it can provoke active reflection on the part of the learner who has to consider alternatives, manage concepts and representations and so on...' (p. 154). The degree to which the reflection provoked by the feedback is active, however, can perhaps be seen to be, in part at least, dependent on the kind of feedback given by the software; as Balacheff and Sutherland (1994) point out in their example above, the feedback given by *Logo* provides a more fragile basis for students to decide whether the parallelogram they have constructed is indeed the one they intended to construct, whereas in *Cabri* the feedback can be seen to provide a more robust basis for such a decision.

Students sometimes interpret feedback in unexpected ways, which may have a negative or distracting impact on developing the understandings the teacher intended (Hoyles and Noss 2003; Sutherland 2007), and which may lead to the development of strategies which are at odds with the intended learning, such as trial and error, trial and improvement and 'intellectual passivity' (Hillel 1992, p. 217). This point is clearly made by Säljö:

> ...what technologies provide are experiences, but they do not guarantee a specific inter-
> pretation of these experiences that would amount to learning what was intended. (1999,
> p. 158)

The important point, perhaps, is that students do not always use feedback in the ways in which it is intended and, further, teachers tend to overestimate students' ability to use this feedback (Laborde 2002).

Feedback from the computer can be seen to have a major influence on students' modes of production; action, formulation and validation. For example, as described by Noss et al. (1997) students used a microworld to test a prediction about the number of matchsticks in a given sequence. The feedback from the computer allowed them to evaluate their prediction; negative feedback led to further suggestions and, later, positive feedback led to the conclusion of the task. In these cases, the feedback can be seen as the 'dialectical partner' in the *milieu* in situations of formulation (and sometimes action). However, when the feedback allows the students to test a prediction, the students may not make the transition to the mathematical/systematic field, which, as argued above, is necessary for learning mathematics. In terms of Brousseau's modes of production, the feedback from the computer could be seen to 'validate' the students' predictions, and therefore the students do not need to engage in the dialectics of validation.

In the example quoted above, the students can be seen to have some expectations about the feedback. It is possible, however, that they have no expectations, and the feedback takes the role of 'oracle' (Sutherland and Balacheff 1999) in scenarios where the students explore. For example, Olivero (2003) describes how students, working with figures in *Cabri*, use 'wandering dragging' which she describes as 'moving the basic points on the screen randomly in order to discover configurations or regularities in the figures' (p. 98). The students did not seem to have any expectations about what would happen; they used the feedback to tell them. This exploring activity, which can be seen as an action dialectic, however, is not productive mathematically, unless it is accompanied by more focused explorations (which would include 'guided dragging' Olivero 2003), in which conjectures are made and tested (formulation dialectics) and include transitions between the pragmatic/empirical field and the mathematical/systematic field (which may lead to validations) (op cit). Further considerations on feedback provided by dynamic geometry environments can be found in Chapters "Designing Assessment Tasks in a Dynamic Geometry Environment", "Designing Non-constructability Tasks in a Dynamic Geometry Environment" and "The Planimeter as a Real and Virtual Instrument that Mediates an Infinitesimal Approach to Area" of this book.

Computer feedback can be seen, to a greater or lesser extent, as complementing the teacher's role. Balacheff and Kaput (1996) use the notion of the 'didactic directiveness' (p. 483) of feedback. They suggest that microworlds (such as dynamic geometry software) and tutoring systems represent two extremes of didactic directiveness; microworlds offer environments in which students can explore freely but tutoring systems give 'strong guiding feedback' (p. 484). What is useful about this way of conceptualising feedback is that it relates directly to the intended role of the software and to the degree to which teachers can devolve a problem to the students (in the sense of Brousseau). This highlights the importance of taking into account the contribution of the software as a 'third player' in the didactical situation; without it, the teacher is completely in charge of the degree of devolution to the students, whereas now the computer has some influence as well.

4 Designing Tasks

This chapter has set out a theoretical framing of the relationship between student activity in the mathematics classroom and mathematical learning. This theoretical position suggests that student activity that includes dialectics of action, formulation and validation with some movement between the pragmatic/empirical field and the mathematical/systematic field is desirable. However, as pointed out above, the assumption is that the students' agenda is to complete the task (they are not concerned about dialectics or movement between fields); and as a result a task should be designed to require the mathematical thinking and reasoning that are '*strictly necessary and sufficient to complete the task*' (Sierpinska 2000, p. 12 italics in the original) also forcing dialectics of action, formulation and validation and movement between the pragmatic/empirical and mathematical/systematic fields. This notion is discussed in detail by Brousseau, who thinks in terms of the need for students to adapt strategies in order to reach target knowledge; and he suggests that they will not do so unless the task forces them to do so.

4.1 Obstacles

Such an adaptation may take place, Brousseau suggests, if the students encounter and overcome 'obstacles' as they work through the task. He describes an obstacle as:

> a previous piece of knowledge which was once interesting and successful but which is now revealed as false or simply unadapted (p. 82).

Obstacles can take a variety of forms; Brousseau, for example, identifies obstacles of ontogenic origin, of didactical origin and of epistemological origin. The first of these relates to the 'student's limitations' (p. 86), and can also be described as 'developmental' limitations (Swan 2006). For example, the lack of prior learning can be seen as an obstacle to completing the task because the student is in some way not ready for the mathematics required to complete the task (Love and Mason 1992).

Obstacles of didactical origin 'seem to depend on a choice or a project in an educational system' (Brousseau 1997, p. 86) and are seen as obstacles for the students because of ill thought out presentation of subject matter, or 'the result of narrow or faulty instruction' (Harel and Sowder 2005, p. 34). The example Brousseau provides is of the way in which decimal numbers are taught by convention in French elementary schools and Harel and Sowder give the example of the didactical practice of teaching students to look for 'key words' in mathematics problems (such as 'altogether' signals that addition is required).

Both ontogenic and didactical obstacles can be seen to inhibit mathematical learning, and should and can be avoided (Brousseau 1997; Harel and Sowder 2005). The third type of obstacle, however, the epistemological obstacle, should not be avoided and is, in fact, key to the design of good tasks. Brousseau's epistemological obstacles are perhaps most clearly explained by Balacheff (1990, p. 264) who discusses how mathematical concepts are learnt through their use as tools in the process of problem solving with some content; this content is supported by the students' prior knowledge. However, although the old knowledge is a necessary basis for the content, it may cause problems for the students as they work through the problem; in other words it becomes an obstacle which causes the students to stumble. If, in order to overcome the obstacle, the students are required to construct the meaning of the new piece of knowledge, then this obstacle is an epistemological obstacle. Brousseau provides examples: $(a + b)^2 = a^2 + b^2$; $0.a = a$, $(0.2)^2 = 0.4$. Harel and Sowder (2005) suggest that 'MMB' (multiplication makes bigger) can often be seen as an epistemological obstacle.

It is also not always easy to distinguish between didactical and epistemological obstacles. For example, as Harel and Sowder (2005) suggest, many obstacles have elements of both. They provide examples and place them on a set of axes labelled 'epistemological obstacle' and 'didactical obstacle' as shown in Fig. 1 (taken from their diagram on p. 47).

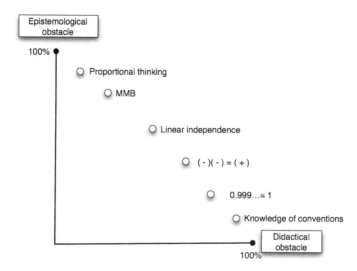

Fig. 1 Examples of obstacles as combinations of epistemological and didactical

The important thing about this idea is that the design of tasks needs to take these dimensions into account, in order to minimise the effects of didactical obstacles. Equally, an analysis of tasks should take both dimensions of obstacles into account and should be grounded in whatever is known about the prior learning and development of the students who complete the task.

The idea of obstacles is useful in thinking about relating the way a task is set up to the mathematical activity of the students, and in particular to the dialectics of action, formulation and validation. As students work on tasks, there will be stages when they know what to do and they do it; this is a dialectic of action. If they encounter an obstacle, however, they will be forced to change their approach and will develop new strategies, make suggestions to one another, conjecture and test; these are dialectics of formulation. If the obstacle has an epistemological dimension, then these formulations will be related to the intended learning.

The section below illustrates these ideas by analysing a task designed by a classroom teacher. The analysis brings together the expected student dialectics and movement between fields, the role of the computer and the obstacles discussed in this section. The example is given not as a 'good' example, as will be discussed later, but in order to provide something concrete to demonstrate not only the theoretical ideas above but also how complex it can be to design a computer-based task for the classroom.

5 An Example: Noticing

In my doctoral research, for which the overall aim was to explore how computers are used in ordinary mathematics classrooms, I observed a sequence of five or six lessons taught by four different teachers. All lessons were designed completely by the teachers themselves. In many lessons computers were used by the students. A careful analysis of all the tasks used in the computer-based lessons, framed by the notion of obstacles outlined above, reveals how the tasks were unlikely to provoke mathematical thinking. Although the students engaged with the task and did as they were asked, they were seldom encouraged to develop the sorts of reasoning that might be evidenced by the formulation and testing of hypotheses or by validation of these hypotheses.

I use one of the case studies to illustrate: an a priori analysis of a task given within the case study provides insight, perhaps, into the hypothetical learning trajectory of the students (Margolinas and Drijvers 2015).

The research took place in 2004 in an English classroom, with a class of about twenty students, of about 12 years of age. The task they were asked to complete had a number of questions. In each question the students were asked to use graphing software to draw a set of straight line graphs of the form $y = mx + c$ (or, in the last question, $y = c + mx$) and then write down what they noticed.

5.1 Intended Learning

The teacher's explicit learning intentions were that the students should make a connection between the graphs and their equations. The sorts of 'connections' it seems the teacher wanted the students to make were: to notice that the y-intercept is the same as the c value in the equation, to notice that there is a relationship between the m value and the gradient, perhaps that a bigger m yields a steeper graph or that graphs sloping one way have a positive m and those sloping the other way have a negative m value. In other words, she wanted them to move between the pragmatic/empirical and the mathematical/systematic fields.

The questions in the task had three parts: drawing the graphs and noticing (which includes finding the language needed to articulate features noticed) then reporting what had been noticed. A priori, drawing the graphs can be seen as a dialectic of action, with some limited feedback from the *milieu* as discussed below. Noticing might involve dialectics of formulation, with students making suggestions and perhaps hypothesising. However, there is nothing in the task that requires the students to engage in dialectics of validation.

To complete the task, the students needed first to construct a set of graphs using the software. In this task, creating the graphs can be seen as easy; the students had been given the equations of the graphs they were required to draw and all they needed to do was to type them in and press the **Enter** key. The graph is automatically drawn on the screen by the software. To create more graphs on the same page, the students only had to repeat the process.

The students had been told that they would be working on straight line graphs; it is likely that their expectations were that the on-screen graphs drawn would be straight lines. It is unlikely that the lines they produced would **not** be straight lines because to get a curved graph using this software the user has to use (for example) the 'squared' or 'cubed' key, which is a deliberate choice (so it is unlikely to happen by mistake), so unless they made a typing or copying error, the graphs will be as intended by the teacher. The task did not call for any discussion of the difference and similarities between the *equations* of the graphs, and nor did it call for any predictions about what the graphs might look like.

Next the students needed to write down 'what they noticed' about the set of graphs. Writing down 'what you notice' can be seen to have two distinct parts (which may take place simultaneously); the first is the noticing and the second is the writing down.

The question on the worksheet was 'Write down what you notice about the set of graphs'. The suggestion is that the way the question was phrased suggests a focus on the **set** of graphs, which may encourage working in the visual field alone because by looking students are able to notice many similarities and differences between the lines. The stated objective, however, was concerned with connecting **individual** graphs to their equations which would require transitions between the visual and theoretical fields. Having sets of graphs on the screen could therefore be seen to be a didactical obstacle, which may confuse the students and inhibit their learning. The fact that the students did not plot points to obtain the graphs could also be seen as a didactical obstacle because it means that they did not need to think about the equation, apart from typing it in.

5.1.1 Set 1

The first set of functions, taking the form $y = x + c$, were: $y = x$, $y = x + 1$, $y = x + 4$, $y = x - 2$ and $y = x - 3$. They were produced on the screen as shown in Fig. 2. Each equation below the graph page is a different colour and the lines drawn on the graph page are each the same colour as the corresponding equation.

When the graphs are produced using the software, the students may notice that each of the five lines is a different colour, corresponding to the text colour in the box below. They may also notice other things: that the blue and black graphs are close together, that all the lines run from the bottom left towards the top right, that the blue and black lines are the same distance apart as the purple and green lines, and so on.

It is likely that the teacher wanted the students to notice that the graphs are parallel. Difficulties involved in noticing the parallel-ness can be seen as an epistemological obstacle, but it does not, in itself, address the learning intentions of the task unless students realise that the fact of being parallel means that *something* is the same about the graphs, and then to look at the equations and notice that the

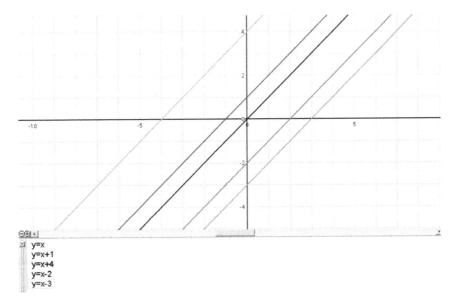

y=x
y=x+1
y=x+4
y=x-2
y=x-3

Fig. 2 Graphs for Question 1

m value is the same. However, here m is 1, so it is implied rather than being written down. It could be that the students notice that the graphs are parallel, but that they overcome the obstacles required to connect this parallel-ness to the (absent) m value is much less likely. Without the experience of this sort of work and with very little experience in working with straight line graphs, the suggestion is that these are ontogenic and didactical obstacles.

The teacher may also have hoped that the students would notice some connection between the intercepts and the value of c, perhaps that the y-intercept is equal to the value of c or that the x-intercept is the same as $-c$. This, however, assumes the prior knowledge and understanding that intercepts may be important, but it may be that the students did not have this prior knowledge.

It also requires a different way of looking at the graphs; instead of looking at what is the same about all the graphs, the students would need to focus on an individual line, read off the value of the intercept, note the colour of the line, find the equation in the same colour and notice that the c value in that equation is the same as the intercept. They would then need to hypothesise that the intercept is the same as the c value, and go and check that this is so for the other graph-equation pairs. Although this process may seem complex, it is, I suggest, not beyond the ability of the students, but I also suggest that it is more unlikely than noticing that the graphs are parallel.

5.1.2 Set 2

The second set of equations are of the form $y = mx$, where m is positive, and are shown in Fig. 3. Where in the previous question the m value is kept the same, here the m value varies but the c value is kept the same. The assumption is that the teacher thought that, by keeping one of the two variables in the equation constant, the students' attention would shift to the other.

In each of these functions, the c value in the equation $y = mx + c$ is zero, and therefore not included in the equation. Even though the students may notice that the lines all go through the origin, to link the value of this point to the absent c value would probably be more difficult and unlikely; this presents a didactical obstacle to their learning.

A second observation the students may make is that the lines are in the first and third quadrants (sloping from bottom left to top right). The teacher may have hoped that they would link this positive gradient to the positive m value in the equations but the suggestion is that, particularly with no negative m values with which to make a comparison, it is unlikely that the students would make the link.

The third observation the students may make is that the steeper the graph is, the higher the value of m is. This last observation is presumably what the teacher wanted them to notice, but it would require the students to have a language for steepness and to compare individual graphs by first noticing that one is steeper than another, then identifying which equation goes with which graph and then observing that the m value in the steeper graph is greater than the m value in the less steep graph. The suggestion is that, with all the graphs already on the screen, the students

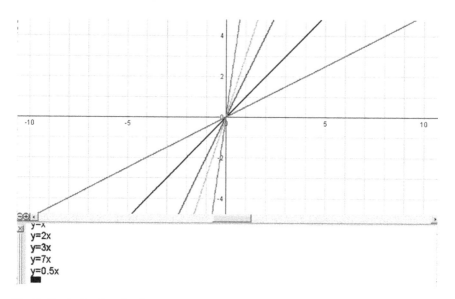

Fig. 3 Graphs for Question 2

would be unlikely to pick out individual lines, compare them and then find the equations. Further, with the question requiring them to notice things about the **set** of graphs, it is probably more likely that they would focus on the whole set, looking for what is the same about the lines rather than picking out individual lines.

Three further sets of graphs were given; again the students were required to draw them and then 'notice'. Overall, the intended learning for the task can be seen as learning to make the transition between the visual and theoretical fields (here between the graphical field and the algebraic) and hence to work out the connections between the graphical and algebraic representations of linear functions. However, there was no mechanism built into the task to encourage this way of working (such as making and a testing a prediction or conjecture, dialectics of formulation) and, further, having a whole set of graphs on the screen may have inhibited these transitions, as suggested above.

5.2 Discussion of the Task

This chapter is about the design of tasks, so the ways in which the students responded to the task are not discussed here. Suffice it to say that they responded very much in the way that is predicted by the analysis above. The interventions of the teacher are perhaps more relevant as she provided some further explanations and questioning during the lesson, thus in some way tweaking the design of the task. Both the teacher and the students reported that, for them, it had been a successful lesson. Certainly the students were engaged throughout and appeared to be working, but as the analysis predicts, their mathematical learning was very limited.

The example given above is not necessarily a badly designed task; as the discussion emphasised, the ontogenic obstacles got in the way of the students' learning, because they had very little prior knowledge about straight line graphs and it seems they did not have the experience to know that they should make connections between the equations of the graphs and what they looked like on the screen. However, students with some experience of working with graphs of straight lines may have benefited more in terms of mathematical learning.

On the other hand, it could be argued that the task is also not *well* designed, both in terms of the dialectics in which the students are forced to engage and movement between the pragmatic/empirical field and the mathematical/systematic field. As pointed out above, there is no requirement for students to engage in dialectics of validation. Also as discussed, there is nothing in the task that requires the students to move between fields by making connections between a graph and its equation.

The software is (almost) necessary to the task. It could be argued that in this case, its power is that it can produce on-screen graphs very quickly, doing some of the mathematics that students otherwise would have done and allowing them the time to look for patterns and connections. This exploits its ability to do the mathematics, but there is little in the way the task was designed that exploits the potential of the feedback from the software. It is perhaps not difficult to think of better ways the computer's power could have been used. One approach, as implicitly suggested above, might be to require the students to predict the shape of the graph before it is drawn by the computer, also justifying their predictions to their partners. This would overcome some of the didactical obstacles discussed above such as the difficulties of focusing on a graph rather than the set of graphs. It would further have encouraged dialectics of formulation and, importantly, validation.

More recent popular software, such as *GeoGebra*, could be used for a similar task. Commonly modern software for graphing includes functionality such as sliders, which allow users to change values incrementally. If *GeoGebra* had been used by this teacher with this class, the teacher may have designed the task differently to enable exploration of what changes and what stays the same as 'm' and 'c' are changed. However, improving the design of the task is not the point.

The point is that using computers in everyday or ordinary classrooms is perhaps not yet well enough understood by teachers, as I found in my research. For example, other tasks observed within the study suffered from similar difficulties. In particular, they did not capitalise on the potential of the computer to enable students to develop and test conjectures. Instead, there was an emphasis on the computer performing mathematical processes, leaving little mathematics for the students to perform. On the other hand, however, the teachers and the students seemed to think that the lessons were successful, and so did I to some extent. Students were actively engaged with the tasks they had been assigned and appeared to 'learn' what the teachers intended, although in fact this mathematical learning was limited by both the tasks and the teachers' interventions. It seems that we all fell into the trap described by Schoenfeld (1988) in his 'disasters of well taught mathematics courses'; the appearance of a successful mathematics lesson may be deceptive and it is not enough for students to be engaged in activities which *look like mathematics* unless they are learning mathematics (this is the purpose of mathematics teaching). It was through the careful analysis of the likely and actual mathematical activity of the students that shortcomings were revealed, particularly in terms of the students' mathematical learning.

6 Conclusion

The theoretical background for task design outlined in this chapter is probably already clearly understood by teachers and task designers, although sometimes tacitly. Making the theory explicit, however, might have value in providing a sort-of tick list against which designers of tasks can evaluate their tasks. For example, does the task force students to engage in dialectics of formulation and validation? Does it require the students to move between the visual and abstract fields? Crucially, what mathematics will the students learn?

The focus of this book is the use of digital technologies in mathematics task design; this chapter argues that the introduction of computers adds significant complexity to the work of task design, illustrating the point with the use of an example taken from empirical research. The tick list might now include questions such as 'What mathematics will the student do and what mathematics will the computer do?' and 'What is the role of feedback from the computer, and in which ways might this affect the dialectics between the student and the *milieu*?' This suggests that teachers need to analyse the likely and actual student activity as they work through the task. This sort of analysis is complex, particularly when computers are introduced into the *milieu,* and teachers often do not have the time and resources to develop the tools to help them make these analyses. This, perhaps, is a key role for the teacher professional development required for the effective embedding of computers in mathematics classrooms.

The arguments developed in this chapter imply that this professional development should include a focus on the intended mathematical learning of the students, the route the students might take through the task (and of the computer's role in determining the route), of the computer's feedback and the students' possible responses to the feedback. Importantly, it needs to raise awareness of the potential and role of the computer, emphasising the need to be clear about what mathematics the computer is intended to do, what mathematics the students are intended to do. It needs to make explicit the need to encourage dialectics of all three aspects, action, formulation and validation, in both the pragmatic/empirical and mathematical/ systematic fields. Finally it should address the sorts of epistemological obstacles that can be built into the task to promote the learning of students and discuss the potential didactical obstacles that can be prevented. This sort of professional development will help teachers design tasks to exploit the power of computer software and, crucially, to plan their own interventions accordingly.

References

Ainley, J., & Pratt, D. (2002). Purpose and utility in pedagogic task design. *Proceedings of the 26th Annual Conference of the International Group for the Psychology of Mathematics Education, 2,* 17–24.

Balacheff, N. (1990). Towards a problematique for research on mathematics teaching. *Journal for Research in Mathematics Education, 21*(4), 258–272. Retrieved from http://links.jstor.org/sici?sici=0021-8251(199007)21:4<258:TAPFRO>2.0.CO;2-U.

Balacheff, N., & Kaput, J. (1996). Computer-based learning environments in mathematics. In A. J. Bishop (Ed.), *International handbook of mathematics education* (pp. 469–502). Dordrecht: Kluwer.

Balacheff, N., & Sutherland, R. (1994). Epistemological domain of validity of microworlds: the case of Logo and Cabri-geometre. In R. Lewis & P. Mendelsohn (Eds.), *Lessons from learning.* Amsterdam: Elsevier Science BV. (N. Holland), IFIP.

Becta. (2004). What the research says about the use of ICT in maths. Retrieved from http://publications.becta.org.uk/display.cfm?resID=25808&page=1835.

Bokhove, C., & Drijvers, P. (2010). Digital tools for Algebra education: Criteria and evaluation. *International Journal of Computers for Mathematical Learning, 15*(1), 45–62. doi:10.1007/s10758-010-9162-x.

Bokhove, C., & Drijvers, P. (2011). Effects of a digital intervention the development of algebraic expertise. *Computers & Education*, (3), 3770–3777. Retrieved from http://www.sciencedirect.com/science/article/pii/S0360131511001886.

Bokhove, C., & Drijvers, P. (2012). Effects of feedback in an online algebra intervention. *Technology, Knowledge and Learning, 17*(1–2), 43–59. doi:10.1007/s10758-012-9191-8.

Brousseau, G. (1997). *Theory of didactical situations in mathematics: didactique des mathematiques, 1970–1990*. Dordrecht: Kluwer Academic Publishers.

Christiansen, B., & Walther, G. (1986). Task and activity. In B. Christiansen, A. G. Howson, & M. Otte (Eds.), *Perspectives on mathematics education* (pp. 243–307). Dordrecht: Kluwer.

Condie, R., & Munro, B. (2007). *The impact of ICT in schools—a landscape review*. Report: Becta.

Dörfler, W. (2000). Means for meaning. In P. Cobb, E. Yackel, & K. McClain (Eds.), *Symbolizing and communicating in mathematics classrooms; Perspectives on discourse, tools, and instructional design* (pp. 99–131). Mahwah, New Jersey: Lawrence Erlbaum.

Goldenberg, E. P. (1988). mathematics, metaphors, and human factors: mathematical, technical, and pedagogical challenges in the educational use of graphical representation of functions. *Journal of Mathematical Behavior, 7*(2), 135–173.

Granberg, C., & Olsson, J. (2015). ICT-supported problem solving and collaborative creative reasoning: Exploring linear functions using dynamic mathematics software. *Journal of Mathematical Behavior, 37*, 48–62. doi:10.1016/j.jmathb.2014.11.001.

Harel, G., & Sowder, L. (2005). Advanced mathematical—thinking at any age: its nature and its development. *Mathematical Thinking and Learning, 7*(1), 27–50.

Hillel, J. (1992). The computer as a problem-solving tool; it gets a job done, but is it always appropriate? In J. P. Ponte, J. F. Matos, J. M. Matos, & D. Fernandes (Eds.), *Mathematical problem solving and new information technologies*. New York: Springer.

Hoyles, C., & Noss, R. (2003). What can digital technologies take from and bring to research in mathematics education? In A. J. Bishop (Ed.), *Second international handbook of mathematics education*. Dordrecht: Kluwer.

Hoyles, C., Noss, R., Vahey, P., & Roschelle, J. (2013). Cornerstone mathematics: Designing digital technology for teacher adaptation and scaling. *ZDM—International Journal on Mathematics Education, 45*(7), 1057–1070. doi:10.1007/s11858-013-0540-4.

Joubert, M. (2007). *Classroom mathematical learning with computers: The mediational effects of the computer, the teacher and the task*. University of Bristol.

Laborde, C. (1998). *Relationship between the spatial and theoretical in geometry—the role of computer dynamic representations in problem solving* (pp. 183–195). London: Chapman and Hall.

Laborde, C. (2002). Integration of technology in the design of geometry tasks with Cabri-Geometry. *International Journal of Computers for Mathematical Learning, 6*(3), 283–317.

Laborde, C., Kilpatrick, J., Hoyles, C., & Skovsmose, O. (2004). *The hidden role of diagrams in students' construction of meaning in geometry* (pp. 1–21). Netherlands: Kluwer.

Laborde, C., & Sträßer, R. (2010). Place and use of new technology in the teaching of mathematics: ICMI activities in the past 25 years. *ZDM, 42*(1), 121–133. doi:10.1007/s11858-009-0219-z.

Love, E., Burton, L., & Jaworski, B. (1995). *Software for mathematics education*. Lund: Chartwell-Bratt.

Love, E., & Mason, J. (1992). *Teaching mathematics: Action and awareness*. Milton Keynes: Open University.

Margolinas, C., & Drijvers, P. (2015). Didactical engineering in France; an insider's and an outsider's view on its foundations, its practice and its impact. *ZDM—Mathematics Education, 47*(6), 893–903. doi:10.1007/s11858-015-0698-z.

Mariotti, M. A. (2000). Introduction to proof: The mediation of a dynamic software environment. *Educational Studies in Mathematics, 44*(1), 25–53.

Martin, L., & Pirie, S. (2003). Making images and noticing properties: The role of graphing software in mathematical generalisation. *Mathematics Education Research Journal, 15*(2), 171–186. doi:10.1007/BF03217377.

Mason, J. (1989). Mathematical abstraction as the result of a delicate shift of attention. *For the Learning of Mathematics, 9*(2), 2–8.

Mavrikis, M., Noss, R., Hoyles, C., & Geraniou, E. (2013). Sowing the seeds of algebraic generalization: Designing epistemic affordances for an intelligent microworld. *Journal of Computer Assisted learning, 29*(1), 68–84. doi:10.1111/j.1365-2729.2011.00469.x.

McNeil, N., & Jarvin, L. (2007). When theories don't add up: Disentangling he manipulatives debate. *Theory into Practice, 46*(4), 309–316. doi:10.1080/00405840701593899.

Monaghan, J., & Trouche, L. (2016). Tasks and digital tools. In J. Monaghan, L. Trouche, & J. M. Borwein (Eds.), *Tools and mathematics* (pp. 391–415). Switzerland: Springer.

Nevile, L., Burton, L., & Jaworski, B. (1995). *Looking at, through, back at: Useful ways of viewing mathematical software*. Lund: Chartwell-Bratt.

Noss, R., Healy, L., & Hoyles, C. (1997). The construction of mathematical meanings: Connecting the visual with the symbolic. *Educational Studies in Mathematics, 33*(2), 203–233.

Olivero, F. (2003). *The proving process within a dynamic geometry environment. Advanced mathematical thinking* (Vol. PhD). PhD thesis. Graduate School of Education: University of Bristol.

Orton, A., & Frobisher, L. J. (1996). *Insights into teaching mathematics*. London: Cassell.

Pimm, D. (1995). *Symbols and meanings in school mathematics*. London: Routledge.

Resnick, L. B. (1984). *A developmental theory of number understanding*. Pittsburg: Learning Research and Development Center, University of Pittsburg.

Romberg, T., & Kaput, J. (1999). Mathematics worth teaching, mathematics worth understanding. In E. Fennema & T. Romberg (Eds.), *Mathematics classrooms that promote understanding* (pp. 3–19). Mahwah, New Jersey: Lawrence Erlbaum Associates.

Roschelle, J. (1997). *Learning in interactive environments prior knowledge and new experience*. Exploratorium Institute for Inquiry: University of Massachusetts, Dartmouth.

Ruthven, K., Hennessy, S., & Brindley, S. (2004). Teacher representations of the successful use of computer-based tools and resources in secondary-school English, Mathematics and Science. *Teaching and Teacher Education, 20*(3), 259–275.

Säljö, R. (1999). Learning as the use of tools: A sociocultural perspective on the human-technology link. In *Learning with Computers: Analysing Productive Interaction Table of Contents*, pp. 144–161.

Schoenfeld, A. H. (1988). When good teaching leads to bad results: The disasters of "well-taught" mathematics courses. *Educational Psychologist, 23*(2), 145–166.

Schwarz, B. B., & Hershkowitz, R. (2001). Production and transformation of computer artifacts toward construction of meaning in Mathematics. *Mind Culture and Activity, 8*(3), 250–267.

Sfard, A. (2000). Symbolizing mathematical reality into being—or how mathematical discourse and mathematical objects create each other. In *Symbolizing and communicating: Perspectives on Mathematical discourse, tools, and instructional design*, pp. 37–98.

Sierpinska, A. (2000). *The "theory of didactic situations": Lecture notes for a graduate course with samples of students' work. master in the teaching of mathematics*. Concordia University. Retrieved 2006 from http://alcor.concordia.ca/~sierp/TDSLecture%202.pdf.

Sierpinska, A. (2004). Research in mathematics education through a keyhole: Task problema-tization. *For the Learning of Mathematics, 24*(2), 7–15.

Sutherland, R. (2007). *Teaching for learning mathematics*. Maidenhead: Open University Press.

Swan, M. (2006). *Collaborative learning in mathematics: A challenge to our beliefs and practices*. In S. M. Wilson & J. Berne (Vol. 24). London: NRDC.

Vygotsky, L. S. (1980). *Mind in society*. Cambridge, Mass: Harvard University Press.

Watson, A., et al. (2013). Task design in mathematics education proceedings of ICMI study 22. In C. Margolinas (Ed.), T*ask Design in Mathematics Education Proceedings of ICMI Study 22*. Oxford.

Task Design Potential of Using an Interactive Whiteboard for Implementing Inquiry-Based Learning in Mathematics

Floriane Wozniak

Abstract This chapter explores the role and potential of using an Interactive Whiteboard (IWB) for inquiry-based learning. A case study on how a French school teacher uses an interactive whiteboard is presented, illustrating how an IWB expands the milieu (Brousseau in *Theory of didactical situations in mathematics.* Dordrecht: Kluwer, 1997) of the learning situation and the collective part of the class investigation and suggests a mesogenesis-topogenesis-chronogenesis heuristic for digital pedagogical task design.

Keywords Interactive whiteboard · Inquiry-based learning

1 Introduction

This chapter proposes a theoretical perspective on task design, by illustrating, a case-study where the Interactive WhiteBoard (IWB) is integrated into a French primary school (10 and 11 years old) and used to discuss theoretical underpinnings of inquiry-based learning. This research study was set up to investigate teachers' practices in proposing and solving a mathematical modelling problem. The purpose of this chapter is to analyse how teachers' use of an IWB encourages or not the implementation of inquiry-based learning in the classroom. More specifically, the chapter attempts to explore the following questions: What might the role and potential of an IWB for inquiry-based learning be? What new dimensions might an IWB bring about in class activities in the context of inquiry-based learning?

In the first part I review theoretical backgrounds for using an IWB and inquiry-based learning. In the second part I present a case study of a teacher who employed an IWB to carry out inquiry-based learning during a mathematical modelling class. In the last parts I will discuss aspects of IWB inquiry-base task design.

F. Wozniak (✉)
Université de Strasbourg, IRIST, EA 3424, Strasbourg, France
e-mail: floriane.wozniak@espe.unistra.fr

© Springer International Publishing Switzerland 2017   41
A. Leung and A. Baccaglini-Frank (eds.), *Digital Technologies in Designing Mathematics Education Tasks*, Mathematics Education in the Digital Era 8,
DOI 10.1007/978-3-319-43423-0_3

2 Theoretical Background

2.1 The IWB and Teaching Practices

The IWB was massively introduced in the UK in order to change the teachers' practices towards greater interactivity between students and their teacher. Consequently many British studies have been conducted on teaching practices in connection with the IWB. Miller et al. (2005) identified three stages of development in the effective use of the IWB[1]:

- Supported didactic: The teacher makes some use of the IAW but only as a visual support to the lesson and not as an integral tool to conceptual development. There is little interactivity, student involvement or discussion.
- Interactive: The teacher makes some use of the potential of the IAW to stimulate students' responses from time to time in the lesson and to demonstrate some concepts. Elements of lessons challenge students to think, by the use of a variety of verbal, visual and aesthetic stimuli.
- Enhanced interactive: This approach is a progression from the previous stage, marked by a change of thinking on the part of teachers. They now seek to use the technology as an integral part of most lessons, and look to integrate concept and cognitive development in a way that exploits the interactive capacity of the technology. These teachers are aware of the techniques available, are fluent in their use and structure lessons so that there is considerable opportunity for students to respond to IAW stimuli—as individuals, pairs or groups—with enhanced interactive learning. The IAW is used as a means of prompting discussion, explaining processes and developing hypotheses or structures; these are then tested by varied application. A wide variety of materials are used including 'home-grown' and internet resources and IAW specific and commercial software (p. 4).

However, Smith et al. (2006) observed that the most common use of the IWB remains as a tool for projecting content and

> traditional patterns of whole class interaction persist despite the emphasis on interactive whole class teaching in the national strategies and the introduction of IWBs in the English primary school classroom (p. 455).

A requirement for taking advantage of the potential of the IWB is to change teacher behaviour: the teacher-instructor who shows the knowledge to be learned must become a teacher-go-between who organizes the meeting between students and knowledge to be learnt. Miller et al. (2008) suggested a new pedagogy for using the IWB which they termed *at the board, on the desk, in the head*:

---

[1]Miller et al. used the abbreviation IAW instead of IWB.

> A typical lesson will have students interacting with the teacher, the IWB and with each other and would involve some of the similar features found in lessons that are typified by the approach of Swan (2005) (p. 3)

This pedagogy aims at leading teachers to question the differences in information processing when the students work on the desk, at the IWB or in "their head". Thus teachers turn their attention to their own practices for improving their understanding on how IWBs can improve learning.

Chevallard (2002a), in the Anthropological Theory of the Didactic, postulates the existence of a close link between mathematical knowledge, mathematical organizations (used by the class and the conditions created by the teacher) and didactical organizations (for using this mathematical knowledge). Thus, the type of teaching activities based on this linkage proposed to students will affect the type of the IWB usages employed. In this chapter, the context for this linkage is a mathematical modelling activity which requires an inquiry-based learning approach.

2.2 Inquiry-Based Learning

The use of inquiry-based learning in science education is a long-standing constructivist pedagogic tradition after John Dewey, Jerome Bruner, Jean Piaget and Lev Vygotsky. Even if there are some differences between the pragmatic philosophy of Dewey and the rationalist philosophy of Bachelard (Artigue and Blomhoj 2013), inquiry-based learning is a pedagogic embodiment of a Bacherlard-like vision of sciences:

> First of all we must know how to state problems. Whatever one might say, in the scientific life, problems do not arise by themselves. It is precisely this sense of problem that gives the mark of the true scientific mind. For a scientific mind, all knowledge is an answer to a question. Without a question, there cannot be scientific knowledge. Nothing goes without saying. Nothing is given. Everything is built. (Bachelard, 1934; p. 17, my translation).

Minner et al. (2010), who synthesised research about the effect on students' learning through inquiry-based science education, noted:

> The term inquiry has figured prominently in science education, yet it refers to at least three distinct categories of activities—what scientists do (e.g., conducting investigations using scientific methods), how students learn (e.g., actively inquiring through thinking and doing into a phenomenon or problem, often mirroring the processes used by scientists), and a pedagogical approach that teachers employ (e.g., designing or using curricula that allow for extended investigations) (p. 476).

In France, inquiry-based learning appears in curricula of science teaching as a teaching method based on "seven essential moments" (BOEN No 5 special issue of August 25, 2005):

(1) Choice of a problem by the teacher;
(2) Appropriation of the problem by the students;

(3) Formulation of conjectures, explanatory hypothesis, possible protocols;
(4) Investigation or the resolution of the problem by students;
(5) Argued exchange on students' proposals;
(6) Acquirement and the structuration of knowledge;
(7) Operationalization of knowledge.

Inquiry-based learning is not only looking for a solution to a problem, it is also a pedagogic approach where inquiry is at the basis of learning. Thus at the end of primary school, the personal skills booklet, introduced on June 14th 2010, attests students' capacity to "practice an inquiry-based method: observe, inquire; handle and experiment, formulate a hypothesis and test it, argue; try several pathways of solution" [my translation].

In this chapter I am interested in the role and potential of using an IWB for the implementation of inquiry-based learning in mathematics classroom. What features of the IWB can be used in the context of inquiry-based task design? First of all, criteria that can be used to determine whether inquiry-based learning has been well implemented in a teaching situation are needed.

2.3 Criteria for Implementation of Inquiry-Based Learning

The Anthropological Theory of the Didactic (Chevallard 2006), like the Theory of Didactical Situations (Brousseau 1997), is based on a postulate: *a student learns by adaptation in interaction with a milieu.* The solution of the studied problem is produced via a student's autonomous confrontation with this milieu. Chevallard (2011) suggested studying milieu through three processes: mesogenesis, topogenesis and chronogenesis. *Mesogenesis*, the genesis of the milieu, is the process by which the milieu of a situation is produced, developed and enriched. *Topogenesis*, the genesis of the positions, is the process by which the duties of the teacher and students in a teaching situation are allocated; that is, how the activity is divided between the teacher and the students. *Chronogenesis*, the genesis of the didactic time, is the process by which the temporality of knowledge acquisition is modified. These three processes form criteria for implementation of inquiry-based learning.

The aim of inquiry-based learning is to search for answers for a given question. Chevallard (2002b) described the process of studying a question through a 5-step cycle:

(1) Observation of already existing resources
(2) Experimental and theoretical analysis of these initial resources
(3) Assessment of these resources
(4) Development of the final answer
(5) Justification and illustration of the answer produced

The function of resources for studying the inquiry process is crucial and Chevallard (2006) differentiates media and milieu as two types of resource. A *media* is defined as "any social system pretending to inform some segment of the population or some group of people about the natural or social world" and a *milieu* is defined as "any system that, as far as the question that you address to it is concerned, is devoid of intentions and therefore behaves like a fragment of nature—a system that intends neither to please or to displease you nor to defeat you of your hopes" (ibid, p. 29). Media and milieu are distinguishable from one another by the didactical intent concerning the acquisition of information. Media is a resource produced with the intention of providing information about something for someone. For instance, the texts in scientific literature are media for a physicist who is searching for existing information about the phenomenon under study. Milieu is a system of objects that produces feedback without any didactic intention towards students. For instance, an experimental process may be used as a milieu for studying a physical phenomenon.

When initially approaching a problem, the first action is to look for different media to find whether the answer, or part of the answer, already exists. Documentary research, experiments, observations are then used to create a milieu to test and validate the information provided by these media. The *dialectic between media and milieu* (Chevallard 2006) is the didactical dynamics that puts to the test the resources to produce the materials from which the answer is developed. Thus, for instance, the outcome of a survey on the Internet (Ladage and Chevallard 2011; Chevallard and Wozniak 2013) is based on a dual assessment of the reliability level and reception quality of the information provided by a media: "Is it right?" and "Do I understand?" respectively. Accumulation and testing of resources contribute to the validation of the produced answer and the construction of a milieu is fed by the validation of information provided by the consulted media. Thus milieus providing feedback to media may combine and evolve into a larger milieu of the problem situation.

The mesogenesis criterion: the milieu of a problem situation is constructed out of the dialectic between media and milieus. In inquiry-based learning, the purpose is to learn how to produce an answer to a problem. Students must find their own ways to validate the information provided by the media. Therefore the teacher must remain in the background. This means that the role of the students in the learning process should grow individually and collectively whereas the teacher is in an assistant position.

The topogenesis criterion: the teacher remains in the background leaving the individual students and the whole class to develop key roles in constructing the milieu from which the answer is developed. Since the milieu is constructed and organized by the class, the issue of controlling the time for doing it becomes crucial. Because of time constraints due to the demand of the curriculum, the teacher sometimes reduces the role of the students in the topogenesis process in order to "move the course onwards." In inquiry-based learning, it is important for the teacher to modify the didactical time allowing students to complete the inquiry process.

The chronogenesis criterion: the teacher gives enough time for students to complete the inquiry process.

Under these theoretical elements, a list of questions can be drawn to evaluate the implementation of inquiry-based learning:

- Mesogenesis: What is the milieu made of? Did the milieu evolve during the inquiry process? Has the dialectic of media and milieus been used? How has the answer to the problem been validated?
- Topogenesis: How and by whom is the milieu made? What are the roles of the teacher and students in building the answer to the problem?
- Chronogenesis: How has the teacher managed the time of the inquiry process? Does s/he shorten the time of the inquiry process?

3   A Case Study on Teachers' Use of an IWB

Wozniak (2012) examined teaching practices and their effects on students' learning during a sequence of problem-based lessons. In the study, teachers were given a larger degree of freedom to design their teaching sequence. In one case, the teacher used an IWB as a tool in the classroom to carry out a sequence of inquiry-based mathematics lessons.

3.1   The Problem

The problem to be solved was introduced by a photo. Figure 1 is a scaled-down version of the original 16.1 cm by 12 cm photo distributed to the students.

This kind of problem is called a *Fermi Problem*:

> Enrico Fermi (1901–1954), who in 1938 won the Nobel Prize for physics for his work on nuclear processes, was known by his students for posing open problems that could only be solved by giving a reasonable estimate. Fermi problems such as how many piano tuners are there in Chicago? share the characteristic that the initial answer of the problem solver is that the problem could not possibly be solved without recourse to further reference material. (Peter-Koop 2004, p. 457)

These problems, based on real world situations, are characterized by a problem statement that does not include numbers and whose solution relies on a modelling activity. Amongst the Fermi problems, the problem of the Giant is of the "Pictorial Problems or Picture Mathematics" type (Herget and Torres-Skoumal 2007) where information required to answer the question must be extracted from a photo or picture.

This photo was taken at an amusement park in England. The leg of a Giant is partly visible. What is roughly the height of the Giant?

Fig. 1 The problem of the Giant [my translation]

3.2 Description of the Case Study

The teacher designed five lessons for a total length of 4 h. During the first lesson (45 min), students were given freedom to conduct individual inquiry starting with three questions:

1. In your opinion, how tall is the Giant?
2. Explain how you obtained this result.
3. What elements are missing to calculate the Giant's height?

Some students asked the teacher about the accuracy level of the answer (in particular whether the answer is an integer or a decimal number). The teacher wrote on the IWB the numerical answers given by the students for the first question and on a paperboard the information that the students would like to know to solve the problem. The teacher ended the lesson with the remark *"I'll look at what you have written on your documents and we will try to see among all the elements that are there, what is useful and what is useless"* [my translation].

The teacher started the second lesson (1 h and 5 min) by showing a selection of four student productions from the previous lesson. The goal was to *"compare these solutions with what we lack and try to see how each of these four solutions attempted to circumvent what we needed"* [my translation]. One production was a mere opinion *"for me it is 12 m"*, the other three solutions were of the same type as what the teacher had in mind. The height of the Giant is calculated by multiplying the foot-length (as measured in the photo) of the Giant by a coefficient k. Afterwards a collective discussion was initiated on identifying the essential elements needed to solve the problem by considering the list set out at the end of the first lesson. Homework was given for the next session: a survey on the heights of adults.

The third lesson (55 min) began with a discussion on the three necessary elements to produce the answer to the problem: the heights of humans, the foot-length of the boot, Giants are human-like (similar in proportion). Then the teacher collected the results of the investigation on the "*average height of a person*" and the class discussed how each student collected and produced this information. Students measured their foot-lengths and their heights. They then established the number of transfer of their foot-length to their bodies to determine their heights. The data thus obtained was collected in a spreadsheet projected on the IWB. Using the Spreadsheet, the students verified that the ratio (height/foot-length) was between 5 and 6. A final discussion started around how to determine the ratio k by transfer, its validation by calculation and the usefulness of knowing k to solve the problem. Afterwards, the teacher gave students homework for the next session: a survey to determine the ratio (height/foot-length) to verify whether the ratio they found was the same for an adult.

In the fourth lesson (1 h and 2 min), the teacher collected the results of the investigation about the relationship k = height/foot-length. A discussion was carried out on the differences between the measurements made on students and adults and the technique that could be used to calculate the height of the Giant. The teacher concluded "*A child is not a miniature adult*". The students made a final individual research structured by three questions:

1. In your opinion, how tall is the Giant?
2. Explain how you reached this result.
3. Explain what enabled you to find the height of the Giant.

Numerical answers were collected on the IWB followed by a discussion focussing on the comparison with the students' answers from the first session.

In the fifth and final lesson, students summarized their findings and wrote in their notebooks the solution obtained.

To assess the implementation of inquiry-based learning in the sequence of lessons described above, in the following section I apply the three criteria discussed in Sect. 2.3 on the students' construction of the answer to the Giant problem.

3.3   Mesogenesis, Topogenis, Chronogenesis

Regarding mesogenesis, the milieu is gradually enriched during the lessons through the survey after lesson 2 and the two data collections on the ratios foot-length to student heights and foot-length to adult height (lessons 3 and 4). To carry out the investigation on the average height of a person, students interviewed their parents and grandparents. Furthermore, some students consulted a website, used the heights of football players or consulted a book. The sharing of different information allowed the implementation of the dialectic of media and milieus. There was a document found on the website of the INSEE (National Institute for Statistics and Economical Studies) which allowed the teacher to validate students' answers:

> I went on the internet and I went to the INSEE. [...] And there is such a study there... Here it is: the currently reported size of men of age 18 to 65 is 1.75 m and the average size of women is 1.63 m. It was you Lisa who found this. You have found the same thing, you have found it in a book. In my case, I am basing [my information] on a study, therefore, on data collected by the INSEE. So if you wish so, do you agree to take 1.75 m? [my translation]

Regarding topogenesis, the teacher guided the lessons by explicitly asking students to perform certain tasks leading gradually to the solution. During lesson 2, a student put forward the idea that a relationship could exist between the size of the shoe and the height of a man. The teacher then organized debates and allowed time in the classroom to make sure that the ideas were well discussed by the whole class. He did not express judgements on the ideas but instead he asked this student to continue the investigation:

> Can you look that up for next time? You'll tell us if there is a link between the foot-size of a person and his/her height. I let you take care of it. [my translation].

Similarly, after the first data collection (lesson 3), the teacher suggested to the students that the ratio may not be the same for an adult. After a class discussion, the teacher concluded:

> Is the same ratio found for an adult? It will be your job for the next lesson. You will do a survey at home. You will try to complete the table with one or two adults. Man or Woman? [my translation]

The milieu is constructed by the class under teacher's management and guidance. The teacher was well aware of the mathematics involved as he said during the post lesson interview:

> Some students let themselves get carried away by the class without understanding why we were looking for the average height of an adult or why the search for a potential invariance of the human body proportions could be important [my translation].

The teacher plays a key role in the study: he helps the students clarify the problem and identify relevant data, organize the comparison of students' answers, coordinate the collective reflection and commission the writing. He indeed used an inquiry-based method in the sense of Dewey.

Regarding chronogenesis, the teacher organized the lessons to be implemented over a longer than usual, but acceptable, duration. In particular he delayed conclusive sharing to allow students to make judgements on their productions first. This drove the lesson in a certain direction. Furthermore, he assigned outside classroom data collection and documentation research activities, and used skilful questioning techniques in collective discussions to guide the students' thoughts.

The milieu for this lesson sequence was made out of ample resources and was being constructed constantly during the lessons. The teacher organized discussions among students until agreeable answers were reached. In this way, the dialectic of media and milieus was pedagogically and fruitfully realized.

4 Discussion on Inquiry-Based IWB Task Design

4.1 Roles and Functions of the IWB

The teacher used the IWB in every lesson and it was a tool that students were comfortable using to conduct surveys or to collect data. The IWB was placed near the teacher's desk and the black board of the classroom to facilitate its use as a classroom tool and students had no difficulty getting their numerical data in the IWB spreadsheet suggesting that they were familiar with using it in the classroom. Rather than just enhancing presentation, the IWB enriched the milieu with respect to sustaining communication in the class and fostering interactivity. Thus, the IWB digitally enhanced collective communication and interactivity.

The IWB was obviously used as a display tool. The Fermi Problem photo was presented using the IWB in lesson 1. Students' procedures were presented and discussed collectively at the IWB before individual work was started (lesson 2). Furthermore the teacher used the IWB to validate the students' research and to gather numerical data on a spreadsheet for computational checking, and to justify the choice of the average size of a man via the Internet (lesson 3).

The IWB was used as a "guardian of collective memory" (lesson 4). Throughout the collaborative lesson sequence, the IWB was a digital environment conducive to producing a collective answer by facilitating the analysis of students' proposals, validating data, keeping track of intermediate results and creating a space to synthesize. The teacher played an important mediating role between the IWB and the students, guiding their investigation with skill and flexibility. It was the teacher who proposed to study the morphology of adults since students did not seem to be aware that there may be physical differences between a child and an adult.

Thus with respect to a mathematical modelling classroom, an IWB can be used as a modelling tool conducive to the struction and formation of solution discourses. Mediation using the IWB can facilitate a constructive implementation of the inquiry-based learning.

4.2 Inquiry-Based IWB Task Design Considerations

Studies have been conducted on using IWBs to support the paradigm shift from a transmissive pedagogy to a pedagogy that focuses on interaction between students and the teacher. Classroom integration of IWBs requires understanding of how the IWB can afford pedagogy. Thus instead of focusing attention on the technology itself, the focus should be on the teachers' pedagogical practices. Wood and Ashfield (2008) made the following observation:

> While initially this study intended to focus upon the way in which the IWB could support whole-class interactive teaching, it became increasingly apparent that the teacher's interpretation of whole-class interactive teaching itself was the primary factor in developing materials and opportunities for children to engage with their own method. In terms of creative teaching, it is essentially the teacher who determines what resource to use and how it will be utilised (ibid, p. 94)

From the above, it seems essential that the teacher uses the IWB as an environment enabling an answer built collectively.

From the point of view of mesogenesis, the IWB clearly enriched the milieu and could be used as a "window on the world", for example when the teacher showed a document from the INSEE website through it. It is uncommon in France that a teacher valorises a student's idea and conducts an Internet query. French teachers usually claim strong reservations about this practice. The IWB provides teachers with a dynamic writing window with access to knowledge beyond the classroom. Teachers should design activities making use of the IWB's features to create a milieu made up of multi-digital resources like photos, maps, software (e.g. spreadsheets, dynamic geometry software), and documental research. An IWB is an effective platform (milieu) to design activities based on sharing that could facilitate the implementation of the dialectic of media and milieus.

From the point of view of topogenesis, the IWB "memorizes" the displays and processes numerical data. A "collective space of student work" can thus be formed where the dialectic between media and milieus takes place by comparing the different student contributions. Teachers should design autonomous activities for students to search and to share under the IWB platform. Teachers may take the role of mediators who guide and organize student-student discussions within the collective space produced by the IWB.

From the point of view of chronogenesis, the IWB "escalates the efficiency" to collect and compare student work and thus speeds up the formation of solution discourse. The teacher should design activities allowing students how to access previous IWB captured data. The task design should make use of the IWB also as a storage space of the class to foster a progressive built up collective answer space to the problem. An IWB task should also be designed to manage the class memory.

4.3 Inquiry-Based Digital Task Design Activity Sequence

I have considered how a teacher made use of an IWB for the implementation of inquiry-based learning for solving a modelling problem. What is observed in an IWB classroom is *a decreased individual topogenesis for the benefit of increased mesogenesis.* By "memorizing" the class activities, the IWB naturally becomes a digital environment for collaborative study. The IWB creates conditions for the establishment of a collective pedagogy and an enrichment of the milieu. For instance, the use of the Internet on the IWB offers simultaneous multiple windows to facilitate inquiry based learning: search engines, translation services, dictionaries, encyclopedias, institutional sites, calculators, dynamic geometry software, spreadsheets, etc. The IWB case study described above confirms an observation of Wood and Ashfield (2008):

> This research seems to indicate that it is the skill and the professional knowledge of the teacher who mediates the interaction, and facilitates the development of students' creative answers at the interface of technology, which is critical to the enhancement of the whole-class teaching and method processes (p. 84).

The IWB is an example of a digital environment that can store and compute students' data to form a collective sample space for students' autonomous learning. Metagenesis, topogenesis and chronogenesis can be regarded as a heuristic triplet for pedagogical digital task design. These features combined suggest that for digital inquiry-based modelling task design, collective interactivity and simultaneous multiplicity should play a dominant role. The case study discussed in this chapter is an example to support such a task design approach. Task design in digital environment like IWB could make use of these two features to organize the classroom dynamic among mesogenesis, topogenesis and chronogenesis.

Base on the theoretical considerations discussed in Sect. 2, I would like to end the chapter by proposing criteria about the inquiry-based digital tasks design.

1. *Activity criterion*: The activity is based on solving a problem and a digital environment (IWB in the case of this chapter) is used to promote a collective study by data sharing.

2. *Mesogenesis criterion*: Students solve the problem by accessing to (digital) ressources and the digital environment is used to implement the dialectic of media and milieus in order to (1) produce an initial milieu of the problem situation by exploring existing (digital) resources; (2) develop the milieu by going deeper into the problem situation via experimental or theoretical analysis of these initial resources; and from this assessment result form a milieu that can provide possible explanations for the problem situation; (3) produce and justify the final answer to the problem situation via formulation of conjectures, explanatory hypothesis and possibly protocols and in this way the solution is validated by students' argumentation and discussion. For example, the IWB features facilitate literature survey and add real value by using resources like photos, maps or suitable digital tools (spreadsheet, dynamic geometry software, for example) for controlling the gradual shaping of the mathematical solution to the problem.

3. *Topogenesis criterion*: The students are autonomous and the teacher encourages students to contact directly with the digital environment (for example, the IWB environment) for gathering and incorporating data and ressources. The teacher is

a study director who organizes discussions between students and does not impose himself as a mediator between the IWB and the students.

4. *Chronogenesis criterion*: The didactic time governs the temporality of knowledge acquisition using the IWB preseres the students' previous works. Thus, the IWB is the memory container of the class that progressively builds a collective solution to the problem.

These activity criteria serve as a guideline to design inquiry-based digital tasks where collective study is essential and investigation is the motor of learning. The genesis of a digital-based (collective) milieu for a problem situation and the ease to shift attention between different resources are key factors enabling students to explore and formulate different possible solutions for a real-life problem situation.

References

Artigue, M., & Blomhoj, M. (2013). Conceptualizing inquiry-based education in mathematics. *ZDM Mathematics Education, 45*, 797–810.

Bachelard, G. (1934). *La Formation de L'esprit Scientifique*. Retrieved from http://classiques.uqac.ca/classiques/bachelard_gaston/formation_esprit_scientifique/formation_esprit.pdf.

Brousseau, G. (1997). *Theory of didactical situations in mathematics*. Dordrecht: Kluwer.

Chevallard, Y. (1989). Le passage de l'arithmétique à l'algèbre dans l'enseignement des mathématiques au collège. *Deuxième partie. Perspectives curriculaires: la notion de modélisation Petit x, 19*, 43–72.

Chevallard, Y. (1992). Fundamental concepts in didactics: Perspectives provided by an anthropological approach. In Recherches en Didactique des Mathématiques, special issue 131–167.

Chevallard, Y. (2002a). Organiser l'étude. Structures et fonctions. In J.-L. Dorier, M. Artaud, M. Artigue, R. Berthelot, & R. Floris (Eds.) *Actes de la 11ᵉ école d'été de didactique des mathématiques* (pp. 3–22). Grenoble: La Pensée Sauvage.

Chevallard, Y. (2002b). Les TPE comme problème didactique. In T. Assude, & B. Grugeon Allys (Eds.), *Actes du séminaire national de didactique des mathématiques 2001* (pp. 177–188). Paris: IREM de Paris 7 et ARDM.

Chevallard, Y. (2006). Steps towards a new epistemology in mathematics education. In *Proceedings of the Fourth Congress of the European Society for Research in Mathematics Education* (pp. 21–30). Barcellona: Universitat Ramon Llull.

Chevallard, Y. (2011). La notion d'ingénierie didactique, un concept à réfonder. Questionnement et éléments de réponse à partir de la TAD. In C. Margolinas, M. Abboud-Blanchard, L. Bueno-Ravel, N. Douek, A. Fluckiger, N. Douek, F. Vandebrouck, & F. Wozniak (Eds.), *En amont et en aval des ingénieries didactiques* (pp 81–108). Grenoble: La pensée sauvage.

Chevallard, Y., & Wozniak, F. (2013). Le calcul proportionnel et le symbole ∝: enquête sur une œuvre mathématique méconnue. In A. Bronner, C. Bulf, C. Castela, J.-P. Georget, M. Larguier, B. Pedemonte, A. Pressiat, & É. Roditi (Eds.), *Questions vives en didactique des mathématiques: problèmes de la profession d'enseignant, rôle du langage* (pp. 421–446). Grenoble: La pensée sauvage.

Herget, W., & Torres-Skoumal, M. (2007). Picture (im)perfect mathematics! In W. Blum, P. Galbraith, H.-W. Henn, & M. Niss (Eds.), *Modelling and applications in mathematics education: The 14th ICMI study* (pp. 379–386). New-York: Springer.

Ladage, C., & Chevallard, Y. (2011). Enquêter avec l'internet Études pour une didactique de l'enquête. *Éducation & Didactique, 5*(2), 85–115.

Miller, D., Averis, D., Door, V., & Glover, D. (2005). *How can the use of an interactive whiteboard enhance the nature of teaching and method in secondary mathematics and modern foreign languages: ICT Research Bursaries*. Report proposed to Becta.

Miller, D., Glover, D., & Averis, D. (2008). *Enabling enhanced mathematics teaching with interactive whiteboards*. Final Report for the National Centre for Excellence in the Teaching of Mathematics.

Minner, D., Jurist Levy, A., & Century, J. (2010). Inquiry-based science instruction—What is it and does it matter? Results from a research synthesis years 1085 to 2002. *Journal of Research in Science Teaching, 47*(4), 363–496.

Peter-Koop, A. (2004). Fermi problems in primary mathematics classrooms: students' interactive modelling processes. In I. Putt, R. Faragher, & M. McLean (Eds.), *Mathematics education for the third millennium, towards 2010. MERGA 2004 conference proceedings* (pp. 454–461). Sydney: Merga, Inc.

Smith, F., Hardman, F., & Higgins, S. (2006). The impact of interactive whiteboards on teacher-student interaction in the national literacy and numeracy strategies. *British Educational Research Journal, 32*(3), 443–457.

Swan, M. (2005) *Improving learning in mathematics: challenges and strategies*. Retrieved from http://www.ncetm.org.uk/files/224/improving_learning_in_mathematicsi.pdf.

Wood, R., & Ashfield, J. (2008). The use of the interactive whiteboard for creative teaching and method in literacy and mathematics: a case study. *British Journal of Educational Technology, 39*(1), 84–96.

Wozniak, F. (2012). Des professeurs des écoles face à un problème de modélisation: une question d'équipement praxéologique. *Recherches en Didactique des Mathématiques, 32*(1), 7–55.

Designing Technology that Enables Task Design

Kate Mackrell and Christian Bokhove

Abstract Although there is considerable interest in the use of technology in mathematics teaching and learning, there has been little focus within mathematics education on the design of the technology itself, or on how technology design might facilitate task design. In this chapter, we address the question of how technology has been designed to enable task design through interviews with four developers of technology environments designed to facilitate the learning of mathematics. Questions ranged from more general ones concerning the purposes and challenges faced in designing the environments to more specific aspects concerned with task design, such as the management of instrumental genesis and the provision of feedback. We found that all designers are facing technical challenges due to rapid hardware and software changes which make it important to identify the crucial aspects of the technology to conserve and develop. Such aspects include maintaining an appropriate balance between flexibility and constraint as well as addressing issues such as the way in which the environment responds to student actions.

Keywords Task · Design · Designers

1 Introduction

In the introduction to the substantial section on the use of technology in the Third International Handbook of Mathematics Education (Leung 2013), a number of significant questions are raised, ranging from the impact of technology on the school curriculum to issues of equity. However, tasks are only mentioned twice and

K. Mackrell (✉)
Institute of Education, UCL, London, UK
e-mail: katemackrell@sympatico.ca

C. Bokhove
University of Southampton, Southampton, UK
e-mail: c.bokhove@soton.ac.uk

© Springer International Publishing Switzerland 2017
A. Leung and A. Baccaglini-Frank (eds.), *Digital Technologies in Designing Mathematics Education Tasks*, Mathematics Education in the Digital Era 8,
DOI 10.1007/978-3-319-43423-0_4

the issue of the design of technology is not raised at all. The aim of this book as a whole is to affirm the importance of considering task design with technology, and this chapter will look at the specific question of what is needed from technology to enable task design.

Our experience working with the designers of two particular educational software environments, Cabri and the Digital Mathematics Environment (DME), has given us an awareness of some of the pedagogical ideals and issues influencing the development of these environments. We are also aware that there is a huge range of other programs that offer far fewer possibilities for task design, and hence felt that it is important to further explore and elucidate some of the design decisions that have been made through interviewing the designers of the above environments, together with two other designers.

We begin this chapter with a brief literature review, followed by a rationale for our choice of technology environments to explore. We then present a series of questions together with responses given by the designers, and some tentative conclusions and directions for further research.

Beyond a commitment to listening carefully to our participants and transparency regarding our questions and assumptions, we have deliberately not adopted a particular theoretical framework in order to interpret our findings, but have hopefully enabled the designers to speak for themselves in a way that will provoke further interest and enquiry.

2   Literature Review

There is currently increasing interest in the design of the technology used in teaching and learning mathematics. As Jackiw (designer of Geometer's Sketchpad and one of the designers of TouchCounts) identifies:

> Design certainly acts as the first doorway and first doorkeeper to any deeper curricular or epistemological innovation an educational technology might offer. For it is not at the structural level, but rather on the surface—at the designed interface—that users interact with technologies, that meanings are negotiated; that cognitive, psychological, educational and social transformation may, or may not, occur (Butler et al. 2009, p. 432).

There is extensive literature on the design of technology for learning from the standpoint of technology design, incorporating areas such as interface design. Of particular relevance for mathematics education is the work of Rabardel (2002), who introduced the well-known idea of instrumental genesis, in which an artifact becomes an instrument as the user develops schemes of use. Another lesser-known concept of Rabardel's is the dimension of operative transparency of an artifact, which has at one of its poles the "black box" in which the artifact's technical system is invisible, so that the person for whom the artifact is an instrument feels that they are acting directly on the environment. At the other pole is the "glass box" in which the artifact is visible and comprehensible to the user. Operative transparency has to do with the transparency of the artifact as appropriate to user action and information needs. For example, a learning situation, or a situation in which the artifact may break down, requires greater visibility.

There is substantially less literature with regard to designing for mathematics learning. An early set of design principles is given by Beeson (1998) in considering the design of an algebraic learning environment. Many of these are specific to facilitating the solving of algebraic equations, but several, such as mathematical correctness, the user making decisions about actions, and the provision of scaffolding when required, are relevant to general mathematics learning environments. Sedig and Sumner (2006) also incorporate considerations of relevance to mathematics, giving a characterization of possible interactions with visual mathematical representations (geometric structures, graphs, and diagrams) in terms of common characteristics, goals, intended benefits, and features. Mor and Winter (2007), working from a design-based research perspective that draws heavily on research in mathematics education, review a number of current projects based on design patterns, which are methods for solving recurrent problems which describe the problem and the context in which the method is applicable, but do not include precise directives. An example is the model-view-controller pattern, in which a model (internal storage of e.g. data), view (the way in which the data is displayed) and controller (the means by which the data are manipulated) are encapsulated separately. This was used in the design of the ToonTalk programming language. They also stress the importance of participatory design. Bokhove and Drijvers (2010) developed a comprehensive framework for the evaluation of technology used in teaching algebra, with criteria, which may also be considered as design principles, divided into those relevant to the mathematics (e.g. "the tool is mathematically sound and faithful to the underlying mathematical properties"), the use of the tool (e.g. "the tool is easy to use for a student"), assessment (e.g. "the tool caters for several types of feedback") and general features (e.g. "the stability and performance of the tool"). Mackrell (2011, 2012) explored a number of the design decisions taken in different dynamic geometry programs in the context of a task exploring the relationship between the radius and area of a circle and showed that subtle differences in the design of the interface and affordances of the programs could significantly affect the outcomes when performing the task.

However, apart from Sangwin and Grove (2006) who discuss the design of an algebraic system that enables teachers to create their own questions, we have been unable to locate any research that looks specifically at the ways in which technology design may facilitate task design in general. This chapter is hence an initial exploration of this question in which we identify possibilities that may form the basis for further research.

3   Technology Environments for Task Design

We deliberately define "task" as loosely as possible, as the focus of a learner's activity. This may arise from a demand made of the learner by a teacher, from a resource such as a textbook or an app, or may be generated by the learner herself. A mathematical task is simply a task which involves mathematics, even if the mathematics is not the focus of the task for the learner. Different task designers working within a particular task design environment are likely to elaborate this definition further in response to their own purposes. In particular, different task designers will have different views on what constitutes an effective task.

In this chapter, we begin the process of identifying the ways in which technology can be designed in order to facilitate task design by interviewing the designers of a number of programs. As there are a huge number of programs which may be used to present mathematical tasks to students, we made a number of choices to limit the programs we considered.

Our first choice was to focus on technology that provides an environment within which the student acts and gets feedback on their actions rather than technology, such as a calculator,[1] which acts primarily as a tool for action within a non-technological environment, as we feel that designing feedback is an important part of task design.

Our second choice was that, while we recognize that generic tools such as spreadsheets can be very rich environments for task design, we confined ourselves to technology that has been specifically designed for mathematics education. One reason for this choice is that mathematics educators are likely to be able to have more impact on the design of such software than on the design of more generic software. Another reason is that most generic software is a tool for doing, designed for efficiency rather than for facilitating learning. An example of the distinction is the Autograph "slow plot" feature, where the graph of a function is drawn slowly and may be stopped at any time to enable the teacher to ask questions. Another example is the Sketchpad dilation tool, where each object defining a dilation (center and scale factor) must be defined separately, which is time-consuming but focuses student awareness on what is required to perform a dilation.

The third choice was to not consider software which has significant deviations from conventionally accepted mathematical norms. Mackrell (2011) points out, for example that in one particular dynamic geometry program, the label for a segment is also used as a variable which represents its length, which can lead to issues with the understanding of the concept of variable.

We are also committed to the view that task design should potentially involve all who participate in the teaching and learning processes:

---

[1]We note however that many highly complex graphical calculators such as the TI-Nspire do provide environments.

- The person or people engaged in the task (e.g. school student, or research mathematician)
- A person or people directly facilitating those engaged in the task (e.g. teacher)
- "Outsiders", who are people not directly engaged in the performance of the task (e.g. textbook author, or app creator)

This means that we were not interested in systems in which task design was only accessible to the "outside" designer, with teachers and students always being presented with set tasks. Enabling student task design can take the form of providing open-ended tasks where students can choose the direction that they take, or the form of asking students to pose their own questions which can be explored within the technology environment.[2] We were hence only interested in systems that enabled open-ended tasks and allowed students to pose and investigate their own questions.

The first two environments we will consider have deliberately been created in order to provide a range of possibilities for task design across the mathematics curriculum and, while fitting the criteria above, also are the ones we have personally used most extensively for task design. Both of these environments provide a task design environment, in which the task is designed, and a separate task environment, in which the task is performed.

3.1 The Digital Mathematics Environment

Peter Boon is the chief designer of this environment. At the beginning of the millennium, the Freudenthal Institute already had a rich library of applets (see Bokhove et al. 2006). The first version of the DME, in which the applets were embedded in an environment that stored the work that students did with them, was created in response to requests from teachers (including the second author of this chapter, in the Galois and Sage project[3]). This, however, caused a new feature request to emerge: authorability. An authoring layer was implemented gradually, first incorporating algebra applets and then other applets. The DME is now a digital learning and assessment environment for mathematics in secondary and higher education, in which "interactive teaching methods and feedback play a central role". Students can work at any time on modules that have been selected for them and receive feedback on their answers. Teachers can view the students' work and adapt modules and activities to meet the needs of the class. DME is currently being extended with further components, or "widgets", in particular in the MC squared project in which Bokhove is involved.

---

[2]Students may also act as "teachers" in e.g. designing tasks for younger students.

[3]See bokhove.net/galois-and-sage-projects/.

3.2 Cabri

Jean-Marie Laborde is the chief designer of this environment. Cabri was one of the two original dynamic geometry environments (the other being Geometer's Sketchpad) created in the late 1980's to enable exploration of Euclidean geometry by taking advantage of the first graphical user interface created by Xerox for the Star Machine. This type of interface was later widely popularized by Apple with the Macintosh and the mouse. Later versions of Cabri added graphing (Cabri II and II Plus) and 3D geometry features (Cabri 3D). However, until the development of the new Cabri (originally named Cabri Elem, but now shortened to just Cabri), beginning in 2007, Cabri was seen as a microworld: an environment for student mathematical exploration and construction, rather than an environment in which students could be constrained to perform structured tasks. The new Cabri has additional features for number and algebra and also a range of options for task designers to control the behavior of objects. In the design of the new Cabri, the idea was not to create two separate environments, but instead to create one common environment, presenting different levels of possibilities to different users (author-teacher-student). Mackrell has worked with Cabri since 1992 and is currently engaged in the Number Stories project at CEMSE, University of Chicago, developing activities involving real-world interactive problem-solving.

We decided to consider in addition two environments which focus on handling data, as this is an area in task design which was neglected in the ICMI—22 study, represented by only one out of the fourteen papers in the technology section. The chosen environments, Fathom, with chief designer Bill Finzer, and Data Workshop, with chief designer Jim Flanders, do not have separate task and task design environments, but are otherwise very different: Fathom focuses on data analysis, while Data Workshop focuses on experiment design in order to collect or generate data. They are also at very different stages of development: Fathom was developed in the mid-1990s, and, owing to the shift to web-based technology, and despite being widely known and used, will not be further developed. Data Workshop is still in the process of development and is not yet publicly available. This gave us the opportunity to compare issues arising in the ongoing development of software with issues faced in initial design.

4 Questions and Responses

The lack of research in this area was a major issue in identifying appropriate questions to ask; hence many of our questions arose from our own experience. We aimed to be comprehensive; however, in retrospect, our choice of questions was not unproblematic. We are hence giving our questions verbatim in order to facilitate criticism.

Our first three questions were designed to explore the purposes, aspects identified as most important, and challenges faced in designing the different environments, without particular reference to task design. Our further questions focused on various aspects of task design. The rationale for each of these questions is given in its introduction. The questions were given to each of the designers in advance of the interview. Interviews, which lasted about an hour, were conducted in person with Laborde and Boon, and online with Flanders and Finzer, and responses were recorded and transcribed or summarized. Transcriptions and ultimately the content of this chapter were also sent to each participant for approval.

1. *What is the main purpose of this environment?*

It was clear from the clarity and depth of all the responses that Beeson's (1998) hypothesis that the starting point for the design of any technology is a clear statement of its purpose was corroborated.

Both Flanders and Finzer stressed that their software was designed primarily for students, as learning environments. They each gave the main focus within handling data that their software was designed to address: Fathom to enable students to get into the flow of working with and understanding data, and Data Workshop to facilitate the design of experiments for students new to experimental design in order to collect their own data. Fathom additionally has facilities for data visualization, although Tinkerplots, (published by the same company originally and designed for younger learners) focuses on this area. Data Workshop additionally has data generation and data analysis options.

Both designers gave a justification for their purpose. Flanders is concerned that data analysis is being pushed out of the early elementary curriculum in the U.S. and that most online statistics technology focuses on looking at other people's data. Data Workshop, in contrast, enables students to learn about experiment design and implementation. Finzer situated the importance of the software in a broader context: "all significant problems that we face in this world require people who understand about how to work with data to reach solutions".

Neither Laborde nor Boon mentioned specific curriculum areas, and both mentioned the needs of designers and learners. DME is described as "an online platform for designing and using rich interactive content for mathematics." The new Cabri is designed partly to better address teacher needs by making it easier to use the technology through providing content that they can change and adapt to student needs. However, there is also an emphasis on the learner; the earlier Cabri environment has been further developed, with the aim of immersing the user in the world of mathematics, with no barrier between what they are doing and what is happening on the screen. There are similarities here with Finzer's aim of "drawing students into data so that they don't just see Fathom as a tool, but they see it as a way into understanding data".

2. *What are the most important aspects of this environment?*

The answers here were closely linked with the purposes identified for the environments. Flanders elaborated on the means by which Data Workshop would achieve its purpose: by requiring students to focus on the nature of variables, defining their type and measures before being able to enter any data, with the consequence that clean data is produced and the software can suggest appropriate representations and disallow inappropriate representations. In addition he elaborated that the environment gives students ways to generate their own data through simulation as well as survey design and implementation.

In contrast, Finzer, who focused on the nature of the user experience, stated that Fathom is "all about reaching in and touching stuff", with direct manipulation, dynamic linking, drag and drop of attributes and the "scraping" of data from html. "You can just reach into the graph and drag your data or change the axes and click on something in a table" without changing mode or shifting to a different page, and the use of dialogue boxes is minimized. "Fathom also gives the user a sense of further possibilities, from the depth of the data but also from its rich facilities: formulas, units, meters, experiments, census micro-data…" He also mentioned "a consistent model for simulation of sampling and collecting measures".

Laborde also focused on the user experience: Cabri aims to be as efficient, easy, and natural as possible, so that what the user sees happening when they act on any part of the environment is what they expect—constrained by the mathematics underlying the environment. Objects are acted on flexibly and directly rather than through command lines. In this way unexpected implications of the mathematics may be revealed. He also stressed the mathematical fidelity of Cabri: "if you expect something that is contradictory to mathematics it will never be realized by the environment".

Boon elaborated on the affordances of DME, focusing on the needs of both the end users and the task designers (teachers and authors). One key feature is the fact that student work is stored and that the environment therefore serves as a "Learning Management System" (LMS) in which teachers can see the work students have done. Boon elaborates that in recent projects such as "MC squared" emphasis has been on extending the existing capabilities with learning analytics features. However, to allow teachers to tailor content to their own needs, the DME also provides features for designing and authoring rich interactive content. In Boon's view "interactive" implies that the system should react to user inputs. Boon specifically mentioned the importance of allowing for both open-ended and more closed tasks; both approaches have their place in the learning process and Boon thinks it is imperative that an environment provides a rich toolbox to cater for different teaching approaches. In Boon's words: "In the DME we try to support the learning process as a whole. At least we try to: digital curriculum as ambition."

3. *What have been the most challenging issues faced in developing the environment?*

A major challenge faced by all developers apart from Finzer was responding to the need to shift to an online environment. For Fathom, the decision has been made to merely maintain it as desktop software until it is no longer feasible to upgrade it to new operating systems. Finzer is instead working on a new project, CODAP, an NSF funded open-source online data analysis platform, designed for curriculum developers who have as part of their goal getting students to work with data which will incorporate many of the ideas developed in designing Fathom.

For the new software, Data Workshop, the challenge has been to find a sufficiently dynamic programming environment that works within a browser; Silverlight has been chosen. Although tablet computers offer new opportunities such as handwriting recognition, Cabri and DME require that code be rewritten in html5, a lengthy and costly process. Laborde also expressed particular frustration at the huge amount of time spent keeping Cabri working with new operating systems for the Mac and for Windows.

Finzer and Flanders both mentioned user expectations as challenges. With Data Workshop, teachers have expressed concerns that, without the facility to misrepresent data, it was difficult to consider what data representations were appropriate. Finzer identified the tension between responding to the users who wanted particular new features and keeping the interface uncluttered, particularly important in light of the challenge of making learning to use Fathom depend on discovery rather than help systems. When Fathom 2 was developed, the choice was made to put most of the software development effort into improving usability.

Finzer also mentioned two specific design challenges: deciding how to represent data (and then convince people that the representation chosen was a good idea), and how to design the formula editor, identified as "the least loved part of Fathom."

Implementing the DME authoring layer for a wide range of existing applets proved to be a big challenge, according to Boon, and meant the whole architecture of the DME had to be revised. The challenge continues, as further components are added.

The next questions focused more specifically on the facilitation of task design.

4. *Task design environment versus task environment*

This question arose out of our experience with Cabri and DME, which each have authoring environments and was aimed at clarifying the structure of the environment as a whole for designing and performing tasks.

We define the task design environment as the environment within which the task is designed and created. The task environment is the environment within which the task is performed. These might be very different, as when a programmer uses Flash to write an applet, or they might be identical, as with Logo, when a student is designing and then performing their own task.

Describe the relationship between the task design environment and the task environment.

We knew in advance that Fathom and Data Workshop do not have specific authoring environments. However, the responses concerning these two environments were unexpectedly rich.

In describing Data Workshop, Flanders made a distinction that we were not expecting:

> For surveys, the task design environment is where students/teachers think about what information they want to gather, what questions do that, and what types of responses are amenable to further analysis. The task environment has two parts: (a) getting participants to take the survey (simplest approach is a URL that they respond to online) and (b) analysis of the results in the Workbench.

> For simulations, the design and task environments are together, but not identical. Simulations are chosen from a menu in the Workbench and then the student gets to modify the parameters of the simulation (e.g., number of coins to be tossed, number of tosses, etc.). Then the computer performs the task of the simulation followed by some limited options for the students to change representations of the results, compare different simulations, and so on.

Finzer made the following important distinction:

> You don't design activities *in* Fathom. You design activities that *use* Fathom.

Fathom deliberately does not have a separate authoring mode: as in Logo the task design and task doing environments are identical. However, documents may be created so that students do not start from scratch: the developer uses the environment to go through what the student is going to go through to know what that experience is like and to lower the obstacles that may be found. For example, a document might be created that contains a collection of data and also some text, a table, or a graph or slider as a minimal scaffold in order to help students get started.

The task environment in Cabri is called the student environment. There are two task design environments: the author environment, with full access to all features of the software, in which the student environment is customized, and the teacher environment, where the student environment may be modified according to the options provided by the task author. Laborde came back to his main concern about the ease of use of Cabri:

> The aim is that the task environment is as natural as possible, with nothing to learn in order to use it. You simply perform what you want in the environment and the environment is smart enough to react to your expectations mathematically.

> The task design environment is at a completely different level of creation and use, where many aspects do not feel as natural, and hence require a step for anybody who would like to create a task in this environment. Unlike mathematics, with shared notation, ways of representation, concepts, etc., which feel "natural" to the community, there is no standard for such an environment. For instance, unlike many environments, Cabri does not have a timeline. Time is stopped and started by means of an hourglass and variables that depend on the time can be reset. This is not a metaphor which comes from the everyday world, and hence some people have difficulties with the hourglass.

In response to the question, Boon clearly sees a separation between the task design environment and the task environment. The authoring/task design environment is available to teachers with editing rights; students can then perform these tasks in the task environment. Boon also commented on how task design tools could be useful to students: see question 9 for further detail.

5. *Features of technology to enable tasks*

This question aimed at identifying some of the ways in which the technology could provide a framework within which tasks could be performed. Mackrell (2015) had found the categorisation of possibilities given below (which to a large extent coincide with the categories considered by Bokhove and Drijvers 2010) fruitful in the discussion of affordances for the provision of formative feedback:

Stacey and Wiliam (2013, p. 722) together with Mackrell (2015) identify that in a technological environment there are new possibilities for the way in which

- *tasks are presented to students*
- *students operate in responding to the task*
- *evidence generated by students is identified*
- *students are given feedback (Mackrell 2015)*
- *evidence is accumulated across tasks*

In what ways does this environment incorporate these possibilities? Are there other possibilities that are incorporated?

However, the question did not give rise to the elaborations of each type of possibility that we had hoped for. This was particularly problematic with regard to feedback.

Flanders stated: "It appears that another possibility for the list is that students define the tasks (e.g., they create the problem a survey is intended to study, design the survey, then get data and analyze it)."

Finzer stated flatly that "As far as I can understand your question I would say that Fathom does not incorporate these possibilities." This was because at the time Fathom was developed (coming out first in 1998) such capabilities were less prevalent and more likely to be separate from the tool. When asked specifically about feedback, he mentioned the "trivial" sense in which the appearance and behavior of objects that are constructed is feedback, "but it's not feedback in the sense of 'you're getting closer to the answer' or 'have you thought about such and such'". Typically, students would print out their work and give it to the teacher, or email it, in which case the teacher could manipulate it. In contrast, in CODAP students generate a stream of events which will eventually provide feedback to the student and teacher because it is possible to identify what the student is doing.

Boon identified that all the possibilities were present. The DME presents tasks consisting of several components, some allowing student input. For example, text components are static, while algebra or geometry components are interactive. As mentioned in response to question 2, LMS features enable student work to be stored and hence teachers may identify evidence generated by students. Depending on the inter-activity of the component, feedback, some of which is authorable, can be given to the student, and currently some limited evidence across tasks can be reported. It is hoped that in the future some learning analytics features will augment these possibilities.

Laborde's response mentioned the devolution of the problem, a key concept in French didactique. Here responsibility for solving a problem is transferred from the teacher to the students so that students, instead of trying to work out what the teacher is intending to teach, engage with the mathematical knowledge that is at stake in the problem (Brousseau and Warfield 1999).

> The multipage structure of Cabri makes this easier. On one page the problem, such as creating the tangent to a circle, or constructing the missing wheel for a car, can be solved and presented to the student to show that a solution exists. This page would show a circle with a movable point through which a line passes that is always tangent to the curve, or a car where the wheel remains the correct size and moves with the car, but would not show how the solution was achieved. On a second page the student can be asked to solve the problem for themselves.

He also mentioned feedback. The new Cabri offers tools for the task designer to be able to evaluate and make decisions about the way in which the environment will respond according to what the student has been doing on a given page.

6. *Technology for learning versus technology for doing*

We have mentioned our decision to focus on technology designed for learning rather than doing. However, we recognize that in practice technology needs to do both. Our next question was hence the following:

Technology can be designed to get a job done or to facilitate learning (or both). These different purposes create a tension: if the aim, for example, is to create a cube, then a tool that enables the user to create a cube in three clicks is efficient and (with adequate documentation) easy to use. However, if the aim is to facilitate learning about a cube, then this tool may be too easy to use. The learner might be better off given only a choice of more primitive tools. On the other hand, once the learner understands cubes, the efficient tool is good for using cubes to create more complex structures.

To what extent can the tension between doing and learning be addressed in this environment?

Flanders referred again to issues with teacher expectations: Data Workshop constrains students to define and represent data accurately, and teachers had expressed concerns that these constraints could get in the way of learning. His view was that it was more valuable for beginning students to see accurate models. Once they understood these, they would have a reference system for evaluating less accurate models. He felt that most statistics software allowed the students to make both sensible and nonsensical representations from the beginning, meaning that students needed to rely on a teacher or other source outside the software in order to decide on the best representation.

Fathom was designed to explore this tension in some aspects of the program but not others. As its companion program, Tinkerplots, was designed to build up representations of data from primitives, the decision was made that Fathom would simply give the student a choice of possible graphs, which would then appear. In contrast, in data analysis some options were provided for learning and others for simply "doing". An example is least-squares fitting. The line of best fit can be found by showing the squares of residuals and dragging a movable line to minimize their sum, but a menu item is also provided that adds the least squares line to a scatterplot.

> A particular issue was whether to provide such an item for non-linear least squares – we felt that giving the student a button-push way of doing an exponential fit meant losing the opportunity to experience dragging a slider and seeing the curve go through the points well or less well. We did implement this in version 2, but students still had to decide whether to attempt to fit a particular curve or whether to use the log form. We did not want the technology making inappropriate decisions for students, or decisions that it was important for students to grapple with.

Laborde discussed the tension between too many and too few tools:

> Having a large number of tools is a problem because too many tools means that people will lose sight of how they work. We try to have a balance between the two, looking at what is crucial and what isn't in order to have a very limited number of tools but powerful tools, versatile tools, tools that can be used in different ways. For example, I was against having a square tool in the first Cabri, but this has turned out to be quite useful and is implemented in the new Cabri.

Another important aspect of Cabri is that the task designer, with complete control over which tools are available in the task environment, can choose to make available tools appropriate to the learning and doing required of the task, and can create and make available new tools. This type of control is not possible in Data Workshop or Fathom.

The tension between doing and learning is described as a "very important feature" by Boon. In the DME Algebra Arrows component, for example, normally the system acts as a "function machine" and does the calculations. However, this can also be customized by the task designer to ask the student to fill in the answer. The contrast between two 3D solids components, both of which involve constructing the polygon that results when a cuboid is intersected by a plane, is another example. With one, the user clicks to create three points on the edges of the cuboid, and the polygon is automatically constructed. With the other, the user must use geometric tools such as parallel lines to construct the polygon. It is Boon's view that both tools are valuable at their own level. The task of authoring and designing a learning path is seen as "selecting the proper tools".

7. Degree of open-endedness

We knew that open-ended tasks were entirely possible with the software we were considering, but were interested in whether the degree of open-endedness could be varied. We were also aware of the difficulty of giving feedback to open-ended tasks in a technology environment (Mavrikis and Gutierrez-Santos (2010). The next question was hence

To what extent is it possible to create tasks with varying degrees of open-endedness? How possible is it to give feedback to open-ended activities?

Flanders and Finzer unsurprisingly both affirmed the possibility of open-ended tasks. Finzer's elaboration was of interest, however; though most people working on the project had a constructivist orientation (with a tendency to prefer open-ended tasks), Fathom was designed to be pedagogically neutral and able to be used in a wide variety of modes. He was aware of tasks that had been developed using Fathom that were tightly directed, but felt that even such tasks could be opened up.

> It's easy to come up with activities that are open-ended, with all the data in the world available and all kinds of simulations able to be produced. An activity can start out being closed and "follow these steps" mode, but it's easy to open it up, gradually or suddenly, and say okay now take this further yourself. One of the joys of developing activities that use data is that there's no end to it and that real questions pop out of it.

> Part of your job as a curriculum developer or teacher is to get students to tune in to what might pop out. You want students to feel they can try to figure out for themselves what's going on there; is that little blip noise, or part of the pattern, or did something special happen?

However, as Finzer stated in an earlier question, Fathom has no facility for giving feedback on open-ended tasks. In Data Workshop, however, the problem of feedback has been considered. Representations of data in the form of summary statistics, charts and graphs could be seen as feedback, and feedback from other people could be facilitated by the ability for students and teachers to access each other's survey designs and results.

Laborde saw no limitation to the open-ended tasks that could be created, and connected this to the original vision of Cabri as a microworld. He felt that one of the strengths of the new Cabri was that tasks could be constrained more than in earlier versions, through constraining the way objects could be moved or changed and making available only the tools decided by the task designer.

> It seems contradictory to the spirit of open-ended systems but if we want to maximize what is happening during one hour we have to control what can happen a little bit.

He was well aware of the issues involved in giving feedback:

> Giving feedback on open-ended activities is very complex, as it involves analyzing student activity. It's extremely difficult to construct a model of the behavior of an expert in the domain in an open-ended environment, and for a novice you also have to take into account misconceptions, mistakes, lack of knowledge, lack of knowledge of the tools, and lack of knowledge of the environment. If an environment currently claims to give feedback on open-ended activities, a question is whether the environment is as open-ended as claimed.

Boon had already emphasized that he saw an equal role for both open and closed tasks, with the task designer able to decide on the task progression. Within the DME, feedback exists at different levels. Boon gave the example of feedback on constructions in the component "Building Blocks": "every mouse-click shows what the consequences are, for example dragging the mouse or rotating." This is very similar to Laborde's emphasis on direct manipulation feedback. Boon sees the value of this more implicit feedback on student strategy in that students have to make their own interpretations. Similarly to Laborde, he also acknowledged the difficulty of giving explicit feedback in such situations. In contrast, predictable mistakes could be caught through the verification of an answer box or text.

8. *Instrumental Genesis*

Instrumental genesis, the process by which an artifact becomes an instrument for the user, is a huge issue in any use of technology. It is one of the main aspects of the conceptual framework used by Bokhove and Drijvers (2010) in evaluating digital tools used for algebra education. Any task designer must consider whether the learner already has or how they can acquire the awareness of the tools required to perform the task, and we were hence concerned about the ways in which the different environments we are considering here could facilitate this process.

For the user, the potential instrument is the entire artifact: hardware, software environment, and software tools. To ensure that we included the software environment as part of the artifact to be instrumented, our question asked about both the tools and the environment.

How can instrumental genesis (the process by which the learner becomes familiar with the environment and learns how to use its tools) be controlled or managed in the task environment?

Finzer and Flanders had very different approaches to instrumental genesis, with Flanders relying on making available on the web getting started guides, FAQs, information manuals and also example tasks with sample data, which might ultimately supplant the user manual and serve as a sort of curriculum guide. In contrast, Finzer's main approach was to make the required skills assimilable enough so that in the process of doing an activity involving data the students could learn about features such as sliders or data entry.

> We wanted to convince teachers that people could just plunge in and learn to use the software in the process of learning something else.

He also pioneered the development of a large number of one-minute videos to show features of the software which were embedded in the help system. Sample Fathom documents were also mentioned as useful.

Laborde distinguished between the task design level and the level of doing the task in considering instrumental genesis.

> At the level of task design people need to get used to the tools that can be used to create the task but at the level of doing the task we try to let people interact with the mathematical objects, not with the environment.

This reflects his concern with making the environment as transparent as possible. He also mentioned the principle of consistency, for example making tool use as consistent as possible to minimize the learning required to use a tool. It is also possible for the task designer to create and embed short videos in the Cabri environment which, on request, show the students how to do specific actions or use specific tools.

Boon focused on the way in which task sequences could be designed to facilitate instrumental genesis, with the ability to introduce components slowly and with scaffolding, and only as necessary to the learning process. He gave the example of a learning sequence in which one element was a manual which showed how to use a particular component. He stated that one of the decisions involved in task design is whether it is worth learning to use the tool in order to perform the task, and stressed that task design can feature a combination of learning the tool and learning the mathematical content. This is similar to Finzer's approach, in which performing a task can involve both.

It is worth noting that, although both Fathom and Cabri provide specific features such as videos to help learners come to grips with the software, Finzer and Laborde are primarily concerned with minimizing the need for instrumental genesis for the learner through the design of the task environment itself, while in contrast Flanders and Boon focus on the features that can be used to facilitate instrumental genesis.

9. *The task designers*

For the final question, we returned to one of our fundamental issues: is task design possible for all who use the environment?

In what ways is it possible for students or teachers to engage in the task design process in this environment?

Flanders and Finzer essentially answered this question in their consideration of open-ended tasks for Data Workshop and Fathom; both students and teachers were expected to design their own tasks. Flanders also mentioned survey and data sharing features which allow students to build on other students' designs. For Cabri and DME the question was also whether teachers and students had access to the task design environment. Both had means of giving teachers access to this environment and both Laborde and Boon felt that student access was an interesting possibility that should be promoted. In Cabri, students may be given arbitrarily many of the geometric and arithmetical tools available in the task design environment; however, the ability to program actions is not available.

Boon acknowledged that the tools in the task design environment are also useful for students. Particularly for open-ended tasks, students could be asked to create a task and report or document it themselves, rather than just performing the task designed by the teacher. The implication is that students should also be able to design; Boon likes this possibility, but sees it as a challenge from a software point of view. Some steps have been taken; for example answer boxes now allow options such as. Eventually, Boon would like to make a large set of the existing tools available in the editor for students; the boundary between task design environment and task environment will become more and more blurred.

5 Conclusion

Let us return to our original question: how can technology design facilitate task design? Our results indicate the urgency of this question. Most of the designers mentioned technical challenges in implementing their ideas in desktop environments, and the current shifts to online and touchscreen devices add further challenges. While certainly opening up many opportunities for new approaches to the use of technology in teaching mathematics (see Sinclair and Heyd-Metzuyanim 2014; Ladel and Kortenkamp 2014 for examples of innovative touchscreen applications for learning about number) the changes, including changes to desktop operating systems, necessitate the expensive and time-consuming process of rewriting code. It is hence important to identify what is most crucial to keep and what is most crucial to develop further.

One of the themes to emerge from our results is that of flexibility: the importance of providing a variety of features and tools, and enabling choices on the part of the task designer. One important area of choice is the degree of open-endedness of a task. Another is the possible variation in operative transparency; the ability to provide tools that perform the mathematics for the student or to ask the student to use more primitive tools to develop an understanding of the mathematics.

A rather different theme is that of constraint. Despite offering a large amount of flexibility to task designers, each of the programs has a number of constraints. Some constraints are due to the stage of development of the software: both DME and Cabri are adding new features to broaden the range of curriculum that can be effectively addressed. However, some constraints are choices on the part of the designers of the programs; Fathom and Data Workshop choose to focus on particular curriculum areas. A major tension is created by the demand for new or different features on the part of users. The designers (in particular Laborde and Finzer) are aware of the way in which too many tools may complicate the interface and make using the software more difficult. Another constraint is the extent to which the student can be a task designer. All the designers see this as valuable, and all enable open-ended tasks. However, both DME and Cabri normally ask students to work in a task environment without access to all the tools available to the task designer. Another constraint is the mathematical fidelity of the software. Only Laborde and Flanders commented on this (Laborde valuing it very highly), but it may well be a constraint taken for granted by the other designers.

Another theme is the importance of the design of the task environment. Some of this is under the control of the task designer, in particular in Cabri and DME, but much of it is due to the designers of the programs themselves. One aspect of this is the way in which the environment reacts to user actions. Boon, Finzer and Laborde each comment on this type of feedback and see it as highly important. Another aspect is the intent to minimize the need for instrumental genesis, stressed by Laborde and Finzer in particular. Unfortunately, there is a common perception that instrumental genesis is inevitably complex (see Hegedus 2010) for a recent elaboration of instrumental genesis in which the complexity of the process is assumed) and that this complexity does not depend on the complexity of the artifact. These designers are challenging this perception. Another important aspect of instrumental genesis is the provision of features to familiarize learners with aspects of the programs such as documentation, sample documents, and videos. Both DME and Cabri have specific features to enable task designers to develop their own means of introducing new tools or other aspects of the program.

Another theme is the features required. Apart from Laborde, each of the designers mentioned a number of features and affordances when discussing the most important aspects of the environment. Such features included the specific tools and actions available to the student, but also features for task design, such as the way in which student work can be stored, in particular for DME.

6 Further Research

We have conducted preliminary interviews with the designers of four programs which can be used for task design using technology in mathematics education. We are now in a position to ask more specific questions in order to elaborate further. One area for further elaboration would be the role of specific features in task design. We would in particular like to consider the way in which feedback can be provided.

Sequences of activities were mentioned by Boon in connection with instrumental genesis and by Laborde in connection with devolution of the task to the student. The extent to which Data Workshop and Fathom allow for sequences of activities was not explored, and in general the purposes of and means of creating sequences of activities in the different programs could be elaborated further.

Another area for future research would be the influence of theory upon the design of the programs. Although we did not ask about this specifically, both Finzer and Laborde made reference to theoretical frameworks that influenced their design (constructivism and the theory of didactic situations), but we did not seek to elaborate on this.

In conclusion, although we found many differences in approach, each of the designers we interviewed were deeply interested in creating programs that would enhance the learning of mathematics in the best ways possible, both through features for learners and also features for task designers.

References

Beeson, M. (1998). Design principles of Mathpert: Software to support education in algebra and calculus. In N. Kajler (Ed.), *Computer-human interaction in symbolic computation* (pp. 89–116). New York: Springer.

Bokhove, C., & Drijvers, P. (2010). Digital tools for algebra education: Criteria and evaluation. *International Journal of Computers for Mathematical Learning, 15*(1), 45–62.

Bokhove, C., Koolstra, G., Heck, A., & Boon, P. (2006). Using SCORM to monitor student performance: experiences from secondary school practice. In *LTSN MSOR CAA Series*. Retrieved April 2006 from http://mathstore.ac.uk/articles/maths-caa-series/apr2006/.

Brousseau, G., & Warfield, V. (1999). The case of Gaël. *Journal of Mathematical Behavior, 18*(1), 7–52.

Butler, D., Jackiw, N., Laborde, J., Lagrange, J., & Yerushalmy, M. (2009). Design for transformative practices. In C. Hoyles & J.-B. Lagrange (Eds.), *Mathematics education and technology—rethinking the terrain: The 17th ICMI study* (pp. 425–438). New York: Springer.

Hegedus, S. (2010). Accommodating the instrumental genesis framework within dynamic technological environments. *For the Learning of Mathematics, 30*(1), 26–31.

Ladel, S., & Kortenkamp, U. (2014). Number concepts—processes of internalization and externalization by the use of multi-touch technology. In U. Kortenkamp, B. Brandt. C. Benz, G. Krummheuer, S. Ladel, & R. Vogel (Eds.), *Early Mathematics Learning: Selected Papers of the POEM 2012 Conference* (pp. 237–253). Dordrecht: Springer.

Leung, F. (2013). Introduction to section C: Technology in the mathematics curriculum. In M. Clements, A. Bishop, C. Keitel, J. Kilpatrick, & F. Leung (Eds.), *Third international handbook of mathematics education* (pp. 517–524). New York: Springer.

Mackrell, K. (2011). Design decisions in interactive geometry software. *ZDM: The International Journal on Mathematics Education, 43*(3), 373–387.

Mackrell, K. (2012). Introducing algebra with interactive geometry software. *Electronic Journal of Mathematics & Technology, 6*(1), 96–114.

Mackrell, K. (2015, February). Feedback and formative assessment with Cabri. Paper presented at CERME 9, Prague, Czech Republic.

Mavrikis, M., & Gutierrez-Santos, S. (2010). Not all wizards are from Oz: Iterative design of intelligent learning environments by communication capacity tapering. *Computers & Education, 54*(3), 641–651.

Mor, Y., & Winters, N. (2007). Design approaches in technology-enhanced learning. *Interactive Learning Environments, 15*(1), 61–75.

Rabardel, P. (2002). *People and technology: A cognitive approach to contemporary instruments*. Retrieved from https://hal.archives-ouvertes.fr/hal-01020705.

Sangwin, C., & Grove, M. (2006). STACK: Addressing the needs of the neglected learners. In M. Seppalal, S. Xambo, & O. Caprotti (Eds.), *WebALT 2006 Proceedings* (pp. 81–96). Eindhoven, Netherlands: Technical University of Eindhoven.

Sedig, K., & Sumner, M. (2006). Characterizing interaction with visual mathematical representations. *International Journal of Computers for Mathematical Learning, 11*(1), 1–55.

Sinclair, N., & Heyd-Metzuyanim, E. (2014). Learning number with TouchCounts: The role of emotions and the body in mathematical communication. *Technology, Knowledge and Learning, 19*(1), 81–99.

Stacey, K., & Wiliam, D. (2013). Technology and assessment in mathematics. In M. A. Clements, et al. (Eds.), *Third international handbook of mathematics education* (pp. 721–751). New York: Springer.

Software

Autograph [Computer software] (2015). Retrieved from http://www.autograph-maths.com/.
Cabri [Computer software].
Fathom [Computer software].
Geometer's Sketchpad [Computer software].
Data Workshop [Computer software].
Digital Mathematics Environment [Computer software].
Tinkerplots [Computer software].

Part II
Task Design in Dynamic Geometry Environments

Designing Assessment Tasks in a Dynamic Geometry Environment

Marta Venturini and Nathalie Sinclair

Abstract Despite the widespread use of Dynamic Geometry Environments (DGEs) in mathematics classrooms, they feature very little in most teachers' assessment practices. Indeed, many researchers have acknowledged the lack of research on how DGEs can and should be used in the context of assessment, and on how the learning that is developed through the use of DGEs in mathematics can be evaluated. Digital technologies include a range of mathematical and technological competencies that are not assessed in a paper-and-pencil environment. Moreover, the feedback provided by DGEs involves a whole new dynamic of action/interaction during assessment. This paper draws on previous work on task design in DGEs to provide a framework for identifying and designing different types of assessment tasks according to the specific goals of the teacher. These types of tasks will be exemplified using tasks designed by the first author for the iPad-based, multi-touch *Sketchpad Explorer*.

Keywords Dynamic geometry · Digital technologies · Formative assessment · Feedback · Circle geometry · Task design

1 Task Design in a DGE

In recent years, there has been growing attention to the importance of task design in mathematics education, as evidenced by the 22nd ICMI Study on *Task Design in Mathematics Education*. Of particular interest to this chapter is the research on task design in the context of digital technologies, especially in terms of how it might relate to assessment. We are interested not only in how task design might be affected by the use of DGEs, but also in what particular constraints and affordances

M. Venturini (✉) · N. Sinclair
Simon Fraser University, Burnaby, BC, Canada
e-mail: marta.venturini87@gmail.com

N. Sinclair
e-mail: nathsinc@sfu.ca

© Springer International Publishing Switzerland 2017
A. Leung and A. Baccaglini-Frank (eds.), *Digital Technologies in Designing Mathematics Education Tasks*, Mathematics Education in the Digital Era 8,
DOI 10.1007/978-3-319-43423-0_5

might be involved in developing and using such tasks in assessment situations. We therefore begin by summarising some of the research around task design as well as DGE-based task design. We then adapt the constructs that emerge from the summarised literature to the context of student assessment by showing some examples of DGE-based assessment tasks designed for *Sketchpad Explorer*. The description of these tasks is followed by an analysis of the mathematical and technological competencies that they are designed to assess, and of the role that the DGE assumes in the tasks. Finally, we examine the opportunities and limitations of DGE-based assessment. Our primary goal is to explore the way that task design can be carried out in order to enable the use digital technologies as part of teachers' assessment practices.

1.1   On Mathematical Tasks and Task Design

Joubert (2013) points out that "the literature distinguishes three main task types: *exercises (or routine problems)*, *problems* and *investigations*" (p. 69). She also observes that these types of task can be distinguished by their goals, and also by the context and the prior learning of the students. We are going to describe these types of task, as well as their relevance to the particular context of DGEs:

- *Repetitive exercises (or routine problems)* include processes like giving results, using well-known procedures and stating concepts. These practices have little in common with most uses of DGEs. However, Thomas and Lin (2013) observe that "other tasks that do have well known by-hand techniques can quickly assume the character of procedural tasks when digital technology is used", for example *constructing objects* in a paper-and-pencil context could be considered as an exercise, but in a DGE there is a change of technique, and students have the possibility to test the validity of their construction (Laborde 2001).
- The '*Problem*' category includes many kinds of tasks: exemplifying definitions, creating counter-examples, solving single-stage and multi-stage problems, deciding between two possibilities. A DGE is the ideal environment for reasoning and trying to solve problems, even with trial-and-error techniques, because students can 'make experiments' with the tools, test their conjectures and come up with counter-examples.
- *Investigations* include digital tasks help students reason in activities like exploring, discovering, proving properties and finding invariance. Many students struggle during this kind of activity in a paper-and-pencil context. In a DGE, processes such as guessing, pattern-seeking, making connections, predicting, hypothesising and proving, are supported by the tools and the possibilities of the software (visualisation, dragging, calculation, etc.) (Mariotti 2006). 'Noticing', intended as developing conjectures based on observations and testing the conjectures, is seen as a key formulation activity in a DGE:

An important implication of the computer's ability to 'do the mathematics' is in the opportunities which can be developed for the students to work inductively rather than deductively as is more usual in mathematics classrooms" (Joubert 2013, p. 73).

Moreover, Joubert states that in an investigation task "students should move between the pragmatic/empirical field and the mathematical/systematic field in order to reach the goal of the task" (p. 75).

As with the word 'task', the word 'design' can involve a wide range of materials (necessary instruments, task sequences, list of misconceptions that could emerge), actions (ways of working, whole lesson sequences, teachers' reactions to possible students' actions) and verbal interventions (things that the teacher might say, answers to possible students' comments or questions). Sometimes the design of the task includes pedagogic advice for the teachers on effective choices. Therefore, task design can look like a script for a drama with designers as scriptwriters, teacher and students as actors, but while the teacher knows the lines, the students have improvise (though teachers can usefully improvise as well, as Zazkis et al. 2013 have suggested).

If digital technologies are involved, the design of the task includes also tools, colours, figures, movement, visualization and much more. Laborde (2001) states that, "the context (and in particular a technological context) deeply affects the task carried out by the student" (p. 292), while Thomas and Lin (2013) point out that:

One of the central issues in the use of technology is the design and implementation of tasks that will encourage the learning and understanding of mathematics, and in particular mathematical thinking (p. 109).

Sinclair (2003) investigated the benefits and limitations of using pre-constructed, web-based, dynamic geometry sketches. She analysed the relationship between the activities and the development of geometric thinking skills, and the connection between the design of the materials, and the exploration process. She highlighted particular characteristics that a task designed in a DGE should have depending on the aim of the task, and provided some hints to design the sketches in order to address the questions and the tools: "When a question aims to focus student attention, the sketch must provide the visual stimulus. It must draw attention through colour, motion, and markings" (p. 312).

Especially in an exploration task, if students should be concentrated on a particular aspect of the task, then the sketch should include some clues through movements or buttons that let the students know where the core of the problem is.

When a statement prompts action, such as asking students to drag, observe or deduce, the sketch must contain the necessary provisions. It must provide affordances so that the student can take the required steps (p. 312).

If students need to follow some steps in order to carry out the task, the sketch should provide the crucial information to guide them along the path. The task should give students the hints to foster the mathematical reasoning through buttons, tools and dynamic objects.

Questions that invite exploration are open-ended. In order to explore uncharted territory, the student requires a sketch that allows options. Thus, when a question invites exploration, the sketch must provide alternate paths (p. 312).

The options for the students could be provided by a choice among different tools or buttons, which offer different possibilities of action, in order to foster students' exploration.

A question can surprise—which may lead to further exploration; however, the teacher is not necessarily there to correct any misinterpretation. Thus, the sketch must support experimentation to unmask the confusion. It must be flexible enough to help students examine cases, yet constrained enough to prevent frustration (p. 312).

In an assessment situation, students are not monitored by the teachers, thus if the sketch shows something unexpected, it should also include the information to figure out the explanation for the 'surprise'. Students need to feel comfortable enough to explore the environment, but also intrigued by some unpredicted situations. The sketch must contain the necessary information and tools to test any correct or incorrect hypothesis that could emerge.

Questions that check understanding are important parts of any learning situation. In the study tasks, the checking involved students looking together for the answer. Study results showed that the sketch aided the process of peer-interactions by providing a shared image for students to consider and discuss (p. 312).

Multi-touch technology (such as *Sketchpad Explorer*) allows students not only to share the screen of the tablet, but also to use their fingers simultaneously on the sketch. They can work together in an exploration activity, but also check their understanding through the communication of their reasoning among peers on the same screen (Ng and Sinclair 2015).

Sinclair (2003) underlines the importance of the decisions made about the design of the tasks in a DGE, because they "have the potential to support or impede the development of exploration strategies and geometric thinking skills" (p. 313). She concludes by affirming that, "through the materials we may be able to improve the context in which students learn the mathematics of dynamic geometry" (p. 313).

2 Different Types of Assessment Tasks

Laborde (2001) describes a case study on teachers designing tasks for a DGE, it analyses every task considering the choices made by the teachers with respect to the following aspects:

- the place of the task in the mathematics curriculum
- the role that teachers assigned to the DGE in the tasks
- the creation of new tasks linked to technology, which means what degree of change has the task designed for the DGE compared to the paper-and-pencil context.

In her research, Laborde identified four different categories of tasks that were used to drive the teachers' tasks. As part of a larger research project, we have been working on designing DGE-based tasks that could be used in assessment situations. We have decided to follow Sinclair's (2003) guidelines, but we also wanted to better understand the affordances and constraints of the different types of tasks described by Laborde (2001). Our particular context relates to basic theorems in Circle Geometry (aimed at students of about 14 years old in the British Columbia curriculum) using *Sketchpad Explorer*. Here we describe DGE-based assessment tasks designed by the first author, one for each category of Laborde (2001).

2.1 Tasks in Which the DGE Facilitates the Material Aspects of the Task

This category includes the tasks in which the DGE is used mainly as facilitating material aspects of the task while not changing it conceptually. The difference lies in the *drawing facilities* offered by the DGE. The solution strategies of both tasks (DGE and paper-and-pencil) do not differ deeply. In these tasks the digital technology could help solve the problem, but it is not part of the solution of the task.

2.1.1 The Counter-Example

If you think this statement is true, make a drawing to represent it; if you think it's not, create a counterexample.
The centre of any circle is the intersection of the perpendicular bisectors of any two chords in the circle.

This sketch is particularly subtle, because there is only one example that does not satisfy the statement: when the two chords are parallel (Fig. 1). A deep understanding of the theorem is necessary in order to answer the question correctly.

Students know exactly what to do, because they have to choose one of the two options: drawing a diagram as example, or a diagram as counter-example. The task, following Sinclair's (2003) indications, prompts students' reflection and action through the tools. The sketch contains the necessary tools to draw the diagram students choose to draw, it helps students reflect through the geometrical objects they can drag around the screen, trying different positions for the chords on the circle.

This task belongs to the first category of Laborde (2001), because *Sketchpad* facilitates the material aspects of the task in making the drawing. The task is not changed conceptually compared with a paper-and-pencil environment. The solution strategies of both tasks do not differ significantly: the only difference could be that students can move the chords all around the circle, and they can accidentally find the case in which the two chords are parallel.

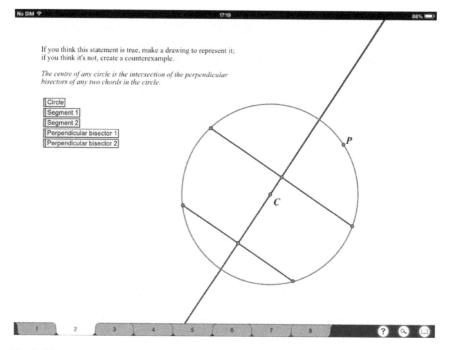

Fig. 1 The counter-example

2.2 Tasks in Which the DGE Facilitates the Mathematical Task

In these tasks the DGE is supposed to facilitate the mathematical task, which is considered as unchanged. The role of DGE is to help students make conjectures about the relations using the drag mode. It is not really used as a tool for solving a task, it is used as a *visual amplifier* in the task of identifying properties, thus the "visual power of technology is used, but mainly for seeing and conjecturing and not for experimenting, in order better to understand the mathematical situation" (p. 289).

2.2.1 The Dog

In this task, *Sketchpad* acts as a visual amplifier for students as they explore the situation by dragging the dog around the screen (Fig. 2). *Sketchpad* allows students to see where the dog can go within the constraints set by the rope and offers visual cues into the problem's solution that would be difficult to obtain through paper-and-pencil alone. Students can drag the dog around the screen and notice the limits of where it can go without the rope breaking.

Fig. 2 The dog

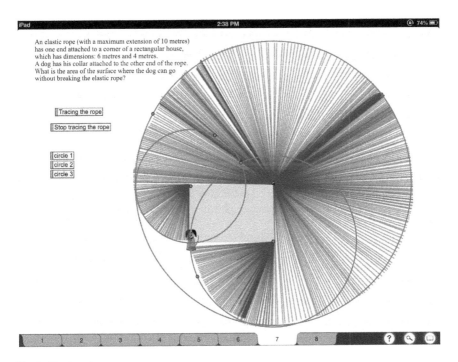

Fig. 3 Tracing the rope

To gain a better sense of the bounds imposed by the rope, students can press the button 'Tracing the rope', so that the rope leaves behind a trace of all its locations as they drag the dog (Fig. 3). Pressing the buttons 'circle 1', 'circle 2', and 'circle 3' students view three circles, whose location and size they can change simply by dragging them. They are supposed to position the circles so that they represent the bounds imposed by the rope. Thinking about the radii of the circles and their placement may help students determine the area where the dog can roam.

Following Sinclair's (2003) suggestion, the sketch focuses students' attention on spatial reasoning trough the visual stimulus of the dog roaming around the house and the colored trace left by the rope. The representation of the rope breaking when the dog is going too far or inside the house is a clear image for students' understanding. They see immediately where the problem is, but they still have some difficulties in representing the area with the three circles, and in finding the exact number of the area.

This task belongs to the second category of Laborde (2001), because the mathematical task is considered unchanged, but the DGE facilitates it: *Sketchpad* is used as a visual amplifier in the task of solving the problem.

2.3 Tasks Modified When Given in a DGE

Within this category, the DGE is supposed to modify the solving strategies of the task due to the use of some of its tools and to the possibility that the task might be rendered more difficult.

2.3.1 The Right Triangle

For this task, students are supposed to know that if a central angle and an inscribed angle of a circle are subtended by the same chord and on the same side of the chord, then the central angle is twice the inscribed angle (Fig. 4). In this sketch students do not have the measurement tool for the angles, so they have to explain how to obtain a right triangle inscribed in a circle depending on the position of the points. The

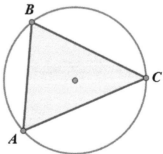

Drag the points *A,B,C* so that the triangle △*ACB* is right.
Explain your reasoning.

Fig. 4 The right triangle

three vertices of the triangle are constructed on the circle: students can drag the points only on the circle.

In this task, the aim is to focus student attention on the invariance of the measure of the inscribed angle when the subscribed arc is the same, thus the sketch provides the visual stimulus through the motion of the points along the circle. As suggested in Sinclair (2003), the sketch contains the necessary provisions to prompt action, since the task asks students to drag and observe.

This sketch belongs to the third category of Laborde (2001), because the task is modified in *Sketchpad*, compared to a paper-and-pencil context: the solving strategy is different, because students have to drag the points on the circle so that the triangle *ABC* is right. In this example the mediating function of the drag mode is used as a search mode to find the right triangle. Students need to know the property, and to notice that in a right triangle inscribed in a circle the hypotenuse is the diameter, but the task in *Sketchpad* actually requires more mathematical knowledge: students can move the third point around the circle, thus they have to know that wherever they decide to place it, the triangle will be right, and this is something that students usually find difficult to put into action.

2.4 Tasks Only Existing in a DGE

In this category, the task itself takes its meaning or its "raison d'être" from the DGE, in particular from the drag mode which preserves geometrical relations; it necessitates reasoning and knowledge. Such tasks require identifying geometrical properties as spatial invariants in the drag mode and possibly performing experiments with the tools of the DGE on the diagram. The identification of underlying properties is not easy and constitutes the question. These are tasks in which the environment allows efficient strategies that are not possible in a paper-and-pencil context, or tasks that are raised by the digital technology, which means tasks that can be carried out only in a DGE. Typically, these tasks appear in two forms:

- *'Black box' situations*: students have to explore a certain environment, and find properties or relations in order to reconstruct a dynamic diagram; the invariance properties here become remarkable rather than routine phenomena, because they are tools for identifying the 'hidden construction'.
- *Prediction tasks*: students have to predict the behaviour of a certain system/construction. As Laborde (2001) states, the DGE "allows a confrontation between what is predicted and what is observed" (p. 305).

2.4.1 The Ball

In this sketch, students are supposed to explore the situation pressing the button 'Rotate the ball', and observe what happens (Fig. 5). They have to find the right

You are rotating clockwise a ball with a lacrosse stick.
Where do you have to stop rotating the stick so that the ball hits the tree?
Drag the ball in the right position and rotate it with the button.
Then explain your reasoning.

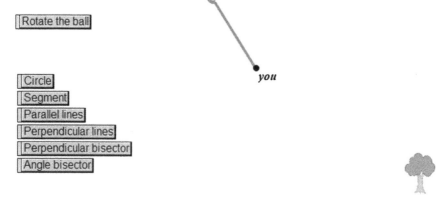

Fig. 5 The ball

initial position for the stick, so that the ball hits the tree after one rotation of the stick. It is quite reasonable to expect that students will try to rotate the ball until they find the solution, but then they need to explain why that one is the correct position. At this point, they will use the tools to try to explain the solution, and they will find that the trajectory of the ball is the tangent to the circle whose centre is the point 'you', and radius is the length of the stick (Fig. 6).

In this task, students are invited to explore the situation, thus following Sinclair (2003), the sketch provides different tools and allows options. This question can also surprise students, since some of them could expect the ball going along a circular path after the stick has stopped. Students could try different configurations for the path of the ball with the tools, and then test them. This sketch supports experimentation, since the student can select different tools and try different actions with them.

The task belongs to the fourth category of Laborde (2001), because it can exist only in a DGE, and it takes its meaning from it. Students have to guess where the ball is going when the stick stops, and they can check their answer with the button. Then, they have to find the 'hidden construction' of the situation using the tools provided. This task requires reasoning and knowledge: students need to know that a tangent to a circle is perpendicular to the radius at the point of tangency. They have to identify the geometrical properties as spatial invariants in the drag mode, because as long as they drag the stick, the trajectory of the ball is always tangent to the radius of the circle, and they can perform experiments with the provided tools on the diagram. The identification of the underlying property that the trajectory of the ball is the tangent is not easy and constitutes the question, because they have to reconstruct the dynamic diagram of the simulation.

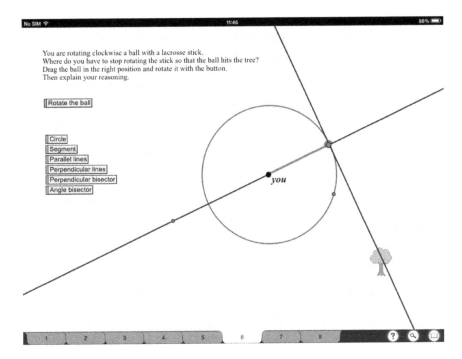

Fig. 6 The tangent

2.5 Evaluating the Tasks

In the tasks illustrated above, we described the ways in which they follow Sinclair's suggestion in the design of the sketch depending on the aim of the task. Is there something that makes a task better than another one? A good task is composed by a good question and a good design. We contend that the task on the Counter-Example is a good question, because it asks students to think about a property of the circle they are supposed to know, to see if they are able to find an exception, or if the property is always correct. The sketch aims to make students reflect through the tools, but since there are not pre-constructed diagrams, students would have to draw the diagram that represents the property or the diagram that represents the exception to the property. In this context the digital technology does not have an essential role, because students could draw a diagram also with paper and pencil, without using the tools of the DGE.

The task with the dog makes students reflect on an image of a dog roaming around a house. In order to find the area of the surface where the dog can go without breaking the rope, students need firstly to figure out where the dog is allowed to go, and then to represent that surface with geometrical shapes with known area. Since all the sketches are related to circle geometry, and this task in particular offers three circles as tools to find the area, then it is easy for students to recognize that they need to use circles to represent the area. However, it is not immediately clear where to place the three circles; also, finding the exact number of the area is not a simple request, because students need to add and subtract portions of the circles. Here we have a good questions and a good design, and the aim of the design is helping students exploring the situation with a dynamic representation of the problem.

The task on the triangle asks students to think about a particular case of a general property. The question is quite simple, but is formulated in a way that does not imply the direct connection to the property of the central angles and the inscribed angles subtended by the same arc. The DGE has a fundamental role, since the questions prompt students to drag the points on the circle. The task could be seen also as an exploration task for students who do not remember the property, they could drag the vertex on the circle and find the invariance of the right inscribed angle when the other two points are the end points of a diameter.

The ball task is definitely a good question and the DGE is the core of the problem: the movement and the tools are the key elements of the sketch. There may be some doubt as to whether it is an assessment question or not. It is an exploration task where students are asked to investigate the situation and explain a certain behaviour of the sketch using a property of the circle. This task evaluates the 'noticing', and the problem solving competence, since students need to observe and to make conjectures. It also evaluates the technological competence of exploring with the tools, and using them to draw the dynamic diagram that represents the hidden construction of the situation.

2.6   Comparison and Discussion

Categorizing the tasks following Laborde's scheme draws attention to the meanings teachers might give to digital technologies, as well as to mathematics. If a teacher wants to use digital technologies to help students in their usual work, they would prefer to use tasks of the first and second category; if a teacher wants 'solving tasks in a DGE' to be a fundamental part of the activity, and a competence to be evaluated, then they would design tasks of the third and fourth category. If teachers do not want to change the meaning of the tasks compared to a paper-and-pencil context, then they would use tasks of the first and second category; if they would like their students to develop different strategies for problem solving, they would prefer tasks of the third category; if teachers value prediction and exploration tasks, they would design tasks belonging to the fourth category.

Teachers may choose to evaluate only the mathematical competencies needed to answer the task, or to evaluate also the technological competencies required to carry out the task in a DGE. A teacher might thus choose tasks of the first category if he/she wants students to be able to use the tools in a DGE to solve the task, but their use is not part of the evaluation. Tasks of the second category would be chosen by teachers who wish to use the DGE to help their students solve problems they struggle with, problems that students do not understand, or that are difficult to be represented. Tasks belonging to the third category would be designed by teachers who expect their students to be able to use the tools to show different solving strategies. Finally, the fourth category would be preferred by teachers who want their students to feel confident observing, solving problems and making conjectures in a DGE.

Teachers could associate tasks to situations: they would use tasks of the first and second category for formal assessment, and they would prefer tasks of the third and fourth category for informal assessment, like classroom activities. Sometimes digital technologies would be optional; other times they would be necessary to complete the task. Sometimes the DGE can be a tool to help students, other times it would be a fundamental part of the assessment. Laborde (2001) observes that teachers did not frequently design tasks with prediction situations for conjecturing and proving. The situation would probably be exacerbated in an assessment situation, where "knowledge" may be valued over "performance," as Madison (2006) suggests:

> Mathematics faculty members are accustomed to formulating learning goals in terms of mathematical knowledge rather than in terms of student performance in using mathematics. This creates tension between testing what students know and testing for what students can do. Since judging student performance is usually far more complex than testing for specific content knowledge (p. 6).

In Table 1, we summarise the mathematical and technological competencies that could be evaluated for each of the tasks described above.

We note that the same task could be an exploration for one person and an exercise or application of a well-known property for another. The competencies that a task aims to evaluate could be different for different classes or students; only familiarity with students and their 'history of learning' can allow a teacher to design a task that evaluates the competencies that he/she wants to test.

3 Task Design in a DGE for Student Assessment

Designing tasks for assessment, especially in a DGE, depends on the kind of assessment being used, as well as on the ideas and practices being assessed.

Teachers usually use the term *formative assessment* to indicate the comments and prompts they provide to the students during an activity in class, for example when they are solving a task. Students use these suggestions to improve their work and modifying their knowledge. In this chapter, *formative assessment* is used as in the definition of Taras (2010):

Summative Assessment + Feedback = Formative Assessment.

Table 1 Mathematical and technological competencies

Tasks	Mathematical competencies	Technological competencies
The counter-example	Correct use of examples in proving or refuting conjectures; generalizing theorems and finding exceptions; applying mathematical reasoning; constructing mathematical representations	Making a draw with the tools; appropriate use of the instruments; selecting and using technological tools to construct a diagram
The dog	Exploring; problem solving; applying mathematical reasoning; pattern-seeking; ability of converting a diagram in algebraic operations; connecting mathematical ideas to everyday experiences	Exploring the situation with the tools; appropriate use of the instruments; ability to use effectively digital technologies in mathematics to solve unfamiliar problems and make rational conjectures; developing visualization skills to assist in processing information
The right triangle	Reading a diagram; explaining the mathematical reasoning with own words; using a property in a particular example; stating concepts; generalizing; proving; 'noticing'	Dragging objects to find invariance; dragging to test the 'stability' of a property as along they are working on a diagram; developing visualization skills to assist in processing information
The ball	Understanding what is going on (interpreting the situation); exploring; predicting; finding invariance and properties; problem solving; making assumptions; using a property in a particular context; developing and apply new mathematical knowledge through problem solving; explaining the mathematical reasoning with own words; generalizing; proving; guessing; pattern-seeking; making connections; 'noticing'; connecting mathematical ideas to everyday experiences, and to other disciplines	Exploring the situation; 'make experiments' with the tools; trial-and-error techniques; selecting and using appropriately technological tools; interpreting the 'behaviour' of a construction to make inferences and deductions about it; using the tools to test the validity of conjectures; ability to use effectively digital technologies in mathematics to solve unfamiliar problems and make rational conjectures; developing visualization skills to assist in processing information

In this 'equation', *summative assessment* is the evaluation of student understanding, knowledge and competence; it becomes *formative assessment* when teachers give comments (feedback) on student performance in relation to their learning goals. This feedback should be used to "update, change and improve the work" (Taras 2010, p. 3) both of the teacher and of the students.

3.1 Assessment with Digital Technologies

Educators and teachers affirm that digital technologies could help students in some mathematics learning goals that are difficult to reach, such as problem solving, reasoning, making deductions and conjectures, and conceptual understanding. If a teacher's goal is to support students to learn to use digital technologies for purposeful mathematical activity, then they should find a way to assess this competence; otherwise students will not see how to effectively use them in mathematics as a learning goal:

> If a teacher encourages students to make extensive use of tools in a course but does not allow their use on the end-of-course test, are students being given the opportunity to show what they learned with the use of such tools? (Sangwin et al. 2010, p. 229).

Drijvers et al. (2010) explain that one of the themes that served to frame the 17th ICMI Study, *Mathematics Education and Technology—Rethinking the Terrain* was on assessing mathematics with and through digital technologies, and on balancing use of mental, paper-and-pencil, and digital tools in both assessment and teaching activities. This question was formulated as follows:

> How can the assessment of students' mathematical learning be designed to take into account the integration of digital technologies and the ways that digital technologies might have been used in the learning of mathematics? (p. 82).

However, these authors observe that much of the question remains open:

> An explicit discussion of how to take into account those different uses for assessment purposes, or how to develop assessment methods that evaluate the learning that is developed through the use of digital technologies, is not included, and remains an area that requires still much research (p. 85).

If students are accustomed to using digital technologies in the learning of mathematics, then they will be comfortable in being assessed in the same way. On the other hand, "it is difficult to integrate a given tool into assessment before having integrated it into the corresponding teaching" (Trouche 2005, p. 31).

3.2 Designing Assessment Tasks

In an assessment situation, a task is an activity for the students, which is proposed by the teacher in order to verify the learning and the understanding of some specific mathematical concept(s) or practice(s). Both in classroom activity, and in test situations, the goal for the student is to answer questions in order to complete the task. For the teacher these two goals are significantly different: in the first situation, the aim of the task is to foster the understanding of a new mathematical concept, and promote learning, while in the second one the goal is to evaluate student knowledge and competence. Therefore, it seems reasonable to infer that the design of such tasks will be different.

In the proceedings of the 22nd ICMI Study, several articles dealt with designing tasks to support student learning, such as Job and Schneider (2013), who note that: "teachers, researchers and the mathematical community in general have an interest in designing tasks to help students acquire mathematical knowledge" (p. 203), and Thomas and Lin (2013), who point specifically to this in the concept of digital environments: "many educators promote digital technology as having a role to play in helping students to develop mathematical thinking" (p. 109).

In most of the tasks teachers are a fundamental part of the activity: teachers usually introduce the task, explain the situation and give prompts while students are going along the activity. However, in an assessment situation, teachers usually play a very different role. This will affect task design because it changes the participation of the teacher. The task should be 'self-consistent' in that students should be able to solve the task by themselves, without the teacher's intervention. In a formative assessment situation, the design of the tasks often excludes interactions among the teacher and the students (this is not always the case, as in the Ontario provincial exam initiative of 2002, where assessment occurred over a three day period and where teachers had specific roles in introducing and guiding the students' work). In this situation, the teacher acts as the designer, the students as the actors, and there is no script. Students have to show what they learned and understood by themselves.

In such a context, therefore, some of the characteristics of an assessment task should look as follows (adapted from Savard et al. 2013):

- The *goal of the task* should be explicitly communicated in the instructions of the task.
- The *text of the task* should be very short, clear, and it should contain simple words and expressions that the students are familiar with.
- All the *instructions* and the *necessary information* should be provided in the text.
- The task should provide all the *instruments* and the *tools* that the teacher wants to incorporate.
- If it is an exploration task, it should include an *intriguing element*, which would foster students' investigation.

3.3   Technology Feedback in the Assessment

Laborde et al. (2006) observe that feedback through technology offers a great deal of opportunity for new ways of understanding mathematics, because feedback from student interactions with digital tools could have a strong impact on their mathematical understandings and practices. It can be used so that tasks take advantage of the computer's potential to provoke situations of validation as well as action and formulation (Joubert 2013, p. 75). Moreover, Olive et al. (2010) affirm that, "feedback provided by computational tools can shift the focus of the student from micro-procedures (that the tool performs) towards macro-procedures that involve higher-level cognitive processes" (p. 167).

However, students sometimes interpret feedback from the computer in unexpected ways. During the mathematics lesson the teacher can intervene to 'put the students back on the path', but in a formative assessment situation the teacher wouldn't be there, students should figure out their way by themselves. In a classroom activity, when students' reasoning is not correct, technology feedback gives evidence that the solution is inadequate showing a sort of inconsistency, or providing a new situation, students can also refine their thinking iteratively as they design, rather than at the end of the design process (Laborde et al. 2006). Moreover, "research on the role of feedback provided by technological tools suggests that learning is most likely to occur when the feedback is unexpected" (Olive et al. 2010, p. 167).

During formative assessment, technology feedback is limited, just as is the teachers' role, in order to avoid the possibility that students try to guess the answer or to solve the problem without thinking. If the teacher's goal is to assess the students' investigation competence, the digital technologies can take on the role of the teacher (Sinclair and Jackiw 2010), because they are not supposed to intervene: the feedback of technology should be sufficient in giving students what they need to find the solution, and it should foster exploration.

Trouche (2005) observes that sometimes "the objective of assessment seems to be to bypass the calculator's existence" (p. 31). It is important that teachers establish the aim of the assessment, and the specific competencies they want to test, taking into account the use of the digital tools: they should have a clear idea of the mathematics the computer will do and the mathematics the students will do in order to avoid digital tools taking the role of the students.

3.4 The Role of Digital Technologies in Assessment

In her paper entitled "Using computers in classroom mathematical tasks: revisiting theory to develop recommendations for the design of tasks" (p. 69), Joubert highlights the importance of paying attention to the intended mathematical learning of students as they work through the task, adapting their strategies as they negotiate epistemological obstacles.

In the same way, in formative assessment, teachers need to know what mathematical and technological competencies they want to evaluate while they are using a DGE to assess their students' understanding, because, as Joubert points out:

> The fact that software can perform some of the mathematical processes can be confusing; if the computer does the mathematics, what learning is there for the students to do? (p. 71).

The fact that digital tools carry out some mathematics procedures should not be a disadvantage: teachers can assess particular mathematical concepts knowing that the computer does some of the mathematics while students do *some other* mathematics, which could be more meaningful than calculating a product, drawing a graph, or computing an area. Moreover, teachers have the opportunity to design tasks that enable certain mathematical thinking that is not accessible with paper-and-pencil tasks, as Olive et al. (2010) observe:

> Several researchers have focused on the importance of task design (e.g. Sinclair 2003; Laborde 2001) in technological environments. They argue for designing tasks that are transformed by the technology, leading to new mathematical practices (e.g. modeling real-life phenomena, making deductions based on observations), rather than tasks that could be just as easily completed without the technology (p. 167).

This 'new' kind of tasks could really "engage students in a mathematical practice that is empowering, meaningful, and coherent" (Caron and Steinke 2005, p. 4). Keeping in mind that designers should pay attention to avoid making the task too easy through the technology feedback:

> Changes that make it easier for the student to complete the task may have the effect of undermining the designers' intentions, and reinforcing students' attention of completion (of the task) as the priority (Ainley and Margolinas 2013, p. 151).

Some tasks lose their meaning if digital tools are used, because technology could prevent some elementary learning processes, or could reduce mathematics to an experimental practice. There is also the risk that a task in a DGE might suffer from constraints of the technology, which may limit the students' exploration space, such as requirements for input formats and styles, and pre-designed tools that may incorporate too much guidance. Careful consideration is required in order to design tasks for the purposes of assessment, in order to give students the opportunity to express their knowledge and to show their competencies.

Based on the research carried out with DGEs, these are some mathematical and technological competencies that can support the use of a DGE in formative assessment:

1. *Communicating in order to express their understanding.* Through the 'actions' that students do in a DGE teachers can see their reasoning and recognize possible misconceptions:

> Even without sophisticated constructions, a student's simple action of manipulating a dynamic figure can already be a meaningful mode to demonstrate their understanding of geometric concepts (Sangwin et al. 2010, p. 235).

Through the different possibilities of answer recording that digital technologies offer, students can explain their mathematical understanding using tools like screenshot, script and recording voice or video while they are working in a DGE. These instruments allow teachers to see broader aspects of student thinking: "by studying a student's script, a teacher can infer ways that the student is thinking about the object or procedure" (Wilson 2008, p. 417).

2. *Connecting mathematical ideas to other concepts in mathematics, to everyday experiences, and to other disciplines.* Through the measure and the simulation tools of a DGE, students can study and model real life phenomena, since the ease with which students can represent, explore and manipulate data with these tools allows them to use technology to solve interesting problems (Olive et al. 2010, p. 168).

3. *Generalizing properties or theorems.* In a DGE the process of generalizing is fostered by the drag mode, because students can test the 'stability' of a property as along they are working on a diagram. Anthony (2013) gives examples of 'soft constructions', which are constructions in a DGE where the action of dragging is not intended to verify some properties, but part of the construction itself:

> Through dragging, the general can emerge from the specific by searching empirically for the locus of figures fulfilling the given conditions. Soft constructions offer a transition from an empirical approach to a theoretical approach in solving a geometry problem (p. 91).

4. *Exploring, finding invariance and properties.* In a DGE students can explore a domain in order to find invariance and relationships among objects, or the laws that drive a certain construction. Students need to know how to interpret an answer or a non-answer from a machine in order to make inferences and deductions, for example how a certain construction behaves as long as students are using the drag mode. Anthony (2013) affirms that "a task in soft construction could foster operative apprehension" (p. 95), interpreting Duval's 'operative apprehension' as the following:

> Operative apprehension of a mathematical concept or problem in DGE is the insights into the concept or the solution of the problem revealed by operating on a pre-designed figure in the environment through dragging (Anthony 2013, p. 91).

5. *Developing and apply new mathematical knowledge through problem solving.* In a DGE students can put forward conjectures and predictions, and test their validity or functionality. If a teacher wants to assess students' ability to use effectively digital technologies in mathematics to solve unfamiliar problems and make rational conjectures, then students can also continue learning (new mathematical concepts) while they are taking a test through technology feedback.

6. *Developing mathematical reasoning.* Mathematical reasoning doesn't consist in doing calculations and improving practical skills, in a DGE students can focus on concepts, and consequences, leaving the symbolic and numerical computation to the tool: "expressive tools (such as DGEs) assist students in the move from action and visualization to conjectures and reasoning" (Olive et al. 2010, p. 167).

7. *Selecting and using technological tools for solving problems.* Students need to choose the right tools in a DGE and use them in an appropriate way to carry out the task.

8. *Developing visualization skills to assist in processing information, making connections, and solving problems.* Through the visualization affordance of a DGE, students can observe objects, graphs, and phenomena, and make deductions or inferences about them; moreover, students have the possibility to visualize abstract mathematical concepts in a DGE:

> Students can model, experiment, and test their emerging mathematical understandings using dynamic visualization software in many mathematical domains (Olive et al. 2010, p. 166).

4   Concluding Remarks

Having assessment tasks that evaluate different kinds of competencies, and that include digital tools as a main and essential component of the problem-solving process, helps students understand the value of using digital technologies in mathematics. The goals of assessment would need to change in order for the use of digital technologies in formative assessment to be warranted. In order for technology to be a valid part of formal assessment, a teacher would want to assess not only what students *know*, but what students *can do* with the technology, like make and test conjectures. A teacher would also need to value technological competencies, because students would require these in order to carry out explorations. And, a teacher would want to identify or create exploratory problems, such as 'black box' and prediction tasks. Such problems would be warranted if assessment is seen as an opportunity for learning, so that students continue to learn during the assessment through the activity feedback of the technology.

While many teachers value technology competencies and mathematical processes—as evidenced in Venturini (2015)—the challenge of designing tasks for student assessment remains an important barrier. Designing and implementing tasks requires time, mathematical knowledge as well as technical knowledge of the software. Moreover, the development of technology is very fast, and it is difficult to keep up with the newest enhancements of digital tools in mathematics education. One of the goals of this chapter has been to provide exemplars of the kinds of tasks that might be useful in an assessment situation, and thus move the research field forward so that researchers and teachers might find more fruitful ways of designing and sharing suitable, technology-based tasks.

References

Ainley, J, & Margolinas, C. (2013). Introduction to theme B: Accounting for student perspectives in task design. In C. Margolinas (Ed.), *Task design in mathematics education: The 22nd ICMI study.*

Anthony, C. M. O. (2013) Designing tasks to foster operative apprehension for visualization and reasoning in dynamic geometry environment. In C. Margolinas (Ed.), *Task design in mathematics education: The 22nd ICMI study.*

Caron, F., & Steinke, T. (2005). Learning in the presence of technology: Report of the CMEF working group. In *Proceedings of the 2005 Canadian Mathematics Education Forum, Québec, Canada.*

Drijvers, P., Mariotti, M. A., Olive, J., & Sacristán, A. I. (2010). Introduction to section 2. In C. Hoyles & J.-B. Lagrange (Eds.), *Mathematics education and technology—rethinking the terrain: The 17th ICMI study.*

Job, P., & Schneider, M. (2013). On what epistemological thinking brings (or does not bring) to the analysis of tasks in terms of potentialities for mathematical learning. In C. Margolinas (Ed.), *Task design in mathematics education: The 22nd ICMI study.*

Joubert, M. (2013). A framework for examining student learning of mathematics: Tasks using technology. In *Eighth Congress of European Research in Mathematics Education (CERME 8).*

Laborde, C. (2001). Integration of technology in the design of geometry tasks with cabri-geometry. *International Journal of Computers for Mathematical Learning, 6*(3), 283–317.

Laborde, C., Kynigos, C., Hollebrands, K., & Sträßer, R. (2006). Teaching and learning geometry with technology. In A. Gutierrez & P. Boero (Eds.), *Handbook of research on the psychology of mathematics education: Past, present and future* (pp. 275–304).

Madison, B. L. (2006). Tensions and tethers: Assessing learning in undergraduate mathematics. In L. A. Steen (Ed.), *Supporting assessment in undergraduate mathematics* (pp. 3–10). Washington, DC: The Mathematical Association of America.

Mariotti, M. A. (2006). Proof and proving in mathematics education. In A. Gutiérrez & P. Boero (Eds.), *Handbook of research on the psychology of mathematics education* (pp. 173–204). Rotterdam: Sense Publishers.

Ng, O., & Sinclair, N. (2015). "Area without numbers": Using Touchscreen dynamic geometry to reason about shape. *Canadian Journal of Science, Mathematics and Technology Education, 15*(1), 84–101.

Olive, J., Makar, K., Hoyos, V., Kor, L. K., Kosheleva, O., & Sträßer, R. (2010). Mathematical knowledge and practices resulting from access to digital technologies. In: *Proceedings of the 17th ICMI Study* (Vol. 8, pp. 133–177).

Sangwin, C., Cazes, C., Lee. A., & Wong K. L. (2010). Micro-level automatic assessment supported by digital technologies, Chap. 10. In *The 17th ICMI study.*

Savard, A., Polotskaia, E., Freiman, V., Gervais, C. (2013). Tasks to promote holistic flexible reasoning about simple additive structures. In C. Margolinas (Ed.), *Task design in mathematics education: The 22nd ICMI study.*

Sinclair, M. P. (2003). Some implications of the results of a case study for the design of pre-constructed, dynamic geometry sketches and accompanying materials. *Educational Studies in Mathematics, 52*, 289–317.

Sinclair, N., & Jackiw, N. (2010). Learning through teaching, when teaching machines. In R. Leikin & R. Zazkis (Eds.), *Learning through teaching.* Dordrecht: Springer.

Taras, M. (2010). Assessment for learning: assessing the theory and evidence. *Procedia—Social and Behavioral Sciences, 2*(2), 3015–3022.

Thomas, M. O. J., & Lin, C. (2013). Designing tasks for use with digital technology. In C. Margolinas (Ed.), *Task design in mathematics education: The 22nd ICMI study.*

Trouche, L. (2005). Calculators in mathematics education: A rapid evolution of tools, with differential effects. In D. Guin, et al. (Eds.), *The didactical challenge of symbolic calculators: Turning a computational device into a mathematical instrument* (pp. 9–40). Dordrecht, The Netherlands: Kluwer Academic Publishers.

Venturini, M. (2015). How teachers think about the role of digital technologies in student assessment in mathematics (Ph.D. thesis). Simon Fraser University, Canada and University of Bologna, Italy.

Wilson, P. (2008). Teacher education: Technology's conduit to the classroom. In K. Heid & G. Blume (Eds.), *Research on technology in the learning and teaching of mathematics, volume 2: Cases and perspectives*. Charlotte, NC: National Council of Teachers of Mathematics/ Information Age Publishing.

Zazkis, R., Sinclair, N., & Liljedahl, P. (2013). *Lesson play in mathematics education*. New York: Springer.

Designing Non-constructability Tasks in a Dynamic Geometry Environment

Anna Baccaglini-Frank, Samuele Antonini, Allen Leung
and Maria Alessandra Mariotti

Abstract This chapter highlights specific design features of tasks proposed in a Dynamic Geometry Environment (DGE) that can foster the production of indirect argumentations and proof by contradiction. We introduce the notion of *open construction problem* and describe the design of two types of problems, analysing their potential a priori, with the goal of elaborating on the potentials of designing problems in a DGE with respect to fostering processes of indirect argumentation. Specifically, we aim at showing how particular open construction problems, that we refer to as *non-constructability problems*, are expected to make indirect argumentations emerge.

Keywords Dynamic geometry environment · Indirect argumentation · Non-constructability problems · Proof by contradiction

1 Introduction

This chapter discusses the potential offered by specific tasks designed in a Dynamic Geometry Environment (DGE) of leading to the production of indirect argumentations and eventually to proof by contradiction. We will attempt to highlight the specific design features that characterize these tasks. We start by introducing two

A. Baccaglini-Frank (✉)
Department of Mathematics "G. Castelnuovo", "Sapienza" University of Rome, Rome, Italy
e-mail: baccaglinifrank@mat.uniroma1.it

S. Antonini
Università degli studi di Pavia, Pavia, Italy
e-mail: samuele.antonini@unipv.it

A. Leung
Department of Education Studies, Hong Kong Baptist Univeristy, Kowloon Tong, Hong Kong, SAR, China
e-mail: aylleung@hkbu.edu.hk

M.A. Mariotti
Università degli studi di Siena, Siena, Italy
e-mail: mariotti21@unisi.it

© Springer International Publishing Switzerland 2017
A. Leung and A. Baccaglini-Frank (eds.), *Digital Technologies in Designing Mathematics Education Tasks*, Mathematics Education in the Digital Era 8,
DOI 10.1007/978-3-319-43423-0_6

main aspects, emerging from previous studies: open problems, and open construction problems in particular, and explorations in a DGE. Then we characterize the design of two types of open construction problems and analyse their potential a priori. The main objective of this chapter is to elaborate on the potentials of designing problems of non-constructability in a DGE with respect to fostering processes of indirect argumentation. Such problems, indeed, withhold potential for fostering the emergence of argumentations referring to logical dependency between constructed properties and derived properties. Specifically, we aim at showing how non-constructability problems are expected to make indirect argumentations emerge. Our discussion is consistent with classical results coming from previous studies where the dragging strategies were described (Healy 2000; Hölzl 2001; Leung and Lopez-Real 2002; Arzarello et al. 2002), but aims at elaborating on them to support the didactic hypothesis that designing and solving non-constructability DGE tasks may offer a rich context for introducing proof by contradiction.

2 Indirect Argumentation

Studies in mathematics education have revealed students' specific difficulties with proof by contradiction (Thompson 1996; Antonini and Mariotti, 2008, 2006; Antonini 2004), at every school level. However, on the other hand, some studies underline that students spontaneously produce argumentations with a structure that is very similar to that of a proof by contradiction:

> The indirect proof is a very common activity ('Peter is at home since otherwise the door would not be locked'). A child who is left to himself with a problem, starts to reason spontaneously '… if it were not so, it would happen that…' (Freudenthal 1973, p. 629).

With the term "indirect argumentation" we intend, in line with Freudenthal, argumentations that are developed starting from the negation of what is to be supported. That is, for example,[1] of the type "…if it were not so, it would happen that…". The transition from indirect argumentation to a (direct or indirect) proof is beyond the scope of the analyses included.

Freudenthal concludes that "before the indirect proof is exhibited, it should have been experienced by the pupil" (Freudenthal 1973, p. 629) and, along the same lines, Thompson writes:

> If such indirect proofs are encouraged and handled informally, then when students study the topic more formally, teachers will be in a position to develop links between this informal language and the more formal indirect-proof structure (Thompson 1996, p. 480).

---

[1]For a more articulated and refined analysis of argumentation supporting mathematical impossibility see Antonini (2010).

Assuming this last hypothesis proposed by Thompson, in this chapter we propose and analyse tasks that have the aim of fostering the production of indirect argumentations in Euclidean Geometry.

3 Open Construction Problems

The term 'open problem' is common in the mathematics education literature (Arsac 1999) to express a task that poses a question without revealing or suggesting the expected answer. When assigned an open problem, students are faced with a situation in which there are no precise instructions, but rather they are left free to explore the situation and make their own conclusions. Frequently reaching a solution involves processes of generation of conditionality after a mental and/or physical exploration of the problematic situation (Mariotti et al. 1997). In the literature, open problems have frequently been characterized by the presence of an explicit request to produce a conjecture (e.g., Boero et al. 1996; Olivero 2000; Arzarello et al. 2002; Boero et al. 2007). In these cases we will use the terminology *conjecturing open problem* (as in Baccaglini-Frank 2010, p. 84).

In Geometry, a conjecturing open problem can take the following form, as described in Mogetta et al. (1999):

> The statement is short, and does not suggest any particular solution method or the solution itself. It usually consists of a simple description of a configuration and a generic request for a statement about relationships between elements of the configuration or properties of the configuration (ibid, pp. 91–92).

Typically, when solving an open problem, the student must first advance one (or more) conjecture(s), as a culmination of what is referred to as the exploration phase or conjecturing phase (Baccaglini-Frank and Mariotti 2010), and then s/he is expected to engage in a proving phase that results in a proof supporting the validation of the conjecture (whether it turns out to be true or false). We will consider tasks that make use of conjecturing open problems that inquire about the *constructability* of a certain figure. Therefore we need to preliminarily discuss construction problems.

3.1 Construction Problems

Construction problems constitute the core of classic Euclidean Geometry. The use of specific artifacts, i.e. ruler and compass, can be considered at the origin of the set of axioms defining the theoretical system of Euclid's *Elements*.

As stated by Heath (1956, in Arzarello et al. 2012),

Euclidean Geometry is often referred to as 'straight-edge and compass geometry', because of the centrality of construction problems in Euclid's work. Since antiquity geometrical constructions have had a fundamental theoretical importance in the Greek tradition (ibid, p. 98).

Accordingly, any geometrical construction corresponds to a theorem, which means that there is a proof that validates the construction procedure that solves the corresponding construction problem. As a matter of fact, the relationship between construction and theorems is very complex, and such complexity is witnessed by the discussions by the classical commentators of Euclid's Elements (Heath 1956, p. 124 et seq.). Proclus distinguished between problems and theorems, "the former embracing the generation, division, subtraction or addition of figures, and generally the changes which are brought about in them, the latter exhibiting the essential attributes of each." (Proclus, quoted by Heath, ibid, p. 125). While the 'theoretical' character of geometric constructions made them similar to theorems, the specificity of construction problems, as open problems, seemed to reclaim the need to maintain the distinction between the two types of statements. The distinction was to be further underlined by the expressions that Euclid put at the end respectively of a theorem and of a problem: in the case of a Theorem he wrote "that which was required to prove" and in the case of a construction he wrote "that which was required to do" (ibid, p. 126). However, the substantial unity of the Euclidean statements led some authors to use a unique term for both types of statements. In some of the later editions of the Elements we can find the term "Proposition" referring to any statement of the theory, followed or not by the specification of the theorem or by a problem (see for instance, Cametti 1755; Legendre 1802).

Thus in classic Euclidean Geometry the *theoretical nature* of a geometrical construction is clearly stated, in spite of the apparent practical objective, i.e. the accomplishment of a drawing following a certain construction procedure. We note that the "non-constructability" of a figure may become manifest in fundamentally two different ways: a figure may be non-constructible with certain (predefined) theoretical tools, mostly straightedge and compass; or non-constructability may derive from the non-existence of the figure of which one requires the construction, that is, from the contradiction that follows once its existence is assumed. Historically, there are many examples of the first case such as the trisection of an angle, doubling a cube or squaring the circle. The problems of constructability with straightedge and compass were solved definitively in the XIX Century with tools developed in analytic geometry and through algebraic extensions. The second case of non-constructability does not depend on the tools used to accomplish the construction because it is a consequence of the theoretical non-existence of the object. The latter is the context we will be working in throughout this chapter.

3.2   Conjecturing Open Problems of Constructability and Non-constructability

In this chapter we will be working with construction problems that involve the formulation of a conjecture, so they are *conjecturing open construction problems*. From the point of view of design, the main aspect we are interested in discussing here, it is useful to distinguish two subtypes within these problems based on whether the construction *is* or *is not* actually possible in Euclidean Geometry. If the construction *is* possible we will speak of *constructability problems*, while if the construction is *not* possible, of *non-constructability problems*. Clearly the solver initially does *not know* whether the construction problem s/he is addressing is a constructability or non-constructability problem, while the designer does.

We will be working, in particular, with non-constructability problems of two types: one in which the solver is asked whether a figure with described properties is constructible or not, and in either case s/he is required to provide an argumentation; second one in which steps of the construction of a figure are given and the solver is asked what kinds of figures of a specific type (e.g., of quadrilaterals) can/cannot the figure become, providing conjectures and argumentations in each case. In either case, the solver will probably attempt to construct the suggested or hypothesized figure. The solution can be provided either producing the construction procedure and its validation according the theory available (in this case Euclidean Geometry), or proving the fact that no construction procedure can be exhibited. This latter case, because of its very nature, may lead to an indirect argumentation, sowing seeds that may lead to a proof by contradiction. As a matter of fact a non-constructability statement expresses the fact that it is impossible to display a valid procedure for constructing a certain figure.

4   The DGE Dragging Phenomenon

Literature over the last 20 years has been filled with examples of how a DGE can be used for the exploration of open problems, and, more in general, in exploratory learning (e.g., Yerushalmy et al. 1993; Di Sessa et al. 1995). In particular, research has shown that a DGE impacts students' approach to investigating open problems in Euclidean Geometry, contributing particularly to students' reasoning during the conjecturing phase of open problem activities (e.g., Leher and Chazan 1998; Mariotti 2000; Arzarello et al. 2002; Leung 2008; Leung et al. 2013). The dynamic nature of the exploration in open problems is particularly evident in a DGE. Any DGE figure that has been constructed using specific primitives can be *acted upon* through dragging hence determining the phenomenon of *moving figures*. A Dragging Exploration Principle was proposed (Leung et al. 2013) to epitomize the DGE dragging phenomenon:

> During dragging, a figure maintains all the properties according to which it was constructed and all the consequences that the construction properties entail within the axiomatic world of Euclidean geometry (ibid, p. 458).

The perception of a *moving figure* in a DGE is the phenomenon on the screen that something about the figure changes while something is preserved under dragging. What is preserved under dragging (the *invariant*) becomes the identity of the object/figure in contrast with what changes that determines its *variation* and consequently its movement. "Dynamic geometry exteriorizes the duality invariant/variable in a tangible way by means of motion in the space of the plane." (Laborde 2005, p. 22). The invariants correspond to the properties that are preserved and allow the user to recognize the sequence of images as the same figure in movement. Perceiving and interpreting the interplay between variation and invariants under dragging is the core of the process of *discernment* in DGE whereby we recognize quite different objects as belonging to the same category (Leung 2008; Leung et al. 2013; Mariotti 2014).

In a DGE, it is possible to distinguish between two kinds of invariants appearing simultaneously as a dynamic-figure is acted upon and therefore "moves". First there are the invariants determined by the geometrical relations defined by the commands used to construct the figure which are called *direct invariants*. Second there are the invariants that are derived (*indirect invariants*) as a consequence within the theory of Euclidean Geometry (Laborde and Sträßer 1990). The relationship of dependency between these two types of invariants constitutes a crucial point in the process of exploration in a DGE, and the experience of dragging constructed figures allows the user to interpret what appears on the screen in terms of logical consequence between geometrical properties; in particular, derived invariants will be interpreted in terms of consequences of the direct invariants. Familiarity with explorations in a DGE will mean for a user to have high confidence of this kind of interpretation of images and transformations of images on the screen.

Solving constructability and non-constructability problems in a DGE presents specific visual features. Drawings realized with a straightedge and compass and theorems validating a construction statement have specific counterparts in a DGE. This can be described in terms of visual theorems (Davis, 1993).

> Briefly, a visual theorem is the graphical or visual output from a computer program— usually one of a family of such outputs—which the eye organizes into a coherent, identifiable whole and which is able to inspire mathematical questions of a traditional nature or which contributes in some way to our understanding or enrichment of some mathematical or real world situation (ibid, p. 333).

> It [visual theorem] is the passage from the mathematical iteration to the perceived figure grasped and intuited in all its stateable and unstateable visual complexities (ibid, p. 339).

Therefore a dynamic visual moving figure in a DGE stands for an interesting epistemic aspect of experimental mathematics where both a visual and theoretical dimensions are present. This duality has been discussed, for example, by Leung and Lopez-Real (2002):

> During any dragging episode, the boundary between exploring new geometrical situations and justifying a theorem is a blurred one .... The holistic nature of the dynamic visual representation in DGE allows variation in meaning when a DGE entity is observed (via dragging) from different points of view. Hence the dragging modality can be interpreted as a kind of "random access" to different cognitive modes (making conjecture, formulating proof) in the mind of the person who is interacting with DGE. This duality in interpretation in DGE ... facilitates the acquisition of deeper insight into the task at hand that could lead to further generalization (ibid, p. 159).

Thus the user is let free to explore the possibility of realizing the requested properties. Different possible situations may occur leading to different possible exploration processes or strategies. As discussed by Sinclair and Robutti (2013), dynamic figures can be interpreted in two fundamentally different ways: one according to which the dynamic figure constitutes a "whole" whose behaviour is analysed all together; and a second way according to which the figure constitutes a (very large and discrete) set of static "examples". The authors remarked on how

> It is still unclear whether learners somehow naturally see the draggable diagrams as a series of examples or as one continuously changing object, and whether this depends on their previous exposure to the static geometric discourse of the typical classroom [...] (ibid, p. 574).

The second modality described may be more present in explorations of non-constructability problems. Now let us consider a conjecturing open construction problem in a DGE that consists in asking to realize an image with a required set of properties. First let us look at the case in which a (robust[2]) construction is possible. The order of construction of the required properties may be important, in that it may not be possible to invert the order of robust construction of the properties and still reach the desired figure. For example, constructing a parallelogram with a right angle is not possible starting from a robust parallelogram. Instead, the solver needs to first construct a right angle and from there proceed to define the three other vertices and two sides of the parallelogram. So the possibility of realizing a figure with specific properties may be subordinated to selecting a certain order of construction of the properties. If the user starts with a robust parallelogram and then tries to impose a right angle in one of its vertices, all s/he can obtain is the right angle as a soft property.

In the case of impossibility of the construction, no matter in what order the solver chooses to construct the properties, s/he will not be able to generate a figure with the desired properties. However, the choice of which property to start constructing robustly may heavily influence the exploration. This issue is touched upon in the paper by Baccaglini-Frank et al. (2013) and will be further elaborated on in the present chapter, as it is key in capturing aspects of the didactical potential of the types of activities proposed in explorative learning contexts. Let us analyse examples of two paradigmatic types of tasks for non-constructability problems. We will give an a priori analysis of possible solution processes showing how indirect argumentations might emerge.

---

[2]The terminology "robust" and "soft" comes from Healy (2000) and refers to the fact that certain properties are or are not invariant under dragging.

5 Two Types of Non-constructability Task

5.1 Type One

The first type of non-constructability task can be given in the following form:

> Is it possible to construct a figure of type X with properties Y_1, Y_2, ... Y_n? If so
> construct it robustly. If not explain why not.

Here "figure of type X" indicates a class of figures such as triangles, quadrilaterals, etc., and Y_i are properties of figures in Euclidean Geometry.

5.1.1 Example Task 1a

The task is formulated as follows: "Is it possible to construct a triangle with two perpendicular angle bisectors? If so, provide steps for a construction. If not, explain why not." The answer to the question posed by the problem is "No. A triangle with two perpendicular angle bisectors cannot be constructed".

Figure 1 depicts a robust construction of the triangle with soft angle bisectors. A proof by contradiction might go along the following lines (refer to Fig. 1).

On the one hand, let $\angle CDA$ be right and CD be the bisector of $\angle BCA$ and AD the bisector of $\angle CAB$. Then, passing to the angle measures, $\frac{1}{2}m\angle BCA + \frac{1}{2}m\angle BAC = 90°$, so $m\angle BCA + m\angle BAC = 180°$. On the other hand, $m\angle BCA + m\angle BAC < 180°$ because $\angle BCA$ and $\angle BAC$ are two angles of a triangle. Therefore, we have a contradiction, that is the conjunction between a proposition and its negation.

In a DGE the solver can choose to construct and reason in one of two fundamentally different ways as follows.

Fig. 1 Possible attempt at constructing a suitable triangle

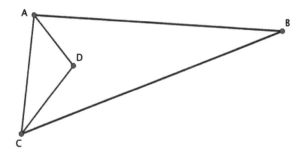

(1) Construct the angle bisectors meeting at a right angle first, then construct the angles of which these are the bisectors and drag to try to "close" the triangle (see Fig. 2).

The solver drags the base points, but his/her attempt at constructing the triangle fails. At this point s/he may ask him/herself why s/he cannot close the triangle. S/he could discover that two sides of the triangle are parallel and so it is possible to construct other figures (like parallelograms, rhombuses ...) but it is not possible to obtain a triangle. S/he could also continue to look for a particular configuration that satisfies the requirements and produce degenerate figures making the sides overlap in a single segment. The problem could move to accepting or not the obtained figure as in Fig. 2 as a triangle. If the solver accepts it as a triangle, what was requested has been constructed; otherwise s/he may conclude that the only way to obtain the requested figure is to make it degenerate, therefore excluding all together the possibility of constructing a triangle. In this second case, the argumentation supporting the conclusion may take an indirect form.

(2) Construct the triangle first, then the angle bisectors, and drag to force the angle at their intersection to become right (objective-property) (see Fig. 3).

Fig. 2 Possible construction with robust angle bisectors intersecting at a robust right angle. One could drag to see if it is possible to make the lines AC′ and CA′ intersect to close the triangle

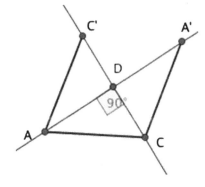

Fig. 3 Possible construction with a robust triangle and angle bisectors, but soft perpendicularity. One could drag to force the angle at the intersection to become right

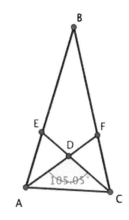

The exploration leads to observing that it seems possible to make the angle a right angle, without however obtaining a single soft instantiation of this property. To check whether the angle is right, the solver may construct an additional element, for example the perpendicular line to the bisector CF through D or s/he might activate the measure of the angle. The fact that the angle can get closer and closer to a right angle can lead the student to thinking that a construction is in fact possible. This can lead him/her to trying to understand what the triangle should be like, and therefore it can lead to assuming that the figure *is already* properly constructed and searching for hypothetical additional properties to add to it (a typical process of analysis in Euclidean Geometry) in order to obtain a robust version of the desired figure. Starting from the assumption of having constructed the figure could lead to an argumentation like "if the triangle had perpendicular bisectors, then…" leading to indirect argumentations that can end in a contradiction or, at least, in properties that are unacceptable for the solver.

Different argumentations could be developed starting from the properties of the bisectors of the triangle, reaching a consequence that comes into conflict with the request of being perpendicular. For example, one can reach a conclusion that the angle between the bisectors has to be strictly greater than a right angle. Finally, theoretical considerations and the observation of the configurations emerging through dragging can lead to particular cases in which the properties are satisfied, but this happens only in degenerate cases in which the triangle collapses into a segment. Although obtaining the contradiction from a theoretical point of view is sufficient to prove that the triangle does not exist, from a cognitive point of view, we could have the necessity to see the consequence of the proposition $m\angle BCA + m\angle BAC = 180°$ which implies that sides BC and BA either coincide or are parallel. Then either B does not exist and so the initial triangle does not exist, or A, B, and C must be collinear, and so again the triangle cannot exist in a non-degenerate form. In other words, a determining difference of how this situation may be seen is how the figure degenerates. In one case the triangle can be seen to degenerate, breaking into an open figure (when BC and BA are seen as becoming parallel, see Mariotti and Antonini 2009), or it can be perceived as turning into a single line (for example, BC and BA are seen as collapsing onto the same line).

5.1.2   Example Task 1b

Task 1a can be given in a slightly different form: "Is it possible to construct a triangle with two perpendicular external angle bisectors? If so, provide steps for a construction. If not, explain why not." The answer to the question posed by the problem is "No. A triangle with two perpendicular external angle bisectors cannot be constructed".

Figure 4 depicts a robust construction of the triangle with soft external angle bisectors. A proof by contradiction might go along the following lines (refer to Fig. 4). Let $\angle ADC$ be right and AD be the bisector of the external angle of the triangle in A(α), and CD be the bisector of the external angle of the triangle in C(γ).

Fig. 4 Possible attempt at
constructing a suitable
triangle

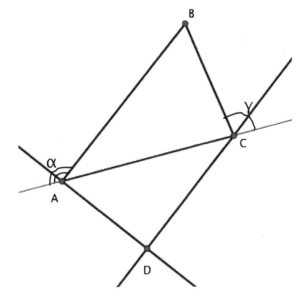

Then, passing to the angle measures, $\gamma = 180° - \alpha + \angle ABC$. Considering the sum of
the internal angles of triangle ACD,

$$\frac{1}{2}\alpha + \frac{180° - \alpha + \angle ABC}{2} = 180° - \angle ADC$$

$$\frac{1}{2}\alpha + \frac{180° - \alpha + \angle ABC}{2} = 180° - 90°$$

$$\frac{\alpha}{2} + 90° - \frac{\alpha}{2} + \frac{\angle ABC}{2} = 90°$$

$$\frac{\angle ABC}{2} = 0°.$$

Therefore, we have a contradiction, because $\angle ABC$ is not zero in a non-degenerate
triangle.

In a DGE the solver can choose to proceed in one of two fundamentally different
ways, as follows.

(1) Construct the external angle bisectors meeting at a right angle first, then
    construct the angles of which these are bisectors and try to drag B_1 to B_2 to
    "close" the triangle (see Fig. 5).
(2) Construct the triangle first, then the external angle bisectors, and drag to force
    the angle at the intersection D to become right (objective-property) (see
    Fig. 6).

Fig. 5 Possible construction
with robust external angle
bisectors intersecting at a
robust right angle

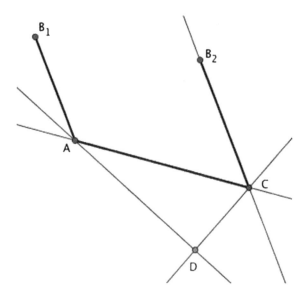

Fig. 6 Possible construction
with robust external angle
bisectors intersecting at a soft
right angle

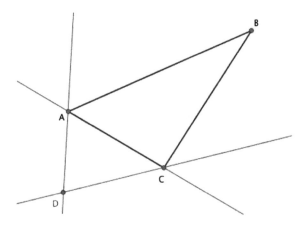

Summing up, in both cases the difficulties in trying to obtain what is requested can
prompt a search for a number of different arguments, at different moments, and with
different objectives:

- understanding, explaining, verifying failure (or the difficulties) of the search,
  and therefore explaining why the two properties cannot coexist at the same
  instant;
- identifying "when" the objective-property is satisfied;
- analysing the acceptability of the anomalous cases obtained.

Whatever the objectives, we expect both direct and indirect argumentations.
Direct argumentations may stem from a certain property to identify consequences

that can be incompatible with the second property. In other cases the solver may start from *the* triangle with all the desired coexisting properties, using processes of analysis and synthesis to see whether the construction is possible, or to motivate the impossibility of the construction. In both cases indirect argumentations may arise.

5.2   Type Two

The second type of non-constructability task can be given in the following form:

> Given the construction with steps S_1, S_2, … S_n, consider figure F originating from the steps. Which kinds of figures of type X is it possible for F to become? Make conjectures and explain.

Here S_i corresponds to a command in the DGE, F is a subset of elements originating from the construction which the solver's attention is called upon, and "figure of type X" indicates a class of figures such as triangles, quadrilaterals, etc.

First, the robust construction of a figure is required, the solver is asked to explore possible specifications of the original figure. Geometrically speaking, this will correspond to asking the solver to identify possible properties that can be consistently added to the construction properties that have been already realized. Let us discuss possible solutions in the following case.

Construct the following figure:

- a point P
- a line r through P
- the perpendicular to r through P
- a point C on the perpendicular
- point A symmetric to C with respect to P
- a point D on the semi plane opposite to C with respect to r
- line through D and P
- a circle with centre C and radius CP
- B as the 2nd intersection of the circle with the line through DP
- the quadrilateral ABCD.

Once the construction is achieved, an image appears like that in Fig. 7. What kinds of quadrilaterals can ABCD become?

As soon as the exploration begins, it will be easy to realize that ABCD can become a parallelogram (Fig. 8). Exploring this case, the solver can discover how to make ABCD into a robust parallelogram by only adding one new property to the construction, adding the following construction steps:

- a circle with centre in A and radius AP
- redefine D on this new circle.

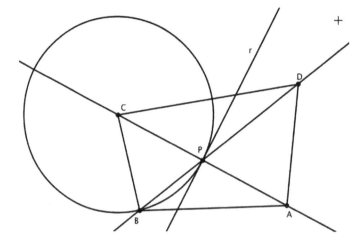

Fig. 7 Quadrilateral ABCD arising from the steps of the task

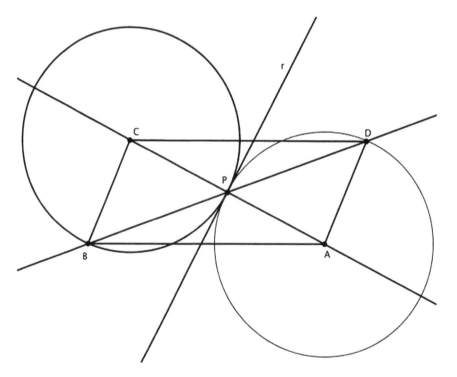

Fig. 8 The solver has discovered a way to transform ABCD into a robust parallelogram

The new properties are geometrically consistent with the previous properties and the construction is successfully achieved. At this point, the exploration could continue in two different directions. The solver decides either to come back to the original figure or to address the problem of constructing new quadrilaterals as subcases of the case of the parallelogram. In the latter case, a square would seem to be possible, since it is a particular kind of parallelogram.

The solver may notice that now the figure has new robust invariants PB congruent to PD; BC parallel and congruent to DA; BA parallel and congruent to CD; etc. The solver might attempt to obtain a figure that visually could be perceived as a square and to do this s/he may decide to see when ABCD has right angles, obtaining such configuration at specific instances. This is in fact possible, however the property is not sufficient for ABCD to be a square, but only a non-square rectangle (Fig. 9).

However, the solver may not grasp the theoretical reasons of such impossibility, therefore acknowledging the failure of his/her attempt. Instead s/he may search for another way of obtaining a square, identifying another property to add to the previous ones. For example, the solver may search for configurations in which the parallelogram has perpendicular diagonals. This happens only when the whole parallelogram collapses onto segment CA (Fig. 10).

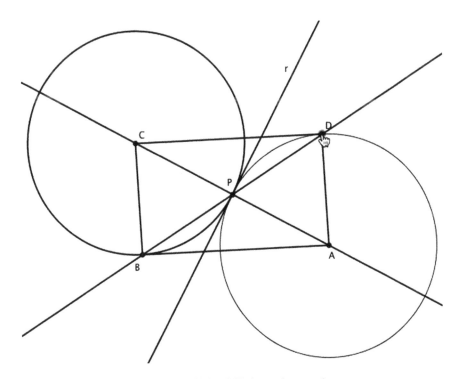

Fig. 9 The solver finds a position at which ABCD is a soft rectangle

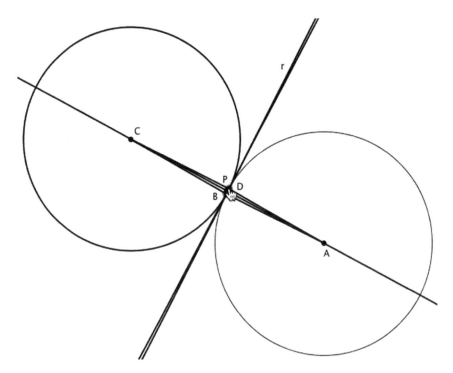

Fig. 10 ABCD has perpendicular diagonals only when the whole parallelogram collapses onto segment CA

The solver has found a particular configuration for which the desired property is visually verified. The solver may also become convinced that there is no other way to obtain the desired property (no matter where s/he places D on the circle). However s/he may now be concerned with which might be the other properties that the figure assumes when the desired property is visually verified. Why is this the case? Is the collapsed quadrilateral a square? These questions may trigger a rich production of argumentations.

Similarly, another issue could be the fact that in *no other* placement of D on the circle is it possible to obtain the desired configuration and thus a square. Finally, the solver may try to drag other points such as P or C to see if the desired property can be obtained for other—less awkward—configurations. In this case, more argumentations about why the configuration is not obtainable may follow.

Even if the solver had not constructed a robust parallelogram and started to explore the possibilities of obtaining a square by overlapping *r* and the line through PD, s/he would have ended up with a strange figure, such as the one below (Fig. 11), in which B and P coincide, thus new pressing questions might arise. Does this always happen? Why? These are more triggers for indirect argumentation processes. All these questions may originate further argumentation processes.

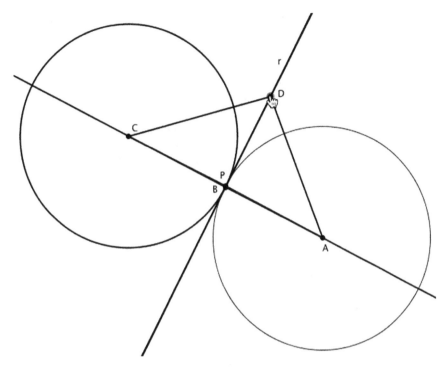

Fig. 11 Figure resulting from the solver's attempt of overlapping *r* and the line through PD

In summary, because of these two types of non-constructability task, it is likely that the arising argumentations will be indirect.

6 Nature of DGE Non-constructability Tasks and Design Considerations

In contrast to doodling with pen and paper to somehow draw what can appear to be impossible geometrical figures, in a DGE one cannot construct a "wrong" (Euclidean) figure! This makes a DGE a possible, and maybe even powerful, digital environment to explore and develop different types of argumentation in Euclidean Geometry. The visual robustness of DGE figures can force a certain desired property or condition into a visual anomaly which may produce experiential aspects that do not have immediate conceptual counterparts in the realm of Euclidean Geometry. The anomaly (here, possibly, a degenerated figure resulted from dragging to impose a condition) opens up a rich epistemic space for the solver to come up with logical argumentations to make sense out of it. Leung and Lopez-Real (2002) discussed a student exploration case about how to use a "biased DGE figure" (mentally projecting a condition on a robust DGE figure) to come up with a proof by contradiction and a related visual theorem under a drag-to-vanish strategy. Baccaglini-Frank et al. (2013) continued and expanded this discussion using tasks of the first type. In particular, they showed how a DGE can offer guidance in the solver's development of an indirect argumentation thanks to the potential it offers of both constructing chosen properties robustly. Therefore asking students to solve non-constructability tasks in a DGE can be conducive to developing their skills related to geometrical reasoning, proof and argumentation. Here we discuss the nature and considerations for this type of task design.

6.1 Task Nature

In Sect. 5, two task types were discussed:

1. Is it possible to construct a figure of type X with properties Y_1, Y_2, ... Y_n? If so construct it robustly. If not explain why not.
2. Given the construction with steps S_1, S_2, ... S_n, consider figure F originating from the steps. Which kinds of figures of type X is it possible for F to become? Make conjectures and explain.

"Is it possible?" is the common theme of these task types. Rather than the usual aiming to construct a DGE figure to ascertain a conjecture or to validate a theorem, an uncertainty is given as the main driving force for the task. In our experience we have noticed that the solver seems to initially be under the impression that a DGE *can* construct anything, possibly because of the Euclidean fidelity provided by a DGE. When the solver encounters a visual conflict with what s/he is expecting, or when s/he is unable to obtain an objective-property, s/he is prompted towards a dragging reasoning/discourse to re-solve the situation. The types of reasoning/discourse that the solver develops to re-solve the visual uncertainty are the main didactical goals of the task. In Sect. 5 the a priori analyses of the different tasks gave a glimpse of what possible dragging discourses can be developed due to the design of the tasks.

6.2 Visual Anomaly

The crux of this type of task design is to lead the solver to seeing a DGE phenomenon that does not seem to make sense at the first instant during a construction/dragging activity. That is, a cognitive conflict is created by a visual anomaly. Take, for instance, the case described in Figs. 10 and 11 in which B and P coincide, while the solver was expecting P to be the point of intersection of a square's (ABCD) diagonals. The anomaly forces the solver to combine concepts in Euclidean Geometry with her/his dragging strategies and the figures they lead to. In this case the solver would like to see a square (and may be seeing one mentally) but is forced by the DGE to recognize an isosceles right triangle which could be interpreted as "half of the square". In the task analyses in Sect. 5, we saw how this can happen for other figures (e.g., a triangle) that degenerated (e.g., into a line segment) when the solver was dragging in the attempt at realizing a desired condition/property. In these cases of degeneration, the anomaly seems to appear through a continuous dragging process that, in a certain sense, culminates with the generation of the anomaly: the objective property is obtained and in that instant something else is lost.

In general, visual anomalies can be generated when a certain condition is imposed on a construction, and the expected figure becomes something else. This can be the case when the solver chooses to robustly construct perpendicular angle bisectors and proceeds "backwards" to construct the sides of the triangle using reflections on the bisectors. The triangle's sides end up being robustly parallel, all of a sudden, and no matter how the solver drags, these sides will never intersect. As before, the solver may be mentally seeing a triangle, but actually with the DGE s/he will never be able to generate one. From these visual anomalies, the solver needs to resolve to Euclidean Geometry to explain the visual phenomena (Antonini and Mariotti 2010). Using the idea of figural concept (Fischbein 1993) as a "harmony" between a figural and conceptual component (Mariotti and Antonini 2009), an anomaly can be thought of as a break between the two components (figural and conceptual). It may be possible to restore the harmony within the figural concept by dragging to make a certain configuration vanish or degenerate, or by re-interpreting the obtained figure, rectifying the anomaly. This kind of solver-DGE interactive phenomenon should be typical in the solution of tasks designed as DGE non-constructible tasks.

We have been investigating the actual argumentations provided by students when solving tasks such as the ones analyzed in this chapter (Baccaglini-Frank et al. 2013), and we are currently working on associating specific types of dragging experiences and interpretation of the dynamic figures to the production of indirect argumentation. Our previous studies and preliminary results of our current research study suggest that specific types of dragging experiences and of interpretation of the dynamic figures seem to be associated to the production of indirect argumentation. Moreover, the non-constructability tasks analyzed in this chapter have proven to be particularly rich for gathering interesting data in this respect.

6.3 Didactical Reflections

We wish to conclude the chapter with some didactical reflections on the two types of task discussed. We find the two types of task to have different degrees of openness. The first type of task asks about the possibility of constructing a well-defined type of figure. The second type asks the solver to make conjectures on possible types of figures that might be obtainable given a certain (explicit) construction.

Though tasks of the first type are open, tasks of the second type appear to have a higher degree of openness, in that it is up to the solver to think of a particular configuration and then decide whether it is obtainable or not. Also, while in solving tasks of the first type the solver almost necessarily will explore (some form of) the impossibility of constructing a figure with the required properties; in solving tasks of the second type, the solver may concentrate on possible configurations that s/he encounters using wandering or guided dragging (Arzarello et al. 2002). This may occur for various reasons, for example: the solver is attracted to configurations s/he "recognizes", since it may be easier to "read" the figure interpreting it theoretically (ascending process[3]) as opposed to "impose something theoretical on the figure" (descending process); the search for ways to robustly impose a new condition on the figure and obtain a particular (possible) configuration may be time and energy consuming, and leave little time for the exploration of impossible cases; the solver thinks the teacher expects certain types of explorations from him/her because of the didactical contract, and such expectations may not include "impossible" cases since these might not be a typical aim of dynamic explorations; the student may not have developed a "mathematical eye" that allows him/her to attend to aspects that an expert mathematician would deem interesting (e.g., Hölzl 2001); etc.

Therefore, when proposing tasks of the second type, the teacher should consider the possible necessity of reformulating the task (maybe after some time or only for some students) in a more guided way, though maintaining the exploratory nature of the task. For example, in the case of the problem analysed in Sect. 5.2, the teacher might explicitly ask whether it is possible to obtain a square, thus making it clear for the students that "square" is a configuration considered interesting/relevant by the teacher and worth spending some time on.

On the other hand, we expect that tasks of the first type will relatively quickly put students in front of the fact that "it might not be that easy" to construct the desired figure, immediately opening the terrain to processes of argumentation. Moreover because the formulation of the task can guide the solver's attention to the contradictory properties, since these are stated explicitly in the task—although it is not stated that they are contradictory—some students may actualize processes of indirect argumentation.

---

[3]Ascending and descending processes are presented in Arzarello et al. (2002), referring to Saada-Robert (1989).

References

Antonini, S. (2004). A statement, the contrapositive and the inverse: Intuition and argumentation. In *Proceedings of the 28th PME, Bergen, Norway* (Vol. 2, pp. 47–54).

Antonini, S. (2010). A model to analyse argumentations supporting impossibilities in mathematics. In M. F. Pinto & T. F. Kawasaki (Eds.), *Proceedings of the 34th Conference of the International Group for the Psychology of Mathematics Education* (Vol. 2, pp. 153–160). Belo Horizonte, Brazil: PME.

Antonini, S., & Mariotti, M. A. (2006). Reasoning in an absurd world: Difficulties with proof by contradiction. In *Proceedings of the 30th PME Conference, Prague, Czech Republic* (Vol. 2, pp. 65–72).

Antonini, S., & Mariotti, M. A. (2008). Indirect proof: What is specific to this way of proving? *Zentralblatt für Didaktik der Mathematik, 40*(3), 401–412.

Antonini, S., & Mariotti, M. A. (2010). Abduction and the explanation of anomalies: The case of proof by contradiction. In V. Durand-Guerrier, S. Soury-Lavergne, & F. Arzarello (Eds.). *Proceedings of the 6th Conference of European Research in Mathematics Education, Lyon, France, 2009* (pp. 322–331).

Arsac, G. (1999). Variations et variables de la démonstration géométriques. *Recherches en Didactique de Mathématiques, 19*(3), 357–390.

Arzarello, F., Olivero, F., Paola, D., & Robutti, O. (2002). A cognitive analysis of dragging practises in Cabri environments. *ZDM, 34*(3), 66–72.

Arzarello, F., Bartolini Bussi, M. G., Leung, A., Mariotti, M. A., & Stevenson, I. (2012). Experimental approaches to theoretical thinking: Artefacts and proofs. In G. Hanna & M. de Villiers (Eds.), *Proof and proving in mathematics education—The 19th ICMI study* (pp. 97–137). New York: Springer.

Baccaglini-Frank, A. (2010). Conjecturing in dynamic geometry: A model for conjecture-generation through maintaining dragging. *Doctoral dissertation*, University of New Hampshire, Durham, NH. ProQuest.

Baccaglini-Frank, A., Antonini, S., Leung, A., & Mariotti, M. A. (2013). Reasoning by contradiction in dynamic geometry. *PNA, 7*(2), 63–73.

Baccaglini-Frank, A., & Mariotti, M. A. (2010). Generating conjectures through dragging in dynamic geometry: The maintaining dragging model. *International Journal of Computers for Mathematical Learning, 15*(3), 225–253.

Boero, P., Garuti, R., & Mariotti, M. A. (1996). Some dynamic mental process underlying producing and proving conjectures. In *Proceedings of 20th PME Conference, Valencia, Spain* (Vol. 2, pp. 121–128).

Boero, P., Garuti, R., & Lemut, E. (2007). Approaching theorems in grade VIII. In P. Boero (Ed.), *Theorems in school: from history epistemology and cognition to classroom practice* (pp. 249–264). Sense Publishers.

Cametti, O. (1755). *Elementa Geometrie quae nova, et brevi methodo demostravit D. Octavianus Camettus.* Firenze.

Davis, P. (1993). Visual theorems. *Educational Studies in Mathematics, 24,* 333–344.

Di Sessa, A. A., Hoyles, C., & Noss, R. (1995). *Computers and exploratory learning.* Berlin, Germany: Springer.

Fischbein, E. (1993). The theory of figural concepts. *Educational Studies in Mathematics, 24,* 139–162.

Freudenthal, H. (1973). *Mathematics as an educational task.* Dordrecht, Holland: Reidel Publishing Company.

Healy, L. (2000). Identifying and explaining geometric relationship: Interactions with robust and soft Cabri constructions. In *Proceedings of the 24th Conference of the IGPME, Hiroshima, Japan* (Vol. 1, pp. 103–117).

Heath, T. L. (Ed.) (1956) *Euclid. The thirteen books of the elements* (vol. 1). Dover.

Hölzl, R. (2001). Using dynamic geometry software to add contrast to geometric situations—a case study. *International Journal of Computers for Mathematical Learning, 6*(1), 63–86.

Laborde, C. (2005). Robust and soft constructions: Two sides of the use of dynamic geometry environments. In *Proceedings of the 10th Asian Technology Conference in Mathematics* (pp. 22–35). Cheong-Ju, South Korea: Korea National University of Education.

Laborde, J. M., & Sträßer, R. (1990). Cabri-Géomètre: A microworld of geometry for guided discovery learning. *Zentralblatt für Didaktik der Mathematik, 22*(5), 171–177.

Legendre, A. M. (1802). *Elementi di geometria di Adriano M. Legendre per la prima volta tradotti in italiano.* Pisa: Tipografia della Società Letteraria.

Leher, R., & Chazan, D. (1998). *Designing learning environments for developing understanding of geometry and space.* Hillsdale, NJ: Lawrence Erlbaum Associates.

Leung, A. (2008). Dragging in a dynamic geometry environment through the lens of variation. *International Journal of Computers for Mathematical Learning, 13*, 135–157.

Leung, A., & Lopez-Real, F. (2002). Theorem justification and acquisition in dynamic geometry: A case of proof by contradiction. *International Journal of Computers for Mathematical Learning, 7*, 145–165. Netherlands: Kluwer Academic Publishers.

Leung, A., Baccaglini-Frank, A., & Mariotti, M. A. (2013). Discernment in dynamic geometry environments. *Educational Studies in Mathematics, 84*(3), 439–460.

Mariotti, M. A. (2000). Introduction to proof: The mediation of a dynamic software environment. *Educational Studies in Mathematics Special Issue, 44*, 25–53.

Mariotti, M. A. (2014). Transforming images in a DGS: The semiotic potential of the dragging tool for introducing the notion of conditional statement. In S. Rezat, et al. (Eds.), *Transformation— A fundamental idea of mathematics education* (pp. 155–172). New York: Springer.

Mariotti, M. A., Bartollni Bussi, M., Boero, P., Ferri, F., & Garuti, R. (1997). Approaching geometry theorems in contexts: From history and epistemology to cognition. In *Proceedings of the 21th PME Conference, Lathi, Finland* (Vol. 1, pp. 180–195).

Mariotti, M. A., & Antonini, S. (2009). Breakdown and reconstruction of figural concepts in proofs by contradiction in geometry. In F. L. Lin, F. J. Hsieh, G. Hanna, & M. de Villers (Eds.), *Proof and Proving in Mathematics Education, ICMI Study 19th Conference Proceedings* (Vol. 2, pp. 82–87).

Mogetta, C., Olivero, F., & Jones, K. (1999). Providing the motivation to prove in a dynamic geometry environment. In *Proceedings of the British Society for Research into Learning Mathematics* (pp. 91–96). Lancaster: St. Martin's University College, Lancaster.

Olivero, F. (2000). Conjecturing in open-geometric situations in Cabri-geometre: An exploratory classroom experiment. In C. Morgan, & K. Jones (Eds.), *BSLRM Annual Publication of Proceedings.*

Saada-Robert, M. (1989). La microgénèse de la representation d'un problem. *Psychologie Française, 34*, 2/3.

Sinclair, N., & Robutti, O. (2013). Technology and the role of proof: The case of dynamic geometry. In A. J. Bishop, M. A. Clements, C. Keitel, & F. Leung (Eds.), *Third international handbook of mathematics education.* Dordrecht, The Netherlands: Kluwer Academic Publishers.

Thompson, D. R. (1996). Learning and teaching indirect proof. *The Mathematics Teacher, 89*(6), 474–482.

Yerushalmy, M., Chazan, D., & Gordon, M. (1993). Posing problems: One aspect of bringing inquiry into classrooms. In J. Schwartz, M. Yerushalmy, & B. Wilson (Eds.), *The geometric supposer, what is it a case of?* (pp. 117–142). Hillsdale, NJ: Lawrence Erlbaum Associates.

The Planimeter as a Real and Virtual Instrument that Mediates an Infinitesimal Approach to Area

Ferdinando Arzarello and Daniele Manzone

Abstract Drawing on a didactic gap detected between the elementary concept of area and the infinitesimal approach to it within the Italian secondary school curriculum, the notion of swept area is introduced in grades 10–11. The idea of swept area is introduced through the mediation of an artifact, the Polar Planimeter, both as a concrete physical-tool and as a virtual-object. It triggers and supports the semiotic productions of the students so that they can grasp the new concept. The notion of didactic cycle is used for designing students' learning sequences. The activities in such sequences are of two types: sensory-motor and symbolic. The mediation of the artifact allows intertwining the two types so that the one can constantly be built on the other. Indeed, the practices mentioned above show a deep intertwining between their cultural and cognitive components.

Keywords Planimeter · Swept area

1 Introduction

In the PISA definition of mathematical literacy we find the ability of "using [...] tools to describe, explain, and predict phenomena". Indeed, many national curricula at all grades suggest involving students in the use of (concrete or virtual) tools to model phenomena and to enter into mathematical ideas. This is not a novelty at all: the links between mathematics, natural sciences and technology, as well as the role of basing mathematics teaching on intuitive and empirical stances have been put at the foreground ever since the early documents of the International Commission on

F. Arzarello
Dipartimento di Matematica "G. Peano", Università di Torino, Turin, Italy
e-mail: ferdinando.arzarello@unito.it

D. Manzone (✉)
Istituto Sociale and Scuola Secondaria di I grado E. Artom, Turin, Italy
e-mail: manzone.daniele@gmail.com

© Springer International Publishing Switzerland 2017
A. Leung and A. Baccaglini-Frank (eds.), *Digital Technologies in Designing Mathematics Education Tasks*, Mathematics Education in the Digital Era 8,
DOI 10.1007/978-3-319-43423-0_7

Mathematical Instruction (Bartolini Bussi et al. 2010; Ruthven 2008; see also Smith 1913) and constitute a widely investigated topic in current studies in mathematics education. As a significant example, two of the ICMI Studies within the last 30 years concern the role of new technologies in mathematics teaching. As pointed out by many scholars, "in mathematics education, the availability of Information and Communication Technologies (ICT) has changed the landscape, including the belief that digital objects can substitute for the references to the concrete world where we live" (Bartolini Bussi et al. 2010, p. 20; also see the website http://nlvm. usu.edu/en/nav/vLibrary.html). However, these changes in the landscape do not mean that we have to throw away all the past: we would risk throwing out the baby with the bathwater. In other words, modeling and applications can be pursued within "an approach that does not neglect, but rather emphasizes, the cultural aspects of mathematics, going back to the prominent founders of modern mathematics and taking advantages of the ICT support" (*ibid.*). This program is widely present in many studies all over the world (for a summary see: Bartolini Bussi et al. 2010). Our claim is that in order to design suitable learning situations in the classroom, where manipulative materials and instruments can be used to support learning, it is necessary to carefully investigate the cultural, epistemological, and cognitive roots of mathematical concepts (Tall 1989; Boero and Guala 2008). This investigation will clarify how manipulative materials, instruments and ICT, suitably combined together in real and virtual environments, can help students grasp those concepts, also basing learning on what today, grounding on fresh research results (Hall and Nemirovsky 2012), is called an embodied approach to mathematics learning.

Using instruments in mathematics classes immediately poses a problem: how do they link with the rigorous formal aspects of the discipline, in particular how do they support the evolution from empirical observations to more formal arguments? We will illustrate this crucial point in the final sections discussing how the use of a planimeter can trigger and support students' understanding of area according to an infinitesimal approach. Answering this question in a proper way is crucial in order to avoid misunderstandings, some of which are common in several research articles: they are at the origin of a sort of comedy of errors about proof, which we think is absolutely necessary to avoid. For example, in the Nineties, a number of developments in mathematical practice, most of them reflecting in some way the growing use of computers, caused some mathematicians and others to call into question the continuing importance of proof or indeed to announce its imminent death (Horgan 1993). One of the developments that prompted Horgan's announcement was the use of computers to create or validate enormously long proofs, such as that of the four-colour theorem by Appel and Haken, or of the solution to the party problem by Radziszowski and McKay (1995).

These speculations had strong consequences on some curricula: they caused a serious turn away from proof (Hanna 1996). For example, in the 1989 NCTM Standards proof is explicitly de-emphasized. These explicitly cite the difficulties for teaching and learning proofs: at the time of the publication of the Standards (1989) the concept of proof had almost disappeared from the curriculum (Greeno 1994) or shrunk to a meaningless ritual (Wu 1996). However, this de-emphasis on proof in the 1989 version of the Standards created a tension within the document. The 2000 version of the Standards (NCTM 2000) ameliorated this tension: moving away from the standard idea of proof, as a purely formal object they made explicit fresh functions of proof that should feature its teaching in the school, and stated goals of treating and teaching mathematics "as reasoning" and "as communication".

This revised outlook on proof is, no doubt, a response to a great deal of literature generated in the decade after the publication of the first Standards document. This body of work sprang up partly in explicit defense of proof (e.g. Epp 1994; Greeno 1994; Hanna 2000), and partly to support and fill in the NCTM's overall picture of what mathematics education should be. In light of that research, the NCTM was able to revise and hone its aims. Assurance of truth is only one of proof's roles in mathematics, in the classroom or in professional practice. We should note that presenting justification as the sole reason to do proof has a few weaknesses, and some argue that because of these weaknesses, there is no need to teach proof in schools. The reply to this argument is twofold; there are so to say, ethical arguments. First, of course it does not matter that students are more convinced by empirical arguments; they shouldn't be, and part of the point of education is to teach them not to be. They should value rationality over authority. Second, students can be led astray from intuition and perceived patterns. But there are also more concrete arguments: proofs can become the essential part of mathematical activities in the classroom, provided they become an integrated process in the process of discovering mathematical concepts and truths: a classroom climate can be created so that the students themselves become the mathematical authority. They can argue about problems and solutions, bringing reasons to bear on the problem, and accepting a proof only when they themselves are convinced by it. In a word, teachers can create a classroom climate, according to which students enter into what we call the *logic of inquiry*. This approach is the rationale behind our project, as it will be made explicit below.

When such a climate is introduced in the classroom students learn to rely on arguments and reasoning rather than authority, they make use of their factual knowledge, and they come to a deeper understanding of the way mathematical facts are related. Experimental and theoretical features will not be seen any longer as contrasting but as complementing components of processes that coach students to investigate, conjecture, and prove.

The manifesto of this approach, based on the logic of inquiry (Dewey 1938; Hintikka 1999), is featured by the following keywords:

- Finding **if** ...
- Establishing **that** ...
- Ascertaining **why** ...
- Settling **why not** ...
- Investigating **what if** ...

Teaching situations can be designed to guide students' processes of inquiry according to these steps, and ICT can support them. We will show an example of this type of processes in the final sections. At this point we limit ourselves to observing that the "experimental" dimension introduced into mathematics by the use of instruments can facilitate the logic of inquiry:

> Experimental mathematics is the use of a computer to run computations – sometimes no more than trial-and-error tests – to look for patterns, to identify particular numbers and sequences, to gather evidence in support of specific mathematical assertions that may themselves arise by computational means, including search. Like contemporary chemists – and before them the alchemists of old – who mix various substances together in a crucible and heat them to a high temperature to see what happens, today's experimental mathematicians put a hopefully potent mix of numbers, formulas, and algorithms into a computer in the hope that something of interest emerges (Borwein and Devlin 2008, p. 1).

In this manner a productive dynamic tension is generated between the *empirical nature* of activities with instruments, which encompasses perceptual and operational components, and the *deductive nature* of mathematics, which entails a rigorous and sophisticated formalization. This link between the two aspects has been widely discussed in Arzarello et al. (2012), where it is claimed:

> The main goal of our chapter centres on the dynamic tension between the empirical and the theoretical nature of mathematics. Our purpose is to underline the elements of historical continuity in the stream of thought today called experimental mathematics, and show the concrete possibilities it offers to today's teachers for pursuing the learning of proof in the classroom, especially through the use of their computers. Specifically, we examine how this dynamic tension regulates the actions of students who are asked to solve mathematical problems by first making explorations with technological tools, then formulating suitable conjectures and finally proving them.

In this chapter we further exploit this goal, basing on an example, where the tension empirical-theoretical is based on the dialectic between a concrete tool (the planimeter), its emulation in a virtual environment (its model through GeoGebra), and the students' actions and interactions (with their classmates, with the teacher, with themselves, with tools), their productions (e.g. answering questions, posing other questions, making a conjecture, introducing a sign to represent a situation, and so on) and communications (e.g. when the discovered solution is communicated to a classmate or to the teacher orally or in written form, using suitable representations).

We will show the pedagogical possibilities offered by this tension with an emblematic example taken from a teaching experiment in Italy. It shows how a concrete tool can help dig into deep mathematical ideas and support the transition from an empirical to a theoretical side. Indeed, this concerns an approach to the notion of the area of a surface as a "swept area": the project is developed from the ideas of Kepler about the nature of the planets' rotation around the sun (first and second law) and even arrives to calculate the area of irregular surfaces. To achieve this goal, a key tool is used, the *Amsler planimeter* (Fig. 1): it embodies the Gauss divergence theorem in dimension 2, and shows the possibility of using old technology intertwined with ICT to make students encounter into important mathematical ideas.

Fig. 1 The Amsler
planimeter

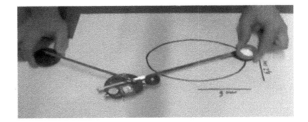

2 Amsler Planimeter

The planimeter was a professional tool used for measuring the areas of flat shapes. Through the centuries several kinds of planimeters have been conceived. For our research we have used the polar planimeter, built by Amsler (Amsler 1856). One can see in Fig. 1 that the Amsler planimeter is an artifact made of:

- two joined arms whose constraints allow only reciprocal rotation,
- a fixed constraint (fixed point) to which one of the arms is attached and which allows only rotation,
- a lens, called tracer that follows the contour of the figure whose area is to be measured,
- a wheel physically constrained to rotate only perpendicularly to the second arm,
- a counter that keeps track of the distance travelled by the wheel.

Following Rabardel (1995) we distinguish between *artifact* (sometimes we use also the word tool) and *instrument*: an artifact is a material with its own physical and structural characteristics made for specific tasks; it is different from an instrument, namely an artifact with a specific utilization scheme (for example the compass as a physical object and the compass as an artifact to draw circles). The utilization scheme for measuring with the planimeter is the following: the fixed point is chosen outside the figure, the tracer is placed on a point on the contour of the figure, the counter is reset and the contour is followed for an entire cycle. The counter will return a number that is proportional to the area of the figure. The functioning of the planimeter relies on two key ideas:

1. The distance covered by the wheel is proportional to the area swept by the second arm. The proportionality relies on the fact that it is possible to split every possible movement of the arm into a translation and a rotation, so that:

   a. motion in the direction of the arm does not sweep any area,
   b. the area swept by a translation is proportional to the distance covered by the arm,
   c. the algebraic sum of all rotations is null because the planimeter must return to the initial position.

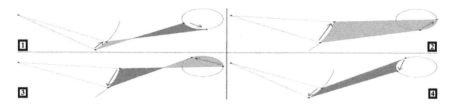

Fig. 2 A utilisation model

2. The area swept by the arm corresponds to the area of the measuring flat shape (a circle in Fig. 2), provided a concept of *swept positive or negative area* is introduced according to the direction of the movement of the arm. For example in Fig. 2, the area outside the figure, which is swept twice but in opposite directions, has a null value and only the area inside the closed curve is evaluated.

Thanks to the planimeter it is possible to measure the area of any plane shape, be it regular or irregular. In the 19th century this tool was wide-spread among many professionals: geographers and cartographers used it to measure extended territories drawn in topographic plants or maps; artisans, especially in the textile sector, used it to evaluate irregular forms of leather or fabrics. Planimeters also helped people in the medical field: cardiologists used them to calculate the integral of the function blood-pressure/ventricular-volume in coronary bloodstream in order to weigh the work done by a ventricle.

With the last decade's technological development, electronic devices, programmed applying planimeter concepts have replaced this old mechanical tool. For example, many APPs for smartphones or tablets, which measure areas, resemble the planimeter in the name or in the programming algorithms (for example, *GooglePlanimeter, AndMeasure*).

The planimeter is very interesting from a mathematical point of view. Indeed, it is a concrete application of Green's theorem, in particular according to the formulation of Gauss and Stokes. From the one side, it is very helpful to convey specific concepts of infinitesimal calculus, and specifically the idea of swept area, while from the other side it can have important practical applications, i.e. in estimating numerical integration.

3   A GeoGebra Planimeter

Concrete planimeters and a virtual model built in GeoGebra, a Dynamic Geometry Software, (Fig. 3) have been used in our teaching experiment. The planimeter virtualisation was implemented to introduce new mathematical knowledge through the construction and the exploration of real situations with the employment of technological tools.

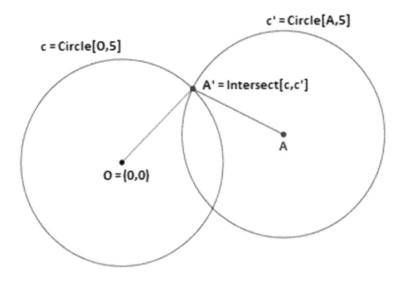

Fig. 3 The GeoGebra planimeter

The composition and the utilization scheme for the GeoGebra Planimeter are the same as for Amsler's one. Let us now illustrate the GeoGebra file, which is the virtual model of the planimeter: to highlight the great analogy between the real instrument and its virtual representation the language of the file description will fit match the language used to describe the real planimeter:

- two segments, $\overline{OA'}$ and $\overline{AA'}$, are the radii of the circles c and c'; the segments are constrained: they are consecutive because they are radii at the intersection point A';
- point O is fixed, chosen external to the figure to be measured. O is an endpoint of one of the segments, hence allowed to perform only rotations around the point;
- a free point A, which will be constrained at the contour of the figure that we want to measure;
- a slider (not shown in Fig. 3), which makes discrete and limits the planimeter's motions, activated by the user;
- a spreadsheet, out of control of the user, (Fig. 4) in which:
  - in columns $A - D$, all the 102 positions of points A and A' are recorded,
  - in cells E_i with $3 \leq i \leq 103$, the software calculates the positive or negative distance between two consecutive positions of the segment $\overline{AA'}$, which moves in a discrete way.

⊞ A	⊞ B	⊞ C	⊞ D	E	F
1	x(A')	y(A')	x(A)	y(A)		
2	?	?	?	?		?
3	?	?	?	?	?	
4	?	?	?	?	?	
5	?	?	?	?	?	
6	?	?	?	?	?	
7	?	?	?	?	?	
8	?	?	?	?	?	
9	?	?	?	?	?	
10	?	?	?	?	?	

Fig. 4 The spreadsheet in the GeoGebra planimeter

– in the cell $F2 := \sum_{i=3}^{103} E_i$, the distance covered by the segment at the end of a complete round of the point A is calculated.

During the lectures we used the GeoGebra Planimeter to measure the area of figures, but we did not ask students to create the virtual tool, because of its complexity. The main objective in using GeoGebra was to introduce the concept of infinitesimal. We led the students to prove the good approximated measurement of this planimeter, so that they could appreciate the core of the proof: if two successive positions of the planimeter's arm are infinitesimally close, then the area swept by the arm is directly proportional to the value in column E of the spreadsheet.

4 Historical Evolution of Swept Area

Measuring with a planimeter is based on the concept of swept area, which makes it possible to measure irregular surfaces. The idea of swept area has been discussed from an epistemological point of view by I. Newton and from a didactic point of view by E. Castelnuovo (1958). Newton writes in his "Tractatus de quadrature curvarum":

> I don't here consider Mathematical Quantities as composed of Parts extremely small, but as generated by a continual motion. Lines are described, and by describing are generated, not by any apposition of Parts, but by a continual motion of Points. Surfaces are generated by the motion of Lines, Solids by the motion of Surfaces, Angles by the Rotation of their Legs, Time by a continual flux, and so in the rest. These Geneses are founded upon Nature, and are every Day seen in the motion of Bodies. And after this manner the Ancients by carrying moveable right Lines along immoveable ones in a Normal Position or Situation, have taught us the Geneses of Rectangles (Newton 1704, p. 1).

From her side, Castelnuovo points out that:

> The child "senses" the notion of area as dynamic; he "senses" area in its "becoming", to use
> the expression of Jacques Hadamard. He wants to build up this area, he does not like to
> have it as a sum of quantities known apriori (Castelnuovo 1958, p. 56: translation from
> French by the authors).

Many scientists trough history used this idea to demonstrate their discoveries.
Archimedes used a similar concept to discover many formulas, proved by the
exhaustion method; he considered the surface of figures as covered (swept) by the
motion of a segment. Kepler was the first to formalize this idea in the construction
of his second law of the motion of Planets around the Sun. He also applied the
infinitesimal motion of a line covering a surface, or the motion of a surface covering
a volume, to find a formula to measure the volume of a barrel. Galileo, ignoring
Archimedes' manuscript found in 1906, utilized the same reasoning to measure
areas.

Archimedes (287 a.C.–212 a.C.), precursor of the integration methods born in
1600s, used this heuristic method like a mathematical *officina* to discover results
differently proved, and explained this in the introduction of his "*Method*":

> The proofs then of these theorems I have written in this book and now send to you. Seeing
> moreover in you, as I say, an earnest student, a man of considerable eminence in philos-
> ophy, and an admirer [of mathematical inquiry], I thought fit to write out for you and
> explain in detail in the same book the peculiarity of a certain method, by which it will be
> possible for you to get a start to enable you to investigate some of the problems in
> mathematics by means of mechanics. This procedure is, I am persuaded, no less useful even
> for the proof of the theorems themselves; for certain things first became clear to me by a
> mechanical method, although they had to be demonstrated by geometry afterwards because
> their investigation by the said method did not furnish an actual demonstration. But it is of
> course easier, when we have previously acquired, by the method, some knowledge of the
> questions, to supply the proof than it is to find it without any previous knowledge
> (Archimedes 1912, p. 13).

To explain his infinitesimal calculation methods, Kepler (1571–1630) took the
cue from a measuring question: how much wine is contained in a barrel? Kepler
began his book, titled "*Nova steriometria doliorum vinariorum*" (1615), finding the
circle area using a decomposition of the circle into infinitely many infinitesimal
isosceles triangles in which the bases are on the boarder and the heights have the
same length as the radius (Fig. 5). In the same way, Kepler calculated the volume of
a sphere as being composed of infinitely many infinitesimal cones covering it.

Galilei (1564–1642), like Archimedes and Kepler, developed some topics related
to the concept of swept area, as we can read in his masterpiece "*The Systeme Of The
World In Four Dialogues*": "Therefore we shall be the better able to exemplify our
intentions by describing a Triangle, which let be this ABC, (Fig. 6) taking in the
side AC, as many equal parts as we please, AD, DE, EF, FG, and drawing by the
points D, E, F, G, right lines parallel to the base BC [...]; therefore to represent unto
us the infinite degrees of velocity that precede the degree DH, it is necessary to
imagine infinite lines successively lesser and lesser, which are supposed to be
drawn by the infinite points of the line DA, and parallels to DH, the which infinite

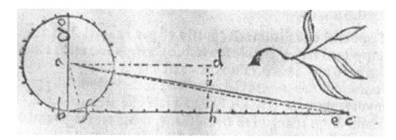

Fig. 5 Original Kepler's picture

Fig. 6 Original Galileo's
picture

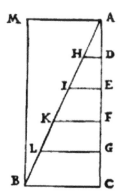

lines represent unto us the superficies of the Triangle AHD" (Galileo 1632/1661, pp. 219, 220).

Cavalieri (1598–1647) gives to Archimedes' method a proving value through the Method of Indivisibles. He presents his Principle in "*Geometria indivisibilibus continuorum nova quadam ratione promota*" (1953): "Suppose two regions in a plane are included between two parallel lines in that plane. If every line parallel to these two lines intersects both regions in line segments of equal length, then the two regions have equal areas" (Eves 1991) (Fig. 7).

However all these approaches are statical, possibly establishing a bijection between the same segments of two figures. The added value in Kepler was the dynamical approach, which introduced motion and introduced the idea of a swept area. From this point of view Kepler is within the stream of the incoming scientific revolution, which in a few years would elaborate the mathematical tools, which were necessary to explain the new science. Motion was its main focus: after Galilei and Kepler, Newton (1643–1727) made a crucial step forward: see his quotation above. Many of these historical aspects were inserted into our teaching design to give the students a deep sense of the mathematical concepts they were learning while using a planimeter. The reasons why we introduced historical concepts into

Fig. 7 Original Cavalieri's picture

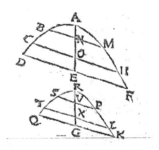

the mathematics lectures will be exposed in the theoretical framework (see the concept of CAC); the historical topics conveyed to students will be presented in the section on the general structure of lessons (see in particular the last lecture).

5 Theoretical Framework

Let us frame the setting of our approach starting from Hasan's definition (Hasan 2002) of *mediation* and on the notion of *semiotic mediation* introduced by Bartolini Bussi and Mariotti (2008). In our case the planimeter plays the role of the *mediator*, in its different use, tangible or technological. The *content of mediation* is the concept of swept area and the *mediatees* are the students that have attended the set of lectures introducing the area by means of the planimeter.

The mediation has been performed mainly through the use of the planimeter in order to exploit the close relationship between the bodily experience and the learning process. For this reason, before the beginning of lectures the students received a package containing Lego bricks with an assembly manual for the Lego Planimeter (Fig. 8) that we had prepared. This was done in order to stress the embodied construction of mathematical meaning and to make the best use of Experimental Mathematics. Indeed, as recalled in Arzarello (2006), along the lines of cognitive studies on embodiment (Lakoff and Nunez 2000), the mental

Fig. 8 The Lego planimeter

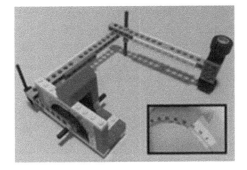

construction of mathematical concepts strongly benefits from the actual use of the body and of concrete tools. According to Papert (1980), the possibility to refer to models can help in any learning process, so to create some bodily model is the best way to support pupils in their cognitive construction. In our research we convey the concept of swept area and an initial approach to infinitesimals with the manipulation of a concrete tool, the planimeter. The construction of mathematical concepts through concrete models becomes a bodily process for each student and not only a purely cognitive activity.

According to the definition of semiotic mediation given by Bartolini Bussi and Mariotti (2008), "within the social use of artifacts in the accomplishment of a task (that involves both the mediator and the mediatees) shared signs are generated." Consequently the lectures have been designed according to the notion of *didactic cycle* (*ibid.*): to this aim a series of *activities with artifacts* were designed for students working in pairs or in small groups. The activities promoted and supported the emergence of specific signs in relation to the use of the planimeter. More precisely we designed an alternation between the following activities and the generation of signs:

(i) *Activities with the instruments*: small groups of students used the planimeter and were pushed towards a production of specific signs related to the use of the instrument;

(ii) *Individual production of signs*: the students were invited to describe their experiences or their reflections on their activities with the instruments;

(iii) *Collective production of signs*: discussion were orchestrated by the researchers and the teacher, in which the different individual productions of the students are collectively criticized and pushed towards the shared mathematical signs.

The mathematical concepts that were the goal of our teaching situation (swept area, infinitesimals) were approached using the planimeter as a mediating tool (Bartolini Bussi and Mariotti 2008; Arzarello and Robutti 2008): the signs built with the tool with the successive movements of its arm while it swept the surfaces (that are internal and external to the figure to be measured) generate the idea of an area as a swept surface. We observe an interesting similarity between the situation with the different positions of the planimeter arms and the original figures of Cavalieri and Galilei above. Moreover, the idea of infinitesimal quantity is given exploiting the dynamic situation of the difference between the successive positions of the arms of the planimeter, while it is sweeping the area.

This semiotic mediation activity gave origin to an *Individual production of signs* from the students, who wrote individual reports on their own experience and reflections including doubts and questions related to the previous activities with the artifact. The cycle was concluded by a *Collective production of signs*, in particular based on mathematical discussions, where the various solutions were discussed collectively and converged towards shared mathematical signs, because of the orchestration promoted by the teacher.

For the analysis of videos, we have adopted three lenses: a mathematical approach, based on the *Cultural Analysis of the content to be taught* (CAC: Boero and Guala 2008), the educational consideration of cognitive construction of the concept, based on the *didactic cycle* by Bartolini Bussi and Mariotti, and the role of gestures in the actions and productions of the students. The first lens CAC is used to justify historical (see Sect. 4) and epistemological discussion about the concept of swept area.

> (CAC) adds to professional knowledge, usually considered in the literature as "subject matter knowledge", "pedagogical content knowledge", and "general pedagogical knowledge" (see Shulman 1986), by including the understanding of how mathematics can be arranged in different ways according to different needs and historical or social circumstances, and how it enters human culture in interaction with other cultural domains (Boero and Guala 2008, p. 223).

The second lens allows to properly design the teaching project which was sketched out above and will be exemplified further below.

The last lens refers to new studies in psychology and in education, in particular in mathematical instruction (Arzarello 2006; Edwards 2003; Goldin-Meadow 2003; McNeill 1992): it focuses on the multimodal construction of mathematical concepts, extending the semiotic analysis of signs produced in the activity beyond the usual verbal register. It will be used in the analysis of the excerpts in the final part of the chapter.

6   The Teaching Activity: General Structure

In the initial lectures we explained the structure, the mechanism and how to use the planimeter and we asked the students to measure the area of different figures (first regular, then irregular), using both a professional planimeter and an instrument they each built using the LEGO blocks (this practical activity fostered their knowledge of the instrument and accelerated the classroom activities). Through a mathematical discussion they were pushed to conjecture proportionality between the area of different figures and the corresponding numbers measured by the instrument. Successively we proved with them the conjecture on proportionality through guided group activities.

The virtual Geogebra version of the planimeter was used in the second part of the project. First we explained to the students how the model works; then we checked with them the effective process of measuring with the virtual instrument, and finally we guided them to prove the reasons why the GeoGebra instrument's approximation was good.

To show this we used a specific dynamic file, which will be discussed in a later part of the chapter. Doing that we were able to introduce the concept of an infinitesimal quantity and of a first intuitive notion of limit, a concept they did not know. We concentrated the didactic activity on this topic since it is important to introduce the modern notion of area according to infinitesimal calculus.

We based the GeoGebra lectures on the manifesto of the *logic of inquiry* (Arzarello et al. 2015): students were led to prove the planimeter's mode of operation, in order to understand that the numerical results given by the instrument are a real measurement of area; students' metacognitive processes were activated in order to foster awareness of basic ideas linked to the planimeter, to solve problems, and ultimately to understand mathematics.

In the last lecture, in line with to the CAC analysis, we described the historical background and the cultural context, which have brought to the genesis of the swept area. We used the knowledge built with the planimeter to discuss the motion of the planets around the Sun. We illustrated the studies of Kepler and his laws, in particular the second one, based deeply bases on the notion of swept area. We based our presentation on the work that Kepler illustrates in his *"Astronomia nova"* (1609) and on the explanations of the Kepler's laws given by Feyneman in a well-known lecture, published and commented in Goodstein and Goodstein (1996). The presence of a Physics lecture in a Mathematics course is justified by the fact that in Italy both disciplines are taught by the same teacher in secondary schools.

We will now discuss some moments of the teaching experiment, concretely showing how the semiotic mediation of instruments can support students approaching into the notions of swept area and of infinitesimals through the logic of inquiry, and within the designed didactic cycle. The space will allow illustrating only two specific moments of the didactic cycle.

7 The Teaching Activity: The Approach to Infinitesimals

7.1 An Important GeoGebra File

Starting from students' own investigation of different examples, we emphasized the importance of the proof after the use of the different planimeters, particularly the virtual version. We led the students to produce a proof of the following (see the GeoGebra planimeter shown above): *the values in the Column E, obtained from measurements with the GeoGebra planimeter, well approximate the distance covered by the arm of the planimeter.* For this proof, we made use of a specific dynamic file construction introduced in class and used by the students to explore the situation (Fig. 9). This point illustrates the way we are using semiotic mediation of the instrument for supporting the transition from observations to a proving approach. While dragging the arm of the virtual planimeter, students observed an unexpected thing happened: they were asking why this could happen and started discussing possible explanations. The steps of the logic of inquiry (Why? Why not? What if?) were activated.

$\overline{A_1B_1}$ and $\overline{A_2B_2}$ represent two consecutive positions of the planimeter, modeled as segments. M_1 and M_2 are midpoints of $\overline{A_1B_1}$ and $\overline{A_2B_2}$ respectively. $\overline{M_1H_2}$ and $\overline{M_2H_1}$ are segments contained in the lines perpendicular to $\overline{A_1B_1}$ and $\overline{A_2B_2}$ through

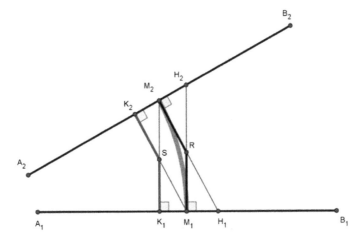

Fig. 9 The starting point of the dynamic file

the midpoints. $\overline{M_1 K_2}$ and $\overline{M_2 K_1}$ are the perpendicular distances from the midpoint of one segment to the other segment.

The students were led to prove the "good measurement" of the virtual planimeter, proving that the distance covered by the arm of planimeter (the curve $M_1 M_2$) is approximated by the length of the two sets of consecutive segments, which will be referred to in the following as "broken lines" $\overline{M_1 R M_2}$ and $\overline{K_1 S K_2}$, whose mean value is given by the GeoGebra planimeter in column E.

The students can improve the approximation by decreasing more and more the inclination of the angle between the two positions of the planimeter. In this way they are introduced to an intuitive idea of an infinitesimal quantity and of the dynamical related process: *the approximation varies because of the infinitesimal features that the angle can take on*. It is the dynamicity of their experience and their previous practices with the real planimeter and with the virtual one that allows them to grasp the meaning of what they see and foresee ideally what will happen imagining this process to continue. This idea is a first approach to a process of transition to the limit. It has been fostered through the semiotic mediation of the instrument: the generated signs through the activity push the students to look for a mathematical explanation of what is happening. In this way a new idea arises. We will explain below how this transition is an example of what Lakoff and Nunez (2000) call the Basic Metaphor of Infinite: a cognitive mechanism through which typically the notion of limit is approached and grasped. In this case the metaphor is generated through the semiotic mediation of the activities with the virtual planimeter.

The key points that led the students to the geometrical and numerical analysis of the presented situation are: the possibility of modifying the angle formed by two successive positions of the planimeter; the zoom options offered by the graphic view of the software; the choice of the decimal numbers calculated in the measurement of the arc and the broken lines.

7.2 Focusing on Some Crucial Episodes

We can now examine the actions, production and communications (Arzarello and Robutti 2008) of two students (S1, put in the foreground in the next frames, and S2) during the periods dedicated to the proof of the "good measurement" with the virtual GeoGebra Planimeter. The students worked in pairs and each one of them was equipped with a computer to work on: this choice was made to encourage the pupils to work more personally and to let their thoughts emerge in the interaction with their classmate, through words and gestures. The episodes illustrate how suitable questions can support the students in the production of individual signs and prepare them for the collective generation of signs.

It is worthwhile noticing how two girls' thoughts evolve from the consideration of a fixed numerical value (zero in our case) to the idea of a continuously changing neighborhood centered at the number itself and of a first intuitive use of infinitesimals and limits. This transition is stimulated by the dynamic file GeoGebra on which they are working, by the questions they have to answer to and by the participation of the teacher. An outline of this process is displayed by presenting extracts of the dialogues between the two girls, snapshots of their gestures and records written by them to answer the questions. We gave the students some sheets to fill out (see the Extracts below), where the questions posed have both guided the work of the students with GeoGebra and promoted their actions and productions according to the logic of inquiry. In the Extracts we have written the questions assigned, the students' answers (Answers) and their interactions each other or with the teacher (resp. S1, S2, and T).

Extract 1 (min 00.55)
Question: In your opinion, is there any chance that the two broken lines [K_2SK_1 and M_2RM_1 in Fig. 9] and the arc [M_1M_2 in Fig. 9] are all of a same size?
Answer: They are of a same size when angle α is $0°$
S1: "because the broken lines are equal if the angle is $0°$, otherwise they're different".

The answer to the first question shows the initial situation of the students, expressed by S1; they see equivalence between the length of the arc and that of the two approximant broken lines only when the angle between the two consecutive positions of the planimeter is zero. Extract 1 shows the answer given by S1 and the comment made while she is writing.

7.3   The Basic Metaphor of Infinity (BMI)

The next steps of the girls' thinking can be explained through *The Basic Metaphor of Infinity (BMI)*, suggested by Lakoff and Nunez in their cognitive interpretation of concepts:

> "We hypothesize that the idea of actual infinity [=infinity conceptualized as a realized "thing"] in mathematics is metaphorical, that the various instances of actual infinity make use of the ultimate metaphorical *result* of a process without end. Literally, there is no such thing as the result of an endless process: If a process has no end, there can be no "ultimate result". But the mechanism of metaphor allows us to conceptualize the "result" of an infinite process – in the only way we have for conceptualizing the result of a process – that is, in terms of process that does have an end. We hypothesize that all cases of actual infinity [...] are special cases of a single general conceptual metaphor in which processes that go on indefinitely are conceptualized as having an end and an ultimate result". Moreover, "the effect of the BMI is to add a metaphorical completion to the ongoing process so that it is seen as having a result – an infinite *thing*" (Lakoff and Nunez 2000, p. 158).

In the table below, which is adapted from that used by Lakoff and Nunez to represent the BMI, we sketch out the processes, through which the students pass as they to build the BMI. The gray part is from the original table: it describes all the steps of the building of the metaphor distinguishing whether they pertain to the Source or to the Target Domain. We have classified all the actions and productions of students while working on the GeoGebra file and the corresponding conceptualization, pointing out if they were working with the value of the angle, or with the relationship between the arc M_1M_2 and the broken lines $M_1R\ M_2$.

The basic metaphor of infinity					
Source domain Completed iterative process	Experimented situation on dynamic GeoGebra file		*Target domain* Iterative processes that go on and on	Conceptualized situation by students	
	Value of $\alpha°$	Arc and broken lines		Value of $\alpha°$	Arc and broken lines
The beginning state			The beginning state		
State resulting from the initial stage of the process	Defined, nonzero	Not coincident	State resulting from the initial stage of the process	Defined, nonzero	Not coincident
The process: From a given intermediate state, produce the next state	Decreasing	Nearer	The process: From a given intermediate state, produce the next state.	Decreasing	Nearer
The intermediate result after that iteration of the process	Defined, nonzero, smaller than previous states	Not coincident, nearer than previous states	The intermediate result after that iteration of the process	Defined, nonzero, smaller than previous states	Not coincident, nearer than previous states

(continued)

(continued)

The basic metaphor of infinity					
Source domain Completed iterative process	Experimented situation on dynamic GeoGebra file		*Target domain* Iterative processes that go on and on	Conceptualized situation by students	
	Value of $\alpha°$	Arc and broken lines		Value of $\alpha°$	Arc and broken lines
The final resultant state	Defined, nonzero, the smallest compared with previous states	Not coincident, the nearest	**"The final resultant state"(actual infinity)**	$\alpha° = 0$	Coincident at a point
Entailment *E*: The final resultant state is unique and follows every non final state			**Entailment *E*: The final resultant state is unique and follows every non final state**		

Below we report on some Extracts of the students' protocols that show students' effective learning processes, through which they elaborate the BMI of Lakoff and Núnez.

Extract 2 (min 03.00)

Question: How can you change the angle measurement so that the broken lines and arc values are more alike?

S1: "Approaching it towards zero the closer the angle is to zero, the more alike are the broken lines".

Extract 2 shows what authors call "The process": the two students act on the slider present in the file and, as one can notice on the computer screen, they see the correspondence between the reduction of the (numerical) value of angle α and the refinements of the differences between the broken line and the arc.

Extract 3 (min 03.26)

Question   Why?

S1   "Because ... because ... I don't know why. Because the broken
            lines get closer to becoming just one thing, to becoming a point".

Following figures show gestures made by the student talking, we see how she stimulates
the situation observed on the screen using her hand as if her fingers, particularly thumb
and index, were the two approximant broken lines within which the arc is squeezed.
When the width of the angle tends to zero everything degenerates into a point.

The next question asks for an explanation of the previous answer: here one can clearly notice the relation between the actual infinity (angle of null width, arc and broken lines degenerate into a point) and potential infinity (angle of adequately small width, broken lines that approximate the arc), described in the BMI final result; Extract 3 shows this situation.

The action performed by the girl is important; indeed one of the objectives of our research has been suggesting a physical-corporeal education and the use the embodiment lens as a teaching instrument that supports what Lakoff and Núñez call creation and conceptualization. The presence of a gesture that simulates the real situation, iconic-metaphorical gesture in McNeill's classification (McNeill 1992), involves a concrete aspect through movement of the student's hand and the shape it assumes because of the position assumed by the fingers and strengthens the transition of the concept from the situation observed to the girl's understanding.

Extract 4 (min 18.19)

Question: What happens geometrically?

Answer: The more the magnitude of α is = to 0, the closer the broken lines
            are to the arc, the three lines will never be the same except that
            $\alpha = 0$, because they are different lines.

(min 29.17)

S1:   "You have to get them closer and closer [...]: repeatedly".

(min 35.24)

S1:   "Look—reading the question—is it possible to obtain the same value?
      You have to make it smaller and smaller".

Extract 4 shows how the girls keep on trying to assimilate the iterative process, acquiring an always more precise terminology and greater affinity with mathematical accuracy both in the expressions and in the choice of the words they use. Mathematically the definition of an infinitesimal depends on the values in the neighborhoods of a certain value: this concept grows from the iteration of an action. In this case the action is the zoom-in, by which it is possible to increase the number of decimal digits. Through this iteration a one "tends" towards a stable situation: it is the final "cap", pointed out by Lakoff and Nunez with their BMI, namely the limit to which the process tends. This is essential in the limit definition, but the students lack this knowledge, hence they use the iteration notion: specifically notice the utilisation of words as "repeatedly" and "smaller and smaller".

Extract 5 (min 39.28)
Question: In your opinion, is it possible to find an angle so that the broken lines and the arc are the same, for all possible zooms and decimal digits? Let's zoom in and add more digital digits before thinking about this question.
S1:   "It's easy".
Answer: No, it's impossible.
S1:   "because the only value would be zero".

It is important to highlight that in the students' processes through which they have arrived to this notion of limit we find a main ingredient of the theoretical frame we discussed above, namely the logic of inquiry. The logic of inquiry is promoted by the questions in each of the Extracts 1–5. The questions guide the students to answer in different ways: at the beginning the answers explain why it is so (Extracts 1 and 2), since things seem clear to them. Then their answers become more problematic (Extract 3) since a contradiction between the idea of a non finishing process versus a finishing one arises (the broken line...a point): their words are not able to clearly explain what is happening and they produce many gestures. In Extract 4 the language of the BMI is made explicit (the more ... the closer; closer and closer ... repeatedly), possibly because of the change of frame suggested by the question (from the numerical to the geometrical one). In Extract 5 the steps "why not?" and "what if?" of the logic of inquiry come to the forth: they allow to state a typical situation of a limit to which a process tends without achieving it. In this step the zoom-in of the instrument has become an ideal tool, with which the students can imagine hypothetical actions.

Towards the end of the activity and of the iterative process the girls have clear the difference between a completed process and a never-ending one, both the conceptualization of a continuous iteration as the infinite repetition of a discrete step (underlined by the alternate utilisation of mouse and keyboard for the reduction of the angle α), and the concept of neighborhood of a point without the point itself. Let us now discuss how things evolve in the successive episodes.

7.4 The Numeral or Geometrical "Precision"

The whole process of proving the good measurement has been based on two options present inside the software:

- the possibility of increasing the calculated decimal number: this allowed the students to evaluate the equality between the measure of the arc to be estimated and the measures of the two approximant polygonal broken lines as a direct consequence of the progressive approach to zero of the angle's value;
- the chance of zooming in and out of the Graphics view: this allowed the students to conduct an analysis of the situation from a geometrical point of view and to arrive at the root of the definition of limit and infinitesimal.

Revising the pathway followed by the students, one can notice a progressive approach to the need of an infinite zoom and the use of infinite significant digits to effectively obtain a good approximation of the arc's length with the one of the two broken lines.

The presence in the work file (see Extract 6) of the explicit visualization of three values coached this route from the beginning. We can see, indeed, S1 dealing with the theme of precision and of the software's digits calculated at first, pointing several times to the part of the screen where the arc's and broken lines' lengths are calculated.

Extract 6 (min 07.22)
S1: "Here—touching the measures—is not very strict".

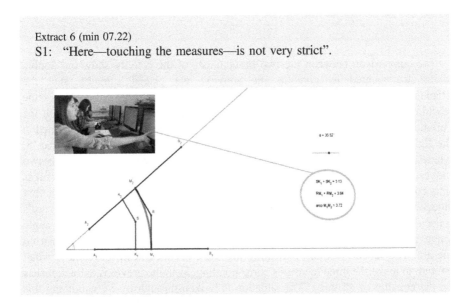

The provocative intervention of the teacher, indicating the equality amongst the three measures with a null angle, as you can see in Extract 7, is an incentive to keep on going along the undertaken route.

Extract 7 (min 08.35)
T: "Look, now the values are the same but the angle is not zero".
S1:   "Because the computer is not very strict".

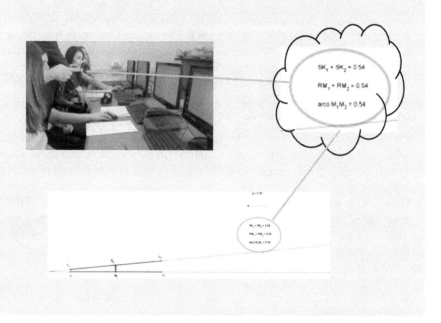

   The comparison between the two protagonists of the activity show the double
vision we wanted to give to the activity: we placed side by side the
graphic-geometrical register and the algebraic-numerical one within the same
teaching frame; during the teaching experiment, we intentionally played with the
variation of *frames* and *registers* following Duval's theories (Duval 1995) treated in
the light of the *jeux de cadres* of Regine Douady (1984). Analyzing Extract 8,
where we analyze images of gestures executed by the students during the two
moves, one can notice that S1 gives a geometrical evaluation, while S2 simply takes
into consideration the three measurements calculated by the program. The first
student states that the rounding up broken lines are necessarily longer than the arc's
trajectory, pointing on the screen to where this situation is displayed with an angle
value α that is adequately large, therefore with the broken lines sufficiently far from
the arc. The second student, indicating her file's situation with the value α small
enough to make the three measures corresponding, as in the previous extract, insists
on the equality of all three. The situation is broken through by S1 validating this
obvious contradiction and combining the work on the trail blazed from an increase
of the precision towards the conception of limit.

Extract 8 (min 15.23)

S1: "but they are the same! Because the computer is not too strict in measurement. In fact, these are never the same, look. Starting from zero they are always different. Indeed this one [a broken line] is always greater than that one [arc]".

S2: "But the values are all the same".

S1: "Because other numbers [= decimal digits] should appear".

A final global idea of the route can be given by the joint analysis of Extracts 9, 10 and 11: the initial situation shows a preconceived analysis of the situations, where S1, a student with remarkable mathematical abilities, foresees that the crux of the matter is the finite dimensional measure of the computer. The activity's evolution presents a relevant step forward when the zoom and the increase of the calculated digits show the diversity of values in any case. It is exactly to overcome this interruption imposed by the tool that S1 finishes her reasoning hypothesizing the need of an infinitely precise computer and of an infinite zoom to have equality of the three values. We can therefore conclude that her reasoning fits into the concept of limit defining the equality of tendency to zero of the angle. The key concept in the theory of limits "tanto più..., quanto più..."[1], through the file mediation built on the base of the planimeter measurement, has migrated from the concrete experience to the theoretical conceptualization through the use of gestures and of a language, which has become more and more precise.

---

[1]The Italian expression is similar but not identical with English expressions like "the more ... the better"; we leave it since, contrary to what can happen in English, it emphasizes the perfect balance between the two sides of the comparisons with the words and their sounds. This effect can be lost or smoothed over in English.

Extract 9 (min 11.50)
Question: Can we have three equal values?
Answer: Yes.
Question: If yes, how? If not, why?
Answer: Three values are the same also if the angle is nonzero, because the computer has a finite measurement.

Extract 10 (min 37.36)
Question: What happens if you zoom in between points R and S?
S1:   "You can see that [although values are the same, the broken lines and the arc] are different. Look, you can see that the points are not coincident".
Question: What happens if you add more decimal digits, for example 5?
S1:   "You can see that they are different [...] you can see that they are very different".

Extract 11 (min 41.20)
Question: In your opinion, what should be possible in order for the broken lines and the arc to be geometrically and numerically coincident? Try to suggest a program improvement to make it possible.

   (S1takes the paper and the pencil and start to gesticulate moving her hands: we interpret this as her understanding the concept of infinity but not being able to explain it in words).
Answer: We need to have a computer infinitively strict, with an infinite zoom.

8   The Teaching Activity: The Swept Area in Two Final Protocols

We show how the concept of swept area has been achieved by the two students, showing and commenting on the answers they gave to a final assessment task, which asked: what is the area of a rectangle?

   F: The area of the rectangle is the product of the base by the height, intended as the continuous movement in which the base "repeats itself along the height". The same principle is used by the swept area, which defines the area of a rectangle through the translation of the rod, which goes to "fill" the area of the surface of the figure. During the translation the caster makes a movement equal to that of the rectangle height and supposing to have a rod so long as the side of the rectangle, the area would be equal to $A = a{\cdot}l$ and hence $A = b \cdot h$.

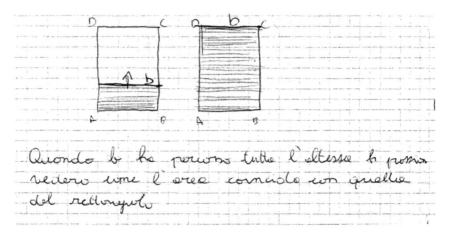

Fig. 10 The solution of F

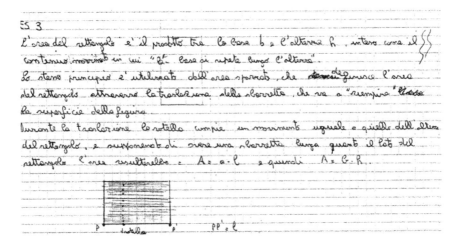

Fig. 11 The solution of A

A: When it has gone through the whole height we can see how the area coincides with that of the rectangle.

A's answer seems more complete than that of F, who has limited himself to repeating the question. However looking at the drawings produced by A and F, we can see that A represents not only the final situation but also an intermediate stage (Fig. 11). This aspect is missing in the protocol of F (Fig. 10). However from the observation we have of F's behavior during the activity solution we know that he has simulated the situation using the lead of his pencil to mimic the movement of a rod sweeping the rectangle. Hence he has drawn only the final situation. In fact he could base his reasoning on the movement he made. On the contrary A had to represent an intermediate situation to draw his reasoning.

The use of drawing to aid their reasoning was a choice of the students. It was not required by the task, but one third of the students made this choice. This can be a result of the way concepts had been discussed in classroom: they were the result of a collective production of signs during the didactic cycle. In a sense for A the drawing represents a visual solution to the task. For the protocol of F we can observe that he uses the idea of movement, in particular he speaks of a "continuous movement" to explain the route of the arm. Moreover F is able to use letters in a rather sophisticated way: b and h are the base and the height of a generic rectangle, while l is the length of the rod and a is the length of the path followed by the caster.

We can summarize these protocols claiming that the concept of swept area has been achieved by these students even if the way they conceive it is typically multimodal, namely it is expressed through a multiple register, where verbal, iconic, and dynamic representations are deeply intertwined in its formulation.

9   Conclusion

In this chapter we have shown how an instrument (in the sense of Rabardel) can support the approach to the concept of swept area and to a first intuitive knowledge of infinitesimal quantities, on which Calculus is based.

One major motivation for this program is the didactical gap existing for the concept of area within the Italian secondary school curriculum (and possibly in other curricula), namely the great distance between the elementary notion of area and the infinitesimal approach through integrals, which in Italy is taught in the last years of Secondary school (grades 12–13). Our teaching program allows bridging this gap starting from grade 11.

We have done this with a teaching experiment in two grade 11 Italian classes of scientifically oriented high schools. The teaching design is based on the following methodological issues, which have been discussed in the first part of the chapter:

- the *logic of inquiry*: the students are asked to investigate how the instrument could be used to calculate the area of figures and to figure out why it could do that;
- the *didactic cycle*, according to which the didactic situation has been designed: activities with the instruments and generation of individual and collective signs;
- the *semiotic mediation* of the instrument for supporting the transition from the empirical side of the inquiry to more formal mathematical statements.

We have also discussed some epistemological aspects of the project according to the CAC frame, underlining how the notion of swept area historically marked an approach to the notion of surface and of its measure, which is closer to the modern notion of measure of surfaces through integral calculus.

In the second part of the chapter we have commented on some protocols of the students, using the Basic Metaphor of Infinity, which allows focusing on their multimodal productions. We have shown how the methodological issues above are instantiated in a specific phase of the didactic cycle to illustrate some moments of the processes in which the students are able to grasp the notion of swept area, and a first intuitive concept of infinitesimals. This can happen because of the rich multimodal intertwined registers simultaneously used by the students to represent the situation, to explain why things are so. The processes through which they reach the final insights is marked by different steps, where the logic of inquiry is used in its positive (why is it so?) and negative (why is it not so?) instances.

References

Amsler, J. (1856). Amsler, über das Polar-Planimeter. *Polytechnisches Journal*, Band 140, Nr. LXXIII, 321–327. http://dingler.culture.hu-berlin.de/article/pj140/.

Archimedes (1912). *The method of Archimedes recently discovered by Heiberg; a supplement to the Works of Archimedes*. (T. L. Heath, Trans.). Cambridge: Cambridge University Press.

Arzarello, F. (2006). Semiosis as a multimodal process [special issue]. *Revista Latinoamericana de Investigacion en Matematica Educativa*, 267–299.

Arzarello, F., & Robutti, O. (2008). Framing the embodied mind approach within a multimodal paradigm. In Lyn D. English (Ed.), *Handbook of international research in mathematics education* (2nd ed., pp. 716–745). NY (USA), Abingdon (UK): Routledge, Taylor and Francis.

Arzarello, F., Bartolini Bussi, M. G., Leung, A. Y. L., Mariotti, M. A., & Stevenson, I. (2012). Experimental approaches to theoretical thinking: artefacts and proof. In G. Hanna & M. de Villliers (Eds.), *Proof and proving in mathematics education* (pp. 97–137). Dordrecht Heidelberg London New York: Springer Science + Business Media.

Arzarello, F., Robutti, O., & Soldano, C. (2015). Learning with touchscreen devices: a game approach as strategies to improve geometric thinking. In *Proceedings of CERME 9, Prague, February 4–8, 2015*.

Bartolini Bussi, M. G., & Mariotti, M. A. (2008). Semiotic mediation in the mathematics classroom. In L. English, M. Bartolini Bussi, G. Jones, R. Lesh & D. Tirosh (Eds.), *Handbook of international research in mathematics education* (pp. 746–783). Lea, USA: Routledge.

Bartolini Bussi, M. G., Taimina, D., & Isoda, M. (2010). Mathematical models as early technology tools in classrooms at the dawn of ICMI: Felix Klein and perspectives from different parts of the world. *ZDM—The International Journal on Mathematics Education, 42*(1), 19–31.

Boero, P., & Guala, E. (2008). Development of mathematical knowledge and beliefs of teachers: the role of cultural analysis of the content to be taught. In P. Sullivan & T. Wood (Eds.), *International handbook of mathematics teacher education: Knowledge and beliefs in mathematics teaching and teaching development* (Vol. 1, pp. 223–246). Rotterdam-Taipei: Sense Publ.

Borwein, J. M., & Devlin, K. (2008). *The computer as crucible: an introduction to experimental mathematics*. Massachusetts: A K Peters.

Castelnuovo, E. (1958). L'object et l'action dans l'enseignement de la géométrie intuitive. In C. Gattegno, W. Servais, E. Castelnuovo, J. L. Nicolet, T. J. Fletcher, L. Motard, L. Campedelli, A. Biguenet, J. W. Peskett, & P. Puig Adam (Eds.), *Le matériel pour l'enseignement des mathématiques* (pp. 41–59). Neuchâtel: Delachaux & Niestlé.

Cavalieri, B. (1953). *Geometria indivisibilibus continuorum nova quadam ratione promota*. Bononiae: ex Typographia de Ducijs.

Dewey, J. (1938). Logic: The Theory of Inquiry. In JA Boydston (Ed.), The Later Works 1925–1953, John Dewey, Vol. 12 (1986 edition ed.). (pp. 1–549).

Douady, R. (1984). Jeux de cadres et dialectiqueoutil-objet dansl'enseignement des mathématiques. Thèsed'État, Univ. de Paris. *Recherches en didactique des mathématiques, 7*(2), 5–31, 1986.

Duval, R. (1995). Quelcognitifretenir en didactique des mathématiques? *Actes de l'Écoled'été,* 1995.

Edwards, A. W. F. (2003). Human genetic diversity: Lewontin's fallacy. *BioEssays, 25,* 798–801. doi:10.1002/bies.10315.

Epp, S. (1994). The role of proof in problem solving. In A. H. Schoenfeld (Ed.), *Mathematical Thinking and Problem Solving* (pp. 257–269). Hillsdale, NJ: Lawrence Erlbaum Associates, Inc., Publishers.

Eves, H. (1991). Two surprising theorems on Cavalieri congruence. *The College Mathematics Journal, 22,* 118–124, March 2, 1991.

Galileo, G. (1661). *The systeme of the world in four dialogues.* (T. Salusbury, Trans.) (pp. 219–220). London (Original work published 1632). Retrieved from http://www.chlt.org/sandbox/lhl/Salusbury/.

Goldin-Meadow, S. (2003). *Hearing gestures: How our hands help us think.* Chicago: Chicago University Press.

Goodstein, D. L., & Goodstein, J. R. (1996). *Feynman's lost lecture: the motion of planets around the sun.* New York: W.W. Norton & Co.

Greeno, J. (1994). Comments on Susanna Epp's chapter. In A. Schoenfeld (Ed.), *Mathematical thinking and problem solving* (pp. 270–278). Hillsdale, NJ: Lawrence Erlbaum Associates.

Hall, R., Nemirovsky, R. (2012). Introduction to the special issue: modalities of body engagement in mathematical activity and learning. *Journal of the Learning Sciences, 21*(2).

Hanna, G. (1996). The ongoing value of proof. In: *Proceedings of the International Group for the Psychology of Mathematics Education, Valencia, Spain* (Vol. I).

Hanna, G. (2000). Proof, explanation and exploration: an overview. *Educational Studies in Mathematics, 44,* 5–23.

Hasan, R. (2002). *Semiotic mediation, language and society: Three exotropic theories—Vygotsky, Hallyday and Bernstein.* Retrieved from http://posner.library.cmu.edu/Posner/books/pages.cgi?call=520_K38PN&layout=vol0/part0/copy0.

Hintikka, J. (1999). *Inquiry as inquiry: A logic of scientific discovery.* Springer Science + Business Media Dordrecht.

Horgan, J. (1993). The death of proof. *Scientific American,* 93–103.

Kepler, J. (1609). *Astronomia Nova ΑΙΤΙΟΛΟΓΗΤΟΣ seu physica coelestis, tradita commentariis de motibus stellae Martis ex observationibus G.V. Tychonis Brahe.* Heidelberg: Voegelin.

Kepler, J. (1615). *Nova stereometria doliorvm vinariorvm [New solid geometry of wine barrels].* Retrieved from http://posner.library.cmu.edu/Posner/books/pages.cgi?call=520_K38PN&layout=vol0/part0/copy0.

Lakoff, G., & Nunez, R. (2000). *Where mathematics comes from: How the embodied mind brings mathematics into being.* New York: Basic Books.

McNeill, D. (1992). *Hand and mind: What gestures reveal about thought.* Chicago: University of Chicago Press.

National Council of Teachers of Mathematics. (1989). *Principles and standards for school mathematics.* Reston, VA: National Council of Teachers of Mathematics.

National Council of Teachers of Mathematics. (2000). *Principles and standards for school mathematics.* Reston, VA: National Council of Teachers of Mathematics.

Newton, I. (1704) *Tractatus de quadratura curvarum* (J. Harris, Trans.). London. (Original work published 1710) from Latin. Retrieved from http://www.maths.tcd.ie/pub/HistMath/People/Newton/Quadratura/HarrisIQ.pdf.

Papert, S. (1980). *Mindstorms: Children, computers, and powerful ideas.* New York: Basic Books.

Rabardel, P. (1995). *Les hommes et les technologies [people and technology]*. Paris: Armand Colin.

Radziszowski, S., & McKay, B. (1995). *R(4,5) = 25*. *Journal of Graph Theory, 19*(1995) 309–322. Retrieved from http://cs.anu.edu.au/ ~ bdm/papers/r45.pdf.

Ruthven, K. (2008). Mathematical technologies as a vehicle for intuition and experiment: A foundational theme of the International Commission on Mathematical Instruction, and a continuing preoccupation. *International Journal for the History of Mathematics Education, 3* (2), 91–102.

Shulman, L. S. (1986). Those who understand: Knowledge growth in teaching. *Educational Researcher, 15*, 3–14.

Smith, D. E. (1913). Intuition and experiment in mathematical teaching in the secondary schools. In *Proceedings of the Fifth International Congress of Mathematicians* (Vol. II, pp. 611–632).

Tall, D. (1989). Concept images, generic organizers, computers and curriculum change. *For the Learning of Mathematics, 9*(3), 37–42.

Wu, H.-H. (1996). The role of Euclidean geometry in high school. *Journal of Mathematical Behavior, 15*, 221–237.

Part III
Task Design in Interactive Digital Platforms

Engagement with Interactive Diagrams: The Role Played by Resources and Constraints

Elena Naftaliev and Michal Yerushalmy

Abstract Interactive textbooks appear to be the tools of choice in mathematics instruction in the foreseeable future. It is important, therefore, to establish the theoretical foundations of design that define student-textbook-teacher interactions. In our long-term research, we suggested, tested, and refined a semiotic framework that offers a set of terms helpful in analyzing how the designed features of interactive diagrams (IDs) function in these interactions. The present chapter summarizes key design decisions about resources and constraints of interactive texts according to various semiotic functions, and discusses the role of designed resources and constraints of the IDs in student engagement with interactive texts.

Keywords Task design · Interactive textbooks · Semiotic · Interactive diagrams · Examples · Representations

1 Introduction

Current technology makes possible the use of a variety of interactive tools and representations in interactive textbooks. Using technology to develop mathematical textbooks and tasks is an attempt to create new venues for engagement with mathematical meaning. An example of a digital interactive web textbook is the VisualMath eTextbook (Yerushalmy et al. 2002/2014). The interactive text in this book provides expositions and instructions in the form of interactive diagrams or of a link to another interactive diagram. The book also provides an implicit suggestion to use other related tasks, exercises, and tools selectable from a menu.

E. Naftaliev (✉)
Achva Academic College, Arugot, Israel
e-mail: elenanaftaliev@gmail.com

M. Yerushalmy
University of Haifa, Haifa, Israel
e-mail: michalyr@edu.haifa.ac.il

© Springer International Publishing Switzerland 2017
A. Leung and A. Baccaglini-Frank (eds.), *Digital Technologies in Designing Mathematics Education Tasks*, Mathematics Education in the Digital Era 8,
DOI 10.1007/978-3-319-43423-0_8

We use the term interactive diagram (ID) to refer to a relatively small unit of interactive text in e-textbooks or another materials. The components of the ID are: the example being provided, its representations (verbal, visual, and other), and interactive tools. The text may be used for different purposes: an exposition, a task, an exercise, etc. Each ID is considered a task, according to Margolinas (2013): "a task is anything that a teacher uses to demonstrate mathematics, to pursue interactively with students, or to ask students to do something. Tasks can also be anything that students decide to do for themselves in a particular situation. Tasks, therefore, are the mediating tools for teaching and learning mathematics" (p. 11). It is a challenge to design tasks that on one hand invite opportunities for active personal learning, and on the other satisfy the requirements of national standards or curricula.

In this chapter, we use the findings of our long-term research[1] to illustrate how the constraints and resources designed into IDs function in the process of developing mathematical knowledge.

2 The Semiotic Framework

In earlier studies, (e.g., Yerushalmy 2005; Naftaliev and Yerushalmy 2011, 2013; Naftaliev 2012) we conducted a semiotic analysis of IDs based on Kress and van Leeuwen's (1996) visual social-semiotic theory. The semiotic analysis proposed three dimensions for defining the functionality of IDs.

The semiotic framework is characterized by three types of ID functions (Table 1) that address a variety of learning and teaching settings: *presentational*, *orientational*, and *organizational*.

2.1 Presentational Functions of IDs

Although examples in an ID are usually designed to be modified by the user, the example that initially appears in the diagram determines the nature of the *presentational* function of the example. Three types of examples are widely used in IDs: random, specific, and generic.

Specific examples present the exact data of the activity of which they are part. They serve as a dynamic illustration that helps analyze the situation without being able to change the information. Random examples are specific examples generated within given constraints, presenting different information at various times and for different users. In a generic example, the diagram is structured to be representative; it presents a situation that can be part of the given task, but it is not

---

[1]https://sites.google.com/site/interactivediagrams/.

Table 1 The semiotic framework: three types defining the functionality of IDs

Presentational function	Orientational function	Organizational function
Specific	Sketchy	Illustrating
Random	Accurate	Elaborating
Generic	Sketchy and accurate	Guiding

intended to present the specific data of the activity but to help learners become acquainted with the generic views of the example through a process of inquiry. Mason and Pimm (1984) noted that generic examples are transparent to the general case, allowing one to see the general through the particular: "A generic example is an actual example, but one presented in such a way as to bring out its intended role as the carrier of the general; this is done by means of stressing and ignoring various key features, of attempting to structure one's perception of it" (p. 287). The art of designing generic examples consists of finding ways to place the focus on generality or representativeness, as elaborated by Goldenberg and Mason (2008). (Davydov 1972/1990) articulated the difficulty: "The real problem is precisely in finding a form for a concept in which the derivation of properties would be possible" (p. 35). Design that offers ways to systematically generate multiple and varied examples, and to preserve and reconstruct processes, provides the basis for conceptual construction of knowledge by generalizations and conjectures (Yerushalmy 1993). It is not usually the case, however, that the generic nature of the example is visible to the learner, and often the example remains a particular case. It is only when the viewer becomes aware of the generality in the specific example that its mission is achieved. The design of the setting of an example as an ID invites the viewer to activate the ID within given limitations in two ways: (a) interacting with components of the examples (the representations, as well as the linking and control tools), and (b) changing the example by generating similar or new ones.

2.2 Orientational Functions of IDs

The tone in which the text addresses the learner is subject to design decisions having to do with the *orientational* function. "Sketchiness" vs. "rigorousness" of the diagrams is an important factor in reader orientation. An example that appears in a diagram can have an accurate appearance and communicate in a strict, distant tone. For example, a graph drawn on paper indicating coordinate values and scale would be interpreted as a specific case. The example can adopt a non-authoritative tone. For example, it may not attempt to provide the complete picture, but rather to highlight important elements, so that it can be used as a plan for a variety of final products that share the same idea or structure. IDs can function both as sketches and as accurate diagrams (Table 2).

Table 2 Twenty seven types of interactive diagrams

	Illustrating ID	Elaborating ID	Guiding ID
Specific example	Sketchy	Sketchy	Sketchy
	Accurate	Accurate	Accurate
	Sketchy/accurate	Sketchy/accurate	Sketchy/accurate
Random example	Sketchy	Sketchy	Sketchy
	Accurate	Accurate	Accurate
	Sketchy/accurate	Sketchy/accurate	Sketchy/accurate
Generic example	Sketchy	Sketchy	Sketchy
	Accurate	Accurate	Accurate
	Sketchy/accurate	Sketchy/accurate	Sketchy/accurate

2.3 Organizational Functions of IDs

The *organizational* function refers to the connection between all the components of the ID: representations, tools, examples, etc. IDs can be organized in three ways: illustrating, elaborating, and guiding[2] (narrating). The three types differ in their settings, each characterized by its own constraints and resources, and intended for a different aspect of inquiry. Illustrating IDs demonstrate the objective of the activity to the reader, usually by offering a single representation and relatively simple actions, such as viewing an animated example. For example, an illustrating ID might allow learners to manipulate rather than read a definition. Elaborating diagrams present occurrences relevant to the problem being explored while working on the task. They attempt to provide a means for students to engage in activities that lead to the formulation of a solution in different ways, and operate at a meta-cognitive level. For instance, the animated example that serves for illustration can also serve for elaboration when it is part of other tools and representations (Table 3). A guiding ID, similarly to an elaborating one, provides a means for learner exploration, but it is designed to also set boundaries for the available exploration options in such a way that it narrates the story to be learned by working on the task. Guiding IDs are designed to point students toward specific actions intended to support them in developing specific mathematical ideas. Although guiding IDs provide tools that promote inquiry, the tools are designed to limit the exploration and serve as boundaries while working on the task.

---

[2]In our earlier publications (e.g., 2005, 2009, 2011, 2011, 2013) we used the term "narrating ID".

Table 3 Comparative view of the three settings of IDs based on organizational, presentational, and orientational functions: modeling series

Organizational functions	Illustrating ID	Elaborating ID	Guiding ID
Presentational functions	Generic example	Generic example	Generic example with an exceptional case
Orientational functions	Sketchy	Sketchy/accurate	Sketchy

3   Design Decisions Based on the Three Organizational Functions

The above analysis classifies IDs into 27 types (Table 2), based on their combinations of features: three organizational functions (illustrating, guiding, and elaborating) × three types of examples (random, generic, and specific) × three types of orientational functions (accurate, sketch, and both).

To study the effect of organizational functions we generated different IDs based on the same content with different organizational functions. Three mathematical foci served as the pivotal points for the design of the series of the tasks:

1. Modeling series (analyzing properties of models and mathematizing outside mathematical phenomena) (Table 3).
2. Formulating mathematical phenomena series (writing expression for linear function) (Table 4).
3. Manipulating series (solving equations) (Table 5).

The tasks were assumed to be challenging and new for students and were designed to support investigation—in other words, formulating and exploring conjectures. These mathematical objectives of the school algebra curriculum are described in the literature (e.g., Schwartz 1999) as key actions undertaken with mathematical objects. Each objective included three comparable tasks, based on an ID of a different design type. In the modeling series, we designed settings of interactive diagrams that shared an example represented as an animation of multi-process motion (Table 3), and a task that required analyzing motion while paying attention to representations and models of path, speed, and pace.

In the formulating mathematical phenomena series, we chose a basic algebra task that required the writing of a symbolic expression to describe a given linear function graph (Table 4). In the manipulating series, we chose a task that focused on performing algebraic manipulations and required to create examples of equations that comply with certain constrains (Table 5).

The sequences chosen represent important issues in school algebra and were intended to reduce the effect of specific content in algebra on the conclusions of the study. Based on the assumption that the design of the ID establishes the context for a variety of learning and teaching settings, the focus of the study was to analyze how the designed constraints and resources of the IDs functioned in developing mathematical knowledge while solving unfamiliar tasks presented by multi-modal texts.

Table 4 Comparative view of the three settings of IDs based on the organizational, presentational, and orientational functions: formulating mathematical phenomena series

Organizational functions	Illustrating ID	Elaborating ID	Guiding ID
Presentational functions	Specific example	Specific example; The design of the ID offers ways to generate multiple and varied examples	Specific example; The design of the ID offers ways to systematically generate varied examples
Orientational functions	Sketchy/accurate	Sketchy/accurate	Sketchy/accurate

Table 5 Comparative view of the three settings of IDs based on organizational, presentational, and orientational functions: manipulating series

	Illustrating ID	Elaborating ID	Guiding ID
Organizational functions			
Presentational functions	Specific example	Specific example; The design of the ID offers ways to generate varied examples	Specific example; The design of the ID offers ways to systematically generate varied examples
Orientational functions	Sketchy/accurate	Sketchy/accurate	Sketchy/accurate

4 Mathematical Engagements with Interactive Texts Within Given Resources and Constraints

We illustrate the students' mathematical engagement with interactive texts concerning the modeling series, and the role played by the resources and constraints in the design of the text. We designed three ID settings (Tables 3, 4 and 5) over the course of three studies, as part of our broader research. The IDs share an example represented as an animation of multi-process motion, but they differ in their organizational functions. In these studies, we reported on the work of 14-year-old students from the same public school, who interacted with different IDs that had distinct organizational functions: illustrating (Naftaliev and Yerushalmy 2009), guiding (Naftaliev and Yerushalmy 2013), illustrating and elaborating (Yerushalmy and Naftaliev 2011).

4.1 Student Engagement with the Illustrating ID

The illustrating ID was simple to operate and provided the minimal control necessary for using the animation: at any time, users could freeze the positions on the track, continue the run, or initialize the race. The generic example provided the sketchy nature of the ID and the inclusion of only one representation were important resources and constraints in the mathematical engagement with the interactive text. In the following episode the students looked for ways to sidestep the design constraints of the ID. For example, Dan's sequence of static diagrams (Fig. 1) prompted him to mentally recreate and describe the entire motion process, pointing to changes of speed of the dots (or "runners") in correlation with changes in their relative positions:

Fig. 1 Sequence of static diagrams

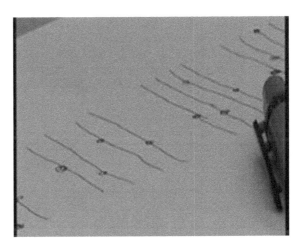

Dan: So in the end it shows that the pink that at first advanced, that began to gain acceleration, and the blue that passed him later, who also began to be the fastest; actually the black accelerated and passed him. The blue and the red started slowing a bit and the red continued at the same pace, and in the end passed the blue and came in third. The black was first. The pink came in second and the red came in third place. And the blue stayed... came in last, even though in the middle he started leading in the distances, and then the black began to pass everyone, and won actually.

Using paper and pencil, the ID was extended in a schematic way that served as a static model (Fig. 1), from which students were later able to describe the dynamic process without activating the ID. In sum, the influence of design constraints and resources on student engagement with the illustrating ID were: (a) the dynamic and sketchy nature of the ID presentation promoted comparative descriptions of the motion and made it easier for the students to distinguish between the runners, to address each one using colors, and to identify their relative progress; (b) the ID was designed as a generic example with an exceptional case that became pivotal in the description of the race; and (c) the inclusion of only one representation in the ID, and the minimal control needed to operate it stimulated looking for ways to bypass the designed constraints. To construct a picture of the motion process, the students resorted to complementing the ID using the representations and tools they created themselves.

4.2   Student Engagement with the Guiding ID

The guiding ID was designed around a known conflict concerning time-position graphs that describe motionless objects while time passes continuously. Analysis shows that a set of constraints and resources contributes to making the task an interesting challenge. Among these are the small number of animated representations in the ID, the partial linking between the various visual representations, the absence of representations and controls that could turn the sketchy nature of the representations into an accurate diagram, the absence of discrete information, and the exceptional example in a list of examples aimed at focusing on absence of motion over time.

We illustrate the students' mathematical engagements with the guiding ID by analyzing the following episode. The students, Lior and Daniel, started their work with the ID by activating it and asking questions such as why are there only six dots moving, whereas in the graph the dots move along seven lines:

Lior: If this doesn't move [points with the mouse at the static car] and here all are moving [points with his finger at the graphs] it doesn't make sense!

The students reflected on their current mathematical understanding with the guidance of the ID, which emphasized a well-known conflict, and they modified their understanding as they came across the various constraints and resources of the guiding ID. The students continued the discussion, reaching the conclusion that time goes on even when the dot is motionless: "Time does move, it [the dot] simply does not move at this time." The discussion took place without activating the animation in the diagram but based on its static mode, which students expanded using body movements and verbal descriptions. The students activated the animation to verify their hypotheses and conclusions.

The following conversation is the students' attempt to explain the correct result they arrived at regarding the static point:

Daniel: But here all the other five... Time moves and the position moves.
Lior: Because they actually move (points at the slanted graphs) but it—it doesn't move. This is the position and it doesn't move (the position dimension of the graph remains constant): it doesn't go up or down... only the time moves for it. This is it! The orange dot (on the linear constant graph) is the green (motionless) dot (in the animation)!

The students seemed to be able to conceptualize the motion or the absence of motion of the green dot, and focused on the analysis of the graphs and on the dimensions of position and time as they appeared on the axes of the graphs:

Lior: I understand. Usually when they move in place, if they move to here then this goes down (moves his hand to the left over the animation and then down on the graph).
Lior and Daniel: ...and if they move here, then it moves upwards (Lior and Daniel move their hands left to right over the animation).
Lior: And if it goes neither here nor here [moves his hand to the left and to the right of the static dot] then it... It doesn't change position either up or down [performs a gesture up and down along the graph window], but its time does [moves his hand left to right along the constant line], like all of them, as if the time didn't pass, then it would have stayed at the beginning [marks the initial spot of the line on the Y-axis], but time does pass, so because of that there's the entire line [moves his hand along the constant line].

This conversation indicates progress in the understanding of the graphic representation and of the roles it has assumed in solving the problem. The students described the motion by imagining rather than executing the animation. They were able not only to describe the change in distance over time of a static dot in the graph, but also to identify two directions of motion in the animation, right and left, as increasing and decreasing lines in the distance-time graph.

According to the data, constraints and resources of the design affected student engagement with the guiding ID in the following ways: (a) Finding the invariance and the variability within the processes in the given set of examples was a foremost theme in all problem-solving processes (e.g., "And if it goes neither here nor here [moves his hand to the left and to the right of the static dot] then it… It doesn't change position either up or down"); (b) The presence of a static object among the seven moving objects played a central role in triggering the exploration of the differences between the representation of motion by animation and its representation as change in the distance over time graph ("If this doesn't move [points with the mouse at the static car] and here all are moving [points with his finger at the graphs] it doesn't make sense!"); (c) The transformation of the graph into a meaningful representation for describing the motion process was made possible by using a combination of the two representations: the animation and the graph (e.g., "… if they move to here then this goes down. And if they move… (moves his hand to the left over the animation and then down on the graph)"). Most of the discussion in the interview excerpted above took place without activating the animation. Students used the animation less than we had expected, and carried out most of the conjecturing mentally. We found, however, that the animation played an important role in coping with the task. As a concrete representation, it drew the students' attention to the conflicts concerning motionless objects over continuous time, and prompted questions and conjectures that were not raised in the task. Students used the animation also to check assumptions and to illustrate conclusions. (d) The animation and the graph were designed to be partially linked but they were not color-matched, and the identification process required extracting data from the animation and the graph in order to link them. The partial link ended up being an important component in the mental analysis that the students performed. (e) The possibility of viewing only the complete motion, without stopping or focusing on discrete events, was an important component in the development of meaning for the graph.

4.3   Student Engagement with the Elaborating ID

The elaborating ID provided four adjacent linked representations (as opposed to one in the illustrating ID and two in the guiding ID): a table of values that represented distance and time in 0.1 s intervals; a 2D graph of distance over time; and a 1D graph of traces of positions at each time unit, with an animation. The variety of linked representations and rich tools in the elaborating ID made possible various options for personal choices concerning how the ID was viewed, for example: a sketch, and/or an accurate diagram, discrete and/or continuous flow of information. It also provided a variety of opportunities, as demonstrated by the significant differences that were observed between the three interviewed groups. Below we present in some more detail only one approach, but note the paths followed by others.

At the beginning of the interview of the first group concerning the elaborating ID, the students activated the animation. A green dot in the animation attracted their attention because it stood out as different: at the beginning of its motion it was very slow, and yet it finished first. The students described the change in speed of the green dot: "initially the green [dot] is the slowest," "the green [dot] begins to accelerate." Without using the stop option, they described the change in the relative positions of the dots in the animation of the race and indicated the finishing positions. The students looked for a way to improve the interpretation, pressed various buttons such as Run, Stop, Initialize, and Traces, they checked boxes, and activated the animation with traces:

May: According to this, the red had reasonable speed, approximately the same speed all the way, the green at the beginning, he was, which means he was really slow at the beginning, and afterwards, when there are bigger spaces between the circles, then the...

Sara: He began to increase the pace. And here, he and the blue, he was faster at the beginning and towards the end he was really slow, you can see that the circles are really close together here, and the pink, so in the beginning he was fast, in the middle of the race he began to slow down, and at the end of the race he began to be fast.

They decided to integrate the two-dimensional graph and began to work with a combination of the two graphs, the 1D and the 2D, in a static state (Fig. 2). They focused on ascribing meaning to the 2D graph reflecting the speed of the motion, and used the description of speed that appeared in the 1D graph to attribute meaning to the 2D graph by analyzing the distance between the tracer dots: "the red is a straight line because its speed was uniform throughout the whole race, and the green is curved, curved because at the beginning it was slow."

To verify the way in which speed was reflected on the graph, they decided to reactivate the animation. After observing the animation, they described the speed of the dots based on the shape of each graph:

Fig. 2 The 1D (traces) and the 2D graphs

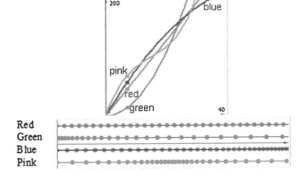

May: Because you can see, if the line is straight like the red one, then you can see that it is a uniform pace.

Sara: In the beginning it ($/$) was not a uniform pace and then it ($/$) was a uniform pace, the blue ($\curvearrowright$) it has, at the beginning it had a uniform pace and then it curves and then it was the one in the last place. The pink ($\diagup$) at the beginning it has uniform pace and then it has a drop in speed and then it has a little increase and then it has a uniform pace, that's why it came in second place.

The description showed the students' attempt to use meaningful items they created for themselves in previous work with the green graph $/$ and the red graph $/$ in order to ascribe meaning to similar items on other graphs: the part of the graph that is close to a straight line describes uniform pace, the part that "curves" describes a change of speed, and the part that looks like the beginning of the green graph describes deceleration.

Analyzing the work of the two other groups, we found different trajectories of mathematical engagement. The second group chose to start working with an animation and a graph, and gradually changed the students' concept image of the lines in the graph from motion paths to graphic representations of motion with changing rates of speed. In the beginning, the students treated the graph as a motion path. Next, they used the stop tool to monitor the change in the respective positions of the dots simultaneously across the two representations. The students proceeded examining a variety of examples in the diagram, some of which contradicted the erroneous assumption they made while examining other examples. The third group focused on the table of values and how it corresponded to the animation. The stop tool helped them match the discrete data in the table and in the animation. After analyzing the characteristics of the respective positions of the dots and the numbers in the table, they progressed from the incorrect assumption that the numbers in the table described time to considering the table values as a description of distance.

In sum, the constraints and resources affected learner engagement with the elaborating ID primarily as follows: (a) Work with the ID is characterized by a wide range of problem-solving choices that have some common elements but involve using different tools or different representations. (b) A carefully planned interactive example helped reveal its generic qualities in describing the various aspects of motion. The components of the example became significant in particular because they represented something exceptional for the students: the unique motion of the green dot relative to the other dots helped the students ascribe meaning to the 1D and 2D graph as descriptions of deceleration. Extracting the few pieces of information that were essential for developing the students' stories concerning the motion process in the task proved greatly useful for their work. (c) The link between the representations allowed students to ascribe meaning to unique situations in other representations. At times, the link between the representations was obvious, as, for example, in the case of the animation and the 1D graph. At other times, establishing the link between the representations using the tools included in a diagram (the stop tool, the clock, and the active line in the table) was another aspect of the process of motion description. (d) The combined use of discrete items of information that described the situation at moments when the action was stopped and of continuous information concerning the entire process was an important component in the students' engagement with the mathematics of motion.

5 Discussion

The present chapter focuses on students' ways of developing knowledge by identifying and defining relevant components of complex, new, digital environments. The following discussion summarizes: (a) the key design decisions concerning resources and constraints of the interactive text as reflected in various semiotic functions, and (b) the role played by ID resources and constraints in the development of mathematical knowledge when reading about and solving unfamiliar tasks. In the following summary and discussion of the conclusions we focus on (a) representations and tools for interacting with the representations and (b) examples and tools for interacting with the examples.

5.1 Key Design Decisions About Resources and Constraints

ID design must support a variety of purposes in the course of learning and teaching. The intentional design of what may be viewed as incomplete tools was based on the principle enunciated by Schwartz (1995) for designing software for mathematical inquiry: finding an "interesting middle," where the setting lets students "interact with and manipulate aspects of a subject that are complex enough to be interesting and simultaneously simple enough to be understood" (Schwartz, *ibid.*, p. 180).

The IDs in our studies varied in the design choices of what was included in the given example and how it was represented and controlled. Designing constraints and resources with a *focus on representations* (graphs, tables, animations, etc.), and designing tools for interacting with these resources involves making decisions about (a) the number of representations, (b) the sketchy or accurate nature of the representation, (c) the kind of links to be made available between the representations, (d) the choices available for reducing the amount of information presented, (e) and the discrete or continuous nature of information. Similarly, designing constraints and resources with *focus on examples* and on the tools for interacting with the examples involves making decisions about: (a) the initial given set of example; (b) the tools available for changing an initial example by creating similar examples or new ones. Table 6 shows a comparative view of the resources and

Table 6 Comparative view of the resources and constraints in the modeling ID series, with a focus on representations and examples

	Illustrating ID	Elaborating ID	Guiding ID
Resources and constraints in the settings of representations			
Number of representations	1	4	2
Intended tone of the representation	Sketchy	Sketchy/accurate	Sketchy
Links between the representations	X	Linked	Partially linked
Options to change the amount of information presented in the representations	X	V	Partial
Mode of information presentation	Discrete/continuous	Discrete/continuous	Continuous
Resources and constraints in the settings of examples			
Initial set of given examples	Combination of the four types of accelerated motion	Combination of the four types of accelerated motion	Combination of the seven types of constant speed motion; static object among the seven objects
Tools for changing an initial example	X	X	X

constraints in the modeling ID series, with a focus on representations and examples that define each of the three organizational functions.

5.2 The Role that ID Resources and Constraints Play in Learners' Engagements: Representations, Tools, and Examples

We showed how ID resources contributed to the active reading of the mathematical text. The processes supporting learners' mathematical engagement with interactive texts position the learners as active readers who approach the text in an exploratory mode. Learners explore the interactive text, which becomes an instrument that assists them in their thinking and problem solving. Using the terms of Borasi et al. (1998), the exploration is characterized by negotiation, the reader and text shaping and being shaped by each other throughout the reading experience. Providing learners with opportunities for personal adaptations of the interactive mathematical text makes this exploratory negotiation more explicit because learners are encouraged to use various resources to interact with the text.

5.2.1 Representations and Tools for Interacting with Them

We begin by discussing the effect of the resources and constraints on engagement with the IDs in the three series (modeling, formulating mathematical phenomena, and manipulating; Tables 3, 4 and 5) with a *focus on representations* (graphs, tables, animations, etc.) and on the tools needed to interact with them. The illustrating IDs present the objective of the activity to the reader by offering a single representation and relatively simple actions for interaction with it. Students who worked with the illustrating IDs looked for ways to bypass the constraints built into the tool: they changed the representation of the data in the given example, expanded the given representation, or constructed new ones. We found that even the minimal interaction designed into the illustrating IDs can be helpful in consolidating relevant knowledge that is not yet adequately structured. The IDs can help present the parts of the less structured ideas to make them more coherent, meaningfully visible, and concrete in a problem-solving process. Following Vygotsky (1978) and Murata (2008) noted that the process of making students' ideas meaningfully visible and concrete helps students focus on core aspects of the problem and engage in their own meaning-making process. We found that personal attention paid to details in the ID presentation, awareness of these details, and the personal choices students made in the construction of additional details for the original presentation played an important role in students' work with illustrating IDs.

In the design of elaborating IDs (Tables 3, 4, 5 and 6), linked representations and rich tools for interacting with them played an important role. The learners' engagement with the elaborating IDs included use of linking tools and representations, and choosing the items considered to be significant in the example, the representations to work with, the order in which to work with the various representations, and whether to not to use the available tools. The differences between the engagement with illustrating and elaborating IDs reveal the pedagogical settings that elaborating IDs can support. The needs and choices of the students related to the exploration of a variety of unfamiliar representations and the interpretation of the links between them were addressed throughout students' engagement with the elaborating ID.

Guiding IDs are almost at the opposite pole from the elaborating IDs. Their design must be carefully adjusted to support development of knowledge and at the same time constrain students to the principal ideas of the task. It is possible to see the similarities in the constraints of the guiding and elaborating IDs with respect to the development of new mathematical ideas by students. Students in our studies started with a situation in which there was a mismatch between their knowledge and components of the IDs. The mismatch had to do both with the mathematical topics displayed in the IDs and with the resources and constraints designed into the IDs. The students spent time trying to learn the representations and tools that the IDs offered, to bypass the constraints of the IDs, and to expand their capabilities. Within the constraints of the IDs the students raised new ideas with respect to the tasks and tested them.

5.2.2 Examples and the Tools for Interacting with Them

Below we consider the role played by ID constraints and resources, with *focus on examples* and on the tools required for interacting with them. To do so, we refer to different settings of examples of IDs that invite viewers to activate them, with certain limitations, in two areas: changing given examples by generating similar examples or new ones, and interacting with components of the given examples.

The design of the three IDs in the modeling tasks supported interaction with components of the given examples but not the generation of new examples. The choice of types of motion was a key design decision. According to (Davydov 1972/1990), "the completeness and adequacy of the generalization depend on the breadth of the variations of the attributes that are combined, on the presence in the raw material of highly 'unexpected' and 'unusual' combinations of the common quality with the concomitant attributes or form of expression" (p. 6). Our intention was to include a repertoire of types of motion that would offer a general view of possible combinations of motion for the purpose of supporting the development of awareness of kinematic phenomena (such as rate of change, constant and changing speeds, two directions of movement, and different starting positions) and of their mathematical descriptions. Our findings show a process of development of a representative example that matches Davydov's argument (*ibid.*), according to which generalization is the result of a comparison of examples. The students revealed the salient features of the characteristics of motion by comparing special cases using the three IDs: they compared the motion in the animation, in the segments of the graphs, and in the value table. An important design feature of the example in the guiding ID was the motionless situation in the animation: one of the seven runners was represented by a steady dot, whereas all seven dots on the linked graphs were moving. Creating awareness of a conflicting image of this nature, which presents a difficult situation (a lack of information of the type described by Nemirovsky and Tierney (2001)), contributed to the ad hoc solution of the task of identifying the runners, and even more so, to understanding the Cartesian distance-time graphs.

The two other series of tasks, formulating mathematical phenomena and manipulating, differ from the modeling series in that they allow learners to change a given example by generating similar or new ones while getting feedback. Our studies concerning these two other series (e.g., Naftaliev and Yerushalmy 2011; Naftaliev 2012) highlight the importance of examples generated on the students' own initiative for clarifying the representativeness of the example as a carrier of the general meaning. The problem-solving process occurred when students were working with elaborating and guiding diagrams, which allowed examples to be entered freely. Problem solving was manifest when students used the given, specific example as a subject for comparison with the new example, which led students to conjectures and conflicts. It was also manifest when students generalized an example they created to produce an example space, in other words, a range of examples seen as instances of a generality based on that specific example (Goldenberg and Mason 2008). The students' strategy to solve the problem was comparison, and presumably it helped them perceive the structures, dependencies, and relationships that characterize any mathematical abstraction, as noted by Davydov (1972/1990).

Working with the guiding IDs, students treated the given example as a carrier of the general meaning and were able to reach a generalization in a process of systematic change and comparison. The variety of tools and representations offered in the elaborating IDs produced various strategies: students constructed, without guidance, various examples and initiated further inquiry that at times resulted in the systematic construction of examples, although the IDs provided no tools for systematic change. Initially, we hypothesized that illustrating IDs, which do not support the creation of new examples, would not be more helpful than a paper diagram because their design is similar to that of the paper diagram and offers only a limited choice of representations and tools. But we found that even the minimal interaction provided by the illustrating ID can be helpful in consolidating relevant knowledge that is not adequately structured yet. Students who worked with the illustrating IDs created their own examples only when it was required to do so by one of the tasks.

5.3 Concluding Remarks and Further Questions

Across our studies we found that similar tasks addressed with different IDs should be considered as different learning settings. The constraints and resources designed into the IDs contributed to making the tasks an interesting challenge for exploration by limiting the students' actions and by supporting guidance, while at the same time maintaining an open space for students' ideas. Based on our study, we find ourselves in a better position to raise relevant yet unresolved questions about the functions of IDs in teaching. In our past studies, we did not create a setting for observing teaching but rather focused on what we considered to be mostly spontaneous problem-solving processes. But the findings may have implications for teaching as a guiding mathematical inquiry, and the pedagogical situations that the tasks in the research appear to support should be studied further.

With regard to the related field of teacher learning, we adopt the approach suggested by Shulman (1986) and by Remillard and Bryans (2004), and assume that curricular resources are part of teacher learning and not intended to be used by students directly and independently of the teacher. The main purpose of teachers' engagement with curricular material is to guide student learning of subject matter during instruction. Teachers are taking further responsibility for their curricular resources, bringing Web materials to their textbooks, flexing and remixing their interactive textbooks. This raises questions about the decisions that educators should take as to whether and how they could use or import new IDs for different purposes in teaching and learning.

Studying such attempts is becoming increasingly important, especially given that the ability to use interactive textbooks and similar resources is growing, and that there are increasing opportunities for teachers to act as designers and authors of interactive materials. Teaching with an interactive textbook should be considered not merely a technological change but an attempt to create new paths for the construction of mathematical meaning. We conjecture that exploring IDs within a social semiotic framework could be useful for the professional development of teachers in analyzing curriculum materials and in examining the mathematical and pedagogical assumptions embedded in their design.

Acknowledgments This study was supported by the I-CORE Program of the Planning and Budgeting Committee and The Israel Science Foundation (1716/12).

References

Borasi, R., Siegel, M., Fonzi, J., & Smith, C. F. (1998). Using transactional reading strategies to support sense-making and discussion in mathematics classrooms: An exploratory study. *Journal for Research in Mathematics Education, 29*(3), 275–305.

Davydov, V. (1972/1990). Types of generalization in instruction. *Soviet Studies in Mathematics Education, 2.*

Goldenberg, P., & Mason, J. (2008). Shedding light on and with example spaces. *Educational Studies in Mathematics, 69*(2), 183–194.

Kress, G., & van Leeuwen, T. (1996). *Reading images the grammar of visual design.* London: Routledge.

Love, E. (1995). The functions of visualisation in learning geometry. In R. Sutherland & J. Mason (Eds.), *Exploiting mental imagery with computers in mathematics education* (pp. 125–141). Berlin: Springer.

Margolinas, C. (2013). Task design in mathematics education. In *Proceedings of ICMI Study 22. ICMI Study 22.*

Mason, J., & Pimm, D. (1984). Generic examples: Seeing the general in the particular. *Educational Studies in Mathematics, 15*(3), 227–289.

Naftaliev, E. (2012). *Interactive diagrams: Mathematical engagements with interactive text.* Ph.D. Thesis, University of Haifa, Faculty of Education, Haifa.

Naftaliev, E., & Yerushalmy, M. (2011). Solving algebra problems with interactive diagrams: Demonstration and construction of examples. *Journal of Mathematical Behavior, 30*(1), 48–61.

Naftaliev, E., & Yerushalmy, M. (2013). Guiding explorations: Design principles and functions of interactive diagrams. *Computers in the Schools, 30*(1–2), 61–75.

Nemirovsky, R., & Tierney, C. (2001). Children creating ways to represent changing situations: On the development of homogeneous spaces. *Educational Studies in Mathematics, 45*(1–3), 67–102.

Remillard, J. T., & Bryans, M. (2004). Teachers' orientations toward mathematics curriculum materials: Implications for teacher learning. *Journal for Research in Mathematics Education, 35*(5), 352–388.

Schwartz, J. L. (1995). The right size byte: Reflections on educational software designer. In D. Persinks, J. Schwartz, M. West, & S. Wiske (Eds.), *Software goes to school* (pp. 172–182). New York: Oxford University Press.

Schwartz, J. L. (1999). Can technology help us make the mathematics curriculum intellectually stimulating and socially responsible? *International Journal of Computers in the Mathematical Learning, 4*(2/3), 99–119.

Shulman, L. S. (1986). Those who understand: Knowledge growth in teaching. *Educational Researcher, 15*(2), 4–31.

Siegel, M. (1995). More than words: The generative power of transmediation for learning. *Canadian Journal of Education, 20*(4), 455–475.

Yerushalmy, M. (1993). Generalizations in geometry. In J. Schwartz, M. Yerushalmy, & B. Wilson (Eds.), *The geometric supposer: What it is a case of?* (pp. 57–84). NJ: Erlbaum Inc.

Yerushalmy, M. (2005). Functions of interactive visual *representations* in interactive mathematical textbooks. *International Journal of Computers for Mathematical Learning, 10*(3), 217–249.

Yerushalmy, M., & Naftaliev, E. (2011). Design of interactive diagrams structured upon generic animations. *Technology, Knowledge and Learning, 16*(3), 221–245.

Yerushalmy, M., Katriel, H., & Shternberg, B. (2002/2014). *The VisualMath functions and algebra e-textbook.* Israel: CET—The Centre of Educational Technology. http://www.cet.ac.il/math/function/english. New version http://visualmath.haifa.ac.il/. Accessed 12 Oct 2014.

Everybody Counts: Designing Tasks for *TouchCounts*

Nathalie Sinclair and Rina Zazkis

Abstract *TouchCounts* is an open-ended multi-touch App, which provides unconventional opportunities for engagement with the concept of a number, counting, and number operations. We describe a series of tasks designed for use in *TouchCounts*, which take advantage of the affordances of this environment. We elaborate on various aspects of the tasks as related to their pragmatic and epistemic values. We discuss the learning potential of the tasks, compare *TouchCount* tasks with similar tasks performed with physical manipulatives and provide a few illustrative examples of children's engagement with the tasks.

Keywords Counting · Number operations · Cardinal number · Ordinal number · Subitising

1 Introduction

For many open-ended, expressive digital environments for mathematics learning, the role of the task can be very important. In a Logo environment, for example, or a dynamic geometry environment (DGE), the learner starts with a blank screen and infinite possibility for engagement. In such environments, designing tasks that enable purposeful mathematical engagement, without becoming overly prescriptive, can be challenging. The challenge is increased by the impetus to design tasks that are not already doable, or even possible, in non-digital environments. In other words, good tasks in these environments should take advantage of the affordances of the given tools. Having students draw five different triangles can be done in a DGE, but having them drag one triangle into five different configurations is

N. Sinclair (✉) · R. Zazkis
Simon Fraser University, Burnaby, BC, Canada
e-mail: nathsinc@sfu.ca

R. Zazkis
e-mail: zazkis@sfu.ca

© Springer International Publishing Switzerland 2017
A. Leung and A. Baccaglini-Frank (eds.), *Digital Technologies in Designing Mathematics Education Tasks*, Mathematics Education in the Digital Era 8,
DOI 10.1007/978-3-319-43423-0_9

something that takes advantage of the continuous and direct manipulation affordance of most DGEs.

In this chapter, we elaborate on several tasks that we have designed for use in a particular open-ended multi-touch App called *TouchCounts* (Jackiw and Sinclair 2014), which provides unconventional engagement with the introductory concept of number and number operations. Learning to count in a contemporary world is as basic as learning to walk and talk. However, it is known that young children often experience difficulty in creating a one-to-one correspondence between the counted objects and assigning the number attributed to the last counted object as an enumerator of the total. Furthermore, initial experiences with arithmetic operations may present a challenge for learners, especially when the operations are approached by means of direct modelling (Coles 2014). How can technology assist with these challenges? This chapter describes a series of tasks that have been specifically designed to take advantage of the affordances of *TouchCounts*. We analyse these tasks in terms of their novel potential for supporting the development of number, as well as the different functions they draw on in terms of how children are invited to count, operate and attend to both ordinal and cardinal dimensions of number.

2 Theoretic Perspectives on Task Design in Expressive Environments

While there are many features of the App design that are of importance to shaping the kinds of tasks that are possible and productive, our focus in this paper is on task design. In our analysis of the tasks, we consider on two different aspects of the task. The first relates to its use of the digital technology. The second relates to the type of values offered by the task.

To begin, we adapt Laborde's (2001) typology of tasks developed by secondary teachers using the dynamic geometry software *Cabri*. She found that the teachers designed the following type of tasks:

- The technology is "used mainly as facilitating material aspects of the task while not changing it conceptually";
- The software is "supposed to facilitate the mathematical task that is considered as unchanged";
- The software "is supposed to modify the solving strategies of the task due to the use of some of its tools and to the possibility that the task might be rendered more difficult";
- The task itself "takes its meaning" from the software.

Tasks that do not change the mathematical activity conceptually can be said to make weak use of the technology. We are thus interested in identifying tasks that make strong use of technology, as well as in better understanding how these tasks change solution strategies or ways of thinking. Tasks that make strong use of technology will probably differ from tasks designed for non-digital environments. While we will highlight some of these differences, our main focus in this paper will be on task design.

In discussing the use of software in mathematics education, (Artigue 2002) distinguishes between their epistemic and pragmatic values:

> Epistemic (what you learn while you are doing this; as they contribute to the understanding of the objects they involve), pragmatic (what you achieve; I would like to stress that techniques are most often perceived and evaluated in terms of pragmatic value, that is to say, by focusing on their productive potential (efficiency, cost, field of validity).) (p. 248).

Similarly, tasks can have epistemic and/or pragmatic value. That is, they can change the techniques that are used, particularly in making a task easier to solve or more precise. They can also have epistemic value in terms of contributing to mathematical understanding in a certain way. We assume that there is some relation between the values of the software and those of the tasks, that is, that tasks that have epistemic value will draw on the epistemic values afforded by the software's design.

A final consideration relates to feedback. Mackrell et al. (2013) distinguish among different kinds of feedback: evaluation feedback is related to completion of a task or part of a task; strategy feedback aims to support or amend student approaches while she is engaged in a task; and, direct manipulation feedback, which "is the response of the environment to student action" (p. 83). One of the benefits of working with computers is that it provides a neutral form of feedback that the teacher cannot, often providing a sufficient indication of whether the task was completed successfully or what can be adjusted to achieve a successful completion. However, this is not always the case. Therefore, a guiding feature in our task design is to allow direct manipulation feedback to serve as evaluation feedback.

3 A Multi-touch Application for Counting and Operating

The multi-touch device is a novel technological affordance in mathematics education. Through its direct mediation, it offers opportunities for mathematical expressivity by enabling children to produce and transform screen objects with fingers and gestures, instead of engaging and operating through a keyboard or mouse. This makes it highly accessible, but also opens the way for new, tangible forms of mathematical communication (Jackiw 2013). In this section, we describe *TouchCounts*, whose design was motivated by multi-touch affordances.

Unlike many 'educational games' that can be found for the iPad, *TouchCounts* is open-ended and exploratory, rather than practice- and level-driven—it follows in the tradition of constructionist and expressive technologies in mathematics education (Papert 1980; Noss and Hoyles 1996) and supports the development of number by offering modes of interaction with objects that involve fingers and gestures. Specifically, it aims both (1) to engage one-to-one correspondence by allowing every finger touch to summon a new sequentially-numbered object into existence, one whose presence is both spoken aloud and symbolically labelled and (2) to enable gesture-based summing and partitioning, by means of pushing objects together and pulling them apart in ways that expose very young children to arithmetic operations. With these new affordances, however, come new questions related to design decisions (such as "What touch-based actions on the screen might better support and enable mathematical activity?"), as well as questions related to the development of number and how this particular technology may shape current curricular trajectories and, in the process, potentially disrupt them.

Currently, there are two sub-applications in *TouchCounts*, one for Enumerating and the other for Operating. After we describe each of the two worlds, we present and analyse a series of tasks, where the first set are to be used in the Enumerating world and the second set in the Operating world. In our analysis we refer to some comments or actions that we have observed children make. These are drawn from an ongoing study that involved iterative testing of the application with children (aged three to eight) in four different educational settings (one day-care and two primary school children either at school or in after-school care). Some of this research has been reported elsewhere (see Sinclair and Heyd-Metzuyanim 2014; Sinclair and Pimm 2014).

3.1   The Enumerating World

In this world, a user taps her fingers on the screen to summon numbered objects (yellow discs). The first tap produces a disc containing the numeral '1'. Subsequent taps produce successively numbered discs. As each tap summons a new numbered disc, *TouchCounts* audibly speaks the number word for its number ("one", "two", …, if the language is set to English). Fingers can be placed on the screen one at a time or simultaneously. With five successive taps, for instance, five discs (numbered '1' to '5') appear sequentially on the screen, which are counted aloud one by one (see Fig. 1a). However, if the user places two fingers on the screen simultaneously, two consecutively numbered discs appear at the same time (Fig. 1b), but only the higher-numbered one is named aloud ("two", if these are the first two taps). One small instance of opportunity lies in a new sense of the times-two table: the number of 'times' two fingers simultaneously touch the screen. The entire 'world' can be reset, to clear all numbered discs and return the 'count' of the next summoned disc to one. Note that the discs always arrive in order, with their symbolic names imprinted upon them.

From an adult perspective, the number of taps (whether made sequentially or simultaneously) is also the number of discs on the screen, a fact which can tacitly reinforce the cardinality principle, since the last number 'counted' (spoken aloud by *TouchCounts*) is exactly "how many" numbered discs there are to be seen. In traditional research in the area of early counting, it is a well-documented finding that even after children have counted a set of things (up to five, say), when they are asked "how many" objects are in that set, they will often count the objects again

(a)   **(b)**

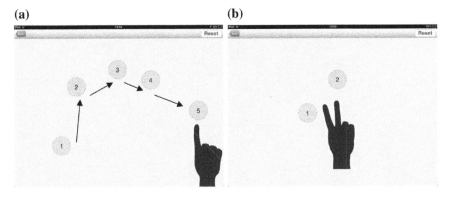

Fig. 1 **a** Five sequential taps—"one, two, three, four, five" is said (the *arrows* are only to indicate the sequence; they are not shown on the screen). **b** A simultaneous two-finger tap—only "two" is said (both discs appear simultaneously)

(Baroody and Wilkins 1999). The "how many?" question seems to provoke a routine of sequential counting.

In *TouchCounts'* Enumerating World, however, the child is engaged in a somewhat different practice—rather than counting a *given* set, she is actively *producing* a set with her finger(s) (perhaps aiming at a pre-given total) and the elements of that set seem to count themselves (both aurally and symbolically) as they are summoned into existence. One distinction that *TouchCounts* makes is that, orally, each number word in succession replaces (and eradicates) the previous one. At the end of the spoken count, no trace is left of what has been said. On the screen, however, each action leaves a visual trace, in the form of (one or more) numeral-bearing discs, of what has once been summoned into being.

If the 'gravity' option for this World is turned on in the App, then as long as the learner's finger remains pressed to the screen, the numbered object holds its position beneath her fingertip. But as soon as she 'lets go' (by lifting that finger), the numbered object falls toward and then disappears "off" the bottom of the screen, as if captured by some virtual gravity. With 'gravity' comes the option of a 'shelf', a horizontal line across the screen (in Fig. 2). If a user releases her numbered object above the shelf, it falls only to the shelf, and comes to rest there, visibly and permanently on screen, rather than vanishing out of sight 'below'. (Thus, Fig. 2 depicts a situation in which there have been four taps below the shelf—these numbered objects were falling—and then a disc labelled '5' was placed above the shelf by tapping above it.) Since each time a finger is placed on the screen a new numbered disc is created beneath it and, once released by lifting the finger, it begins to fall, one cannot "catch" or reposition an existing numbered object by re-tapping it. This is not a conventional "dragging" world.

Discs dropping away (under 'gravity') mirror the way spoken language fades rapidly over time, with no trace left—the impermanence of speech. Also, with discs disappearing, any sense of cardinality goes too: in the absence of the presence of

(a)   **(b)**

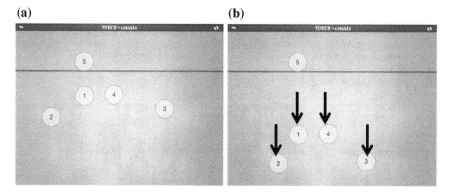

Fig. 2 **a** Five sequential taps—"one, two, three, four, five" is said (*the arrows are only to indicate the sequence; they are not shown on the screen*). **b** A simultaneous two-finger tap—only "two" is said (both discs appear simultaneously)

'1', the disc labelled '2' is simply the second one to have been summoned. So the Enumerating World with 'gravity' enabled (it is an option) is almost entirely an ordinal one, with the shelf acting as a form of visible memory.

One of the characteristics of *TouchCounts*, then, is that the computer handles the counting (the iPad is the one who announces and manages the arrival of various figures onto the ritual scene). The design intent was to help move young users towards transitive counting, even though the general setting provides a mix of cardinal and ordinal elements.

3.2 The Operating World

Whilst tapping on the screen in the Enumerating World creates sequentially numbered objects, tapping on the screen in the Operating World creates autonomous numbered sets, which we refer to as herds. The user's creation choreography starts by placing one or several fingers on the screen, which immediately creates a large disc that encompasses all the fingers and includes a numeral corresponding to the combined number of fingers touching the screen. At the same time, every one of the fingers in contact with the screen creates its own much smaller (and unnumbered) disc, centred on each fingertip. When the fingers are lifted off the screen, the numeral is spoken aloud and the smaller discs are then lassoed into a 'herd' and arranged regularly around the inner circumference of the big disc (Fig. 3a shows herds of 3 and 4). The small discs all move in either a clockwise or counter-clockwise direction to emphasise that they are to be seen as one unit. Herds of size one wander around the screen in order to make them more difficult to place one's finger on, in order to encourage children to operate with herds that are greater than one in number.

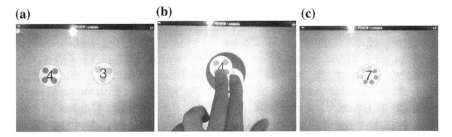

Fig. 3 a The herds. **b** Pinching two herds together. **c** The sum of two herds

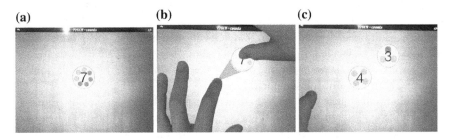

Fig. 4 a An initial herd of 7. **b** Left finger (in this instance) swiping outside the herd. **c** Resulting separation of 7 into herds of 4 and 3: *TouchCounts* announces "four"

Unlike in the Enumerating World, herds can be interactively dragged, either to move them around on the screen or to operate upon them. After two or more such arrangements have been produced (as in Fig. 3b) they can either be pinched together (addition) or 'unpinched' (subtraction or partition). In the case of pinching together, two fingers are required—one on each herd—to make the herds merge. Dynamically, they then become one herd that contains the 'digital' counters from each previous herd, thus adding them together. The new herd is labelled with the associated numeral of the sum (Fig. 3c), which *TouchCounts* announces aloud. Moreover, the new herd keeps a distinguished trace of the previous herds, which can be seen by means of the differentiated colours of the individual small discs. Multiple herds can be pinched together simultaneously. Note that the pinching gesture is entirely symmetric, both with respect to the pinching fingers and with respect to the herds, so that adding does not have the kind of order implied by the directionality of verbal or written expressions such as 'two plus three' or '2 + 3'.

An inverse pinch gesture ('unpinching') can be made in order to decompose a given herd into two herds. The gesture can be described either as 'separating', which supports the idea of partitioning, or as 'taking out' or 'removing', which supports the idea of subtracting. In both cases, two fingers are placed in the herd—

while one stays put, the second swipes out of the herd. This distinction of roles between the two fingers supports the needed directionality of subtraction. The further the swipe travels, the more will be taken out from the starting herd (and of course, at the extreme, everything can be taken out of the starting herd) (Fig. 4b). When the swiping finger is lifted, two new herds are formed and *TouchCounts* announces the number that has been taken out (Fig. 4c). In the extreme case (where everything is removed), a new herd is formed under the finger that has swiped, while in the location of the previous herd the numeral '0' appears briefly but then fades away.

The pinching gesture draws on one of the four grounding metaphors for addition, that of *object collection* (see Lakoff and Núñez 2000). Both adding and either subtracting or partitioning offer children the *action* of operating without necessarily requiring them to calculate the result. Unlike with the calculator, which can also perform addition and subtraction, *TouchCounts* first requires the production of herds that will be labeled by a numeral (indicating "how many" are in the herd) and then enacts the gathering/splitting mechanisms in which the two herds join or separate, both visually and temporally.

Children can pinch two herds together or split a herd apart relatively easily (though some children find it challenging, at least initially, to place their fingers right on the herds and often produce new herds of one). They can do this, obviously, without knowing what the sum or difference will be, without knowing that the transformation occurring reflects the operation of addition or subtraction and, most importantly, without thinking of those herds as cardinal numbers. In this sense, *TouchCounts* invites the children into a gesture-mediated form of operations. We note that while a teacher might introduce the word 'adding' to describe the process, neither that word nor its symbolic counterpart (e.g., '+') appears on the screen: the iPad only announces the result of the operation. As such, language such as "making" or "putting together" or "joining" can all be used to accompany the action of pinching discs together.

4   *TouchCounts* Tasks

In this section, we describe and analyse six tasks that have been created for use with *TouchCounts*. They have been developed over the course of on-going work with young children in a variety of settings and geographic locations. In developing the tasks we consider what engages the children and also what can focus attention on the mathematics of counting and operating. Some of the tasks were initiated by the children, which are of particular interest because of their adidactical nature.

4.1   Plucking Out Numbers for the Shelf

Put 36 above the shelf

This is an extension and variation on the previously explored task in which a child was asked to put 5 on the shelf. 36 has no particular attributes other than being a relatively big number. It is expected that a child will not count up by ones, but find a more efficient way.

Attending to the task requires a continuous control and comparison of the number that is on the screen and the target number. For example, if a child repeatedly increases the number of discs "counting by 5's", there is a point at which she will have to stop and evaluate a situation. The task is a good introduction to developing ideas related to addition and subtraction, considering a "relative distance" from the current number to the target number. If a screen has 30 on it, a child, maybe implicitly, starts evaluating whether to put another 5 or whether to "play it safe" and reach 36 increasing by ones.

This task provides a teacher with an opportunity to observe children's learning. If a child's preferable method is to increase the number by 1s, she can be encouraged to use a different way to "get there faster". Changing the task to a bigger number, 360 for example, may serve as a motivation for a child to seek a more efficient strategy. Also, it is interesting to observe if a child semi-randomly increasing the count or is using some kind of a strategy, like counting by threes.

The analog outside of the *TouchCounts* environment is making available to a child a large amount of counters in some container and asking her to put 36 counters on the table. One can definitely count by ones, or put some amount on the table, count up and adjust. Such a task is made both easier and harder within *TouchCounts*. It is easier because the child does not have to produce the number names or symbols. It is also harder because the target number in this case cannot be adjusted both up and down. The constraint in *TouchCounts* is that there is no option for adjusting down. Consider the case that by some oversight a child reached 37 or any other number bigger that 36. Working with counters, some can be returned to the container. Working with *TouchCounts*, the only way to complete the task is to start over. This requires a "calculated" approach, which is the epistemic value of the task.

If the task is repeated, one may focus on a minimal number of steps. I can complete the task in 4 steps: 10, 10, 10, 5–36! Less than 4 may require collaboration (or use of toes). The task is also appropriate for a group work. (Think of it as a simplified NIM game.) 2 or 3 children sharing a screen and taking turns. The "winner" is the one who puts 36 on the shelf. Each child, in turn, can touch the screen once or twice, and can use 1 or all his fingers.

Put numbers with 0 at the end on the shelf

We are purposefully avoiding the language of 'multiples of 10' in setting this task. However, it is expected that a child will develop to idea of counting by 10's. The epistemic value here is connecting the multitude and the sound to the written representation. That is, a child learns that the number that comes after 9 (or 19, or 39) is the one that has zero at the end. The same of course can be requested with ANY digit at the end. A challenge is to do this with eyes closed.

Put numbers that have digits 3 or 7 on the shelf
This is a more complex variation, especially when several children work on the task. This can be a game of concentration, when the iPad is shared between two children or more. A child has to predict whether the next number has in it one of the two given digits. Note that this task does not focus on the last digit, but any digit.

4.2 Continue the Pattern

A teacher repeats 3 times the following: taps twice below the shelf and then taps once above the shelf. The numbers 3, 6, 9 appear on the shelf.

Can you put those numbers on the shelf like I did?
The pragmatic value of this task is to place the same numbers on the shelf as the teacher, and to try to mimic the finger choreography of the teacher. The epistemic value is in the embodiment of the skip counting, that is, the opportunity to connect rhythmic taps to a sequence of multiples of 3. Another pragmatic value, particularly if the child has mainly been using one finger at a time to make numbers, is for the child to use two fingers simultaneously. This connects to the an added epistemic value, which is in becoming familiar with different strategies for making numbers more efficiently (a two-tap followed by a one two is quicker than a one tap followed by a one tap and then another one tap), especially for bigger numbers. If children have developed adequate tool fluency, the teacher might ask whether 30 will ever appear on the shelf, for example.

This task resembles hand clapping tasks that teachers use to help children develop a more rhythmic sense of the multiples. It changes somewhat the emphasis only on the multiples since the number preceding the multiple is also said aloud by *TouchCounts* ('two, three, five, six, eight, nine...'). It also puts the fingers in charge of the production of the multiples, so that the actual numbers do not have to be known in advance—it is enough for the rhythm of the fingers to remain constant. An extension to this task might involve placing the sequence 4, 8, 12 on the shelf by tapping a triplet below the shelf and a single above.

After putting the required numbers on the shelf, one first grade child decided to place 5, 10 and 15 on the shelf. However, instead of placing four fingers below the shelf simultaneously, he continued using two fingers at a time. This produced a different kind of pattern (two tap below, two tap below, one tap above, repeat) that was successful in terms of achieving his goal. Once the teacher suggested a different approach (a four tap below followed by a one tap above), the child tried making a ten tap below followed by a one tap above, and was delighted to produce the sequence 11, 22, 33.

4.3   Inverse Gestural Subitising

Making 4 all-at-once
This task, which is best performed in the Enumerating world, preferably with no-gravity, involves the children pressing four fingers simultaneously on the screen. It is a task that is related to subitising. In subitising tasks, students must determine quickly, without counting, the number of objects in an array, which they then either say or type using a keyboard. Instead of producing a spoken or alphanumeric action based on a visual prompt, inverse gestural subitising requires that the children produce an action (quickly lifting up their fingers and pressing them on the screen, instead of pressing fingers one by one) based on an oral prompt. Unlike conventional subitising tasks, which rarely extend beyond five, inverse gestural subitising with *TouchCounts* has no upper limit, in the sense that a child may use all her fingers to make ten/10, but she can also work collaboratively with other children to produce even higher targets.

The making of 4 all-at-once can also be used in the Operating World as a quick way of producing and operating on numbers. The pragmatic value is clear in that the children know that they have to hear *TouchCounts* say 'four' (and only 'four'). The epistemic value is in the use of a finger gesture that expresses cardinality because 'four' is the number of fingers that are lifted and that will touch the screen at the same time. If more fingers touch the screen, *TouchCounts* will not say 'four', which provides immediate feedback to the student, who can then reset and try again, perhaps even guided by the fact that the number *TouchCounts* said was too high.

In one episode involving a four-year-old boy as well as several other children aged 4 or 5, the teacher asks "Make 7 all-at-once". The boy looks at his fingers and counts to seven on them, unfurling them one at a time palms facing him. He then turns his hands around and places the unfurled fingers on the screen. *TouchCounts* says "eight", indicating that he actually touched the screen at eight different places (perhaps accidentally touching with an unfurled finger or with his palm). The teacher asks if he wants to try again, which he does. He then immediately stretched out seven fingers (without counting them out) and places them on the screen. *TouchCounts* says "seven". It is clear in this case, and in many others we have observed, that the temporal counting out of a number quickly turns into a gesture (both communicative and manipulative) for expressing cardinality.

4.4   Count by n in Both Worlds

Count by 3s (in the Enumerating world)
Count by 3s (in the Operating world)

This task is often done in early years school settings, and involves "skip-counting". It is a primarily oral task in that the student must utter the correct sequence of numbers, a sequence, which is often learned by heart (like the counting sequence) at the younger ages. The only way for students to know that they are wrong is if the teacher tells them, and their options for self-correcting are limited to them trying to remember the correct answer.

In *TouchCounts*, the task involves taking actions that makes *TouchCounts* produce the oral sequence of numbers. The task itself thus changes, as do the solution strategies and the opportunity for feedback. Although the hand gesture for doing so can be quite similar in both worlds, the visual display on the screen looks very different. In the Enumerating World, one can count by threes, for example, by repeatedly tapping three fingers on the screen simultaneously. *TouchCounts* will say "three, six, nine, twelve, …". In the no-gravity setting, numbered yellow discs will appear where the fingers have tapped the screen so that the total number of discs will be equal to the value of the last multiple created. In the gravity setting, the yellow discs that have been created below the shelf will have fallen away, leaving only the yellow numbered discs that were created above the shelf. Therefore, there may very well be less numbered discs on the screen than the value of the last multiple created. A dexterous tapping of the fingers could also leave all the multiples of three on the shelf while the other numbers fall away.

In the Operating World, tapping three fingers simultaneously will produce a herd of three. In order to count by 6, a child might either create a three with three fingers, then a six with six fingers, then a nine with nine fingers and so on. This gets quite challenging once the count gets to twelve, though children could work together to produce 12, 15, 18, etc. Another method would be to create a second herd of three, join it to the first herd so as to obtain six, then create another herd of three, join it with the herd of six so as to obtain nine, and so on. Thus, *TouchCounts* would be heard saying "three, three, six, three, nine, three, twelve, …" Similarly, a child could produce many herds of three and then begin to join herds of three to a running count in order to get *TouchCounts* to say "three, six, nine, twelve, …"

The pragmatic function of the task is clear, in that students have to produce a certain sequence in the right order, without skipping any elements. But the epistemic value resides in the multiple ways in which the task can be solved, which children then are invited to compare. In each of the ways of solving the task (in both worlds), the three-fingers-lifted gesture functions as a pragmatic and epistemic ways. Pragmatically, it is the way to get *TouchCounts* to say just three, without having to count up to three. Epistemically though, it also expresses three as a single action, which relates it to the cardinality of 3, rather than the ordinality. While in the Enumerating world, counting by threes is a question of succession, in the Operating World, an additional action is required, which is the combining of two herds in order to produce a sum.

The importance of this additional action is evident in the interaction of a 5-year-old called Chloe, who had decided that she wanted to make a really big number. She began by making a 5 in the Operating World by tapping the screen with a five-fingers-lifted gesture. She then made another 5 and combined it with the first one. Then she made a third five and combined it with the 10 and, finally, combined a fourth five with the 15. Once she saw the new herd, which was labeled with a 20, she said "That's why they say five, ten [short pause] fifteen, twenty". Chloe had clearly engaged in skip-counting before but now, having produced the sequence of numbers 5, 10, 15, 20 by successive addition of herds of 5, she made a connection between skip counting and adding.

There are two important aspects of *TouchCounts* that differentiate it from other environments. First, it takes care of the computation so that Chloe can attend to the result of her successive adding. She may well have been able to perform the additions herself, but that would likely have shifted her focus of attention away from the pattern she was producing. It is important to note that in doing the calculation, *TouchCounts* offers both symbolic and aural results, and it is perhaps the latter that helped Chloe make a connection to skip-counting, which is most often a ritual, spoken aloud event in the classroom. This distinguishes the task from what Chloe might have done on a calculator, which would also take care of the computation, because the calculator does not announce the sums out loud. The second distinguishing feature is the gestural interface for performing the addition. This gesture, which has both pragmatic and epistemic functions, draws Chloe's attention to the adding operation, which is very different from the successive counting that might occur in the Enumerating World.

4.5 Make Them Equal

A teacher puts on the screen 2 herds, for example 4 and 6.
A student is asked to "make these two equal".

Imagine this task outside of the *TouchCounts* environment. You have in front of you two piles of marbles, 4 in one and 6 in another. A solution that appears obvious initially is to move one marble from the six-pile to the four-pile. In a way, you created the following equation: $4 + 1 = 6 - 1$.

Is there another way? Of course one can think of hiding 2 marbles in a pocket, an action that can be modelled as $4 = 6 - 2$. Adding more marbles to the table is another option of course, if those are available. However, the immediate action, and also a self-imposed restriction, is that of creating a balance using only what is available and all of what is available.

Now turn to the *TouchCounts* task. Obviously, the two options described above are available. In this sense, the task may be seen as facilitating the mathematics since the students do not need to actually perform the operations, but can instead focus on strategy. But the environment easily affords a variety of other solutions, at times unintentional or self-correcting. For example, Tiki wanted to pull out 1 from six and join it with 4. However, unintentionally, she pulled out 2. She immediately recognized that the desired outcome had been achieved. In this sense, the task also modifies the solving strategies, thereby offering a form of strategy feedback.

While availability of additional marbles is uncertain, creation of new numbers is a matter of a touch. As such, it opens many options for achieving a balance. For example, a child can "make 1" and "make 3" and then rejoin, which can be modelled by $4 + 3 = 6 + 1$.

If this is a preference, a constraint can be introduced:

8 and 4 on the screen. Make those equal, without creating more numbers.

This constraint can be examined with an "impossible" task

4 and 7 on the screen. Make those equal, without creating more numbers.

This could be done in a more elaborate way by proposing the following sequence of tasks:

Make equal herds from:
Given: 8 and 4
Given: 8 and 12
Given: 8 and 5.

The pragmatic value of the tasks is clear: equal herds are created. Direct manipulation feedback of the symbols provides children with quick feedback as to whether or not they have achieved their goal, as does the aural feedback to some extent. However, the epistemic value is far reaching. The task(s) open the exploration of equalities and equations. In a way, what a child is concerned with can be modelled as $4 + x = 6 + y$. And, of course, the epistemic value is enhanced if a teacher is asking for alternative solutions. The last task invites initial considerations of parity.

A possible variation is to start with a larger number and ask a child to split it into two equal parts, or 3 equal parts. The epistemic value of such an exercise is that it can serve as initial informal introduction to the concepts of division, division with remainder or divisibility. Of course we do not intend to say that a child who successfully splits 9 into 3 equal groups has acquired the concept of divisibility. But we do claim that this is an experiential hands-on—in fact, fingers on—initiation into the multiplicative structure.

4.6 Families of Partitions

How many different ways can you make 7?

This task, which is used in the Operating World, invites children to use pinching (addition) to make 7 in different ways. This task is frequently undertaken at the primary school (sometimes with physical manipulatives), where students are asked to come up with different combinations such as $3 + 4$ and $5 + 2$. The task is important in drawing attention to partitioning and in preparing for work with subtraction. Strategies for solving this task involve looking for different combinations of number that sum to 7, and then perhaps writing the sums as equations. The task is used with children who have already been introduced to addition and perhaps know some addition facts.

In *TouchCounts*, there are three main differences. The first is that *TouchCounts* performs the addition, so that students are focused more on experimenting with different combinations of numbers. The second is the visual display of the sum, which looks both like a new number because it came from the addends, but also like any other number that can be used to perform operations with. The third is that the output of the addition is given as a new number that retains the trace of its composition (by colour). That means that the 7 that one makes from pinching 3 and 4 looks different than the 7 that one gets from pinching 2 and 5. This provides some visual feedback on how to produce more combinations.

The pragmatic value of this task might not be as straightforward in that *TouchCounts* does not tell you when you have made all the combinations, and nor does the task. Indeed, there can be some vagueness about the task since 7 made all-at-once, for example, could be considered as a way of making 7 that is equivalent to 7 + 0. The epistemic value of the task is in the seeking of strategies for producing different combinations as well as in the strategies used to adjust combinations that do not produce the target number of 7. So, for example, if a student puts 5 and 3 together to get 8, they might use the feedback to reduce one of the two addends.

5 Discussion

We have described a series of tasks that have been designed for use with *TouchCounts*, based in part on the functionalities of the App, but also on interactions with young children. In fact, there were several tasks that we tried with children and did not analyse above, and this occurred primarily for reasons related to feedback. For example, one of the tasks that we tried early on was to show children a repeated sequence of touching with two fingers below the shelf and then one finger above, and then to invite them to continue. The goal was to develop a rhythmic sense of the skip counting by three. However, the children sometimes touched the screen with an extra finger, which meant that the numbers on the shelf were no longer multiples of three. The feedback offered by *TouchCounts* was thus not well aligned with the pragmatics and epistemic goal of the task. This led to the design of the 'Counting the pattern' task we discussed above. In general, we have found that given the nature of the *TouchCounts* feedback, it is imperative for feedback to provide information that enables the learner to assess (either through seeing or hearing) her action *in relation to the goal*, a type of feedback that has been called direct manipulation feedback (see Mackrell et al. 2013). This is true of exploratory environments more generally. When a learner drags the vertex of an isosceles triangle, the feedback is not evaluative, but can provide visual information about whether the given triangle can indeed be dragged into an equilateral configuration. While the importance of goal-aligned feedback is especially true when working on a given task, we emphasize that children can also develop goals based on the feedback from *TouchCounts*. So, for example, a child who notices the numeral 44 on a disc (even if she was not trying to get to 44) might wonder how to make numbers that have two fives or two eights.

One of the important features of feedback is that it offers immediate information, which is directly related to one's actions, and which can guide further actions, especially if a goal has not been reached. In the case of the 'Put 5 above the shelf' task, when a child taps for the fifth time below the shelf, she can see that she has not succeeded in the task, but can also use the oral feedback provided to notice that "four" comes before "five", which may in turn result in a change in strategy. In the Enumerating world though, she cannot simply "undo". She must press Reset and start all over again. In a sense, the Enumerating World is unforgiving because it does not allow for much tinkering. This contrasts with most other software programs, from Word to DGEs, which almost always allow the last action to be undone. It also contrasts with the Operating world, where undoing is often possible. For example, if a child wanted to make a herd of 5, but mistakenly only made a herd 4, she can make another herd of 1 and pinch it together with the herd of 4. Or, she can simply push it off the visible screen. These differences are important to take into account when designing tasks and when assessing the learning potential of tasks. Having to try many times to put 5 on the shelf may serve an important purpose if a child is still struggling with the counting sequence from 1 to 5. However, in the extended task where a child is asked to put 5, 10, 15, 20 on the shelf, but mistakenly places 5, 10, 15 and 19 on the shelf, there may be less value in starting over again.

In the Operating world, it is the possibility to tinker that opens up a multiplicity of solutions to certain tasks (like Make two herds the same). If children were only allowed to use the existing herds, there would be a highly constrained focus to the task, but given that the child can make new herds, the number of solution strategies increases. While this might be challenging for teachers with a specific learning outcome in view, it likely offer the children a greater sense of agency.

6   Conclusions

In our analyses, we highlighted both the pragmatic/epistemic values of the tasks as well as the nature of the task in terms of its use of *TouchCounts*. As is evident in these analyses, the pragmatic value of a task is almost always equivalent to the completion of the task itself, which may in part be due to the nature of mathematics involved and the age of the children. Further, the epistemic value of each task usually depended strongly on the making of certain bodily actions that, in turn, entailed a particular aspect of number. For example, in the task "Making 4 all-at-once", a child can learn the physical action of lifting four fingers and touching them to the screen, and it is precisely this physical action that is intended to bring about the cardinality of four.

Finally, each task made use of *TouchCounts* in a way that either offered new ways of thinking about number, as compared to similar physical manipulatives-based tasks, or derived its meaning from *TouchCounts* altogether (so that equivalent tasks in a non-digital environment do not exist). As Laborde (2001) notes, it can be very difficult to teachers to design such tasks because they are accustomed to certain ways of working with number that involve different tasks, different questions and different challenges. In an exploratory environment, it is thus very important for teachers to have access to well-designed tasks. A further challenge for teachers and parents will be to achieve a fine balance between offering the kinds of tasks we have described in this chapter and enabling children to engage in self-directed mathematical exploration as well, so that they are not exclusively following a set of given tasks.

References

Artigue, M. (2002). Learning mathematics in a CAS environment: The genesis of a reflection about instrumentation and the dialectics between technical and conceptual work. *International Journal of Computers for Mathematical Learning, 7*(3), 245–274.

Baroody, A., & Wilkins, J. (1999). The development of informal counting, number, and arithmetic skills and concepts. In J. Copley (Ed.), *Mathematics in the early years* (pp. 48–65). Reston, VA: National Council of Teachers of Mathematics.

Coles, A. (2014). Ordinality, neuro-science and the early learning of number. In C. Nichol, S. Oesterle, P. Liljedahl, & D. Allen (Eds.), *Proceedings of the joint PME 38 and PME-NA 36 conference* (Vol. 2, pp. 329–336). Vancouver, BC: PME.

Jackiw, N. (2013). Touch and multitouch in dynamic geometry: Sketchpad explorer and "digital" mathematics. In E. Faggiano & A. Montone (Eds.), *Proceedings of the 11th international conference on technology in mathematics learning* (pp. 149–155). Bari, Italy: University of Bari.

Jackiw, N., & Sinclair, N. (2014). *TouchCounts [software application for the iPad]*. Burnaby, BC: Simon Fraser University.

Laborde, C. (2001). Integration of technology in the design of geometry tasks with cabri-geometry. *International Journal of Computers for Mathematical Learning, 6*(3), 283–317.

Lakoff, G., & Núñez, R. (2000). *Where mathematics comes from: How the embodied mind brings mathematics into being*. New York, NY: Basic Books.

Mackrell, K., Maschietto, M, & Soury-Lavergne, S. (2013). The interaction between task design and technology design in creating tasks with Cabri Elem. In A. Watson, M. Ohtani, J. Ainley, J. Bolite Frant, M. Doorman, C. Kieran, A. Leung, C. Margolinas, P. Sullivan, D.R. Thompson, & Y. Yang (Eds.), *Task design in mathematics education. Proceedings of ICMI study 22, Oxford* (pp. 81–89).

Noss, R., & Hoyles, C. (1996). *Windows on mathematical meanings: Learning cultures and computers*. Dordrecht, The Netherlands: Kluwer Academic.

Papert, S. (1980). *Mindstorms: Children, computers and powerful ideas*. New York: Basic Books.

Sinclair, N., & Heyd-Metzuyanim, E. (2014). Learning number with *TouchCounts*: The role of emotions and the body in mathematical communication. *Technology, Knowledge and Learning, 19*(1–2), 81–99.

Sinclair, N. & Pimm, D. (2014). Number's subtle touch: Expanding finger gnosis in the era of multi-touch technologies. In *Proceedings of the PME 38 Conference, Vancouver, BC*.

Designing Innovative Learning Activities to Face Difficulties in Algebra of Dyscalculic Students: Exploiting the Functionalities of *AlNuSet*

Elisabetta Robotti

Abstract In this chapter I discuss students' difficulties in algebra, considering in particular those students affected by *developmental dyscalculia* (DD) (Butterworth in *Handbook of Mathematical Cognition*. Hove, UK: Psychology Press, 2005; Dehaene in *The number sense: How the mind creates mathematics*. New York, Oxford University Press, 1997). Focusing on algebraic notions such as *unknown*, *variable*, *algebraic expression*, *equation* and *solution of an equation*, I will describe possible processes of meaning making in students with low achievement in mathematics, or even diagnosed with DD including adult learners. This involves considering algebra not only in its syntactic aspects but also in its semantic ones. The assumption on which the work is based, is that some difficulties in learning algebra could be due to the lack of meaning attributed by the students to the algebraic notions. Basing the analyses on studies both in the domain of cognitive psychology and in the domain of mathematics education, I will show how students with DD can make sense of the algebraic notions considered above, thanks to tasks designed within AlNuSet exploiting its semiotic multi-representations based on visual, non-verbal and kinaesthetic-tactile systems. AlNuSet (Algebra of Numerical Sets) is a digital artifact for dynamic algebra, designed for students of lower and upper secondary school.

Keywords Algebra · Developmental dyscalculia · AlNuSet · Task · Variable · Solution of an equation · Algebraic expression

1 Introduction

For a significant percentage of students the current teaching of algebra does not seem to be sufficient for helping them effectively develop the necessary skills and knowledge to master this domain of knowledge (Sfard and Linchevsky 1992; Kieran 2006). Here I will focus on students manifesting low achievement in mathematics, or even diagnosed with developmental dyscalculia (DD) (Butterworth 2005; Dehaene 1997).

E. Robotti (✉)
Università della Valle d'Aosta, Aosta, Italy
e-mail: elisabetta.robotti@gmail.com

© Springer International Publishing Switzerland 2017
A. Leung and A. Baccaglini-Frank (eds.), *Digital Technologies in Designing Mathematics Education Tasks*, Mathematics Education in the Digital Era 8,
DOI 10.1007/978-3-319-43423-0_10

   The need to deal with different cognitive demands and in particular with those of students having learning difficulties in mathematics is discussed in the mathematics education research, in the cognitive psychology and in the literature on learning disorders. In Italy, students with learning disorders are estimated to be between 3 % and 5 %, and recent data disclosed by the Italian Ministry of Education, indicate that only 0.9 % of the school population has obtained diagnoses, so the number of certified students with learning disorders is likely to increase. A conscious use of specific teaching strategies suitable for students diagnosed with learning disorders, and in particular with developmental dyscalculia, is also important for those students who, although uncertified, show learning difficulty profiles very similar to those of dyscalculic students.

   Students' difficulties in algebra seem to be due to lack of meaning developed for algebraic notions (Arzarello et al. 1994). Having acquired meanings of algebraic notions seems to be very important also in order to have better control over algebraic manipulations (Radford 2005; Robotti and Ferrando 2013). Recent studies in mathematics education indicate that the construction of mathematical knowledge, as a cognitive activity, is supported by the sensory-motor system activated in suitable contexts.

   According to Arzarello's definition of *semiotic bundle* (2006), in addition to the standard semiotic resources used by students and teachers (e.g. written symbols and speech), I consider other important resources, such as graphic and extra-linguistic modes of expressions. These can be particularly useful both for teachers in designing effective tasks and for students in learning algebra.

   Thus, the construction of meaning in mathematical activities is based on a rich interplay between three different types of semiotic sets: speech, gestures and written representations (Arzarello 2006). In this respect, Radford (2005) underlines that the understanding of the relationship between body, actions carried out through artifacts (objects, technological tools, etc.), and linguistic and symbolic activity is essential in order to understand human cognition in general, and mathematical thinking in particular.

   The design and use of tasks for pedagogic purposes is at the core of mathematics education (Artigue and Perrin-Glorian 1991). Tasks generate activities, which afford opportunity to encounter mathematical concepts, ideas, strategies, and also to use and develop mathematical thinking. Following Mason and Johnston-Wilder's idea (2006), I mean by "task", what students are asked to do.

   To understand how tasks are linked to one others in order to support teaching, it is important to understand the nature of the transformation of knowledge from implicit knowledge-in-action (see Vergnaud 1982) to knowledge which is formulated, formalized, memorized, related to cultural knowledge, and so on. This work is often undertaken by using a textbook and/or other resources designed by outsiders. I will show how *AlNuSet* provides teachers with a new and innovative environment to design tasks, which also support inclusive education.

   Therefore, it is my belief that to make algebraic notions explicit, ensuring that students grasp the meaning of the algebraic notions used, teachers need artifacts, which make available new semiotic representations of the algebraic objects. For this reason, I will examine the software AlNuSet and analyse its potential in designing

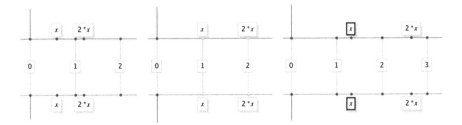

Fig. 1 The algebraic expressions containing x move accordingly with x

activities that take into account students' difficulties in algebra, as described in the literature, and, at the same time, that are aimed at engaging all students in the class, as much as possible (Baccaglini-Frank and Robotti 2013). In particular, I report on a case study with a 26 year old DD student, which shows that tasks in AlNuSet can be designed to support the construction of algebraic notions using in particular the visual non-verbal and kinaesthetic channels of access to information.

In the following section I will present a short description of the software.

2   Description of AlNuSet

AlNuSet was developed in the context of the ReMath (IST - 4 - 26751) EC project and it was designed for students of lower and upper secondary school (from age 12–13 to age 16–17). It was developed by the research group of the ITD (Istituto per le Tecnologie Didattiche)- CNR (Centro Nazionale di Ricerca) of Genoa (Italy) to which the author belongs.

AlNuSet is made up of three tightly integrated components: the Algebraic Line, the Symbolic Manipulator, and the Functions component (for more details see www.alnuset.com). Since this paper concerns tasks in which only the first component is used, I will describe only the Algebraic Line component.[1]

The main characteristic of the Algebraic Line component is the possibility of representing an algebraic variable as a mobile point on the line, namely, a point that can be dragged along the line thanks to the mouse. The point can be labelled with a letter (Fig. 1). By dragging the mobile point along the line, the letter associated to the point assumes the values of numerical set instantiated. This new visuo-spatial approach, which exploits dynamic representations, allows making explicit the notion of *variable* as a mobile point on the line that can assume all values within the numerical set instantiated. Therefore, by dragging the mobile point on the line, all algebraic expressions containing such a variable, move accordingly (Fig. 1).

---

[1]For a detailed description of algebraic activities developed within the Manipulator component, which allows the teacher to approach algebraic manipulation in an innovative way, see Robotti and Ferrando (2013).

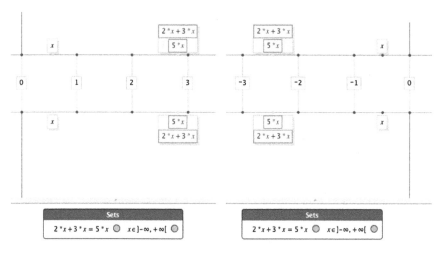

Fig. 2 Variable and expressions on the line. By dragging x along the line, it is possible to verify the equivalence of $2x + 3x$ and $5x$ because they belong to the same post-it for all values of x

This feature has transformed the number line into an algebraic line where it is possible to operate with algebraic expressions and propositions in a quantitative and dynamic way.

This visuo-spatial approach to algebra allows the student to handle dynamic representations as new semiotic representations of algebraic objects on the Algebraic Line. This makes dynamic algebra possible and it supports students in the conceptualization of algebraic objects. The most important new semiotic representations available in the Algebraic Line of AlNuSet that are involved in the tasks presented in this paper are:

- the yellow square named "post-it": two expressions belonging to the same post-it can be connected to the notions of *equation* seen as equivalence between expressions (see Figs. 2 and 3a);
- the colour of the dot associated to a proposition (equality/inequality) and/or to the truth set built by the user (see Figs. 2 and 3a, b): the colour match between the two dots can be used to validate the constructed numerical set as the truth set of the proposition.

In the Algebraic Line it is possible to explore equations, inequalities and systems of equations and of inequalities. Their solution sets are visualized in a specific window, labelled "Sets", and they are associated to a coloured dot: green if the instantiated value of x belongs to the set, red otherwise. This way, dragging the mobile point along the line, the colour of the dot changes depending on the value of x.

Mediation provided by AlNuSet is profoundly different from mediation offered by other software used for the traditional teaching of algebra: new dynamic representations, based on a visuo-spatial approach, offer the possibility of reifying

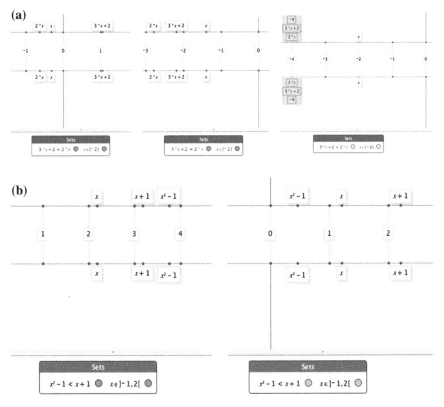

Fig. 3 **a** By dragging x along the line, it is possible to explore the solution of the equation $3x + 2 = 2x$. The truth set of the equation is the value -2. **b** By dragging x along the line, it is possible to explore the solution of the inequality $x^2 - 1 > x + 1$. The truth set of the inequality is $]-1, 2[$

semiotic representations and of constructing meaning for algebraic notions linking the semantic and symbolic nature of algebraic objects.

Several studies (Chaachoua et al. 2012; Chiappini et al. 2010; Robotti 2013; Leung and Bolite-Frant 2015) have shown the educational potential of this software indicating how the new approach described above can be effective in fostering understanding of the basic mathematical concepts (fractions, expressions, equations,…).

3 Developmental Dyscalculia and Algebra

According to Butterworth (2005), Developmental Dyscalculia (DD) is a *learning disability* that affects the acquisition of knowledge about numbers and arithmetic: "DD children have problems with both knowledge of facts and knowledge of arithmetical procedures […], although Temple (1991) has demonstrated, using case studies, that the knowledge of facts and grasp of procedures and strategies are dissociable in the developmental dyscalculia" (Butterworth 2005, p. 459).

Thus, it is known that students with DD have severe difficulties in arithmetic, that is, in the areas of mathematics that depend on quantity (Butterworth 2003).

However, there are also areas of mathematics that do not depend so much on manipulating quantities—algebra, geometry and topology, for example. It may be that students with DD can in fact become proficient in these areas, even though their arithmetic is poor. As a matter of fact, some studies on dyscalculic learners showed that there is a dissociation between the recovery ability of arithmetic facts, which is compromised, and algebraic manipulation, which is intact (Hittmair-Delazer et al. 1995; Dehaene 1997). Dehaene analysed the mathematical performances of dyscalculic subjects: they presented difficulties in simple calculations such as $2 \cdot 3, 7–3, 9:3, 5 \cdot 4$, but they were able to transform and simplify algebraic expressions such as:

$$\frac{a \cdot b}{b \cdot a} = 1$$
$$a \cdot a \cdot a = a^3$$

and they were able to judge the non equivalence between algebraic expressions such as:

$$\frac{d}{c} + a = \frac{d+c}{c+a}$$

These results have been interpreted as evidence for the existence of two independent processing levels of mathematics: a formal-algebraic level and an arithmetic-numeric level (Dehaene 1997). Moreover, neuroimaging results, focusing on the algebraic transformations, have highlighted how the visual-spatial areas of the brain are activated at the expense of language. For example, it has been shown that in solving equations, the expressions are manipulated mentally by means of a visual elaboration rather than of a verbal one (Landy and Goldstone 2010).

Those results help us highlight, from a neuro-scientific perspective, the difficulties of students with DD in algebra. In the next paragraph I will describe the nature of such difficulties from a strictly didactical point of view.

4 Difficulties in Algebra of Students with DD

Research in mathematics education characterizes as semantic difficulties in algebra, the difficulties to give meaning to algebraic notions (Sfard and Linchevsky 1992; Thomas and Tall 2001; Arzarello et al. 1994) among the major difficulties encountered by students. Now, the question is: what about difficulties of students with DD in algebra?

In my research, I have identified some main algebraic difficulties of students with DD (Robotti and Ferrando 2013; Robotti 2013):

- constructing meaning for the algebraic symbols, e.g. giving the correct meaning to the expressions $a \cdot a$ and $2 \cdot a$;
- recovering skills of an arithmetical nature, e.g. recovering number facts, for instance the times tables.

Of course arithmetical difficulties influence algebraic performance, but these are of a different nature. Students with DD could have difficulties in developing and using new skills for the rules of algebraic transformation. Indeed, in general they find it hard to efficiently use long and short term memory. Therefore they have difficulties in memorizing and recovering facts:

- algebraic rules; for example, factorization formulas used to factor algebraic expressions, such as

$$(a+b)(a-b) = a^2 - b^2$$

or the quadratic formula for finding the roots of a quadratic equation,

$$x_{1,2} = \frac{-b \mp \sqrt{\Delta}}{2a}$$

- algebraic facts, such as, $a \cdot a = a^2$.

Once some main algebraic difficulties for students with DD are identified, the question is: How can we didactically intervene in effective ways?

In the following section I present some research results, which allowed me to answer this question.

5 Some Results from Research in Neuroscience, Cognitive Psychology and Mathematics Education

Research in cognitive psychology has identified four basic channels of access to and production of information: the visual-verbal channel (verbal written code), the visual non-verbal channel (visual-spatial code), the auditory channel (verbal oral code), and the kinaesthetic-tactile channel (Mariani 1996).

Italian research has indicated that most students with specific learning difficulties (or disabilities), not only in mathematics, encounter the greatest difficulties in using the visual-verbal channel and this impacts their development for preferring different channels (Stella and Grandi 2011). The importance of these different channels of access to and production of information shifts the focus from simply "being able or not" to solve a certain task, to different paths and strategies adopted by the individual (whether successful or not) for approaching the task. This allows to explain mathematical difficulties not only in terms of "lacking abilities" but also in terms of necessity to use certain preferred modalities that lead the student to access, elaborate and/or produce information in a certain way.

Moreover, various studies in cognitive science point to a correlation between mathematical achievement, working memory (Raghubar et al. 2010; Mammarella et al. 2010, 2013; Szucs et al. 2013), and non verbal intelligence (DeThorne and Schaefer 2004; Szucs et al. 2013). These findings suggest that non-verbal intelligence may partially depend on spatial skills (Rourke and Conway 1997) and these can be potentially important in mathematical achievement, where explicit or implicit visualization is required.

My colleagues and I (e.g. Robotti and Baccaglini-Frank 2016) have found other theoretical stances advanced in mathematics education that are in line with the idea that means of access to and production of information, different from the visual-verbal one, can be very important in learning. Some studies in this domain have stressed the important role of bodily actions, gestures, language and the use of technological artifacts in students' elaborations of mathematics (Arzarello 2006; Nemirovsky 2003; Núñez 2000) and, in particular, of algebra (Arzarello and Robutti 2001). According to Arzarello's notion of *semiotic bundle* (2006) the construction of meaning in mathematical activities, is based on a rich interplay among three different types of semiotic sets: speech, gestures and written representations (from sketches and diagrams to mathematical symbols). These constitute a semiotic bundle, which dynamically evolves over time.

Thus, important research questions, developed in math education, are related to our understanding of the relationship between body, actions carried out through artifacts (objects, technological tools, etc.), and linguistic and symbolic activity (Radford 2005).

According to Radford, research on the epistemological relationship between these three main sources of knowledge formation is essential in order to understand human cognition and mathematical thinking, in particular. For this reason, he underlines, from a semiotic point of view, the importance of revisiting cognition in such a way that leads to thinking of cognitive activity as something that is not confined to mental activity alone.

Arzarello (2006) refers also to the discoveries in neuropsychology underlining aspects of cognition. His aim is to put semiotic representations in relation with mental ones, in mathematics. He remarks (2006) that a major result of neuroscience is that "conceptual knowledge is embodied, that is, it is mapped within the sensory-motor system" (Gallese and Lakoff 2005, p. 456). The sensory-motor system of the brain is multimodal. This means that imagining and doing use a shared neural substrate. Moreover, "sensory modalities like vision, touch, hearing, and so on are actually integrated with each other and with motor control and planning" (Gallese and Lakoff 2005, p. 456).

Thus, the paradigm of multimodality seems to be crucial in order to alleviate the difficulties of students with DD in maths: "the understanding of a mathematical concept, rather than having a definitional essence, spans diverse perceptuo-activities, which become more or less active depending on the context. [...]. Learning a different approach for what appears to be the "same" idea, far from being redundant, often calls for recruiting entirely different perceptuo-motor resources." (Nemirovsky 2003, p. 108).

A consequence of this approach is that "not only the usual transformations and conversions (in the sense of Duval) from one register to the other must be considered as the basic producers of the mathematical knowledge. Its essence consists, rather, of the multimodal interactions among the different registers within a unique integrated system, composed of different modalities: gestures, oral and written language, symbols, and so on (Arzarello and Edwards 2005; Robutti 2005). Also the symbolic function of signs is absorbed within such a picture." (Arzarello 2006, p. 284).

According to these considerations, the design of tasks is essential as the context in which students are asked to work. In this sense I consider AlNuSet an effective context to foster understanding of algebraic concepts both for students with difficulties and for students with dyscalculia.

In addition to the standard semiotic resources used by students and teachers in teaching and learning algebra (e.g. written symbols and speech), other important resources are considered in the case study which I will treat. In particular, dynamic representations available in AlnuSet (such as the point which can be dragged along the line), symbols (such as the post-it or the coloured dots), and, more generally, extra-linguistic modes of expressions, which turned out to be particularly useful for the student with DD involved in a recent case study.

According to these premises, in the following section I will try to give some suggestions for answering the question "How can we didactically intervene in effective way?"

6 How the Functionalities of AlNuSeT Allow Designing Tasks to Construct Algebraic Meanings

I discuss here if and how this new approach to the meaning of algebraic notions in AlNuSet, can be effective for students with dyscalculia. In particular, I will present how a student with DD was able to make sense of the notions of *unknown* of an equation, and of *variable* of an algebraic expression, exploiting the functionalities of the Algebraic Line.

I refer to task as "what students are asked to do" (Mason and Johnston-Wilder 2006), and I expect the activity to be carried out in AlNuSet, so I am speaking of tasks expressed verbally that are designed to be effective with respect to specific didactical objectives. In this sense, the tasks are designed considering AlNuSet as a tool that allows and favors a multimodal approach to algebra.

The subject of this case study is Eleonora, a student with severe dyscalculia. The case is particularly interesting because, although she had taken algebra in high school (she is 27 years old), she had not been able to construct any (apparent) meaning for the various algebraic notions she had encountered and she was not able to use algebra when solving problems. I will show how the perceptive and dynamic approach, together with the visual non-verbal representations, offered in the Algebraic Line of AlNuSet, were effective in helping Eleonora grasp the desired concepts.

6.1 Methodology

I met Eleonora as a working university student, in 2014, when she was 27 years old. She had obtained her first diagnosis of dyscalculia the year before. Eleonora attended the fourth year of a 5-year undergraduate degree for becoming a primary school teacher. She claimed to have always had a bad relationship with mathematics. Indeed the word "mathematics" immediately created in her a state of anxiety and low self-esteem. She had difficulties in calculating the results of simple arithmetic operations; she found it hard to construct algebraic models and to recall algebraic processes for solving equations (even linear equations) or algebraic facts (for example that $a \cdot a = a^2$).

The experimental activities I proposed to Eleonora were structured in two moments: a pre-test to explore the meanings Eleonora initially attributed to the algebraic notions that would be treated, and, then, the sequences of tasks in AlNuSet. These activities were carried out outside of the customary university lectures, as additional hours in a quiet setting where I was alone with Eleonora, who willingly took part in the study.

During the AlNuSet tasks the researcher (the author) would guide Eleonora in using the software through additional questions.

Each session lasted about one hour and a half and it was video recorded. We worked through three sessions: the pre-test session, and two subsequent sessions using the Algebraic Line of Alnuset.

In the following sections I will analyse Eleonora's performance throughout main moments of each session.

6.2 Pre-test

A pre-test was presented to Eleonora in order to investigate the meaning she attributed to the notions of variable and of expression containing that variable, of unknown and of equation. The tasks *(Tn)* and Eleonora's written answers are in italics; they are followed by a brief analysis in regular font.

(T1) What does the letter "a" represent in the expression " $2 \cdot a$ "?
E: "a" denotes any number which is, here, in relation, through an arithmetic operation, with 2. It [a] can take on any value.

Fig. 4 Eleonora's attempt at solving T2

Note that *"a"* denotes "any number" but no reference is given to the numerical set of reference. Moreover, Eleonora does seem to attribute to the expression $2 \cdot a$ the meaning of a symbolic representation of the arithmetic operation of multiplication but it seems, again, unrelated to a number set (in this case, the set of even numbers): Eleonora seems to think that varying the value of a, the expression 2a could take on any value, not just those of even numbers. In other words, the algebraic expression 2a seems to be, for Eleonora, a relation between a fixed number (2) and a variable (*a*), but it does not seem to be a value that depends on *a*.

(T2) 3 times a certain natural number is equal to 11. Find the number.
E: No, it isn't possible.

[She draws three dots and, at the same time, she says: "This one, plus this one, plus this one...". See the right side of Fig. 4]

The multiplication is interpreted as repeated addition and the equality is solved using an arithmetic pattern.

E: No, it [12] isn't possible [she means that 12 is not the right number] *but, it is possible with a fraction ...*

She writes: $\frac{11}{3}$; $3 \cdot \frac{11}{3}$; 366,666,666,667 (Fig. 4) using trial and error and a calculator to look for a number that multiplied by 3 can give 11. Notice that no equation $[3 \cdot x = 11]$ is used to represent and solve the situation. She only refers to arithmetical expressions: $\frac{11}{3}$ is the number, and $3 \cdot \frac{11}{3}$ corresponds to the arithmetic verification of the fact that she found the number such that 3 times it needs to be 11. Thus, one dot corresponds to 366,666,666,667 [note that 366,666,666,667 is written on one of the circled dots and it refers to a dot] but 3 times 366,666,666,667 is not 11 [she uses the calculator]. She says: "It *is nearly 11*...". It seems that $\frac{11}{3}$ cannot be considered the number she was looking for. This might be a misconception Eleonora holds relative to rational numbers, according to which they are not considered "numbers" unless they are transformed into decimal form (e.g. Fandiño Pinilla 2005).

(T3) When 3 is added to 3 times a certain number, the sum is 28; find the number.

As before, Eleonora is oriented towards computation and not towards the use of algebra (Fig. 5), so she subtracts 3 from 28 (obtaining 25) and then she divides by 3—"undoing" the operations stated in the text of the problem. She writes that the number 25/3 plus 3 is equal to 28. Once again, she uses a trial and error strategy

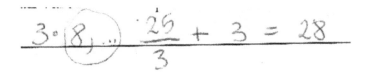

Fig. 5 Eleonora's answer to T3

looking for the number (8, …) that, multiplied by 3 and added to 3, gives 28. Once again, she does not seem to accept $\frac{25}{5}$ as a number. She does not seem to feel the need to use algebra; she does not see algebra as a tool for representing and solving a situation and this appears quite clearly from Eleonora's use of the equal sign (Fig. 5).

This paragraph should give a general idea of the meaning attributed by Eleonora to algebra, to the notion of variable, of unknown, of equation and of solution of an equation. Through this preliminary assessment I was able to determine that Eleonora, very likely, had not constructed proper meanings for the algebraic notions involved, even though she had constructed some meaning for the notion of variable, but one that was not useful for working with algebraic expressions.

In the next paragraph, I will describe the interventions and tasks in the working sessions that were based on the "little" Eleonora seemed to know. I will analyse how the meanings of expression depending on a variable, unknown, equation and solution of equation, are constructed by Eleonora working with the Algebraic Line of AlNuSet. Therefore, I will include excerpts from the dialogue between the researcher and Eleonora.

6.3 Tasks to Construct the Meaning of the Notion of Variable and of Algebraic Expression Depending on that Variable

As described above, in these working sessions Eleonora used the Algebraic Line in AlNuSet. The researcher designed tasks favouring a perceptive approach, which seems to be one of the most effective approaches to helping students with DD build mathematical notions. I did this exploiting the dynamic functionalities of the Algebraic Line in AlNuSet. I started by asking Eleonora to insert, in the Algebraic line of AlNuSet, the letter "a" and to drag the corresponding point along the line.

E: At this moment, we can see that "a" changes value,… it changes value if I drag it. We can see that, when I drag "a", when I drag the corresponding point to "a" along the line, it takes on all values of the numerical set. As we can see, the values can be positive or negative [she drags the point along the positive and along the negative parts of the number line].

The yellow square shows the value that the letter takes on. It is very useful to not "get lost" along the line.

The point corresponding to "a" is dragged along the line. Eleonora observes, in a very spontaneous way, that the point can take on different values in the instantiated numerical set. She states that the yellow square (post-it) plays a role in supporting her memory and in orienting her dragging of the point corresponding to *a* along the number line. We can see this as a new sign that allows Eleonora, by means of visual perception, to build an image for the equivalence between the letter "a" (label), the point on the line, and the values associated to that point on it. The post-it and the mobile point are new available signs in AlNuSet that help Eleonora construct meaning for the notion of variable as a symbol representing *any* quantity in the instantiated numerical domain. In other words, the notion of variable seems to get mapped within the sensory-motor system mediated by the task that exploits the functionalities of AlNuSet. In this sense, understanding of the mathematical concept of variable seems to be fostered, rather than through a definition, through perceptuo-motor activities, implemented within AlNuSet.

The most significant feature of AlNuSet in this activity seemed to be the dragging of the point: indeed the dynamicity allowed Eleonora to carry out actions producing images on the screen linked to visual verbal (the label "2a"), visual non-verbal (the mobile point, the post-it...) and symbolic representations, that were useful for constructing the meaning of variable. The multimodal interactions between the different registers within a unique integrated system made up of different modalities is clear: the gesture (point dragging along the line) and the symbols that make explicit the symbolic function of the signs (post-it, point on the line).

The researcher's aim is now to introduce the dependence of the variable on the numerical set in which it is instantiated. What the researcher asks to do in AlNuSet is still tied to the perception, to the dynamic images and to the manipulation through the mouse.

R: Now, select the Set of Natural numbers. What happens? Why?
E: we can see that now we are able to visualize only numbers on the right side of the number line [Fig. 6], because...because the negative numbers are not present in the Natural numbers! If I drag "a" along the line, I observe that I cannot go on the left side of the line. I observe that "a" takes on integer values; but now it cannot take on values between two natural numbers.[...] The point jumps from one natural value to another. Moreover, we can observe that, even if I forget that I'm working in the set of the Natural numbers, AlNuSet's interface reminds me of it.

Two main considerations can be drawn. Firstly, Eleonora seems to be associating an image to the fact that the set of Natural numbers is not "dense". As a matter of fact, she observes that the point corresponding to "a" "jumps" along the line. This is perceptually evident comparing the movement of the point in the Natural numbers with that in the Full Domain. This visual perception of the movement of the point along the line (Fig. 6), allows Eleonora to construct a new meaning for the structure of the set of Natural numbers. Secondly, AlNuSet seems to be perceived

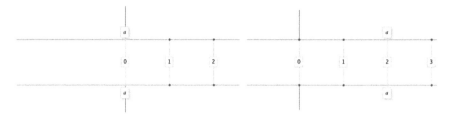

Fig. 6 Different positions of the point labelled "a"; one shows where it takes on the value 0, and the other where it takes on the value 2

as a compensatory tool for Eleonora's memory: *"even if I forget that I'm working in the set of the Natural numbers, AlNuSet's interface reminds me of it"*. This leads to a more "relaxed" approach to the mathematical task and it allows Eleonora to focus on the algebraic task rather than on recalling information that she finds difficult to retrieve.

R: In maths, this "a" is called "variable". So, what is, in your opinion, a variable? In other words, how could you explain to a student the meaning of variable?
E: Variable indicates any value in the numerical set considered.

For Eleonora "variable" seems to denote the mathematical object "number", in a specific numerical set. So, to grasp the meaning of variable, Eleonora mainly uses a visual and perceptual approach (visual-non verbal and kinaesthetic channels to access and elaborate the information) but, in order to explain the meaning of variable, she does not refer explicitly to visual signs such as "mobile point" or "post-it". Once the notion of variable is introduced, the researcher introduces the expression depending on that variable.

R: Now, edit $2 \cdot a$ on the editing bar and press the "enter" button. What happens?
E: It appears on the line. So... what value can we give? [she drags the point corresponding to "a" along the line]. *If I give to "a" the value −1... 2a will be... will be −2, yes, of course!*

We can observe that, in addition to the answer *"it [$2 \cdot a$] appears on the line"*, Eleonora performs actions on the expression "$2 \cdot a$" dragging "a" along the line. This is a realization of the meaning of expression depending on a variable: Eleonora shows that, when the "a" *varies* (that is to say, when the corresponding point is dragged along the line), then the value of the expression "$2 \cdot a$" *varies* accordingly.

R: Ok, so, what does the letter "a" represent in the expression "$2 \cdot a$"?
E: a ... variable? Yes, "a" is a variable! And... $2 \cdot a$,... takes on values, takes on values depending on "a".

Note that Eleonora uses the algebraic term "variable" to refer to "a". She explains the dependence of the expression "$2 \cdot a$" on "a" stressing that the values taken on by "$2 \cdot a$" are dependent on those taken on by "a". So here we see the expression not interpreted exclusively as a symbolic representation of the arithmetic operation (multiplication), as in the pre-test. This answer suggests that Eleonora has constructed a new meaning of variable and she uses it to construct the meaning for expression depending on that variable.

6.4 Tasks to Construct the Meaning of the Unknown Involved in Equation

The researcher's aim is now to construct meaning for the notion of *identity* and *conditioned equality* (equation). To this aim, it is necessary to first construct the meaning of unknown involved in equation.

R: For which value of "a" is the expression 2 · a equal to 8?
E: The expression is equal to 8... that is 2a is equal to 8... If I move "a" along the line, I am looking for the right value to match to the letter. For example, I discovered that if I place "a" on 3 ...if I give to "a" the value 3... 2 · a is [equal to] 6; Instead, if I put "a" on 4, 2 · a is 8...

Dragging the corresponding point to "a" along the line, Eleonora observes that there is only one value of "a" for which the point corresponding to the expression takes on the value 8 (Fig. 7a, b). This dynamic representation contributes to building new meaning for the equal sign between the expressions as *conditioned equality*. Indeed, when Eleonora tries to verify the equality between 2a and 8, the dragging of "a" is performed with a specific aim: to ensure that the expression is associated to the point 8 on the line and it belongs to the same post-it as 8. If dragging is accomplished with this aim, then the meaning of variable can be that of *unknown*, and the action associated to it is searching for a value to be assigned to "a" *so that* the equality is true.

Notice that the expression "If I place "a" on 3...", which refers to the perceptive approach to solving the equation is reformulated as "if I give to "a" the value 3...", which, instead, refers to the mathematical meaning of solving the equation (finding the value of the unknown that makes the equation true). This awareness is also present in the following exchanges. This shows how the sensory-motor system,

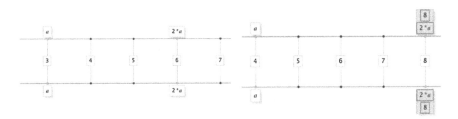

Fig. 7 a "a" takes on value 3, so that 2 · a takes on value 6. **b** "a" takes on value 4, so that 2 · a takes on value 8

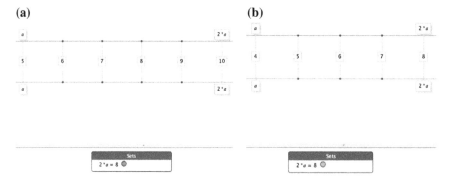

Fig. 8 *a* The *red dot* associated to the equation means that the value of "a" is not a truth-value.
b The *green dot* associated to the equation means that the value of "a" is a truth-value

which acts through the perceptive approach, can contribute to the construction of mathematical knowledge also in presence of dyscalculia.

R: Ok, now insert $2 \cdot a = 8$ *into the edit bar and then, push "enter". What do you get?*
E: A verification …It's a check, if I drag "a", the red dot shows that I'm making a mistake. Because, in this moment, 2a equals 8 is not true [see Fig. 8a]. There isn't equality. Because it's 2a equal to 10, if I give to "a" the value 5. But, if I give to "a" [the value] 4, the green dot shows that it is right [Fig. 8b], because 2a is 8. So, I found the value of "a" which allows me to say that this equality is true. Yes, because I'm multiplying.

The coloured dot next to the equation is interpreted as a visual aid to validate the truth of the equation. Moreover, we can observe how the colour of the dot supports reaching the appropriated mathematical interpretations: verbal expressions referring to the truth of the equation evolve from perceptual (linked to signs) to formal expressions (referred to maths object). For example, "..the red dot shows that I make a mistake" becomes "…the red dot shows that there isn't equality", or "the green dot shows that it is right" becomes "the green dot shows that this equality is true".

Here it is evident that for Eleonora the equality is conditioned by the values of "a" but the stronger meaning for the equal sign is still "give a numerical result" rather than showing a "relation" (probably due to the fact that the second term of the equality is a number). Indeed Eleonora uses the term "multiplying".

This is why I chose to now propose a task addressing this misconception. The task fosters both the construction of the idea that the equality between two expressions is conditioned by the value of unknown and that the equal sign denotes a relation between the expressions.

R: Now, edit the expressions: $2 \cdot a + 3$; $2 \cdot a + 3 \cdot a$; $5 \cdot a$. *Insert them into the Algebraic Line and drag "a" along the line. What happens?*

E: [after editing, without dragging] 5 · *a automatically goes on 5* [the last position of "a" was on the point 1] *and this is written in the yellow square:* 2 · *a* + 3; 2 · *a* + 3 · *a; and* 5 · *a are all together* [they belong to the same post-it] *and they refer to the same value 5. But, for example, if "a" is 2* [she drags the mobile point along the line] *then* 2 · *a* + 3 *is 7 and the others are 10...*

Dragging "a" along the line Eleonora explores what happens to the expressions 2 · *a* + 3; 2 · *a* + 3 · *a;* 5 · *a.* She knows that the expressions depend on the values of "a" (that is, they move because of the movement of "a"), but this exploration allows her to make sense of the *existential quantifier* and the *universal quantifier.* Indeed, dragging point "a" along the line, Eleonora observes that there is only one value of the "a" for which the points of the expressions 2 · *a* + 3 and 5 · *a* take on the same value, that is to say, they correspond to the same value on the line. This dynamic representation contributes to building meaning for the equal sign between the expressions, guiding its interpretation as a conditioned equality. Indeed, she tries to verify the equality between the two expressions dragging "a" with a specific aim: to ensure that the two expressions take on equal values, that is, they are associated to the same point on the line and they belong to the same post-it. This fosters construction of a new meaning for the *existential quantifier* (∃).

In Fig. 9, two moments corresponding to dragging "a" along the line are represented (Fig. 9a, b). The expressions 2a + 3 and 5a refer to the same point, corresponding to the value 5, and they belong to the same post-it, only for a = 1. Since the expressions are equal, the equality is true and the dot associated to the equation is green.

A specific command allows the student to construct and visualize the truth set associated to the equality (Fig. 9). Moreover, a coloured dot is associated to that set: the red (Fig. 9a)/green (Fig. 9b) colour means that the current value of the unknown is/is not an element of the constructed set. So the fact that the colour of the dots

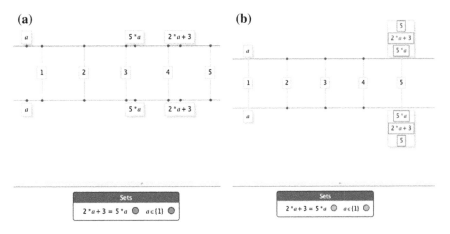

Fig. 9 a The expressions do not refer to the same point on the line. Thus, the equation is not true. **b** The expressions refer to the same point on the line. Thus, the equation is true for a = 1

matches/does not match during the dragging of "a" along the line is a visual representation that allows Eleonora to:

- construct the meaning for truth set for equality, as the set of the values making the equality true,
- check the correctness of the truth set.

Note that usually teachers replace truth-values in the equality with letters in order to make the equivalence explicit (passing through a calculation that forces the equal sign to be seen as a "result" rather than a "relation"). This kind of approach does not seem to be very effective for Eleonora. On the contrary, the dynamic representations of the Algebraic Line of AlNuSet allow Eleonora to elaborate the meaning of "=" found between the expressions as a conditioned equality. This suggests that the visuo-spatial approach rather than a computational or verbal one, can be very effective in helping some students with DD.

6.5 Tasks to Construct the Meaning of the Identity in AlNuSet

The following figure (Fig. 10) shows two moments when a is in different positions.

By dragging "a" along the line it is possible to verify that the expressions 2a + 3a and 5a refer, for all values of "a", to the same point on the line and they belong to the same post-it (Fig. 10). The equality is verified for all values of "a", hence it is an *identity*. This is highlighted by the green colour of the dot associated to the equation 2a + 3a = 5a and by the matching of the colour between

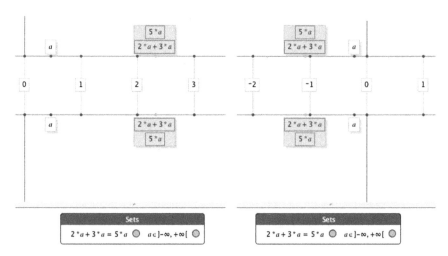

Fig. 10 By dragging *a* along the line, it is possible to verify the equivalence between 2a + 3a and 5a because they belong to the same post-it for all values of *a*

the dot associated to the equation and that associated to the truth set of the equation. Thus, a new meaning for *universal quantifier* (∀) can be constructed through the dragging of "a".

E: 5 · a is inside 2 · a + 3 · a [referring to the same point] and they belong to the same post-it. This means that they can have the same value.
R: Sometimes, always?
E: Always! If I drag "a", they move correspondingly! But...Why don't we have the window with the dot?
R: Because we haven't typed an...
E: yes! We haven't typed the equality!!

Eleonora edits $5 · a = 2 · a + 3 · a$ on the edit bar of AlNuSet and presses the "enter" button.

E: et voilà, so, we can see that, dragging "a" along the line, the expressions belong to the same post-it... they belong always to the same post-it!

The meaning of *universal quantifier* is perceived by means of the "post-it" sign. This sign belongs to the new set of signs introduced by AlNuSet. The post-it can be related to the mathematical meaning expressed by different signs (e.g. the verbal sign "*for every*" associated to a visual sign, ∀). This last connection, between mathematical meanings and different signs, is only partially accomplished because the researcher did not introduce the sign "∀". The same applies to the *existential quantifier*. Here, the "post-it" sign is related to the meaning of "equivalence" between the expressions belonging to it. So the equal sign ("=") can be associated to the meaning of "relation" rather than of "result" of the arithmetical operation. Note that here two different signs (the "post-it" and the "=" sign), referring to different semiotic sets of signs, are related by means of dragging "a" along the line. This allows to construct a new meaning of universal quantifier (and existential quantifier in the previous task). Once again, the sensory-motor system allowed Eleonora to construct meanings for the mathematical objects. In other words, the meaning of *universal* and *existential* quantifiers are built exploiting the perceptive and visuo-spatial approach available in the Algebraic Line.

7   Conclusion

The standard teaching approach to algebra leads to finding, within the algebraic formalism, the meanings of algebraic notions: for instance, the manipulation of an equation allows to finding values that, replaced in the initial equality, make it true; thus, the meaning of the solutions of equation is found in the algebraic manipulation itself. As I tried to show, this does not seem to be an affective approach to algebra for Eleonora, a student with dyscalculia, whose case I discussed as I have found it to be representative of many students with DD that I have worked with or read about in other studies. Referring to studies in mathematics education and neuro-science, I discussed how a perceptual and dynamic approach can be used to effectively construct mathematical knowledge in the case of students with DD. This can be done with the software AlNuSet, designed for teaching dynamic algebra.

In this chapter I considered the Algebraic Line in AlNuSet and I discussed how its possibilities in terms of representation allowed me to design a sequence of verbal tasks that helped a student grasp new meanings of the algebraic notions involved in the solution of the equations and identities. AlNuSet seems to provide a context, in which it is possible to design mathematical tasks that activate particular perceptual-motor activities, as discussed in Nemirovsky, that foster understanding of the algebraic notions involved. Thus, in addition to the standard semiotic representations and registers, (e.g. written symbols, graphs, speech…), there are other important digital resources that can be exploited to design tasks that effectively promote algebraic learning. In particular, the dynamic representations available in AlnuSet (such as the mobile point dragged along the line), symbols (such as the post-it or the coloured dots), and, more in general, extra-linguistic modes of expressions, seem to be particularly appropriate for addressing certain algebraic notions, such as the one analysed.

In conclusion, the new dynamic representations available in the Algebraic Line of AlNuSet allow teachers to design tasks that support the construction of algebraic notions using the visual non-verbal and kinaesthetic channels of access to information. It seems that the dynamicity, expressed by the point dragging along the line, and the correlated representations (post-it, coloured dots, mobile point, truth set,…) are the key functions that allow the student to:

- construct algebraic meanings (for the notions of variable, unknown, solution of equation, truth set of an equation) and algebraic relations among expressions (for example, the equal sign as a relation rather than as a result indicator);
- support fact retrieval from memory when solving algebraic tasks (for example, recalling numerical sets of reference or the rules and the axioms to manipulate algebraic expressions).

These are core aspects of some ongoing and future studies.

References

Artigue, M., & Perrin-Glorian, M. J. (1991). Didactic engineering, research and development tool: some theoretical problems linked to this duality. *For the learning of Mathematics, 11*(1), 13–17.

Arzarello, F. (2006). Semiosis as a multimodal process. *Relime, Revista latinoamericana de investigación en matemática educativa, 9*(1), 267–299.

Arzarello, F., & Edwards, L. (2005). Gesture and the construction of mathematical meaning (research forum 2). In *Proceedings of 29th Conference of the International Group for the Psychology of Mathematics Education* (Vol. 1, pp. 122–145). Melbourne, AU: PME.

Arzarello, F., & Robutti, O. (2001). From body motion to algebra through graphing. In H. Chick, K. Stacey, J. Vincent, & J. Vincent (Eds.), *Proceedings of the 12th ICMI Study Conference* (Vol. 1, pp. 33–40). Australia: The University of Melbourne.

Arzarello, F., Bazzini, L., & Chiappini, G. P. (1994). Intensional semantics as a tool to analyse algebraic thinking. *Rendiconti del Seminario Matematico dell'Università di Torino, 52*(1), 105–125.

Baccaglini-Frank, A., & Robotti, E. (2013). Gestire gli studenti con DSA in classe: alcuni elementi di un quadro commune. In *Convegno Grimed 18 "Per piacere voglio contare-difficoltà, disturbi di apprendimento e didattica della matematica"*, Padova, (pp. 75–86).

Butterworth, B. (2003). *Dyscalculia screening*. London, Uk: nferNelson Publishing Company Limited. (ISBN: 0 7087 0366 6).

Butterworth, B. (2005). Developmental Dyscalculia. In *Handbook of mathematical cognition* (pp. 455–467). Hove, UK: Psychology Press.

Chiappini, G., Robotti, E., & Trgalova, J. (2010). Role of an artifact of dynamic algebra in the conceptualization of the algebraic equality. In *Proceedings of CERME 6, Lyon, France* (pp. 619–628). www.inrp.fr/editions/cerme6.

Chaachoua, H., Chiappini, G., Croset, M. C., Pedemonte, B., & Robotti, E., (2012). Introduction de nouvelles rerpésentations dans deux environnements pour l'apprentissage de l'algèbre. *Recherche en Didactique des mathématiques*, 253–281.

Dehaene, S. (1997). *The number sense: How the mind creates mathematics*. New York, Oxford Unicersity Press.

DeThorne, L. S., & Schaefer, B. A. (2004). A guide to child nonverbal IQ measures. *American Journal of Speech-Language Pathology, 13*(4), 275–290.

Fandiño Pinilla, M. I. (2005). *Le frazioni, aspetti concettuali e didattici*. Bologna: Pitagora Editrice.

Gallese, V., & Lakoff, G. (2005). The brain's concepts: The role of the sensory-motor system in conceptual knowledge. *Cognitive Neuropsychology, 22*(3/4), 455–479.

Hittmair-Delazer, M., Sailer, U., & Benke, T. (1995). Impaired Arithmetic Facts But Intact Conceptual Knowledge a Single—Case Study of Dyscalculia. *Cortex, 31*(1), 139–147.

Kieran, C. (2006). Research on the learning and teaching of algebra. In G. Gutierrez, & P. Boero (Eds.), *Handbook of Research on the Psychology of Mathematics Education. Past, Present and Future* (pp. 11–49). Rotterdam, Taipei: Sense Publishers.

Landy, D., & Goldstone, R. L. (2010). Proximity and precedence in arithmetic. *The Quarterly Journal of Experimental Psychology (Colchester), 63*, 1953–1968.

Leung, A., & Bolite-Frant, J. (2015). Designing mathematics tasks: The role of tools. In A. Watson & M. Ohtani (Eds.), *Task design in mathematics education: The 22nd ICMI study (new ICMI study series)* (pp. 191–225). New York: Springer.

Mammarella, I. C., Giofrè, D., Ferrara, R., & Cornoldi, C. (2013). Intuitive geometry and visuospatial working memory in children showing symptoms of nonverbal learning disabilities. *Child Neuropsychology, 19*(3), 235–249.

Mammarella, I. C., Lucangeli, D., & Carnoldi, C. (2010). Spatial working memory and arithmetic deficits in children with non verbal learning difficulties. *Journal of Learning Disability, 43*, 455–468.

Mariani, L. (1996). Investigating learning styles, perspectives. *Journal of TESOL-Italy, XXI, 2/ XXII, 1*, (pp. 35–49). Spring.

Mason, J., & Johnston-Wilder, S. (2006). *Designing and using mathematical tasks*. Tarquin.

Nemirovsky, R. (2003). Three conjectures concerning the relationship between body activity and understanding mathematics. In N. A. Pateman, B. J. Dougherty, & J. T. Zilliox (Eds.), *Proceedings 27th Conference of the International Group for the Psychology of Mathematics Education* (Vol. 1, pp. 103–135). Honolulu, Hawaii: PME. C. K. Ogden, & I. A. Richards (1923).

Núñez, R. (2000). Mathematical idea analysis: What embodied cognitive science can say about the human nature of mathematics. In XXX (Eds.), *Proceedings of the 24 PME Conference* (Vol. 1, pp. 3–22). Japan: Hiroshima University.

Radford, L. (2005). Body, tool, and symbol: semiotic reflections on cognition. In E. Simmt, & B. Davis (Eds.), *Proceedings of the 2004 Annual Meeting of the Canadian Mathematics Education Study Group* (pp. 111–117). Toronto, Canada.

Raghubar, K. P., Barnes, M. A., & Hecht, S. A. (2010). Working memory and mathematics: A review of developmental, individual difference, and cognitive approaches. *Learning and individual differences, 20*(2), 110–122.

Robotti, E. (2013). Dynamic representations for algebraic objects available in AlNuSet: How develop meanings of the notions involved in the equation solution. In C. Margolinas (Ed.), *Task design in mathematics education: Proceedings of ICMI study 22* (pp. 99–108). UK: Oxford.

Robotti, E., & Baccaglini-Frank, A. (2016). Using digital environments to address students' mathematical learning difficulties. In E. Faggiano, F. Ferrara, & A. Montone (Eds.), *Innovation and technology enhancing mathematics education. Perspectives in the digital era.* Springer Publisher (accepted).

Robotti, E., & Ferrando, E. (2013). Difficulties in algebra: new educational approach by AlNuSet. In E. Faggiano, & A. Montone (Eds.), *Proceedings of ICTMT11*, 250–25. Italy: ICTMT.

Robutti, O. (2005). Hearing gestures in modelling activities with the use of technology. In F. Olivero, & R. Sutherland (Eds.), *Proceedings of the 7th international conference on technology in mathematics teaching* (pp. 252–261). University of Bristol.

Rourke, B. P., & Conway, J. A. (1997). Disabilities of arithmetic and mathematical reasoning perspectives from neurology and neuropsychology. *Journal of Learning disabilities, 30*(1), 34–46.

Sfard, A., & Linchevsky, L. (1992). Equations and inequalities: Processes without objects? In W. Goeslin, K. Graham (Ed.), *Proceedings PME XVI, Durham, NH* (Vol. 3, p. 136).

Stella, G., & Grandi, L. (2011). *Conoscere la dislessia e i DSA.* Giunti Editore.

Szucs, D., Devine, A., Soltesz, F., Nobes, A., & Gabriel, F. (2013). Developmental dyscalculia is related to visuo-spatial memory and inhibition impairment. *Cortex, 49*(10), 2674–2688.

Temple, C. M. (1991). Procedural dyscalculia and number fact dyscalculia: Double dissociation in developmental dyscalculia. *Cognitive Neuropsychology, 8*, 155–176.

Thomas, M. O. J., & Tall, D. O. (2001). The long-term cognitive development of symbolic algebra. In H. Chick, K. Stacey, J. Vincent & J. T. Zilliox (Ed.), *International Congress of Mathematical Instruction (ICMI) Working Group Proceedings—the future of the teaching and learning of algebra, Melbourne* (Vol. 2, pp. 590–597).

Vergnaud, G. (1982). A classification of cognitive tasks and operations of thought involved in addition and subtraction problems. *Addition and subtraction: A cognitive perspective*, 39–59.

What Can You Infer from This Example? Applications of Online, Rich-Media Tasks for Enhancing Pre-service Teachers' Knowledge of the Roles of Examples in Proving

Orly Buchbinder, Iris Zodik, Gila Ron and Alice L.J. Cook

Abstract There is a consensus among mathematics educators that in order to provide students with rich learning opportunities to engage with reasoning and proving, prospective teachers must develop a strong knowledge base of mathematics, pedagogy and student epistemology. In this chapter we report on the design of a technology-based task "What can you infer from this example?" that addressed the content and pedagogical knowledge of the status of examples in proving of pre-service teachers (PSTs). The task, originally designed and implemented with high-school students, was modified for PSTs and expanded to involve multiple components, including scenarios of non-descript cartoon characters to represent student data. The task was administered through Lesson*Sketch*, an online interactive digital platform, to 4 cohorts of PSTs in Israel and the US, across 4 semesters. In this chapter we focus on theoretical and empirical considerations that guided our task design to provide rich learning opportunities for PSTs to enhance their content and pedagogical knowledge of the interplay between examples and proving, and address some of the challenges involved in the task implementation. We discuss the crucial role of technology in supporting PST learning and provide an emergent framework for developing instructional tasks that foster PSTs' engagement with proving.

The erratum of this chapter can be found at under DOI 10.1007/978-3-319-43423-0_17

O. Buchbinder (✉)
University on New Hampshire, Durham, NH, USA
e-mail: orlybuchbinder@gmail.com

I. Zodik · G. Ron
Technion, Israel Institute of Technology, Haifa, Israel

G. Ron
Ohalo College, Katzrin, Israel

A.L.J. Cook
University of Maryland, College Park, MD, USA

© Springer International Publishing Switzerland 2017
A. Leung and A. Baccaglini-Frank (eds.), *Digital Technologies in Designing Mathematics Education Tasks*, Mathematics Education in the Digital Era 8,
DOI 10.1007/978-3-319-43423-0_11

Keywords Teacher education · Reasoning and proof · Examples in proving · Technology-based task · Virtual learning environments

1 Introduction

Examples play an essential role in teaching, learning and doing mathematics at all levels (Bills et al. 2006). In particular, examples constitute important tools of mathematical exploration since they provide empirical grounds for generalization and forming conjectures, and play a crucial role in testing and modifying conjectures[1] (Lakatos 1976; Rissland 1978). Despite the important role examples play in mathematics, research literature consistently shows that students at all levels, prospective teachers and even practicing teachers have difficulties in understanding the status of examples in proving[2] (e.g., Barkai et al. 2002; Healy and Hoyles 2000; Knuth 2002).

One of the main difficulties identified in this line of research is students' reliance on empirical evidence, i.e., examples, for proving a general statement. This phenomenon is often referred to as the *empirical justification proof scheme* (Harel and Sowder 2007) and its limitation stems from the fact that for a general statement to be true it has to be true for *all* objects in the statements' domain; hence, a single counterexample is sufficient to disprove (a false) statement, even if multiple supporting examples exist. However, research shows that students often treat counterexamples as exceptions, rather than sufficient evidence for refuting a false statement (Balacheff 1988). Moreover, even recognizing that a certain example constitutes a counterexample for a given statement can be a non-trivial task for students (Buchbinder and Zaslavsky 2009; Ron 1998), especially when the logical structure of the statement gets more complex (Selden and Selden 1995).

The commonality and persistence of students' difficulties in understanding the status of examples in proving across mathematical areas and grade-levels (Harel and Sowder 2007) suggest that students need significant pedagogical support in order to develop appropriate conceptions of proof and understanding of the role of examples. Researchers also identified similar problems and difficulties among prospective elementary mathematics teachers, and even among secondary prospective teachers (Ko 2010).[3] Stylianides and Stylianides (2009) emphasize that teachers are unlikely to appreciate the importance of proving in mathematics or to support their students' engagement with reasoning and proving unless they themselves have strong knowledge of both mathematical content and teaching practices for implementing reasoning and proof tasks. Therefore, they stress the importance

---

[1]These processes are the focus of our chapter. Discussion of the roles of examples in teaching mathematics is beyond the scope of this chapter.

[2]To simplify communication we use the short term "the status of examples in proving" to denote both examples and counterexamples in both proving and refuting processes.

[3]See Ko (2010) for an extensive literature review on teachers' conceptions of proof.

of providing PSTs with structured learning experiences that would enable them to develop more appropriate views of general proof and recognize the limitation of reliance on empirical evidence for proving.

In this chapter we report on the design and development of the instructional task *What can you infer from this example?*, which aimed to enhance PSTs' mathematical knowledge for teaching proof through the utilization of digital tools provided by the online, rich-media, interactive platform Lesson*Sketch* (www.LessonSketch.org) developed for teacher education and research (Herbst et al. 2016).

The word "task" has multiple meanings in the literature, therefore, we adopt Leung and Bolite-Frant's (2015) definition of a tool-based task as "a teacher/researcher design aiming to be a thing to do or act on in order for students to activate an interactive tool-based environment where teachers, students and resources mutually enrich each other in producing mathematical experiences." In line with this definition we refer to the (technology-based) task *What can you infer from this example?* as a part of an instructional activity which is directly mediated through a technological environment. We use the term *task implementation* to describe a broader spectrum of the instructional activities that encompass the task itself as well as accompanying activities such as post-task whole-class discussion, preparation or follow-up assignments and assessments.

2 Overview of the Task and Design Methods

The task *What can you infer from this example?* was originally designed as a part of a research program investigating high-school students' understanding of the status of examples in proving and refuting mathematical statements (Buchbinder 2010; Ron 1998).[4] The task served a dual purpose as a tool that both assesses and promotes students' understanding of the status of examples in proving by evoking uncertainty and cognitive conflict (Hadas et al. 2000). Uncertainty and cognitive conflict are recognized in the research literature as powerful mechanisms for creating learning opportunities for students and teachers to re-evaluate and refine their mathematical and proof-related knowledge (Buchbinder and Zaslavsky 2011). Our assumption was that the original task for students can be successfully modified for the purposes of teacher education and enriched with research-based student data to create powerful learning opportunities for prospective teachers. Such a modification process required a wide range of considerations that go beyond designing a task for students. In order to address a variety of content and pedagogy-oriented goals we designed an interactive, media-rich experience that consists of four parts: (I) Examination of a given mathematical statement and determining its truth value; (II) Examination of six student-generated examples and determining their status with respect to the given statement; (III) Analysis of a classroom scenario showing students interacting with

---

[4]The same task with minor variations was used in two different studies with similar foci and student populations.

the statement and the examples; followed by requesting PSTs to make a suggestion on how to orchestrate a whole-class discussion; and finally, (IV) Reflection and participation in a discussion forum. All parts of the task were facilitated through Lesson*Sketch* in either individual or collaborative mode, without the intervention of a mathematics teacher educator (MTE). The task was followed up by a face-to-face whole-class discussion facilitated by one or more MTEs. Parts I and II of the task closely resemble the task for students, but with additional elements on which we elaborate later. Parts III and IV were designed specifically for PSTs.

In developing the task *What can you infer from this example?* for PSTs we used a design-experiment research methodology (Cobb et al. 2003) which is considered particularly appropriate for developing technology enhanced learning tasks (Rieber 2005; Chieu et al. 2011). Design-experiment involves multiple cycles of design, implementation and refinement of the task based on participants and instructor feedback. The task *What can you infer from this example?* was implemented over the course of 4 semesters with 96 prospective teachers in Israel and the US, in undergraduate courses taught by the authors of this chapter. In each country the task was implemented in one general course on proof for elementary PSTs, and one Geometry content and methods course for secondary PSTs. While the specifics of each course, the goals and the participants varied across different courses and countries, the technology-based task *What can you infer from this example?* was kept as a core instructional activity. Analysis of data collected in each implementation cycle led to gradual improvement of the task and refined articulation of design principles and the underlying theoretical grounds. Despite the obvious differences between the implementation settings, we were interested in identifying potential *commonalities* in PTS' interaction with the task *What can you infer from this example?* and in developing appropriate instructional support based on different groups' backgrounds and needs. The following questions guided our thinking:

1. To what extent do PSTs' responses to the task prompts provide evidence that different task goals were achieved (across various PSTs groups)?
2. What kinds of learning opportunities stem from PSTs' interaction with the task?
3. How did the technological environment of Lesson*Sketch* afford or hinder PST learning opportunities associated with the task?

The goal of this chapter is to share the lessons we learned in our experience of going through the process of modifying a task for students into a task for PSTs. We hope to contribute to the ongoing effort of the field to develop technology-based instructional tasks for PSTs focused on reasoning and proving. In the following sections we describe four different but interrelated theoretical perspectives that guided the design process of the task for PSTs. We then describe in detail the task itself and illustrate how its design features reflect these theoretical perspectives. Finally, we provide some illustrative data from PSTs' interaction with the task taken from various implementation cycles.

3 Theoretical Perspectives

3.1 Mathematical Knowledge for Teaching Proof

Following the seminal work of Shulman (1986), the nature of professional knowledge for teaching mathematics has been the focus of significant theorizing and empirical research over the last 30 years. Mathematical knowledge for teaching (MKT) has been described in terms of broad categories such as content knowledge —CK (or subject-matter knowledge), and pedagogical content knowledge—PCK. The latter is a special kind of teacher knowledge which reflects the transformation of content knowledge in the context of student learning. Van Dreil and Berry (2010) clarify that teachers use this type of knowledge "to structure the content of their lessons, to choose or develop specific representations or analogies, to understand and anticipate particular preconceptions or learning difficulties in their students" (p. 656).

Recently researchers have turned their attention specifically to mathematical knowledge for teaching of reasoning and proving (e.g., Lesseig, 2012; Steele and Rogers 2012; Stylianides and Ball 2008; Stylianides 2011). Building on the vast literature on teacher knowledge, Stylianides (2011) proposed a "comprehensive knowledge package for teaching proof" which involves at least three interrelated broad kinds of knowledge: (a) robust mathematical content knowledge, (b) knowledge about students' conceptions of proof, and (c) knowledge of pedagogical practices that can support students' development of conceptions of proof which are in line with conventional understanding. The latter two knowledge categories can be viewed as elements of PCK that are specific to teaching of reasoning and proof. Developing this type of knowledge with PSTs is essential, especially considering the crucial influence of teacher knowledge on students' learning experiences (Ball et al. 2005). Hence, it is important to provide PSTs with opportunities to develop both the knowledge of students' conceptions as well as the knowledge of specific pedagogical practices for successful implementation of mathematics instruction focused on reasoning and proving. Researchers highlight the challenges associated with creating such rich learning opportunities for PSTs (Ponte and Chapman 2008) and the critical need for more research informed instructional tasks for developing PST competency for teaching proof (Ko 2010).

The first category of Stylianides's "comprehensive knowledge package for teaching proof" is robust mathematical content knowledge. Within it, we identify two sub-categories: knowledge of particular mathematical concepts and relations among them in a certain proving task, and meta-mathematical knowledge of aspects such as validity of arguments, distinction between premises and conclusions in mathematical statements, the role of examples and counterexamples, and types of proof. We view both these types of mathematical knowledge as vital for teaching reasoning and proof, and assert that instructional tasks for PSTs should create rich opportunities for PSTs to enhance their mathematical knowledge by becoming aware of their pre-existing conceptions, and through analysis, evaluation, refinement and re-organization of their knowledge (Ball et al. 2005). In particular, with respect to PSTs' content knowledge of the status of examples in proving, we build on Buchbinder and Zaslavsky's (2009) framework to outline aspects of content knowledge that a task for PSTs should address. It is important to mention that the original task (for students) *What can you infer from this example?* was designed according to this framework (Buchbinder and Zaslavsky 2013), and was mostly preserved in the modified task for PSTs. Below we present one part[5] of Buchbinder and Zaslavsky's framework which is relevant for the task *What can you infer from this example?,* and illustrate it with the mathematical statement that was used in the task.

3.2   The Mathematical Framework Describing the Status of Examples in Determining the Truth-Value of Universal Statements

In general, every mathematical statement can be characterized by the domain (D) of objects (x) to which it refers and a proposition P(x) that specifies some property[6] of these objects. A general, or universal, statement maintains that a proposition is true for all the objects in the domain: $\forall x \in D, P(x)$. For example, given the domain D: "all quadrilaterals with perpendicular and congruent diagonals" and the property P: "being a kite" we can form a (false) universal statement "All quadrilaterals with perpendicular and congruent diagonals are kites." Note that in this case the domain D is described by a logical conjunction of two properties of quadrilaterals ("having perpendicular diagonals" and "having congruent diagonals"), while the property P involves a definition of a kite (a quadrilateral that has two disjoint pairs of congruent sides). With respect to the given domain D and property P we can define four types of examples based on whether a certain object x belongs to the domain D or not, and whether it satisfies the property P or not. Figure 1 below illustrates the logical status of each type of example.

A *supporting* example is an element of D which satisfies the property P $(x \in D, P(x))$. For instance, a square has diagonals that are both congruent and perpendicular to each other, and it is also a kite. Although it supports the universal statement, it is insufficient for proving it, since in order for a universal statement to be true the property has to hold for *all* objects in the domain. The second type of

---

[5]The complete framework describes the status of examples with respect to two types of mathematical statements: universal and existential. Here we focus on universal statements only.

[6]When presented in the form of a conditional statement (i.e., "if...then..."), the *premises* describe the domain of objects to which the statement refers and the *conclusion* describes the property that these objects have.

Goal / Type of Example	To prove a universal statement $\forall x \in D, P(x)$	To disprove a universal statement $\forall x \in D, P(x)$
Supporting $x \in D, P(x)$	Insufficient	Non applicable
Contradicting $x \in D, \neg P(x)$	Non applicable	Sufficient
Irrelevant $x \notin D, P(x)$	Non applicable	Non applicable
Irrelevant $x \notin D, \neg P(x)$	Non applicable	Non applicable

Fig. 1 A framework for examining the logical status of examples in proving or refuting mathematical statements, adapted from Buchbinder and Zaslavsky (2009)

example is an element of D which does not satisfy the property P ($x \in D, \neg P(x)$). In our case, a general scalene quadrilateral that has congruent and perpendicular diagonals, but is not a kite, constitutes such type of example. This is a counter example, which is sufficient for refuting a false universal statement, hence it is a *contradicting* example for this statement. The other two types of examples describe objects that are not in the domain D: ($x \notin D, P(x)$ or $x \notin D, \neg P(x)$). Regardless of whether they do or do not satisfy the property P, they are irrelevant for either proving or disproving a statement. Although both constitute *irrelevant* examples for this statement, an example of the form $x \notin D, P(x)$ can be potentially misleading since it describes an object that satisfies the property P. For example, a general convex kite that has non-congruent, but perpendicular diagonals might be mistakenly perceived as relevant because it is a kite. Moreover, a general convex kite constitutes a *contradicting* example to the *converse* (false) statement "a kite is a quadrilateral with perpendicular and congruent diagonals," which may add to the potential confusion.

According to Buchbinder and Zaslavsky (2009) "understanding of the logical status of examples in proving and refuting" can be defined operationally, in terms of the framework above. Thus, recognition of different types of examples (without necessarily using the framework terms) with respect to a given statement, and being able to explain what can or cannot be inferred regarding the truth value of the statement based on a certain type of example, can be considered evidence of understanding of the status of examples in proving. The task *What can you infer from this example?* encompasses all aspects of understanding described above and therefore bears a potential for providing PSTs with rich learning opportunities to enhance their mathematical knowledge of this content.

3.3 Pedagogies of Enactment and the Virtual Learning Environment LessonSketch as a Mediating Tool

In addition to the strong focus on mathematical content, an important goal in designing the task *What can you infer from this example?* for PSTs was to provide them with opportunities to contemplate the pedagogical aspects of the status of examples in proving. Teaching is a complex practice characterized by high temporality, and teachers are often required to "think on their feet" and make decisions "in the moment" (Mason and Spence 1999). This is especially true for the facilitation of classroom discussions around high-level mathematical tasks (Stein et al. 2008) such as reasoning and proving tasks. Research shows that developing pedagogical practices for orchestrating meaningful classroom discussion as well as eliciting, interpreting and responding to student thinking have been particularly challenging for prospective teachers (Ponte and Chapman 2008). Consequently researchers and practitioners strive to design pedagogical approaches for bridging theoretical knowledge and teaching practices that allow prospective teachers to analyze, evaluate, reflect on and engage in teaching practice, all while in a safe and controlled environment of *reduced complexity* (Grossman et al. 2009). Grossman et al. identify three such pedagogical approaches: representation, decomposition and approximation of practice, which they term *pedagogies of enactment:*

> Representation of practice refers to the ways in which teaching practice is made visible for the purposes of analysis and reflection. Decomposition, the breaking down of practice into constituent parts, allows for focused attention on discrete components of teaching. Approximation involves engagement in components of practice under conditions of reduced complexity (p. 2055).

Various tools and methodologies, such as the use of video recordings of practice (Santagata and Yeh 2014), have been designed and used by researchers and practitioners in order to bridge between theory and teaching practice. Digital technologies, including virtual environments and online communication tools, brought with them a whole new spectrum of additional affordances for teacher education (Herbst et al. 2011, 2016). To support implementation of pedagogies of enactment in the design of the task *What can you infer from this example?* we capitalized on the technological affordances of the rich-media online environment Lesson*Sketch*. It houses a variety of digital tools that teacher educators can use to create interactive rich-media experiences involving activities such as: analyzing a video or cartoon representation of a classroom scenario; examining student work; participating in discussion forums around specific instructional episodes; and creating one's own representation of teaching which can be shared, evaluated and discussed with others (Herbst et al. 2014).

A distinctive feature of Lesson*Sketch*, which we utilized in the task *What can you infer from this example?* to represent student work and classroom interactions, is the use of cartoon-based representations of teaching. According to Herbst and Chazan (2015) using representations with non-descript cartoon characters eliminates the particularities associated with video recordings such as distinctive characteristics of individuals or of the setting, which allows PSTs to focus more on critical moments of classroom interaction. Chieu et al. (2011) use dimensions of temporality (a sense of time flow in the scenario) and individuality (of represented actors and settings) to classify different representations of teaching such as written cases, cartoon-based representations and video. They conclude that:

> Animations of nondescript cartoon characters […] immerse the viewer in a temporality closer to that of real classroom action but offer an experience of individuality somewhere in between that of video and text because […] people are represented with icons. These kinds of animations of nondescript cartoon characters […] may thus reproduce for the viewer the temporal and tactical demands of real classroom interaction while inviting viewers to project onto the scenarios the individualities of the settings in which and the people with whom they practice (p. 598).

Herbst et al. (2014) maintain that "Lesson*Sketch* cartoon-based artifacts and tools play a crucial role, as 'mediators of cognition,' to help teacher users externalize their thoughts and ideas about instructional practice" (p. 4). The use of non-descript, cartoon-based representations of teaching supports participants' *notion of presence* (Oztok and Brett 2011) through which users associate themselves with the represented practice and its actors. With respect to the task *What can you infer from this example?*, the digital representational tools of Lesson*Sketch* allowed PSTs to examine the practice of teaching under conditions of reduced complexity while maintaining an appropriate level of authenticity of the represented practice; it also allowed PSTs to focus on those aspects of instruction we considered critical in the context of the task.

Another important feature of Lesson*Sketch* used in the task design is participation in reflective discussion via an online forum. Online communication tools provided PSTs with opportunities to reflect on and share with others individual mathematical ideas, views and experiences around representations of practice; these served as shared reference points around which meaningful conversations could evolve (Chieu et al. 2011).

We turn now to describing the task *What can you infer from this example?*, and elaborate on the goals, theoretical grounds and technological design features called on to support these goals.

4 From a Task for Students Towards a Task for Teachers

The task *What can you infer from this example?* aimed to provide PSTs with a wide range of learning opportunities to reflect on and enhance their professional mathematical knowledge for teaching proof as outlined by Stylianides (2011), but with a specific focus on the status of examples in proving. To that extent, the task focuses on PSTs' content knowledge of families of quadrilaterals in geometry, on meta-mathematical knowledge of the status of examples in proving, and two types of pedagogical content knowledge: knowledge of students' understanding of the status of examples in proving, and knowledge of pedagogical practices for supporting students' understanding of this content. As mentioned above, the task consists of four parts followed by a whole-class, face-to-face discussion, facilitated by at least one mathematics teacher educator.

Part I: Examination of a given mathematical statement and determining its truth value

The first part of the task invited PSTs to examine the false mathematical statement "A quadrilateral with congruent and perpendicular diagonals is a kite." The PSTs were required to decide whether the statement is true or false, and to justify their answer. With some groups we included additional prompts asking PSTs to determine the domain and the property of the statement, or the type of the statement: universal or existential. The wording of the statement contains two elements of difficulty. One, it is neither in a conditional form (i.e., if...then... form), nor it is explicitly universally quantified (i.e., does not contain keywords such as "any" or "all"). However, geometrical properties or definitions are often worded this way; for example: a statement "diagonals of a parallelogram bisect each other" is a universal statement, frequently used in school geometry, yet it is not explicitly quantified as universal. The second element that adds to the statement's complexity and can hinder correct recognition of the status of examples with respect to it, is the fact that the domain of the statement is a conjunction of two properties "congruent diagonals" and "perpendicular diagonals." The use of a statement from the school geometry curriculum combined with the two complexity elements aimed to create a balanced task that would be viewed by PSTs as relevant to their future practice, within their reach of solving, but challenging enough to allow PSTs to experience it from the learner's perspective (Ball et al. 2005). The goal of Part I is mainly content-oriented, and interaction with the digital task is individual and untimed.

Part II: Examination of six student-generated examples

Part II of the task involves evaluating six student examples and determining their status with respect to the given statement. This part of the task was embedded in the instructional context—a cartoon depiction of a classroom—with the teaching practice decomposed and represented through individual students' responses. PSTs are asked to imagine themselves as the teacher who is facilitating a geometry lesson in which students investigate properties of diagonals of quadrilaterals by exploring whether a conjecture: "A quadrilateral with congruent and perpendicular diagonals is a kite" is true or false. The students approached this exploration by drawing their own examples, which they then presented to the whole class and contemplated what could be inferred from each example about the truth-value of the conjecture. The collection of the six students' examples (Fig. 2) was carefully constructed according to the mathematical framework. It includes two supporting examples (#1 and #6), two examples that contradict the statement (#2 and #3) and one of each type of irrelevant examples (#4 and #5).

For each student's example PSTs needed to determine whether it: (a) proves the statement, (b) contradicts the statement, (c) only supports the statement, or (d) is irrelevant to the statement (Fig. 3).

#	Example	Design-Analysis of the examples with respect to the statement: *A quadrilateral with congruent and perpendicular diagonals is a kite*	
1.	A square	Diagonals of a square are congruent and perpendicular to each other. A square is a kite	$x \in D, P(x)$ supporting
2.	An isosceles trapezoid with perpendicular diagonals	Diagonals of an isosceles trapezoid are congruent and, in this case, are also perpendicular to each other. An isosceles trapezoid cannot be a kite.	$x \in D, \neg P(x)$ contradicting
3.	A general quadrilateral with congruent & perpendicular diagonals	A general quadrilateral with congruent and perpendicular diagonals $(AC \cong BD, AC \perp BD)$. This quadrilateral is not a kite.	$x \in D, \neg P(x)$ contradicting
4.	A convex kite	Diagonals of a convex kite are perpendicular to each other, but in this case they are not congruent.	$x \notin D, P(x)$ irrelevant
5.	A rectangle which is not a square	Diagonals of a rectangle which is not a square are congruent but not perpendicular to each other. A general rectangle is not a kite.	$x \notin D, \neg P(x)$ irrelevant
6.	A concave kite with congruent diagonals	Diagonals of a concave kite are perpendicular to each other and they can be congruent.	$x \in D, P(x)$ supporting

Fig. 2 Examples used and design-analysis of their status with respect to the statement: *A quadrilateral with congruent and perpendicular diagonals is a kite*

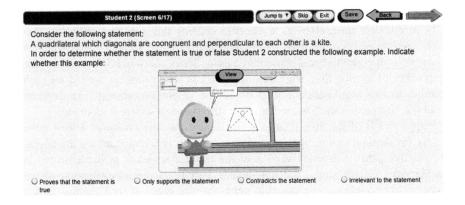

Fig. 3 A screen shot of one example of student work

Based on our prior research experience with implementing this part of the task with students (Buchbinder 2010; Ron 1998) we anticipated that recognizing what can be inferred from certain examples might be particularly challenging. For instance, example #4, a convex kite, is irrelevant to the statement at hand even though it has the specified property—it is a kite. Also, example #1, a square, is a type of kite, which makes it a supporting example for this statement. However, a square is not a prototypical example of a kite, thus, PSTs who do not have a strong knowledge of quadrilaterals might think of a square as a counterexample. Our expectation was that engaging with these particular examples might challenge and stimulate PSTs' reflective thinking.

This part of the task has both content—and pedagogy-oriented goals. Examining the collection of examples above aimed to provide PSTs with a rich learning opportunity to reflect on their mathematical understanding of quadrilaterals and to refresh their knowledge of this topic. Importantly, the task allowed PSTs to contemplate their own mathematical understanding of the status of examples in proving, and to test their initial decision whether the statement is true or false in light of additional, possibly unexpected empirical evidence. We anticipated that PSTs confronted with various students' examples would experience uncertainty and cognitive conflict regarding the truth-value of the statement and regarding the status of these examples with respect to the statement. At the same time, we hoped that the carefully chosen and structured sequence of examples would eventually support resolving the uncertainty, and serve for PSTs as a *pivotal* (set of) *examples*. Zazkis and Chernoff (2008) define pivotal examples as examples that help learners to resolve a cognitive conflict in a way that moves their initial naïve conceptions towards more appropriate mathematical conceptions (p. 197). Examining the collection of examples also evoked the need for common language and systematization of mathematical ideas pertaining to the status of examples in proving. The theoretical framework for the interplay between examples and proving (Fig. 1), which was introduced by MTEs during the post-task whole-class discussion, provided the means to address this need and to bridge between mathematical and meta-mathematical knowledge.

From the pedagogical perspective, Part II of the task provided an opportunity for PSTs to visualize themselves as teachers facilitating this very task in their classroom, confronted with the need to interpret and evaluate students' mathematical thinking. As opposed to a real classroom, Lesson*Sketch* allowed PSTs to control the temporality of events: they were able to spend as much time as needed on each example, as well as go back and forth between examples and change their decision about the statement's truth-value and about the status of different examples.

Parts I and II of the task *What can you infer from this example?* mirror quite closely the original task design for students, but with two important modifications. The original paper-and-pencil version of the task for students, as implemented in Buchbinder's (2010) study, did not include Part I—an initial evaluation of the statement. The students were asked to determine the status of each example in the collection with respect to the given statement prior to determining its truth-value. As a result, some students were still unsure whether the statement is false even after correctly identifying all counterexamples. This surprising observation triggered the inclusion of an initial evaluation of the statement as Part I of the task for PSTs.

Another modification to the task for PSTs was embedding the collection of examples as products of student work in the classroom in which PSTs assumed the teacher role. This design feature aimed to emphasize the importance of analyzing and interpreting students' thinking while orchestrating the whole-class discussion, even though the latter aspect was implicit at this point. Implementation of this design feature was made possible due to the *Depict* tool of Lesson*Sketch*—an advanced authoring tool which allowed us, teacher educators and researchers, to create cartoon representations of a mathematics classroom and introduce particular student work in the context of a whole-class discussion (Herbst et al. 2016).

Parts I and II of the task combine important pedagogical aspects of teacher practice with a strong focus on mathematical content, while maintaining safe environment for PSTs through individual and untimed interaction with the software.

Part III: Analysis of a classroom scenario and making a suggestion for orchestrating a whole-class discussion

The next two parts of the task were developed especially for PSTs. Part III of the task presented PSTs with a scenario[7] in a storyboard format realized with cartoon characters. The scenario depicts a class discussion of the statement "A quadrilateral with congruent and perpendicular diagonals is a kite." Students in the class seem to agree that the statement is false, but they are not sure which counterexample contradicts it. One student, Purple,[8] wrongly asserts that a convex kite (example #4, Fig. 3) is "the best" counterexample, since "it is already a kite with perpendicular diagonals, but they are not congruent, so it contradicts the statement." Another student, Red, maintains that "the most contradicting example is an isosceles trapezoid (example #2, Fig. 3) since its diagonals are congruent and perpendicular, but it is not a kite." Other students in the class express confusion over which of the two examples, or both of them, can be used to refute the statement. The scenario ends with the teacher putting both examples on the board next to each other. Following the scenario PSTs were presented with a prompt:

> It seems that the classroom conversation shifted to the question "what does it mean to contradict a mathematical statement?" How would you lead the discussion to support your students' understanding? Write a short description of how you would continue this scenario if this was your class. Include at least three specific questions to pose to the class.

These are non-trivial mathematical and pedagogical questions that aim to stimulate PSTs' thinking, yet they arise naturally in the context of the scenario.

In this part of the task teaching practice was represented through a cartoon-based classroom scenario. The teaching context is explicit, and although the temporality is still reduced as opposed to a real classroom, the events in the scenario unfold faster

---

[7]Based on student data from Buchbinder's (2010) study.

[8]All cartoon student characters in the scenario are named by the color of their shirt.

than in part II of the task, where each students' work was viewed on a separate screen. The scenario also introduced interactions between different students in class and between the students and the teacher, which made it more representative of a real classroom. At the same time, as opposed to a "real" classroom, the classroom scenario was carefully scripted to draw PSTs' attention to those mathematical and pedagogical aspects of student thinking which we considered critical for PSTs to engage with. In particular, we aimed to evoke a conflict for PSTs without hinting at potential ways to resolve it.

The important aspect of this part of the task is an approximation of teaching practice through engaging PSTs in writing a description of how the scenario should continue from the point it stopped, including specific questions they would pose in class. This provided PSTs with an opportunity to envision themselves as teachers who need to correctly recognize the status of the two examples, identify the source of students' confusion and devise a way to orchestrate a discussion that promotes students' understanding. The mode of interaction with this part of the task was individual and timed, which was crucial for PSTs' analysis of student thinking and planning of the instructional response.

Part VI: Participation and discussion in an online forum
The fourth part of the task *What can you infer from this example?* invited PSTs to reflect on and share their personal impressions, ideas and insights from the first three parts of the task through a discussion forum. The forum prompt encouraged PSTs to reflect on their experiences as learners and also to address any pedagogical issues they felt the task evoked for them. PSTs were required to post their own thread and respond to at least two threads of their peers. Participation in the online forum also served as an initial step for PSTs to reflect on their own learning from different components of the task.

Post-task whole class discussion
After completing all parts of the task *What can you infer from this example?* PSTs participated in a follow-up activity: a face-to-face whole-class discussion facilitated by MTEs. The goal of this part was to create a context for PSTs to reflect on, clarify and enhance both personal and shared understanding of content- and pedagogy-oriented aspects. MTEs played an essential role in this activity as they framed and structured the discussion, led the analysis and supported the articulation of mathematical and pedagogical ideas evoked by the task (Smith 2001). As intended by our task design, the mathematical conflict evoked by the task created for PSTs the need for a shared language and systematization of mathematical knowledge. The framework for the status of examples in proving (Buchbinder and Zaslavsky 2009), which MTEs introduced during the whole class discussion, addressed those needs. It helped to enhance PSTs' content knowledge and also supported the discussion and collective planning of pedagogical approaches for advancing student learning.

4.1 Summary and the Emergent Framework for Designing Digital Tasks for PSTs

We summarize the structure of the four parts of the technology-based task and of the post-task whole-class discussion in Fig. 4. The figure presents an emergent framework for the design of media-rich digital tasks for PSTs on the basis of mathematical tasks for students. It specifies different characteristics of the task, such as the type of interaction (individual or group), the type of interaction with digital technology (direct or indirect) and the presence or absence of MTE facilitation. The figure lays out the pedagogies of enactment utilized in different parts of the task as well as the types of goals and learning opportunities that the task *What can you infer from this example?* afforded.

The framework presented in Fig. 4 reflects our systematic approach of combining theoretical grounds, empirically tested design features and advanced technological tools through the process of design-research to create much needed instructional tasks that address prospective teachers' content and pedagogical knowledge for engaging students in proving with a particular focus on the status of examples in proving.

Task parts / Task characteristics		Part I: Examination of a given statement and determining its truth value	Part II: Examination of students' examples	Part III: Analysis of the classroom scenario and making suggestions for a class discussion	Part IV: Reflection and participation in a discussion forum	Post-task whole class discussion
Pedagogy of enactment		—	Decomposition and representation	Representation and approximation	—	—
Goals and Learning Opportunities	Content-oriented	Engagement with mathematical content and determine truth-value of the statement.	Opportunity to expand personal example space and change decision about the statement in light of new evidence.	Examine questions such as: What does it mean to contradict a universal statement? How many counterexamples can a statement have?	Participation in the community of learners. Opportunity to discuss and clarify content- and pedagogy-oriented ideas. Opportunity collective reflection on the learning process in each part of the task and as a whole.	Opportunity to share, reflect on and enhance both personal and shared understanding of the status of examples in proving by exposure to the theoretical framework, and expanding the repertoire of the relevant pedagogical approaches.
	Pedagogy-oriented	—	Interpretation of students' thinking. Opportunity to envision oneself as a teacher facilitating a proof oriented task. Teacher's role is implicit.	Planning a whole-class discussion and support students' understanding of the status of examples in proving. Teacher's role is explicit.		
Individual / Group interaction:		Individual			Group	
Digital technology interaction: Direct / Indirect		Direct			Indirect (but referenced to the digital task)	
Facilitation type: No MTE facilitation / With MTE facilitation		No MTE (Mathematics Teacher Educator) facilitation			With MTE facilitation	

Fig. 4 The framework for design of media-rich tasks for PSTs

5   Lessons Learned from Task Implementation and the Role of Technology

A comprehensive presentation of results is beyond the scope of this chapter, however, we illustrate some common themes that emerged in PSTs' interaction with the task *What can you infer from this example?* across four cycles of implementation. We present the themes according to the two types of task goals: content-or pedagogy-oriented.

With respect to content-oriented goals, the task evoked a whole range of mathematical and meta-mathematical themes, as anticipated based on the prior research with students and as intended by the task design. As expected, PSTs experienced challenges with identifying a square (example #1, Fig. 3) as a type of a kite, and with recognizing that a convex kite (example #4, Fig. 3) is irrelevant to the statement "A quadrilateral with congruent and perpendicular diagonals is a kite." For instance, on average, 42 % of PSTs across different groups incorrectly considered a convex kite as contradicting the statement. Their justifications resembled the one made by Purple in the scenario: "since diagonals of a kite are not (necessarily) congruent, this example contradicts the statement." However, some PSTs noticed that the example of a convex kite contradicts the converse of the given statement and brought this up in the forum, which consequently led to an extensive whole-class discussion of the relationship between a statement and its converse. Other logical-mathematical themes evoked by the task were: How to identify the logical structure of a statement—its domain and property? How a statement, a converse and a bi-conditional are related to each other? How many counterexamples can a false statement have? What does it mean to contradict a statement? What is the relationship between a counterexample and a proof by contradiction?

As intended by the task design, the task led to extensive discussions of the relationships between different types of quadrilaterals and clarifications of their definitions and properties. For example, a kite, like other quadrilaterals, can have several correct definitions, but it is common to define a kite by the properties of its sides, rather than diagonals (Zaslavsky and Shir 2005). In forum conversations and in the whole-class discussions PSTs frequently brought up questions such as: Which properties of diagonals follow necessarily from a definition of a kite? and What necessary and sufficient conditions must diagonals of a quadrilateral fulfill, in order for it to be a kite? These questions, evoked by individual interaction with the task, were then discussed and resolved during the whole-class discussion. This interaction between Lesson*Sketch* and the in-class discussion set the stage for achieving the pedagogical goals of the task.

With respect to pedagogy-oriented goals, across all implementation cycles, PSTs' interaction with the task led to an increased awareness and appreciation of the logical-mathematical complexity of the roles of examples in proving, and to the increased realization of the conceptual complexity that students face when they encounter this content. The vast majority of PSTs reported that the task exposed them to aspects of student conceptions of which they were not previously aware. For example, one PST wrote:

> This was an eye opening experience for me. I never thought that students could have any problems with refuting any statement, but this task showed me where students might have difficulties or misunderstandings.

Many PSTs, in Israel and the US alike, expressed the view that understanding the status of examples in proving is important for students' engagement in proving, yet it is not sufficiently addressed in schools. Consequently, PSTs agreed that there is a need for pedagogical approaches for supporting students' understanding of this content and proposed a range of ideas, such as using non-mathematical contexts and analogies to illustrate the status of different types of examples. For instance, one group of PSTs came up with the following analogy:

> What kind of evidence would contradict a statement "All strawberries in my store are red and ripe?" Finding a red strawberry in another store or finding a green, unripe strawberry in the same store?

The PSTs explained that the first example is analogous to a convex kite in our task, and is clearly irrelevant to the statement, while the second example corresponds to an isosceles trapezoid in our task and contradicts the statement. Other pedagogical suggestions were the use of Venn diagrams for representing relationships between different groups of quadrilaterals, or to use mathematical statements with simpler logical structures. The common thread in PSTs' suggestions was that deep conceptual understanding of the status of examples in proving, and of related logical aspects, cannot be achieved with a single instructional task, but should be developed gradually through multiple encounters with a variety of tasks and mathematical contents. PSTs expressed their appreciation for the need to develop a repertoire of pedagogical tools for supporting students' learning.

We attribute the richness and the scope of mathematical and pedagogical issues evoked by the task *What can you infer from this example?* to the design of the task and the flexibility of the digital tools in Lesson*Sketch*. It is important to note that these tools are not designed to support the manipulation or creation of mathematical objects, as opposed to dynamic geometry environments. The static images of particular mathematical objects aimed to represent sample student work. The advantage of Lesson*Sketch* is in its ability to embed these images in a teaching context; to associate them with instances of student thinking; to represent interactions between students and a teacher around mathematical content; and to engage PSTs in careful examination of this content, to deepen and refine their understanding of it. These features of Lesson*Sketch* also supported the implementation of pedagogies of enactment as proposed by Grossman and her colleagues (2009). In particular, we *decomposed* the practice of facilitating a proof task in a geometry classroom into several parts and used the *Depict* tool of the Lesson*Sketch* platform to *represent* a few carefully chosen components of this practice with non-descript cartoon characters. Such representation allowed PSTs to envision themselves as teachers called on to manage the depicted classroom interactions, but in conditions of reduced complexity. We used the *Plan* tool of Lesson*Sketch* (Herbst et al. 2014) to create a virtual learning experience for PSTs comprised of sequences of representations, accompanied by questions and prompts to support the study of specific components of teaching practice.

One crucial feature that contributed to the educational value of the task was the balanced combination of an asynchronous mode of interaction through the Lesson*Sketch* platform, with the follow-up face-to-face discussion. The asynchronous mode of interaction provided each and every PST with an opportunity to immerse themselves in the represented situation, while having sufficient time to contemplate the mathematical and pedagogical issues evoked by the task, and to review and rehearse their responses in a safe, virtual environment. Moreover, each PST would then contribute to the online discussion and participate in the community of learners (Putnam and Borko 2000). Hence, the technological tools of Lesson*Sketch* and the particular design of the task allowed for *all* individual PSTs' voices to be heard and ideas to be examined, which would be almost impossible to achieve otherwise. For us, MTEs, such structure provided a unique opportunity to examine PST responses to the technology-based task and analyze the main themes occurring in the online forum *prior* to the follow-up whole-class discussion and to adjust its facilitation accordingly.

Throughout implementation of the task *What can you infer from this example?* in multiple settings we encountered a few challenges. In particular it became apparent that PSTs needed a more deliberate tool for *approximation* of practice than we originally envisioned. In Part III of the task we provided PSTs with a simple textbox on Lesson*Sketch* to draft their suggestions and guiding questions for orchestrating a whole-class discussion. Many PSTs' responses were rather superficial, overly generic and teacher-centered; although they gradually improved and became more focused, specific and student-centered as PSTs discussed them in forums (Stein et al. 2008). This suggested to us that PSTs would benefit from more careful and detailed planning of instructional scenarios to better approximate teaching moves. One way to achieve this is to have PSTs create their own storyboard representations of classroom scenarios using the *Depict* tool.[9] Other alternatives may include the use of the "lesson-play" technique (Zazkis et al. 2013) in which PSTs use simple word processing software to write their proposed plan for classroom discussion in the form of a screen play; or the use of screen-capture with voice annotation (i.e., screencasts). Creating such artifacts as depictions, lesson-plays and screencasts require PSTs to engage in careful planning of teacher prompts and anticipated student responses. These artifacts could then be shared through the Lesson*Sketch* discussion forum and serve as a better starting point for meaningful interaction among PSTs to support approximation of teaching practice (Clay et al. 2012; Herbst et al. 2014).

---

[9]The *Depict* tool was not originally considered for implementation in the task as it was not available in Hebrew, however it has recently became available in languages other than English.

We conclude this chapter by reflecting on our own learning as MTEs and researchers from engaging in the process of designing and implementing the technology-rich task *What can you infer from this example?*. For us, this process was characterized by deep reflection on theoretical underpinnings, and careful adaptation of available technological tools to support PSTs' content and pedagogical knowledge of the interplay between examples and proving. Following the tradition of design research we examined affordances and pitfalls of various technological tools through iterative cycles of design, implementation, analysis and redesign (Cobb et al. 2003) resulting in the emergent framework presented in this chapter.

References

Balacheff, N. (1988). Aspects of proof in pupils' practice of school mathematics. In D. Pimm (Ed.), *Mathematics, teachers and children* (pp. 216–235). London: Holder and Stoughton.

Ball, D. L., Hill, H. C., & Bass, H. (2005). Knowing mathematics for teaching: Who knows mathematics well enough to teach third grade, and how can we decide? *American Educator, 29* (1), 14–17, 20–22, 43–46.

Barkai, R., Tsamir, P., Tirosh, D., & Dreyfus, T. (2002). Proving or refuting arithmetic claims: The case of elementary school teachers. In A. D. Cockburn & E. Nardi (Eds.), *Proceeding of 26th Conference of PME* (Vol. 2, pp. 57–64). Norwich, UK: PME.

Bills, L., Dreyfus, T., Mason, J., Tsamir, P., Watson, A., & Zaslavsky, O. (2006). Exemplification in mathematics education. In J. Novotná, H. Moraová, M. Krátká, & N. Stehlíková (Eds.), *Proceedings of the 30th Conference of the International Group for the Psychology of Mathematics Education* (Vol. 1, pp. 126–154). PME: Prague, Czech Republic.

Buchbinder, O. (2010). The role of examples in establishing the validity of universal and existential mathematical statements. Unpublished dissertation manuscript (in Hebrew). Technion, Haifa.

Buchbinder, O., & Zaslavsky, O. (2009). A framework for understanding the status of examples in establishing the validity of mathematical statements. In M. Tzekaki, M. Kaldrimidou, & C. Sakonidis (Eds.), *Proceedings of the 33rd Conference of the International Group for the Psychology of Mathematics Education* (Vol. 2, pp. 225–232). Thessaloniki, Greece: PME.

Buchbinder, O., & Zaslavsky, O. (2011). Is this a coincidence? The role of examples in fostering a need for proof. *ZDM—The International Journal of Mathematics Education, 43*(2), 269–281.

Buchbinder, O., & Zaslavsky, O. (2013). A holistic approach for designing tasks that capture and enhance mathematical understanding of a particular topic: the case of the interplay between examples and proof. In C. Margolinas (Ed.), *Proceedings of ICMI Study 22: Task Design in Mathematics Education Conference, Oxford, UK* (Vol. 1, pp. 27–35).

Chieu, V. M., Herbst, P., & Weiss, M. (2011). Effect of an animated classroom story embedded in online discussion on helping mathematics teachers learn to notice. *Journal of the Learning Sciences, 20*(4), 589–624. doi:10.1080/10508406.2011.528324.

Clay, E., Silverman, J., & Fischer, D. J. (2012). Unpacking online asynchronous collaboration in mathematics teacher education. *ZDM—The International Journal of Mathematics Education, 44*(6), 761–773.

Cobb, P., Confrey, J., diSessa, A., Lehrer, R., & Schauble, L. (2003). Design experiments in educational research. *Educational Researcher, 32*(1), 9–13.

Grossman, P., Compton, C., Igra, D., Ronfeldt, M., Shahan, E., & Williamson, P. (2009). Teaching practice: A cross-professional perspective. *Teachers College Record, 111*(9), 2055–2100.

Hadas, N., Hershkowitz, R., & Schwarz, B. B. (2000). The role of contradiction and uncertainty in promoting the need to prove in dynamic geometry environments. *Educational Studies in Mathematics, 44*(1 & 2), 127–150.

Harel, G., & Sowder, L. (2007). Toward comprehensive perspectives on the learning and teaching of proof. In F. Lester (Ed.), *Second handbook of research on mathematics teaching and learning* (pp. 805–842). NCTM. Reston, VA.: Information Age Pub Inc.

Healy, L., & Hoyles, C. (2000). A study of proof conceptions in algebra. *Journal for Research in Mathematics Education, 31*(4), 396–428.

Herbst, P., & Chazan, D. (2015). Using Multimedia Scenarios Delivered Online to Study Professional Knowledge Use in Practice. *International Journal of Research and Method in Education, 38*(3), 272–287.

Herbst, P., Chazan, D., Chieu, V. M., Milewski, A., Kosko, K. W., & Aaron, W. R. (2016). Technology-mediated mathematics teacher development: research on digital pedagogies of practice. In: M. Niess, S. Driskell, & K. Hollebrands (Eds.), *Handbook of research on transforming mathematics teacher education in the digital age* (pp. 78–106). Hershey, PA: Information Science Reference.

Herbst, P., Chazan, D., Chen, C., Chieu, V. M., & Weiss, M. (2011). Using comics-based representations of teaching, and technology, to bring practice to university "methods" courses. *ZDM—The International Journal of Mathematics Education, 43*(1), 91–104.

Herbst, P., Chieu, V. M., & Rougee, A. (2014). Approximating the practice of mathematics teaching: what learning can web-based, multimedia storyboarding software enable? *Contemporary Issues in Technology and Teacher Education, 14*(4). Retrieved from http://www.citejournal.org/vol14/iss4/mathematics/article1.cfm.

Knuth, E. J. (2002). Secondary school mathematics teachers' conceptions of proof. *Journal for Research in Mathematics Education, 33*(5), 379–405.

Ko, Y. Y. (2010). Mathematics teachers' conceptions of proof: implications for educational research. *International Journal of Science and Mathematics Education, 8*(6), 1109–1129.

Lakatos, I. (1976). *Proofs and refutations: the logic of mathematical discovery*. Cambridge: Cambridge University Press.

Lesseig, K. (2012). *Mathematical knowledge for teaching proof*. Unpublished dissertation manuscript. Retrieved from: http://ir.library.oregonstate.edu/xmlui/bitstream/handle/1957/23465/LesseigKristinR2011.pdf?sequence=2.

Leung, A., & Bolite-Frant, J. (2015). Designing mathematics tasks: The role of tools. In A. Watson & M. Ohtani (Eds.), *Task design in mathematics education, an ICMI study 22* (pp. 191–225). Switzerland: Springer International Publishing.

Mason, J., & Spence, M. (1999). Beyond mere knowledge of mathematics: The importance of knowing-to act in the moment. *Educational Studies in Mathematics, 38*(1), 135–161.

Oztok, M., & Brett, C. (2011). Social presence and online learning: A review of research. *The Journal of Distance Education, 25*(3), 1–10.

Ponte, J. P., & Chapman, O. (2008). Preservice mathematics teachers' knowledge and development. In L. English (Ed.), *Handbook of international research in mathematics education* (2nd ed., pp. 223–261). New York: Routldge.

Putnam, R. T., & Borko, H. (2000). What do new views of knowledge and thinking have to say about research on teacher learning? *Educational Researcher, 29*(1), 4–15.

Rieber, L. P. (2005). Multimedia learning in games, simulations, and microworlds. In R. E. Mayer (Ed.), *The Cambridge handbook of multimedia learning* (pp. 549–567). New York, NY: Cambridge University Press.

Rissland, E. L. (1978). Understanding understanding mathematics. *Cognitive Science, 2*(4), 361–383.

Ron, G. (1998). *Counter-Examples in mathematics: how do students understand their role? Unpublished dissertation manuscript (in Hebrew)*. Haifa: Technion.

Santagata, R., & Yeh, C. (2014). Learning to teach mathematics and to analyze teaching effectiveness: evidence from a video- and practice-based approach. *Journal of Mathematics Teacher Education, 17*(6), 491–514.

Selden, A., & Selden, J. (1995). Unpacking the logic of mathematical statements. *Educational Studies in Mathematics, 29*(2), 123–151.

Shulman, L. S. (1986). Those who understand: Knowledge growth in teaching. *Educational Researcher, 15*(2), 4–14.

Smith, M. S. (2001). *Practice-based professional development for teachers of mathematics.* Reston, VA: National Council of Teachers of Mathematics.

Steele, M. D., & Rogers, K. C. (2012). Relationships between mathematical knowledge for teaching and teaching practice: The case of proof. *Journal of Mathematics Teacher Education, 15*(2), 159–180.

Stein, M. K., Engle, R. A., Smith, M. S., & Hughes, E. K. (2008). Orchestrating productive mathematical discussions: Five practices for helping teachers move beyond show and tell. *Mathematical Thinking and Learning, 10*(4), 313–340.

Stylianides, A. J. (2011). Towards a comprehensive knowledge package for teaching proof: A focus on the misconception that empirical arguments are proofs. *Pythagoras, 32*(1), Art. #14, 10 pages.

Stylianides, A. J., & Ball, D. L. (2008). Understanding and describing mathematical knowledge for teaching: knowledge about proof for engaging students in the activity of proving. *Journal of Mathematics Teacher Education, 11*(4), 307–332.

Stylianides, G. J., & Stylianides, A. J. (2009). Facilitating the transition from empirical arguments to proof. *Journal for Research in Mathematics Education, 40*(3), 314–352.

Van Dreil, J. H., & Berry, A. (2010). Pedagogical content knowledge. In P. Peterson, E. Baker, & B. McGaw (Eds.), *International encyclopedia of education* (3rd ed., Vol. 7, pp. 656–661). Oxford, UK: Elsevier.

Zaslavsky, O., & Shir, K. (2005). Students' conceptions of a mathematical definition. *Journal for Research in Mathematics Education, 36*(4), 317–346.

Zazkis, R., & Chernoff, E. J. (2008). What makes a counterexample exemplary? *Educational Studies in Mathematics, 68*(3), 195–208.

Zazkis, R., Sinclair, N., & Liljedahl, P. (2013). *Lesson play in mathematics education: a tool for research and professional development.* New York, NY: Springer.

Part IV
Issues in Digital Task Design

Supporting Variation in Task Design Through the Use of Technology

Christian Bokhove

Abstract This chapter describes a digital intervention for algebraic expertise that was built on three principles, crises, feedback and fading, as described by Bokhove and Drijvers (*Technology, Knowledge and Learning. 7*(1–2), 43–59, 2012b). The principles are retrospectively scrutinized through Marton's Theory of Variation, concluding that the principles share several elements with the patterns of variation: contrast, generalisation, separation and fusion. The integration of these principles in a digital intervention suggests that technology has affordances and might be beneficial for task design with variation. The affordances in the presented technology comprise (i) authoring features, which enable teacher-authors to design their own contrasting task sequences, (ii) randomisation, which automates the creation of a vast amount of tasks with similar patterns and generalisations, (iii) feedback, which aids students in improving students' learning outcomes, and (iv) visualisations, which allow fusion through presenting multiple representations. The principles are demonstrated by discussing a sequence of tasks involving quadratic formulas. Advantages and limitations are discussed.

Keywords Task · Design · Sequence · Crisis · Feedback · Fading · Variation

1 Introduction

In recent years task design in mathematics education has become more and more important, culminating in specific conferences and a separate ICMI study devoted to this topic. One challenge in task design is that tasks are often only described vaguely. Furthermore, Schoenfeld (2009) advises on having more communication between designers and researchers. In this way educational research and design can be bridged, as the communities involving task design are naturally overlapping and diverse. One particular focus concerns the observation that tasks are not single

C. Bokhove (✉)
University of Southampton, Southampton, UK
e-mail: c.bokhove@soton.ac.uk

© Springer International Publishing Switzerland 2017
A. Leung and A. Baccaglini-Frank (eds.), *Digital Technologies in Designing Mathematics Education Tasks*, Mathematics Education in the Digital Era 8,
DOI 10.1007/978-3-319-43423-0_12

events, but are often embedded in a sequence of tasks. It is suggested that the design of sequences of near-similar tasks deserves specific attention. In such sequences it is possible to 'vary' specific parts of tasks over the course of a sequence. One example might be task sequences in which the problem formulation remains constant but the numbers used increase the complexity of the task. This approach has been used previously in an earlier article (Bokhove and Drijvers 2012b), whereby the complexity of tasks first increases, and then—with the help of feedback—decreases. In one sense this can be seen as an adaptation of the 'variation' "Watson and Mason (2006) used when coining the term 'micromodelling' to describe 'learners' response to exercises in which dimensions of variation have been carefully controlled, because the aim is to promote generalization of the dimensions being varied in the exercise, and thence to focus on mathematical relationships between dimensions." (p. 104). Furthermore, certainly in using the term 'variation', it draws similarities with Marton's suggestion of 'Variation Theory'. This theory, promoted by Marton and colleagues (Marton and Booth 1997; Marton and Trigwell 2000; Marton and Tsui 2004; Marton and Pang 2006) and extended by Watson and Mason (2002, 2005) proposes that learners must experience variation in the critical aspects of a concept, within limited space and time, in order for the concept to be learnable. The aim of this chapter is to first describe a digital intervention for acquiring, practicing and assessing algebraic expertise (Bokhove 2011), then go into Marton's concept of Variation, and then demonstrate how these principles tie into the idea of 'variation'. It demonstrates how patterns of variation can be used to frame task design to further the discovery of mathematical knowledge. I will specifically emphasize the role and affordances of technology in operationalizing the idea of variation in this specific algebra intervention, supplementing literature that used the lens of variation for other digital environments (e.g. dynamic geometry environments, Leung 2008; Leung et al. 2013). I will conclude with thoughts on what added value, theoretically and didactically, such an approach might have.

2 Digital Intervention for Algebraic Expertise

The starting point for this chapter is an online intervention which was designed at Utrecht University (Bokhove 2011). The intervention was part of a study called 'Algebra met Inzicht' [Algebra with Insight] and was made in the Digital Mathematical Environment (DME http://www.fi.uu.nl/dwo/en).[1] The DME is a digital learning and assessment environment for mathematics in secondary and higher education, in which interactive teaching methods and feedback play a central role. Within the DME, students can work at any time on modules that have been

---

[1]An English translation of part of the module can be found at http://www.fi.uu.nl/dwo/soton. Log in as guest, and choose 'Demo for 22nd ICMI study'. Java is needed.

Fig. 1 Proposed model for crises, feedback and fading

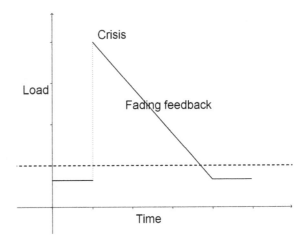

selected for them and receive feedback on their answers. Teachers can view the students' work and adapt modules and activities to meet the class' needs. The DME intervention in the current study consists of a paper-and-pencil pre-test, four digital modules, a digital diagnostic test, and a final digital test and, finally, a paper-and-pencil post-test, and aims to address algebraic expertise. It was deployed in fifteen 12th grade classes from nine Dutch secondary schools (N = 324), involving eleven mathematics teachers. The schools were spread across the country and showed a variation in school size and pedagogical and religious backgrounds. The participating classes consisted of pre-university level 'wiskunde B' students (comparable to grade 12 in Anglo-Saxon countries). As this chapter focuses on the design and sequencing of the tasks, I refer to different articles for more details of the set-up of the study and the actual effects of the digital intervention (Bokhove and Drijvers 2012a, b). The three main design principles behind the design of (sequences of) algebra tasks are crises, feedback and fading. The cohesive argument behind the three principles is depicted in Fig. 1.

I propose that near-similar tasks and repetitive exercises are interspersed by *intentional crises* i.e. tasks that are hard or impossible to solve with skills and knowledge that are available. In other words, the 'load' of the task is too high. I will not go into the word 'load' in detail. There is a vast body of knowledge connected to the term Cognitive Load Theory (Sweller 1988). There also is, rightly so, criticism (De Jong 2010). For the purpose of this model, we will only assume that knowledge that isn't known (novice) potentially will bear a larger load than known knowledge (expert). The intentional crises might be overcome by *providing feedback*. To avoid a dependency on feedback for the summative assessments *feedback is faded* during the course of the sequence of tasks. The three elements will first be explained more extensively.

3   Describing the Three Principles for the Digital Intervention

I will first elaborate on the three elements of the model: crises, feedback and fading. The first element, *crises*, builds on the idea which poet John Keats[2] so eloquently described in the early 19th century as 'failure is the highway to success.' In subsequent centuries this idea that what goes wrong contributes to better learning has been used by several scholars. The principle, for example, seems to underpin Piaget's (1964) concepts of *equilibrium* and *disequilibrium*. These essentially say that, whenever the child's experience/interaction with the environment yielded results that confirmed her mental model, he or she could easily assimilate the experience. When the experience resulted in something new and unexpected, the result was disequilibrium, with a child in some cases experiencing confusion or frustration. Eventually, the child changes his or her cognitive structures to accommodate the new experience and moves back into equilibrium. Tall (1977) refers to *cognitive conflicts*: "one of the distinguishing factors in catastrophe theory is the existence of discontinuities, or sudden jumps in behaviour when certain paths are taken." (p. 6). In his 'levels of thinking' Van Hiele (1985) discerns structure and insight. According to Van Hiele, there can be a *'crisis of thinking'*, which has a link to the Vygotskian zone of proximal development. The common ground between the two is that there is a need for challenge. Recently, drawing on cognitive psychology, Kapur (2010) has used the term *productive failure* and cites Clifford (1984): "However, allowing for the concomitant possibility that under certain conditions letting learners persist, struggle, and even fail at tasks that are complex and beyond their skills and abilities may in fact be a productive exercise in failure requiring a paradigm shift". The difference with my own work (Bokhove and Drijvers 2012b) seems to be whether crises are an inherent part of learning when solving open problems, or actually embedding tasks that could *intentionally* cause a crisis, would be a good thing. It is proposed that intentional crisis tasks are added to sequences of near-similar tasks, for example in the way depicted in Table 1, which illustrates the way in which crisis items are integrated within the current study's intervention. The general structure of such a sequence would then be: first appropriate pre-crisis items, then the item that intends to intentionally cause a crisis (for some students), and then some post-crisis items. The subsequent question then becomes how students can address this crisis. It is suggested that this is done through the second design principle: feedback. Feedback is an integral part of assessment *for* learning, so-called *formative* assessment. Black and Wiliam (1998) define assessment as being 'formative' only when feedback from learning activities is actually used to modify teaching to meet the learner's needs. From this it is clear that feedback plays a pivotal role in the process of formative assessment. Hattie and Timperley (2007) conducted a meta review of the effectiveness of different types of feedback. The

---

[2]It is attributed to Keats but he probably used a different wording.

Table 1 Sequence of items illustrating crises and feedback (Bokhove 2014)

1	Tasks: "Solve the following equation:"	**Pre-crisis items** In the first few items students are confronted with equations they have experience with. Students may choose their own strategy. Many students choose to expand brackets as that is the strategy that they have used often: work towards the form $ax^2+bx+c=0$ and use the Quadratic Formula. There is some limited feedback on the task
2	$(4x-3)\cdot(4x-1)=(4x-3)\cdot 2$	
3	$(x-4)\cdot(3x-5)=(x-4)\cdot(-2x+1)$	
4	$(x-4)\cdot(2x-5)=(x-4)\cdot(-3x+3)$	
5	**Opgave 1.5** Los de volgende vergelijking op: 	 $(5x-13)\cdot(4x-3)-(5x-13)\cdot(-2.$
6	 $(x^2+3x-3)\cdot(8x-6)=(x^2+3x-$ $8x^3+18x^2-42x+18=4x^3+24x$ $4x^3-6x^2-66x=-54$ $4x\left(x^2-1\tfrac{1}{2}x-16\tfrac{1}{2}\right)=-54$	**Crisis item** Some students will be confronted with a crisis if they try to use their conventional strategy of expanding the expression. The yellow tick at the bottom of the screen denotes that the equation is algebraically equivalent to the initial one, but that it is not the final answer. This is accompanied by a partial score for an item and some feedback on correctly rewriting the expression. Although these students showed good rewriting skills, in the end they are not able to continue, as they do not master the skill to solve a third order equation. There is some limited feedback on the task

(continued)

Table 1 (continued)

7	**Opgave 1.7**
	Los de volgende vergelijking op:
	$(2x^2 - 3x - 2) \cdot (7x - 3) = (2x^2 - 3x - 2) \cdot (3x + 12)$
	voorbeeldfilm
8	$(x^2 - 3x - 2) \cdot (6x - 3) = (x^2 - 3x - 2) \cdot (4x + 12)$
9	$\sqrt{3x + 3} \cdot (2x + 4) = \sqrt{3x + 3} \cdot (6x - 5)$
10	$(4x + 4) \cdot \sqrt{-2 + 3x} = \sqrt{3x - 2} \cdot (7x - 5)$
11	$(-5 + {}^2\log(x - 2)) \cdot (6x - 6) = (-5 + {}^2\log(x - 2)) \cdot (3x + 14)$
12	$(4x - 13) \cdot (3x - 3) = (4x - 13) \cdot (-3x + 2)$
13	$(-4x + 5) \cdot (8x - 5) = (-4x + 6) \cdot (3x + 14)$

Post-crisis items

After the crisis item students are offered help by providing a feedback, an instructional screencast, and buttons to get hints ('tip'), the next step in the solution ('stap') or a worked solution ('losop'). These features have in common that they provide feedforward information at the task level and self-regulation (Hattie and Timperley 2007) feedback effects of hints and corrective feedback are deemed best. A meta review of feedback in computer-based learning environments suggested that elaborated feedback, providing an explanation, had large effect sizes for mathematics (Van der Kleij et al. 2015). However, one challenge while providing feedback is that one must make sure students do not overly rely on this feedback, as eventually students often will need to pass a summative test on their own. Assuming that students finally have to pass an exam themselves, it makes sense to address this over-reliance on feedback. In a follow-up paper on his productive failure Kapur (2011) notes that scaffolding implies help to overcome failure (Pea 2004). As a design principle it is therefore proposed that initially a lot of feedback is provided to foster learning, but the amount is decreased towards the end, to facilitate transfer. Using scaffolding this way is based on the concept of *fading* (Renkl et al. 2004). Formative scenarios (Bokhove 2008) are a variation of this concept, starting off with a lot of feedback, and providing a gradually decreasing level of feedback.

Figure 2 shows how this principle was implemented in the intervention. At the start feedback is provided for all intermediate steps of a solution. The subsequent part of the intervention concerns self-assessment and diagnostics: the student performs the steps without any feedback and chooses when to check his or her solution by clicking a "check" button. Feedback is then given for the whole of the exercise.

Finally, students get a final exam with no means to see how they performed, no feedback is given. Just as is the case with a paper test, the teacher will be able to check and grade the exam (in this case automatically) and give students feedback on their performance. A student needs to be able to accomplish tasks independently, without the help of a computer. An implicit advantage of implementing feedback in a sequence of tasks is that teachers and designers have to think upfront about possible student responses (Bokhove 2010). Together the three principles propose

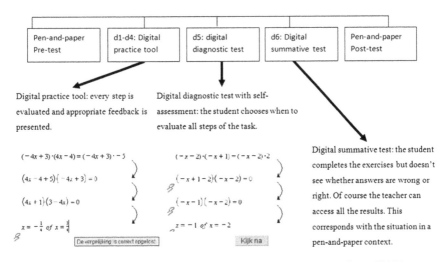

Fig. 2 Outline of fading feedback in formative scenarios (Bokhove and Drijvers 2012b)

embedding *variation* in a sequence of tasks. To demonstrate how the principles might relate to Variation Theory it is first necessary to unpick this term.

4 Unpacking Variation Theories

The idea that invariant structures during changing phenomena often denote the presence knowledge acquisition is an essential part of phenomenology. This is expressed in, among others, the Theory of Variation (e.g. Marton and Booth 1997; Gu et al. 2004). By using variation certain constraints, and associated freedom, give rise to the 'dimensions of possible variation' and 'ranges of permissible change' which are usually at the heart of task design (Mason and Johnston-Wilder 2006). One way of integrating different tasks into pedagogic situations is to make use of 'learner generated examples' and the shared 'example space' (Watson and Mason 2005) or the 'outcome space' (Marton and Booth 1997).

Fan and colleagues (Fan et al. 2004) showed that the "Two Basics" (Basic Knowledge and Basic Skills) in the Mathematics Curriculum of Mainland China can develop into meaningful learning. (Gu 1981) systematically analysed and synthesized the concepts of teaching with variation. He identified and illustrated the two forms of variations: *'conceptual variation'* and *'procedural variation'*. Conceptual variation has as starting point that concepts can be understood from multiple perspectives. Variation is created in several ways. The first way, standard concept variation, is by varying the concept in a standard way via inducing concepts by varying visual and concrete instances. The main purpose of using this variation is to help students establish the connection between concrete experience and abstract concepts. The second way, non-standard concept variation, highlights the essence of a concept by contrasting the concept with a non-standard example. This stresses the teaching strategy that examples should not only be the 'normal' ones, but also the non-standard ones. Finally, the third way of non-concept variation uses non-concepts, for example counterexamples, to reinforce a concept. Procedural variation concerns progressively unfolding mathematics activities. In procedural variation students can arrive at solutions to a problem and form connections among different concepts step by step from multiple approaches. This type of variation is also created in several ways. The first way addresses the formation of concepts and the process of unfolding concepts. The second way uses scaffolding for problem solving. Multiple variations (analyses) of the configuration of a problem do not only help students clarify the *process* of solving the problem and the *structure* of the problem, but also are an effective way of experiencing problem solving and enhancing the competency of problem solving (Gu 1994, as cited in Gu et al. 2004). The third way establishes a system of mathematics experience. Variations make up a system of (hierarchical) experiences and strategies that are internalized into the cognitive structure. The two forms of variation are closely linked to each other, forming a hierarchical system of experiencing process through forming concepts or solving stages of problems. It is this mechanism, where conceptual variation is static and procedural variation is dynamic, that connects processes with previous and new knowledge. Chinese scholars have called this distance between previous and new knowledge 'potential distance' (Gu 1994, as cited in Gu et al. 2004). Effective teachers can judge this distance perfectly, balancing a short distance where new knowledge is acquired, and a long distance which is useful for developing students' exploring competency.

In another vein, the four patterns of variation articulated by Marton in his Theory of Variation (Marton et al. 2004) might provide the best framework for my purpose:

1. Contrast. "… In order to experience something, a person must experience something else to compare it with…"
2. Generalisation. "… In order to fully understand what "three" is, we must also experience varying appearances of three…"
3. Separation. "… In order to experience a certain aspect of something, and in order to separate this aspect from other aspects, it must vary while other aspects remain invariant."
4. Fusion. "…if there are several critical aspects that the learner has to take into consideration at the same time, they must all be experienced simultaneously" (p. 16).

These patterns of variation can bring about discernment and awareness. The focal point of variation is the procedure or form in which problems are proposed. It is *carefully designed* such that only their *non-fundamental elements of knowledge and skills* are changed in a variety of ways. By comparing and differentiating, students struggle to identify invariant properties. In the next section I will argue how these four functions are apparent in the task design for the intervention and what role technology plays in facilitating the four functions.

5 Linking the Patterns of Variation to the Intervention

To demonstrate how the four patterns of variation can be used to design tasks, I take one of the elements of the intervention described previously, namely the sequence with quadratic equations in Table 1. Obviously, this concerns only one mathematical topic, and then only one sub-topic within that topic, but the use of variation can potentially be used for any topic. What variables can we discern? The first variable is the appearance of the equation: basically there are quadratic Eqs. (2, 3, 4, 5, 12 and 13), third order Eqs. (6, 7 and 8) and equations with square roots and logarithms (9, 10 and 11). Almost all the equations have a variation of the pattern $AB = AC$ (2 to 12), only 13 does not have this pattern and tries to confront any new-found assumptions of equations in the sequence always having the pattern $AB = AC$. In my view it possible to describe this sequence of tasks in terms of functions of variation.

When it comes to *contrast*, the third order equations of 6, 7 and 8 were specifically added to provide a non-standard variation. Although they conform to the AB = AC pattern, one of the correct strategies that might have been used in 2 to 5, expanding the brackets, will not be efficient for third order equations.

$$(x - 4) \cdot (2x - 5) = (x - 4) \cdot (-3x + 3) \qquad (4)$$

$$(x^2 + 3x - 3) \cdot (8x - 6) = (x^2 + 3x - 3) \cdot (4x + 12) \qquad (6)$$

A second contrast might be provided by 13 as this equation, although quadratic and visually similar, does not conform to the AB = AC pattern. The amount of contrast in the sequence could further be expanded by including equations with no solutions. Variation is also provided for *generalisation* by presenting the pattern AB = AC in numerous ways, with square roots, with logarithms or even just with all terms at one side of the equality sign.

$$\sqrt{3x + 3} \cdot (2x + 4) = \sqrt{3x + 3} \cdot (6x - 5) \qquad (9)$$

$$\left(-5 + {}^2\log(x - 2)\right) \cdot (6x - 6) = \left(-5 + {}^2\log(x - 2)\right) \cdot (3x + 14) \qquad (11)$$

A further expansion, not in this intervention, could be implemented by not solely presenting factored equations but also the expanded expressions presented in the format $ax^2 + bx + c = 0$. *Separation*, vary an aspect while other aspects remain invariant, is apparent in these examples as well. For example, it is important to note that the coefficients in the items are randomized, something which shall be presented as one of the affordances of technology. Another example was already demonstrated through generalisation: the pattern AB = AC is invariant while the appearance is varied. Potentially, more elements can be varied or kept invariant, which I will demonstrate when I present some affordances of technology in this regard. Finally, *fusion* is obtained by providing multiple representations e.g. through a graphical representation of the equation. Presenting graphs next to equations further emphasizes a crucial aspect of 'solving an equation', namely that it generates coordinates for intersection points of two graphs. This might contribute to the understanding that indeed, for example, Eqs. (4) and (6) have a different number of intersection points and therefore that the Quadratic Formula might not be appropriate. This aspect was under-utilized in this specific study. In my opinion this shows that a sequence of tasks can be designed in such a way that all functions of variation are met. It will often be the case that the four functions are inter-twined rather than distinct functions. In the next section I will describe how technology managed to support these functions.

6 Affordances of Technology for Variation

Technology used in this study supported variation in several ways: through authoring, randomisation, feedback and visualizations.

6.1 Authoring

A prerequisite for any task design is that it's possible to *author* one's own tasks. With pen-and-paper it is evident that this is possible. Digital systems, however, often come with their own non-customizable content (e.g. materials from publishers) or have limited authoring capabilities. If the materials provided already contain aspects of variation then this could serve as appropriate content, but ideally technology would cater for authoring. The DME provides an authoring environment, as depicted in Fig. 3.

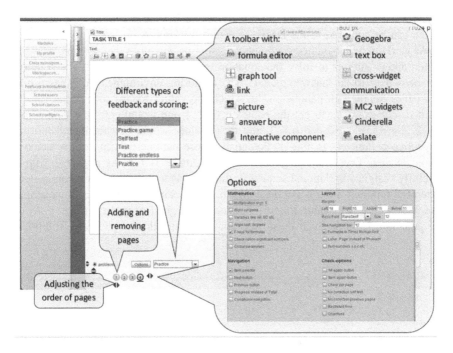

Fig. 3 Overview of the editing window (adapted from: Abels et al. 2013). This is an extended version of the original DME authoring interface, which was part of the MC-squared project, a FP7 EU project which aimed to author creative digital books for mathematics. See http://www.mc2-project.eu/

The main editor allows authors to add and remove pages to a digital book, adjust their order, add different types of feedback and scoring, and—most importantly — add a variety of elements to the pages of the book, ranging from basic static texts to complex, interactive widgets. Potentially, such a feature might allow the authoring of sequences of tasks with variation. In the case of the current intervention these authoring facilities were used to author randomisation, specific *crisis* items and integrate representations.

6.2 Randomisation

A specific example of authoring can be done by using the randomization features in the DME. By 'varying' coefficients within equations it is possible to address the 'separation' function of variation as we 'vary an aspect while other aspects remain invariant'. We can take the quadratic example from 4 to demonstrate this.

$$(x - 4) \cdot (2x - 5) = (x - 4) \cdot (-3x + 3) \tag{4}$$

One starting point could be that this is a specific case of a general equation, which can be authored in the DME, as depicted in Fig. 4.

As working with parameters complicates solving equations the 'possible answer' button allows authors to solve the equation with parameters in place. The solution can be copied to an 'answer model'. The authoring environment also has a box 'Variables for random parameters' in which the values for the parameters can be defined. For example, to get the equation from 4 one would enter b = 1, c = −4, d = 2, f = −5, g = −3 and h = 3, and these values would be substituted into the respective parameters in Fig. 4. Potentially these parameters can be any random whole integer. One interesting observation to make is that, as expected with a carefully designed variational sequence, thought has to go into this randomisation. Often full randomisation is not desirable. In this specific example it is obvious that variables with a zero value might influence the original pedagogical intentions of the equation. It might even mean equations suddenly do not yield any solutions.

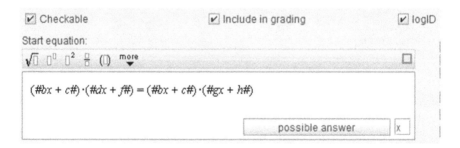

Fig. 4 Using parameters to get variation

With the quadratic equation $ax^2 + bx + c = 0$ one initially would want there to be solutions, even well rounded solutions, for example to practise factoring. Just as with designing sequences of variational tasks one wants to 'control' the values of parameters, but also benefit from the technological affordance of randomisation. This might be typified as *semi-randomisation* for variation: parameters are random but the author/designer carefully chooses the range of values parameters may take. In the final version of the intervention variables were defined as $b = 1...5$; $c = -3, -4, -5, -6, -7$; $d = 1...4$; $f = -5, -3, -1$; $g = -3, -2, -1$ and $h = 1...4$ whereby $1...5$ denotes all whole numbers from 1 to 5. This means there are potentially $5 \times 5 \times 4 \times 3 \times 3 \times 4 = 3600$ different equations a student can get, but they all adhere to the AB = AC pattern because they have been authored that way. If one would choose to expand the terms in the equation with the parameters in place, this would be a useful way to change the appearance of the equation but still ensure there are suitable (and nicely rounded) solutions. In principle we could even start with a third order equation and in the early cases simply choose our parameters in such a way that only lower order terms are generated. Likewise, we could argue that linear terms are nothing more than quadratic terms $ax^2 + bx + c$ formatted with $a = 0$. Anecdotally, in projects in which these features were used, some designers really enjoyed the process of determining appropriate parameters. The feature of randomisation allows a 'scaffolding' of variation by using a similar 'generalized' template for all the tasks, and varying the parameters. Randomisation is not only restricted to algebraic topics parameters in the DME can also be used for other domains, for example generating random coordinates in geometry tasks.

6.3   Feedback

In static paper-and-pencil cases a carefully designed sequence with variation hinges on assumptions about student responses to the tasks. Ideally, sequences are designed in such a way that (most) students can make them. The previously mentioned 'potential distance' should not be too large i.e. students should be enabled to overcome any problems. This, of course, is even more important when an *intentional* crisis is implemented in the sequence of tasks. Normally, in a classroom setting, I would assume this would be part of teacher feedback. If I go with the desire to implement crisis items for variation, and would want to address these by providing feedback, one affordance of technology might be the provision of automatic feedback to overcome such crises (Van der Kleij et al. 2015). I specifically see the design of feedback as an important part of the task design as well (also see Bokhove 2010), allowing not only to design for variation but also the feedback that might scaffold the sequence of tasks. The DME allows authors to design such feedback in several ways. The first feature is the 'built in' feedback

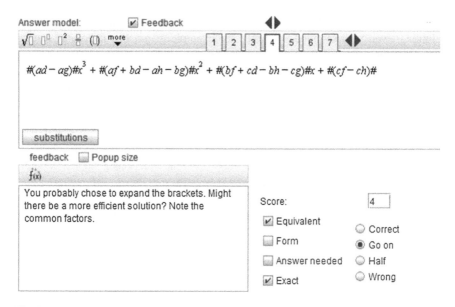

Fig. 5 Feedback might be customized

features which indicate whether a next step in a solution to an equation is (partially) correct. This can be accompanied by a score as well. A second concerns the feature of being able to author custom feedback.

In the context of variation in the previous examples, feedback could be provided to help students notice the AB = AC pattern. Figure 5 shows how for Eq. (7) from Table 1, feedback might be customized to indicate the common factors. There also is a rule-based feedback provision with buttons to get hints ('tip'), the next step in the solution ('stap') or a worked solution ('losop'). Feedback can also be moderated at a more general level by choosing several 'modes': a practise mode gives full feedback, a self-test mode asks students to evaluate their answer when they're ready and an exam mode 'mimics' a summative test setting. This feature is used for the previously mentioned fading of feedback.

6.4   Visualisations

To discern several critical aspects in one go, fusion, the task designer can incorporate several representations in the sequence of tasks. Figure 6 shows how two representations can be authored in the DME. This feature becomes particularly powerful if these representations can be provided for several variational tasks.

This feature can also be 'linked' in that graphs, equations and other representations like a balancing scale can interact: change one representation and the other representation(s) change(s) as well, as demonstrated in Fig. 7.

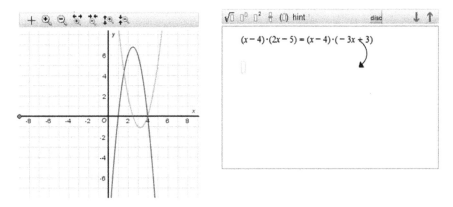

Fig. 6 Multiple representations for one equation

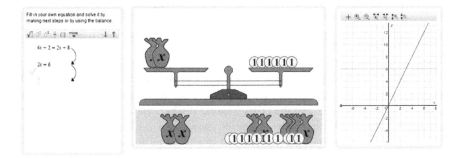

Fig. 7 Three linked representations: equation, scales and graphs

Teachers or students can create an equation (left side of the figure). The equation that is created can be represented as a pair of scales (middle part of the figure). A third representation is provided by the graph. Several critical aspects are experienced together: the algebraic notation of the equation, the fact that 'solving an equation' corresponds to using a model of 'balancing scales' and also that it represents the intersection of two—in this case linear—graphs.

7 A Student at Work

Let's look at one student named Pauline while utilizing the environment. In the first task the student has to get acquainted with the digital environment. The pre-crisis items pose no problem for most students, including Pauline. On arriving at the crisis item 1.6 students exhibit three behaviours, roughly corresponding with the ones already observed in the pre-test: (i) students solve the equation correctly, (ii) students recognize the pattern AB = AC of the equation but subsequently make

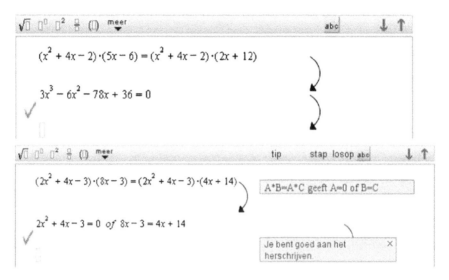

Fig. 8 Pauline's digital work. *Left* crisis item *left*. *Right* post-crisis item

mistakes (for example by losing solutions in the process), and (iii) students do not recognize AB = AC and expand the expressions, getting stuck with an equation of the third power. The design of this sequence, utilizing the affordances of the technology, hypothesized that the crisis item serves as a variational element in the sequence of tasks. The left side of Fig. 8 shows that our case student Pauline demonstrates the third type of behaviour. At this point in the sequence feedback is still restricted to correct or incorrect. In addition, students are allowed to choose their own strategies, even when they aren't efficient or might lead to problems. In the post-crisis items, the feedback correct/incorrect is supplemented by custom feedback, buttons for hints and worked examples, and a movie clip demonstrating the correct solution. From the log-files of the online environment—all student work is stored—it becomes clear that Pauline fails at the crisis-item, but succeeds at the post-crisis item with feedback.

This example demonstrates how the elements of technology use and three design principles (crises, feedback and fading) can be combined with a carefully designed sequence of tasks with variation.

8 Conclusion and Discussion

This chapter sought to demonstrate how three principles, crises, feedback and fading, which were the basis of a digital intervention for algebraic expertise, were retrospectively scrutinised through the lens of Variation Theory with its functions of contrast, generalisation, separation and fusion. I contend that the principles share several elements with this lens. Crisis items primarily aim to *contrast* with the standard procedure students tend to use. By intentionally causing a crisis this contrast is emphasized. This is also emphasized by using varying appearances of the task, aimed at instilling *generalisation* in the students. By carefully varying certain aspects only, and leaving other aspects invariant, *separation* is obtained. Finally, *fusion* is obtained by providing multiple representations e.g. through a graphical representation of the equation. The functions of variation can be supported by technology. In this specific intervention this was done through four features: the feature of being able to author one's own tasks, the feature of using randomisation for these tasks, the feature of authoring and providing feedback, and the feature of being able to use multiple representations. The task designer can really utilize these features to implement a carefully designed sequence of tasks with appropriate variation. In this example the main focus was on algebra, but the DME also implements other domains, like geometry and statistics. It might be beneficial if educators, teachers, designers and researchers alike can adopt these principles when designing and implementing sequences of (near-similar) tasks. There are several advantages to this approach. Firstly, the 'lens' of Variation Theory enables authors, teachers and designers alike to realise the importance of careful task design. Making good instructional materials is an art and should not be taken lightly. Guiding principles for their design can facilitate the creation of quality materials. Secondly, as a consequence of thinking more carefully about task design with technology, using these aspects of variation contributes to more effective learning by students. We must keep in mind that we are talking about web-based tools, basically digital books, which incorporate these features. Their presence greatly enhances the quality of instructional resources. They can incorporate sensible design of task sequences, a vast set of tasks through randomisation, relevant feedback and multiple representations.

There are, however, some points of discussion. One concerns when we are actually talking about variation, as variation depends on variant and invariant elements of the tasks. In other words, the variation needs to be observed. It would be hard to argue that the level of discernment does not also depend on prior knowledge or the difficulty of the task. What can be a simple task for one year-eight student can prove to be difficult for another student, even when at first sight they seem fairly similar. Also, the way in which a crisis is overcome can differ: some students learn from repeating near-similar tasks, others seem to recognize 'a pattern' immediately and apply this to new tasks. Given this diversity, it is important to field-test and evaluate sequences of tasks, again combining the power of teaching, researching and designing. In my opinion, there sometimes also is the wrong assumption to classify certain tasks as 'more creative' and other tasks as 'less creative'. This too depends on the background and context of the learner: a wonderful, new and creative task can become a repetitive task the second time around. In this respect, variation is context-dependent, and this further emphasizes the importance of being able to flexibly change and author materials. One could even go as far to say that the predicate 'near-similar' applies to almost *all* tasks in education: if a student has seen a task before, even the elaborate, creative ones, it becomes part of the cognitive structure. It fits the literature which says the acquisition of concepts and procedures is inextricably linked (e.g. Star 2005;

Rittle-Johnson et al. 2015; or 'deep learning' by Ohlsson 2011). The already cited work by Fan et al. (2004) and my work with Fan on algorithms (Fan and Bokhove 2014) suggests that this might 'explain' some contradictory observations that Asian countries address memorisation and understanding. Variation certainly seems to be a powerful way to combine both, and in this light I think this chapter describes already powerful design principles through the lens of variation.

References

Abels, M., Boon, P., & Tacoma, S. (2013). *Designing in the digital mathematics environment*. Retrieved from http://www.fisme.uu.nl/wisweb/dwo/DWO_handleidingen/2013-10-11manual_DMEauthoringtool.pdf.

Black, P., & Wiliam, D. (1998). Inside the black box: Raising standards through classroom Assessment. *Phi Delta Kappan, 80*(2), 139–149.

Bokhove, C. (2008, June). *Use of ICT in formative scenarios for algebraic skills*. Paper presented at the 4th Conference of the International Society for Design and Development in Education, Egmond aan Zee, The Netherlands.

Bokhove, C. (2010). Implementing feedback in a digital tool for symbol sense. *International Journal for Technology in Mathematics Education, 17*(3), 121–126.

Bokhove, C. (2011). *Use of ICT for acquiring, practicing and assessing algebraic expertise*. Utrecht: Freudenthal Institute, Utrecht University.

Bokhove, C., & Drijvers, P. (2012a). Effects of a digital intervention on the development of algebraic expertise. *Computers & Education, 58*(1), 197–208. doi:10.1016/j.compedu.2011.08.010.

Bokhove, C., & Drijvers, P. (2012b). Effects of feedback in an online algebra intervention. *Technology, Knowledge and Learning., 7*(1–2), 43–59. doi:10.1007/s10758-012-9191-8.

Bokhove, C. (2014). Using crises, feedback and fading for online task design. *PNA, 8*(4), 127–138.

Clifford, M. M. (1984). Thoughts on a theory of constructive failure. *Educational Psychologist, 19*(2), 108–120.

De Jong, T. (2010). Cognitive load theory, educational research, and instructional design: Some food for thought. *Instructional Science, 38*(2), 105–134. doi:10.1007/s11251-009-9110-0.

Fan, L., & Bokhove, C. (2014). Rethinking the role of algorithms in school mathematics: a conceptual model with focus on cognitive development. *ZDM-International Journal on Mathematics Education, 46*(3). doi:10.1007/s11858-014-0590-2.

Fan, L., Wong, N. Y., Cai, J., & Li, S. (Eds.). (2004). *How Chinese learn mathematics: Perspectives from insiders*. Singapore: World Scientific.

Gu, L. (1981). *The visual effect and psychological implication of transformation of figures in geometry*. Paper presented at Annual Conference of Shanghai Mathematics Association, Shanghai, China.

Gu, L. (1994). Theory of teaching experiment: The methodology and teaching principle of Qingpu [in Chinese]. Beijing, China: Educational Science Press.

Gu, L., Huang, R., & Marton, F (2004) Teaching with variation: A Chinese way of promoting effective Mathematics learning. In L. Fan, N. Y. Wong, J. Cai & S. Li (Eds.), *How Chinese learn mathematics: Perspectives from insiders* (2nd ed.). Singapore. World Scientific Publishing.

Hattie, J., & Timperley, H. (2007). The power of feedback. *Review of Educational Research, 77*(1), 81–112.

Kapur, M. (2010). Productive failure in mathematical problem solving. *Instructional Science, 38*(6), 523–550.

Kapur, M. (2011). A further study of productive failure in mathematical problem solving: Unpacking the design components. *Instructional Science, 39*(4), 561–579.

Leung, A. (2008). Dragging in a dynamic geometry environment through the lens of variation. *International Journal of Computers for Mathematical Learning, 13*, 135–157.

Leung, A., Baccaglini-Frank, A., & Mariotti, M. A. (2013). Discernment in dynamic geometry environments. *Educational Studies in Mathematics, 84*(3), 439–460. doi:10.1007/s10649-013-9492-4.

Marton, F., & Booth, S. (1997). *Learning and Awareness*. Mahwah: Lawrence Erlbaum.

Marton, F., & Pang, M. (2006). On some necessary conditions of learning. *Journal of the Learning Sciences, 15*(2), 193–220.

Marton, F., & Trigwell, K. (2000). Variatio est Mater Studiorum. *Higher Education Research and Development, 19*(3), 381–395.

Marton, F., Runesson, U., & Tsui, A. B. M. (2004). The space of learning. In F. Marton & A. B. M. Tsui (Eds.), *Classroom discourse and the space of learning* (pp. 3–40). Mahwah: Lawrence Erlbaum Associates, Inc. Publishers.

Marton, F., & Tsui, A. (Eds.). (2004). *Classroom discourse and the space for learning*. Marwah: Erlbaum.

Mason, J., & Johnston-Wilder, S. (2006). *Designing and using mathematical tasks*. London: QED Publishing.

Ohlsson, S. (2011). *Deep learning: How the mind overrides experience?* Cambridge: Cambridge University Press.

Pea, R. D. (2004). The social and technological dimensions of scaffolding and related theoretical concepts of learning, education, and human activity. *Journal of the Learning Sciences, 13*(3), 423–451.

Piaget, J. (1964). Development and learning. In R. E. Ripple & V. N. Rockcastle (Eds.), *Piaget Rediscovered* (pp. 7–20). New York: Cornell University Press.

Renkl, A., Atkinson, R. K., & Große, C. S. (2004). How fading worked solution steps works—a cognitive load perspective. *Instructional Science, 32*(1/2), 59–82.

Rittle-Johnson, B., Schneider, M., & Star, J. R. (2015). Not a one-way street: Bidirectional relations between procedural and conceptual knowledge of mathematics. *Educational Psychology Review, 27*(4), 587–597.

Schoenfeld, A. H. (2004). The math wars. *Educational Policy, 18*(1), 253–286. doi:10.1177/0895904803260042.

Schoenfeld, A. H. (2009). Bridging the cultures of educational research and design. *Educational Designer, 1*(2).

Star, J. R. (2005). Reconceptualizing procedural knowledge. *Journal for Research in Mathematics Education, 36*(5), 404–411.

Sweller, J. (1988). Cognitive load during problem solving: Effects on learning. *Cognitive Science, 12*(2), 257–285. doi:10.1016/0364-0213(88)90023-7.

Tall, D. (1977). Cognitive conflict and the learning of mathematics. In *Proceedings of the First Conference of The International Group for the Psychology of Mathematics Education*. Utrecht: PME. Retrieved from http://www.warwick.ac.uk/staff/David.Tall/pdfs/dot1977a-cog-confl-pme.pdf.

Van der Kleij, F. M., Feskens, R. C. W., & Eggen, T. J. H. M. (2015). Effects of feedback in a computer-based learning environment on students' learning outcomes: A meta-analysis. *Review of Educational Research*. Advance online publication. doi:10.3102/0034654314564881.

Van Hiele, P. M. V. (1985). *Structure and Insight: A theory of mathematics education*. Orlando: Academic Press.

Watson, A., & Mason, J. (2002). Student-generated examples in the learning of mathematics. *Canadian Journal of Science, Mathematics and Technology Education, 2*(2), 237–249.

Watson, A., & Mason, J. (2005). *Mathematics as a constructive activity: Learners generating examples*. Mahwah: Erlbaum.

Watson, A., & Mason, J. (2006). Seeing an exercise as a single mathematical object: Using variation to structure sense-making. *Mathematical Thinking and Learning, 8*(2), 91–111.

Feedback and Discrepancies of a Physical Toolkit and a Digital Toolkit: Opportunities and Pitfalls for Mediating the Concept of Rotational Symmetry

Yip-Cheung Chan, Allen Leung and Doris Ming Yuen Ong

Abstract In this chapter, excerpts of lessons on using tool-based tasks to teach the concept of 'rotational symmetry' were analyzed. Both the instrumental approach and the theory of semiotic mediation were adopted as theoretical frameworks. We compare a lesson carried out with a tailor-made physical tool and one carried out with the software PowerPoint (a digital tool). The analysis focuses on the opportunities and pitfalls that these two tools offer and on how the tasks could (or could not) exploit the semiotic potential of the tool used. In particular, the notions of feedback and discrepancy are theorized. Hypotheses on these notions in the context of designing and implementing tool-based mathematics tasks are raised. We propose that the critical features of the object of exploration, the discrepancy opportunity and pitfall of the tool and the task as well as the teachers' sensitivity and insights into the discrepancy are important considerations for tool-based mathematical task design. They provide a useful guiding framework for investigating the pedagogical affordances of different mathematical tools. We hope that this chapter can provide insights into how the choice of the tools and the design of tool-based tasks may enhance exploitation of the semiotic potential of the tools.

Keywords Feedback · Discrepancy · Instrumental distance · Rotational symmetry · Tool-based mathematics education task

Y.-C. Chan (✉)
The Chinese University of Hong Kong, Sha Tin, Hong Kong
e-mail: mathchan@cuhk.edu.hk

A. Leung
Department of Education Studies, Hong Kong Baptist Univerisity,
Kowloon Tong, Hong Kong, SAR, China
e-mail: aylleung@hkbu.edu.hk

D.M.Y. Ong
St. Edward's Catholic Primary School, Kwun Tong, Hong Kong

© Springer International Publishing Switzerland 2017
A. Leung and A. Baccaglini-Frank (eds.), *Digital Technologies in Designing Mathematics Education Tasks*, Mathematics Education in the Digital Era 8,
DOI 10.1007/978-3-319-43423-0_13

1   Introduction

The use of concrete physical manipulative objects to teach mathematics has a long history (c.f., Dienes 1960, 1971). Designing tool-based learning tasks has been popular in recent decades because of the developments of digital interactive environments such as Geometer's Sketchpad or Cabri. A tool-based task is a teacher-designed 'thing-to-do' using a tool, either concrete or virtual, for students to experience potential mathematical meanings carried by the tool involved, where the teacher then "orchestrates" a task-based discussion to foster the development of the intended mathematics meanings (Mariotti and Maracci 2012). The theme of this chapter is investigating the differences and similarities between task design with digital tools and task design with physical tools.

In this chapter, excerpts of lessons that make use of tool-based tasks to teach the concept of 'rotational symmetry' were analyzed under the frameworks of the instrumental approach and the theory of semiotic mediation. We compare a lesson carried out with a tailor-made physical tool and one carried out with the software PowerPoint (a digital tool).

The use of PowerPoint instead of a more sophisticated Digital Interactive Mathematics Learning Environment was the teacher's choice, due to an attempt to simulate the tailor-made physical tool with a familiar software environment.

The analysis proposed focuses on opportunities and pitfalls that these two tools may offer and on how teachers may use the tools to set up the learning tasks and post-task mathematics discussions to exploit the semiotic potential of these tools. It is hoped that this analysis can provide some insight into how the choices of tools and the designs of tool-based tasks influence the exploitation of such semiotic potential.

2   Theoretical Perspectives

2.1   Instrumental Approach

The instrumental approach was originally proposed by Vérillon and Rabardel (1995), and Vérillon (2000), in the context of vocational and technology education. Later, it was used extensively for investigating the use of technologies in mathematics learning and teaching (see for example, Drijvers et al. 2010). The central idea it proposes is to differentiate an artifact from an instrument. An artifact is a man-made object or a tool designed for a specific purpose, e.g. plastic shape blocks or computer software. An instrument is a psychological construct composed by an artifact and its associated utilization scheme implemented by a particular user for a specific purpose or context (Vérillon and Rabardel 1995; Vérillon 2000). Depending on the user's utilization scheme, an artifact may or may not be the instrument it is originally intended to be. An artifact may be used in a way that is not as intended or designed; Béguin and Rabardel (2000) called this phenomenon "catacresis". In some situations, a same person may use a same artifact differently in different situations or contexts, and thus, the same artifact can become two different instruments: "a single artifact serves as several instruments in different situations" (Vérillon 2000, p. 7). Furthermore, an artifact may become a different instrument in the hands of different people. Thus, an instrument is situational-dependent and personal-dependent. In some instances, "artifacts may be available but no instruments are elicited" (Vérillon 2000, p. 7). The process of transforming an artifact into an instrument, or put in another way, the process of evolution of a utilization scheme of the artifact, is called "instrumental genesis" (Verillon and Rabardel 1995; Vérillon 2000). It is a long-term and unexpectedly complex process (Artigue 2003) and it is a bi-directional process between the artifact and the users (Trouche 2004).

2.2 Semiotic Mediation

The framework of "semiotic mediation" (Bussi and Mariotti 2008) rooted within the Vygotskian perspective on social construction of knowledge (Vygotsky 1978) highlights the mediating role of an artifact. An artifact which carries mathematical meanings can become a "tool of semiotic mediation" by which the students can experience the development of mathematical concepts. In particular, a tool of semiotic mediation provides a means to express mathematical ideas. Bussi and Mariotti (2008) point out that there is a "double semiotic link" between a tool, a task and mathematical knowledge when the tool is used to accomplish a specific task. They further point out that:

> The main point is that of exploiting the system of relationships among artifact, task and mathematical knowledge. On the one hand, an artifact is related to a specific task … that seeks to provide a suitable solution. On the other hand, the same artifact is related to a specific mathematical knowledge (Bussi and Mariotti 2008, p. 753).

This double semiotic relationship is called the "semiotic potential" of the tool (Bussi and Mariotti 2008, p. 754). In the mathematics classroom, the teacher plays a crucial role in the process of semiotic mediation. Empirical studies suggest that teachers can promote the evolution of mathematics knowledge through "orchestrating" tool-based learning tasks and post-task mathematics discussions. (See for example, Jones 2000; Mariotti 2002; Falcade et al. 2007.) We follow Mariotti and Maracci (2012) in using "orchestration" as a metaphor for classroom discussions with the aim "of developing shared meanings, having an explicit formulation, de-contextualized from the artifact [tool] use, recognizable and acceptable by the mathematicians' community" (p. 60). As "the voice of mathematics culture", the teacher guides the mathematical discussions which aim at bringing out the semiotic potential of the tool: a progression from students' production of mathematical discourse to mathematical knowledge.

2.3 Feedback and Discrepancy

During the process of semiotic mediation, an artifact supports experimental approaches to theoretical thinking via classroom dynamic relationships among the tool, the task, students' productions and the teacher, and mathematical knowledge (Arzarello et al. 2012). In this process, the teacher uses feedback from the tool to open up mathematical discourse. In this sense, feedback plays a mediating role between the students' production and the mathematical concepts intended to be taught. It is a bi-directional process. On the one hand, the tool acts towards the user (teachers or students) through feedback. On the other hand, the teacher can adjust the tool to 'control' the feedback to facilitate mediation between students' discourses and curriculum mathematics or between visualization and reasoning. Thus, designed feedback can be regarded as "didactical intervention" which can be developed into a tool of semiotic mediation (c.f. Leung and Bolite-Frant, p. 193).

Discrepancy is a special kind of feedback given by the tools. It deviates from the standard representations of the intended mathematical concept of the lessons. It has influences on students' learning. Chan and Leung (2013) proposed this notion as a possible way to interpret the semiotic potential of a tool. Leung and Bolite-Frant (2015) elaborate this notion and defined the *discrepancy potential* of a tool as "a pedagogical space generated by (i) feedback due to the nature of the tool or design of the task that possibly deviates from the intended mathematical concept, or (ii) uncertainty created due to the nature of the tool or design of the task that requires the tool users to make decisions" (p. 212). This notion resonates with the notion of *instrumental distance* which is rooted within the instrumental approach. Haspekian (2005, 2011, 2014) introduced and elaborated this notion to highlight the constraints and instrumental needs in integrating a computer tool into mathematics teaching. In particular, he proposed that "the more complex the instrumental process is, with regard to the traditional environment (paper and pencil), that is to say, the bigger is its distance from the 'current school habits', the more difficult the integration of the tool is" (p. 135). From the perspective of semiotic mediation, the notion of instrumental distance can be regarded as the size of the gap between the mathematics represented by the tool and the mathematical concepts intended to be taught. In other words, instrumental distance can be regarded as the measure of the 'length' of the *discrepancy*. Leung and Bolite-Frant (2015) and Haspekian (2011) pointed out that *discrepancy* or *instrumental distance* does not have inherent "good" or "bad" values.

In Chan and Leung (2013) a task based on a tailor-made physical tool designed for developing the concept of rotational symmetry was described and discussed. In this chapter, a similar task using a digital tool (PowerPoint) will be discussed and compared with the non-digital task. Based on the comparison of these two tools and the corresponding tasks, the notion of *discrepancy* on tool-based mathematics education tasks will be hypothesized with respect to *feedback* and *discrepancy potential* in tool-based tasks, and their positions in the frameworks of the instrumental approach and semiotic mediation will be proposed.

3   The Context

The excerpts of lesson episodes chosen for discussion in this chapter were taken from a Lesson Study carried out in Grade 5 classrooms at a Hong Kong primary school[1] based on the Japanese's Lesson Study (Fernandez and Yoshida 2004) and the Learning Study (Lo et al. 2005) models. The research lessons aimed at improving mathematics teaching through tool-based tasks. Five Grade 5 mathematics teachers worked together over a period of five months to design lessons for a selected topic. The topic selected for the research lesson was rotational symmetry. One teacher implemented the lesson whereas other teachers observed and evaluated the lesson. A modified lesson was agreed upon by the teachers and was implemented by another teacher (in another class). This cycle was repeated until all five teachers had taught the lesson to their own classes. A researcher in charge (one of the authors) acted as a participant observer and gave theoretical advice. All the teacher preparation meetings, lessons and the post-lesson discussion were video-recorded.

3.1   The Tool and the Task

The objective of the lesson was to introduce to the students the idea of a rotational symmetric figure; that is, a figure that 'overlaps itself' at least two times during one cycle of rotation. A toolkit was specially designed for this lesson. There were two versions of the toolkit: a physical version and a digital version.

The physical version of the toolkit, which we call the 'transparency toolkit', consisted of blue-tacks, push pins, an overhead transparency, a pen and a styrofoam board. It was designed for the purpose of verifying whether a given/constructed figure has the property of rotational symmetry. Students were asked to copy a figure (or a figure constructed using given plastic shapes) on the overhead transparency. The copied figure acted as an identical copy of the original figure and was placed on top of the original figure. Students used the push pin to locate and fasten the position of the centre of rotation. While rotating the transparency, the original figure and the rotated copied figure could be seen at the same time (see Fig. 1).

The digital version of the toolkit was situated within the software PowerPoint. It was the teacher's choice to use a file in PowerPoint as the digital tool instead of using dynamic geometry software. The design was similar to the transparency toolkit with some built-in commands designed to have the same functions as some components of the 'transparency toolkit'. The polygons under 'basic shapes' in the PowerPoint software were used to create the figures. The 'group' and 'ungroup' commands served the same function as blue-tack in the sense that different shapes can be

[1]The authors would like to express their gratitude to the team of mathematics teachers form St. Edward's Catholic Primary School who designed and implemented this Lesson Study.

Fig. 1 Transparency toolkit

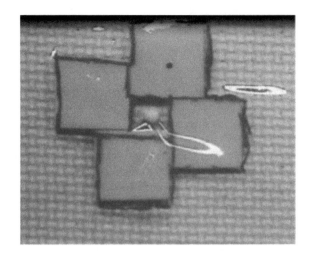

Fig. 2 The 'rotational
control handle' of PowerPoint
software

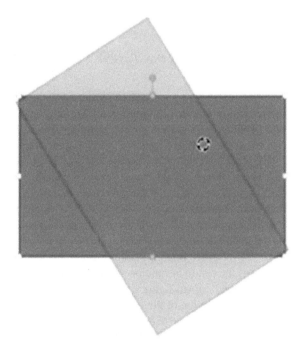

combined as a single figure. The 'rotational control handle' enabled the user to rotate
a shape or a group of shapes. This was useful for figure creation and for figure
verification. While rotating a shape or a group of shapes by using the 'rotational
control handle', the original figure and the rotated image co-exist on the computer
screen (Fig. 2). Thus it served the same function as the overhead transparency in the
'transparency toolkit'. This synchronic simultaneity feature of both the physical and

digital toolkits enables the concept of rotational symmetry to become visible and manipulative. The co-existence of the original figure and the rotated image demonstrates the concept of rotational symmetry which is defined as a figure which appears identically more than once when it is rotated about a certain point (the pushpin in the physical toolkit or the centre embedded in the rotation function of PowerPoint) in one cycle. This constituted part of the semiotic potential of the toolkits.

The lesson structure was basically the same in all the five classes, while there were slight differences in the details; in particular, some classes used the digital toolkit and the others used the physical toolkit. The teacher started the lesson by giving a brief review on line symmetry through a whole-class discussion and, briefly, the idea of rotational symmetry was introduced. Then a figure was given to the students and they were asked to verify/explore whether the figure has the property of rotational symmetry using the chosen toolkit. The last part was the main part of the lesson. Some identical polygons were given to the students. Students (working in pairs) were asked to design rotational symmetric figures using these polygons and used the toolkit to verify their work. Afterwards, a whole-class discussion was led by the teacher along with the students' presentations.

In the next section, excerpts from lessons of three classes (Lesson A, Lesson B and Lesson C) are described. The transparency toolkits (physical tool) were used in Lessons A and B. A sheet of squared paper was used in Lesson A to create the shapes while plastic square pieces were used in Lesson B. A file in PowerPoint (a digital tool) was used in Lesson C.

4 Analysis

In this section, feedback and discrepancies observed from Lesson A, Lesson B and Lesson C will be compared. The opportunities and pitfalls offered by the feedback and discrepancies will be analyzed.

4.1 Feedback from Tool-Use

4.1.1 Feedback as Guidance for Creating Rotational Symmetric Figures

In Lesson A, square grid paper was given to students to draw figures with rotational symmetry. After guidance from the teacher, by rotating the square grid paper while drawing, some students were able to produce simple figures with rotational symmetry.

In Lesson B, besides square grid paper, plastic square pieces were given to the students. The plastic pieces provided students with a tangible experience to comprehend the meaning of rotational symmetry. These allowed the students to rotate the individual square pieces and consequently to be able to produce more complicated figures. Some students could detect and correct mistakes by rotating the individual square pieces. For instance, a pair of students initially proposed an incorrect figure (Fig. 3a). By rotating (some of) the square pieces, they found that the figure did not have the sought for property of rotational symmetry (Fig. 3b). Then they modified the figure to obtain it (Fig. 3c).

(a)

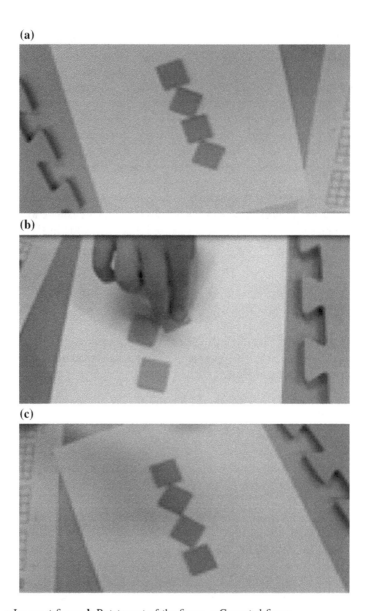

(b)

(c)

Fig. 3 a Incorrect figure. **b** Rotate part of the figure. **c** Corrected figure

In this self-correction process enabled by the *feedback* of the tool (in this case, the plastic square pieces), students experienced that the upper half and the lower half of a rotational symmetrical figure they produced have the same distance from the centre but in opposite directions. This may emerge from students' intuitive understanding of the meaning of a 2-fold rotational symmetry.

In Lesson C, students worked with the PowerPoint file. A number of identical polygons of one type (say a triangle) created from the 'basic shapes' menu of the software were given to the students. Students were required to create rotational symmetric figures by dragging the given type of polygons around and 'stick' them together. If they wished, they could reproduce more polygons of the given type using the 'copy-&-paste' command. Students usually grouped, ungrouped, and re-grouped the polygons alternatively in order to rearrange part of the figure by using the 'rotational control handle'. Figure 4 shows a typical working sequence in which the figure was created by grouping and re-grouping the polygons. During this process, the actions of rotation and grouping-and-regrouping were guided by *feedback* that focused on figural accuracy (e.g. making sure that there is no gap between the sides of two figures when they are dragged to stick).

When comparing lessons A and B, it was observed by the teachers and the researcher that the square grid paper was not as conducive as the plastic square pieces in bringing about the (intuitive) meaning of rotational symmetry. What made the difference? One possibility was that the square grid paper could not be separated into different parts. Whenever the whole sheet was rotated, all the individual squares were changed in the same way. The *lack of variation* of parts in the creation process may result in a limited experience of which features are typical in rotational symmetry and hence the critical to be discerned in a rotational symmetric figure. In contrast, the plastic square pieces could be manipulated as separate entities and changed with respect to each other in different ways. This opened up wider variation and opportunity to produce more complicated figures. As seen in the 'self-correction' example of Lesson B, students could rotate *parts of* the created figure (the middle two squares). This may have lead to discernment of critical features of rotational symmetry (Marton 2015) and hence to an intuitive understanding of the concept. Thus a shift of attention between the parts and the whole of the object of exploration (the rotational symmetric figure) could occur through manipulation of the square pieces but this may not be the case for the grid paper. In Lesson C, the feasibility of swapping the attention between the *whole* and the *parts* was even more conducive, thanks to the 'group' and 'ungroup' commands. As observed in Lesson C, these two (related) commands provided a convenient tool for controlling which parts of the created figure should be changed (rotated) and which parts of the figure kept invariant, and hence the shifting of attention between the *parts* and the *whole* of the object of exploration through manipulation could be easily managed and fortified. Consequently, a possible link between visualisation (an intuitive idea of rotational symmetry) and reasoning (a definition and properties of rotational symmetry) could be established.

Fig. 4 Producing a figure by using group/ungroup commands and the rotational control handle

4.1.2 Feedback Initiated Discussion as a Bridge to Link up Students' Produced Figures with the Concept of Rotational Symmetry

After the group activity that involved creating the figure, the teacher selected a few student groups to report on their works in front of the class and initiated a mathematical discussion which aimed at exploiting aspects of the semiotic potential of the tool. The structure of this phase was basically the same. First, the teacher asked the students whether the figure had the property of rotational symmetry and then verified it by using either the transparency toolkit (we will call this the physical toolkit) or the 'rotational control handle' of the PowerPoint file (the digital toolkit). In Lessons A and B, the transparency toolkit was used. The students were asked to use the pushpin to fasten the centre of rotation. Then, they were asked to demonstrate the figure's rotational symmetry by using the transparency toolkit. While rotating the transparency, the whole class was instructed to pay attention to when the original figure (i.e. the figure composed by the square pieces) and the rotated figure (i.e. the figure on the transparency) overlapped. In Lesson C, PowerPoint was used. The procedure was similar but the 'rotational control handle' was used to do the demonstration. The polygons were combined into one whole figure through the 'grouping' command. Then, the figure was rotated by using the 'rotational control handle'. The synchronic simultaneous appearance of the original figure and the rotated image served the same function as the overhead transparency used in Lessons A and B. When the two figures overlapped, the whole class counted the number of times the overlapping occurred. After a cycle of rotation, the teacher asked the whole class whether the figure had the property of rotational symmetry and highlighted the reason (i.e. the figure overlapped at least two times in one cycle).

Despite the fact that the structures of the post-activity discussions were similar across the lessons, a subtle difference between the lessons using the transparency toolkit and the lessons using PowerPoint was observed. Some students rotated the figure *too quickly* without paying attention to whether the original figure and the image ever overlapped. This problem was more severe in Lesson C (the lesson which used PowerPoint) than Lessons A and B (the lessons which used the transparency toolkit). A possible reason was that it was much easier to rotate a figure using the 'rotational control handle' in PowerPoint than by the manual control of the physical transparency toolkit. The students only needed to hold down one button (the 'rotational control handle') in PowerPoint. Hence, they may have been putting their attention more on the mechanical operation of the created figure rather than on the mathematics behind it. That is, *students may fail to interpret the feedback from the digital tool with respect to the intended mathematical concept due to the more easy to manipulate design of the software*. The role of the teacher in Lesson C was important in the interpretation process. She prompted the students to rotate the figure slowly in order to count the number of overlappings. In this last part of the lesson, the teacher used the feedback from the tool to mediate students' productions into the formal definition of rotational symmetry (that is, a figure appears the same more than once when it is rotated about a certain point in one cycle). The definition was made explicit through the actions in a well-structured group reporting procedure: locating the centre, rotating the figure on the transparency or by using the rotation function of the software, and then counting the number of times of overlapping. In this orchestrated process, the potentials of the transparency toolkit and the rotation function of PowerPoint software as tools of semiotic mediation emerged through evaluation of the students' productions by manipulating the tool and counting the number of times overlapping occurred *at the same time.* The defining property of rotational symmetry was then verbalized.

In Lesson C, due to the nature of the design of the 'rotational control handle', the students had an inclination to rotate the figure too quickly which led to failure of linking up the simultaneity of manipulating the tool and speaking out the key concepts explicitly. It suggests that the influence of the tool design (no matter how minor it is) can cause (unexpected) pitfalls for the emergence of mathematical concepts. This kind of subtle effect deriving from tool design may not be acknowledged unless the task is empirically tested in the lessons. Teachers' sensitivity in identifying this effect is successively required for constructing the intended mathematical knowledge from the feedback of the tool use. In the next section, two more unexpected types of feedback from tool use (one is extracted from Lesson B and another is from Lesson C) will be described. These two episodes can be classified as *discrepancy* caused by the tool utilization. They exemplified the opportunities and pitfalls provided by *discrepancy* in tool-based mathematics education tasks.

4.2 Discrepancy: Opportunities and Pitfalls

The concepts represented by the feedback from the tool use may deviate from the mathematical concepts intended to be taught. This "discrepancy" (Leung and Bolite-Frant 2015) can open up an opportunity to extend students' knowledge development but it can also be a pitfall which hinders students' shaping of the intended learning objective. The following two episodes illustrate these two possibilities. In both episodes, the feedback given by the tools deviated from the standard representations of rotational symmetry (the intended mathematical concept of the lessons) and had influences on students' learning. The discrepancy in the first episode had a positive influence whereas the discrepancy in the second episode had a negative influence. In both excerpts, the teachers played an important role in maintaining the learning effectiveness by changing the "instrumental distances" (Haspekian 2005, 2011) of the discrepancy. We will interpret these two episodes from the perspectives of semiotic mediation and the instrumental approach.

The first episode was extracted from the whole class post-activity discussion in Lesson B. A group of students used three plastic square pieces to create a 3-fold rotational symmetric figure (Fig. 5a). Students in the group reported a routine for locating the centre, rotating the figure on the transparency, and then counting the number of times of overlapping. Although the explanation given by the students was basically correct, the teacher *deliberately* extended the discussion by pointing out that the original figure and the rotated figure did *not* overlap exactly (Fig. 5b). In other words, he *amplified* the instrumental distance (that is, the *size of the gap* between the mathematics represented by the tool and the mathematical concepts intended to be taught) so that the discrepancy became explicit. He proceeded to ask

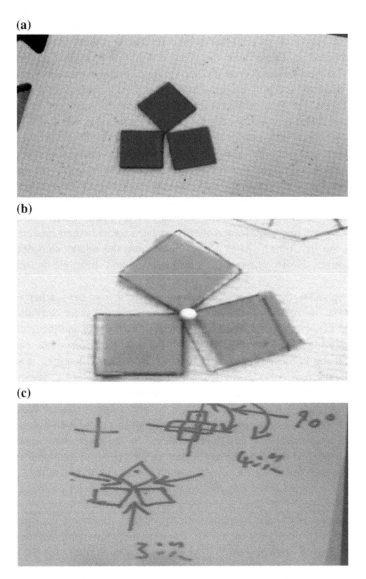

(a)

(b)

(c)

Fig. 5 **a** A 3-fold rotational symmetric figure created by plastic square pieces. **b** Verify the figure by transparency toolkit. **c** Teacher's further elaboration

the whole class how to modify the figure in order to make these two figures overlap exactly. After thinking for a while, a student suggested that the sizes of the angles between each of the adjacent squares should be the same. In order to further elaborate this idea, the teacher compared this figure with a 4-fold rotational symmetric figure which was produced by another group (Fig. 5c). After a brief discussion, it was concluded that the more times overlapping is obtained in one cycle, the smaller the size of the angle is between adjacent squares. This property was actually beyond the mathematics knowledge that the teacher intended to teach.

The second episode is an excerpt from the whole class post-activity discussion in Lesson C. A group of students used three regular hexagons from the 'standard shapes' provided in PowerPoint to create a 3-fold rotational symmetric figure (Fig. 6a). The figure was accurate and the centre of rotation was easily recognized. However, when the students used the 'rotational handle control' of PowerPoint to rotate the figure, the rotation trajectory deviated from the expected locus and the rotated image failed to overlap with the original figure (Fig. 6b).

In order to handle this unexpected disturbance, the teacher decided to *diminish* the instrumental distance by telling the students that the figure was indeed a rotational symmetric figure and the deviation was due to technical error. The teacher continued her teaching agenda and discussed the angle of rotation with her students. She rotated the figure until the original figure and the rotated image had the same orientation in which she 'pretended' that they overlapped. Then, she asked her students, "Of how many angles has the figure been rotated when it overlaps [with the image] the first time?" After a brief discussion, the relationship between the number of times overlapping occurred in one cycle and the angle of rotation was established.

In both episodes, the feedback of the tools deviated from the teacher's expected representation of 'rotational symmetry'. In other words, there was discrepancy between the mathematical representation provided by the tool and the mathematical representation intended to be taught through the task. However, there was a subtle difference in the influences of the discrepancy on students' learning in these two episodes. In the first episode, the teacher made use of the tool's 'inaccurate representation' to extend the conceptual understanding of rotational symmetry from merely recognizing a descriptive definition to discerning a critical feature about angle size in rotational symmetry. The occurrence of this tool-based discourse could be regarded as an incidental opportunity offered by the discrepancy embedded in the tool. It happened that the pair of students created a 3-fold rotational symmetric figure by three identical square pieces in such a way that the resulting figure was difficult to be arranged accurately (by eye). The angle between two adjacent square pieces needs to be 30° in order to create a rotational symmetric figure using three identical squares. For Grade five students, it is difficult to arrange the square pieces visually so that all three gaps are of 30°. Rotating the figure using the transparency toolkit made this discrepancy explicit which gave an opportunity for the teacher to orchestrate meaningful mathematics discussion with the students. From the instrumental approach perspective, the teacher highlighted the discrepancy by amplifying the instrumental distance between the tool representation and the

(a)

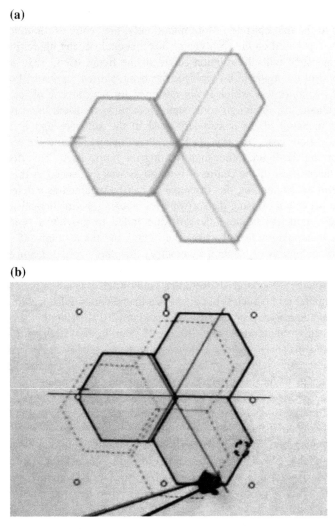

(b)

Fig. 6 **a** A 3-fold rotational symmetry figure created by using PowerPoint software. **b** The rotation trajectory deviated from the expected locus

intended mathematical concepts. The transparency toolkit was *instrumentalized* as a tool of semiotic mediation for the teacher. The pedagogical space was expanded, and in it mathematical rich discourse was brought out.

In the second episode, the source of discrepancy was due to the design of PowerPoint. The figure created by the students in the episode was an accurate rotational symmetric figure but the rotation function of PowerPoint software failed to verify it. The reason was that PowerPoint assigns the centre of rotation automatically and does not allow manual assignment. (In contrast, the centre of rotation can be assigned easily by fastening the location with a pushpin of the transparency toolkit used in the first episode.) More importantly, the centre of rotation assigned by PowerPoint is based on *the rectangular box* that encloses the figure. Its location may be inconsistent with the rotation centre of the figure itself. That is why the rotation centre of the figure in this episode has been 'shifted' upwards. PowerPoint is a general computer tool which is *not* designed for the purpose of learning and teaching mathematics. Although some same vocabulary is used, there is *discrepancy* in the meaning of the vocabulary used in the software and in curricular mathematics. In our case, 'rotation' in PowerPoint means rotating *the rectangular frame* containing the figure rather than rotating *the figure* itself. This discrepancy influences the location of the centre of rotation as was evidenced in this episode. From the semiotic standpoint, this discrepancy can be regarded as a defect (not of the software per se but of using the software for teaching the mathematical concept of rotational symmetry) because the software failed to provide a semiotic link between the manipulation task (rotating the figure) and the mathematical meaning (the standard definition of rotation symmetry). In other words, the instrumental distance between the mathematical knowledge embedded in the tool and in curricular mathematics is too large. Indeed, this kind of defect is not uncommon when a general computer tool, which is not given as a mathematics didactical tool, is used for teaching mathematics. For instance, Haspekian (2011) points out that the distinction between absolute referencing (i.e. the '$' sign in the variable formula) in a spreadsheet and the usual algebraic expressions in the school context may cause difficulties in teaching algebra by using a spreadsheet. The teacher has strong instrumental needs to fix these defects. In the episode of our rotational symmetry lesson, the teacher tried to diminish the instrumental distance by simply telling her students that the figure was in fact rotational symmetric and claiming that the figure would be overlapped if the centre were moved to a further up position. In other words, the teacher gave up using PowerPoint as a tool of semiotic mediation for rotational symmetry. She withdrew her initial intention of enabling the students to experience the abstract concept of rotational symmetry through manipulation of concrete tools but decided (more or less consciously) to transmit facts to her students directly.

Both tools used in Lesson B and Lesson C have embedded *discrepancy* with respect to the task of experiencing the concept of rotational symmetry. However, the discrepancy embedded in the physical tool used in Lesson B had a positive effect on the construction of mathematical knowledge whereas the discrepancy embedded in the digital tool used in Lesson C had a negative effect. It resonates with Leung and Bolite-Frant (2015) in that "the notion of discrepancy potential does not have an inherent good/bad value" (p. 213). In this connection, we distinguish discrepancy which has positive effect towards learning as *discrepancy opportunity* and that which has negative effect as *discrepancy pitfall*. As Haspekian (2011) points out, too large an instrumental distance is a constraint on technology integration whereas suitable distance can lead to the opportunity of opening up new mathematical representations which may not have appeared in paper-and-pencil environments. *Whether a discrepancy is an opportunity or a pitfall relies on the teacher's competence in identifying and modifying the instrumental distance into a suitable 'length'.* As evidenced in these two episodes, teacher-led mathematical discussions can amplify/diminish the instrumental distances to turn discrepancy into an opportunity rather than a pitfall. It is important to point out that we are *not* trying to make an oversimplified conclusion that a physical tool always embeds discrepancy opportunities and a digital tool always embeds discrepancy pitfalls. Indeed, from the perspective of instrumental approach, an instrument is dependent on context and users (teachers and students). Along this line of thought, whether the discrepancy of a tool is an opportunity or a pitfall depends on the intended object of learning (mathematical concept) and on many other contextual factors. However, the teacher plays an important role in *instrumentalizing* the tool so that the discrepancy opportunities can be brought out and the discrepancy pitfalls avoided. While designing a tool-based task, it is important to identify the discrepancy potential embedded in the tool and the possible instrumental distance between the mathematical concept intended to be learnt and the representation offered by the tool. Appropriate questions for amplifying/diminishing the instrumental distance into suitable 'length' through mathematical discussion is an important part of the task design. If possible, these issues should be carefully addressed *before* the task is implemented.

5 Feedback and Discrepancy in Tool-Based Mathematics Education Tasks

In this section, we suggest theoretical perspectives on the notions of *feedback* and *discrepancy* in the context of tool-based task design in mathematics education, particularly using digital technologies in designing mathematics education tasks. The notion of *discrepancy* will be refined. Then, designing and implementing tool-based mathematics education tasks will be discussed from the perspectives of feedback and discrepancy. The discussion will be integrated into the existing theoretical frameworks of the instrumental approach and the theory of semiotic mediation. Some hypotheses related to *feedback* and *discrepancy* in tool-based tasks will be advanced.

5.1 The Notion of Discrepancy

Within the instrumental approach, the choice of tools is crucial in designing a tool-based mathematics task because the affordances and constraints of the tool play a significant role in shaping students' mathematical concepts, as highlighted in the description of instrumental genesis by Drijvers, Kieran and Mariotti (2010):

Instrumental genesis is an ongoing, nontrivial and time-consuming evolution. A bilateral relationship between the artifact and the user is established: while the student's knowledge guides the way the tool is used and in a sense shapes the tool (this is called instrumentalization), the affordances and constraints of the tool influence the student's problem solving strategies and the corresponding emergent conceptions (this is called instrumentation) (pp. 108–109).

Discrepancy embedded in a tool can be regarded as the tool's affordances or constraints. What counts as discrepancy is a relative notion which depends on the *perceived* nature of the chosen tool. In our example of rotational symmetry, the physical toolkit ('transparency toolkit') was expected to be a crude tool. For instance, slight errors such as the case illustrated in Fig. 5a above were usually regarded as acceptable and not as a discrepancy. (If the teacher did not deliberately amplify the instrumental distance, the discrepancy would not be perceived to exist and hence no longer be an affordance of the tool.) On the contrary, the digital toolkit of rotational symmetry (the PowerPoint software) was expected to be an accurate tool. However, as illustrated in Fig. 6b, the effect of the rotation was not 'accurate' enough even if the rotated figure was accurately created. The constraints due to this inaccurate rotation were 'amplified' by a common perception (or expectation) that computer software is always accurate. (In Lesson C, the teacher was sensitive enough in her attempt to diminish the instrumental distance so that the constraints could be minimized.)

Based on the above discussion, it seems that there are two levels of discrepancy. The first level is of *embedded discrepancy*. It is the tool's not being able to perform certain actions, a feature embedded in the tool per se. However, it has *potential* contribution to the affordances and constraints of the tool (and hence to instrumental genesis) which may be conducive to teaching and learning. The second level of discrepancy is *enacted discrepancy*. This type of discrepancy contributes *actually* to the affordances and constraints of the tool via *feedback* given to the user by the embedded discrepancy and hence it has actual influences on the emergence of mathematical knowledge. With respect to the instrumental approach, enacted discrepancy is a result of the process of instrumentation. Thus enacted discrepancy is an *interaction* between the perceived nature of the tool (such as whether the tool is expected to be crude or accurate) and the discrepancy embedded in the tool (that is, the potential discrepancy) *regulated by the user*, hence it is 'subjective' in the sense that it is user dependent. The same embedded discrepancy may be perceived by different people as different feedback and hence may result in different enacted discrepancies. To a certain extent, the teacher's or the students' knowledge guides the way the nature of the tool is perceived and hence how the enacted discrepancy is shaped. In this respect, we suggest a dual instrumental process for the discrepancy. On the one hand, the potential emergence of mathematical knowledge offered by the tool is shaped by the embedded discrepancy. On the other hand, the enacted discrepancy is shaped by the teacher's or students' knowledge already possessed. Mathematical knowledge and discrepancy are shaped together in this process.

5.2 Designing Tool-Based Mathematics Education Tasks from the Perspective of Feedback and Discrepancy

Having chosen an appropriate tool which has appropriate affordances and constraints (including discrepancy) is one thing, designing a suitable task based on this tool is another thing. Based on his previous research studies in dynamic geometry environments, Leung (2011) proposes an epistemic model of task design in technology-rich pedagogical environments. This model provides a guiding framework to think about how to design a tool-based mathematics education task which can capitalize on the affordances and constraints (in particular, the discrepancies) of the tool (digital or physical). The model is made up of a nested structure of three epistemic modes in the sense that the first mode is a "cognitive extension" (p. 328) of the second mode and the second mode is a "cognitive extension" of the third mode. The three epistemic modes, in the nested sequence, are: Establishing Practices Mode, Critical Discernment Mode, and Establishing Situated Discourse Mode. In the following, we will discuss the positions of *feedback* and *discrepancy* in these three modes (see a further discussion of these nested epistemic modes in Chapter One of this book).

The process of instrumental genesis begins in the Establishing Practices Mode in which the utilization scheme of a tool develops. It relates to developing the pragmatic knowledge of how to use the tool. From the instrumental approach point of view, developing this knowledge cannot be taken for granted and could be a complicated process. Take, as examples, fastening the centre of rotation in the transparency toolkit and in the PowerPoint software. In the former case, the pushpin in the transparency toolkit is a convenient tool for fastening the centre accurately. However, as illustrated in the teaching episode described in previous section, there is no similar 'pushpin' in PowerPoint, hence there is (potential) discrepancy embedded in fastening the centre of rotation by using this software. It illustrates the substantial differences between the utilization scheme of PowerPoint and the utilization scheme of the transparency toolkit for the same purpose of developing the concept of rotational symmetry. In designing a tool-based task, more efforts and longer time may be needed for establishing the utilization practice if the tool has a large instrumental distance between the actual effect of the manipulation and the expected effect represented by the intended mathematical concepts. This could be regarded as the first criteria in deciding whether a tool is suitable to be used for a particular task. In retrospect, if dynamic geometry software (instead of PowerPoint) had been used for this task, the whole story may have been completely different. Dynamic geometry software has a built-in command for marking the centre of rotation. This command serves the same function as the pushpin in the transparency toolkit. If a dynamic geometry software had been used, the embedded discrepancy pitfall described above may not have appeared (if the students had been already familiar with the basic skills of using the software).

The second epistemic mode in the model is the Critical Discernment Mode. It refers to discerning critical features of the intended mathematical objects (or concepts). The line of thought of this epistemic mode is rooted in Ference Marton's phenomenography and variation theory of learning (Marton and Booth 1997; Marton and Tsui 2004; Marton 2015) and later Leung's application to studies on dynamic geometry environments (see for instance, Leung 2003; Leung and Chan 2006; Leung 2008; Leung et al. 2013). Learning is considered as seeing or experiencing something (or some phenomenon) in a different way due to the discernment of different *critical features* (or aspects) of the phenomenon under study. "To discern an aspect is to differentiate among the various aspects and focus on the one most relevant to the situation. Without variation there is no discernment" (Bowden and Marton 1998, p. 7). In particular, critical features of something can be discerned by means of discernment strategies that focus on variation and invariance. An efficient tool-based learning task can enable the students to *instrumentalize* the tool in such a way that variation and invariance can be observed. Take the task of rotational symmetry as an example. Both the transparency toolkit (with plastic shape pieces) and the PowerPoint software allow the students to freely shift their attention (a variation strategy) between the parts and the whole of the object of exploration (creating rotational symmetric figures). Thanks to the blue-tack of the transparency toolkit and the group/ungroup commands in PowerPoint. As evidenced from the data, the feedback from the tools while working on the task of figure creation provided an opportunity for the students to experience the part/whole shifting and hence establish the link between visualization and reasoning. In general, it seems that the semiotic potential of a tool may be enhanced if the task based on this tool enables the students to freely shift their attention between the parts and the whole of the object of exploration. This kind of tool feedback gives rise to an opportunity for the students to establish a better grasp on the part-whole relationship and to discern invariant features from the incidental ones.

The third epistemic mode is the Establishing Situated Discourse Mode; it involves the development of mathematical reasoning and arguments which are situated in the tools used and it acts as a bridge connecting the tool-based task to formal mathematics discourse. A tool-based task which allows uncertainty due to tool discrepancy may initiate meaningful situated discourse which could lead to deeper conceptual understanding. Meaningful mistakes are a source for mathematics discussion leading to construction of mathematical knowledge. Some settings of a task have a higher chance of allowing the student to make (meaningful) mistakes than other settings when the same task is used. As evidenced in the first episode of the transparency toolkit in Sect. 4.2, when creating a rotational symmetric figure by using three identical square pieces, it is easier to make 'mistakes' than by using four identical square pieces. Though the 'mistake opportunity' that occurred in this episode was rather incidental, 'mistake opportunity' could be planned in the task design so that the embedded discrepancy can be more likely to be developed into an enacted discrepancy that carries mathematical meaning. Hence the mathematics implied by the 'mistakes' could be an important consideration for task design. Furthermore, the tool used in a task may also influence the chance of making mistakes. When a digital tool (e.g. PowerPoint or a dynamic geometry software) was used for this task (Lesson C), it was observed that the enacted discrepancy that occurred in Lesson B did not occur because the drawings produced by the digital tools are usually accurate (at least the discrepancy cannot be discerned visually). In this connection, it is interesting to note that empirical studies have been conducted where students deliberately construct 'wrong' figures in dynamic geometry environment in the process of exploration and argumentation (See for example, Leung and Lopez-Real 2002; Mariotti and Antonini 2009; Baccaglini-Frank et al. 2011; and Chapter "Designing Non-constructability Tasks in a Dynamic Geometry Environment" in this book). Therefore, there is also *user-created tool discrepancy*.

5.3 Implementing Tool-Based Mathematics Tasks from the Perspective of Feedback and Discrepancy

A well designed and implemented tool-based mathematics education task can amplify the pedagogical potential *of* the embedded discrepancy and diminish the potential pitfalls caused by the discrepancy which in turn increase the probability of bringing about the intended mathematical concepts. In this regard, the teacher plays a deterministic role.

The process from students' performing a tool-based task activity to students' acquisition of mathematical knowledge is usually not automatic. As an expert representative of mathematics culture, the teacher plays a significant role in the process of semiotic mediation by guiding the evolution of mathematical meanings related to the tool and its use within the mathematics classroom. A teacher needs to use the students' productions to foster the processes of semiotic mediation (Mariotti 2002; Bussi and Mariotti 2008). The feedback given by the task has potential to bring out the intended mathematical concepts. However, the correspondence between the feedback and the mathematics knowledge may not be explicit. It is because appropriate mathematics terminology (vocabulary) may not be provided by the tool especially for those tools (either physical or digital) which are not initially designed as a tool for mathematics teaching and learning (for example PowerPoint). This point of view resonates with the idea that the vocabulary involved in using the tool can be a source of "instrumental distance" (Haspekian 2005). It is part of the role of the teacher to make this correspondence explicit. In the lesson episodes described in Sect. 4.1.2, the teachers made use of a well-structured orchestration procedure which involved students' evaluation of their own productions by manipulating the tool and expressing the key mathematics concepts explicitly, at the same time, to create the correspondence. During this orchestration, the teacher deliberately highlighted the mathematical terminology corresponding to function-alities of the tool. (For example, the push pin corresponds to the "centre of rotation".) The correspondence between students' tool-based productions and the mathematics knowledge may be seen as matching a tool-based discussion to the formal (at least curriculum-wise) mathematical discussion. The lesson episodes described in Sect. 4.2 suggest that a tool-based task which can capitalize on the embedded discrepancy potentials in the tool may bring about a higher level of conceptual understanding. This happened due to the teacher's insight and flexibility during the task orchestration. In the first episode described in Sect. 4.2, the teacher made use of the students' incorrect (or not-so-correct) production to extend the mathematics discussion so that a deeper conceptual understanding of rotational symmetry evolved. This was incidental in the sense that it was not part of the teacher's original plan. If the teacher had ignored the discrepancy and simply told the students that their ideas were correct, then the situated mathematics discourse would not have been so rich and fruitful. On the other hand, not all the mistakes were equally as fruitful for extending the discussion. In the second episode described in Sect. 4.2, the centre of rotation was shifted to an incorrect position which caused failure in demonstrating the rotational symmetry of the figure produced by the students. This 'mistake' was not due to the students but to a 'defect' of PowerPoint when it was used for teaching the concept of rotational symmetry. The teacher chose to ignore the 'mistake' and continued the mathematical discussion as initially planned. The former case is a *discrepancy opportunity* and the latter is a *discrepancy pitfall*. Teacher's sensitivity in determining whether a student's (mistaken or unexpected) production (or response) is a discrepancy opportunity or a discrepancy pitfall and the ability in adjusting the "instrumental distance" (Haspekian 2005, 2011) to an appropriate 'length' is one of the factors contributing to successfully bringing about the semiotic potential of a tool-based task. Developing such ability is an important aspect in teachers' proficiency in designing and implementing tool-based mathematics education tasks.

6 Conclusion

In this chapter, the opportunities and pitfalls given by the feedback of tool-based mathematics education tasks are discussed. Two similar tasks (one based on a tailor-made physical toolkit and another based on a digital toolkit) for developing the concept of rotational symmetry are compared. Based on comparing the discrepancy of these two tasks, the notions of embedded and enacted discrepancies and their pedagogical significance in tool-based mathematics education task design are expounded.

Tool discrepancy influences mathematics learning positively or negatively, respectively bringing about discrepancy opportunity and discrepancy pitfall. Embedded discrepancy is objective referring to the 'physicality' of the tool while enacted discrepancy is 'subjective' depending on the interaction between the user-perceived nature of the tool and the embedded discrepancy. Enacted discrepancy is a tool-user feedback, hence it has actual influences on the emergence of mathematical knowledge. Based on our data from the rotational symmetry task, four tool-based mathematics task design considerations are raised.

1. The tool should enable students to shift their attention freely between the parts and the whole of the object of exploration. This can help students discern critical features of the object of exploration and be aware of the mathematical concepts.
2. The task should bring out the *embedded discrepancy opportunity* of the tool (for instance, by providing 'meaningful mistake opportunity') in order to initiate mathematical discussion which may lead to deeper conceptual understanding.
3. If the instrumental distance between the actual effect of the manipulation and the expected effect as represented by the intended mathematical concepts is too large, the tool has an *embedded discrepancy pitfall* in the sense that the students need more time and effort to *instrumentalize* the tool.
4. Teacher's sensitivity and insight in identifying the *discrepancy opportunity* and *discrepancy pitfall* (both embedded and enacted) and the ability to adjust the *instrumental length* are a key factors in successfully exploiting the semiotic potential of the tool-based task.

These four tool-based task design considerations could serve as a guide for a larger scale study on investigating teachers' design and implementation of mathematics education tool-based tasks for different tools and compare the pedagogical opportunities and pitfalls afforded by the tools in the process of mathematics teaching and learning.

Acknowledgments This work is supported by Hong Kong Baptist University Faculty Research Grant 11314030.

References

Artigue, M. I. (2003). Learning mathematics in a CAS environment: the genesis of a reflection about instrumentation and the dialectics between technical and conceptual works. *International Journal of Computers for Mathematical Learning, 7*(3), 245–274.

Arzarello, F., Bussi, M. G. B., Leung, A., Mariotti, M. A., & Stevenson, I. (2012). Experimental approaches to theoretical thinking: artefacts and proofs. In G. Hanna & M. de Villiers (Eds.), *Proof and proving in mathematics education—the 19th ICMI study* (pp. 97–137). New York: Springer-Verlag.

Baccaglini-Frank, A., Antonini, S., Leung, A., & Mariotti, M. A. (2011). Reasoning by contradiction in dynamic geometry. In B. Ubuz (Ed.), *Proceedings of the 35th Conference of the International Group for the Psychology of Mathematics Education* (Vol. 2, pp. 81–88). Ankara, Turkey: PME.

Bussi, M. G. B., & Mariotti, M. A. (2008). Semiotic mediation in the mathematics classroom: Artifacts and signs after a Vygotskian perspective. In L. English (Ed.), *Handbook of international research in mathematics education* (2nd ed., pp. 746–783). New York: Routledge.

Béguin, P., & Rabardel, P. (2000). Designing for instrument-mediated activity. *Scandinavian Journal of Information Systems, 12*, 173–190.

Bowden, J., & Marton, F. (1998). *The university of learning*. London: Kogan Page.

Chan, Y. C., & Leung, A. (2013). Rotational symmetry: semiotic potential of a transparency toolkit. In C. Margolinas (Ed.). *Task Design in Mathematics Education: Proceedings of ICMI Study 22* (pp. 35–44). Oxford, UK. Retrieved from http://hal.archives-ouvertes.fr/hal-00834054.

Dienes, Z. P. (1960). *Building up mathematics* (4th ed.). London: Hutchinson Educational.

Dienes, Z. P. (1971). *The elements of mathematics*. New York: Herder and Herder Inc.

Drijvers, P., Kieran, C., & Mariotti, M. A. (2010). Integrating technology into mathematics education: theoretical perspectives. In C. Hoyles & J.-B. Lagrange (Eds.), *Mathematics education and technology-rethinking the terrain—the 17th ICMI study* (pp. 89–132). New York: Springer-Verlag.

Falcade, R., Laborde, C., & Mariotti, M. A. (2007). Approaching functions: Cabri tool as instruments of semiotic mediation. *Educational Studies in Mathematics, 66,* 317–333.

Fernandez, C., & Yoshida, M. (2004). *Lesson study: A Japanese approach to improving mathematics teaching and learning.* Mahwah, New Jersey: Lawrence Erlbaum Associates.

Haspekian, M. (2005). An "instrumental approach" to study the integration of a computer tool into mathematics teaching: The case of spreadsheets. *International Journal of Computers for Mathematical Learning, 10,* 109–141.

Haspekian, M. (2011). The co-construction of a mathematical and a didactical instrument. In M. Pytlak, E. Swoboda & T. Rowland (Eds.), *Proceedings of the Seventh Congress of the European Society for Research in Mathematics Education, CERME 7,* Rzesvow.

Haspekian, M. (2014). Teachers' instrumental geneses when integrating Spreadsheet software. In A. Clark-Wilson, O. Robutti, & N. Sinclair (Eds.), *The mathematics teacher in the digital era—an international perspective on technology focused professional Development* (pp. 241–275). New York: Springer-Verlag.

Jones, K. (2000). Providing a foundation for deductive reasoning: Students' interpretations with using dynamic geometry software and their evolving mathematical explanations. *Educational Studies in Mathematics, 44*(1–3), 55–85.

Leung, A. (2003). Dynamic geometry and the theory of variation. In N. A. Pateman, B. J. Dougherty & J. Zilliox (Eds.), *Proceedings of PME 27: Psychology of Mathematics Education 27th International Conference, Hawaii, USA* (Vol. 3, pp. 195–202).

Leung, A. (2008). Dragging in a dynamic geometry environment through the lens of variation. *International Journal of Computers for Mathematical Learning, 13,* 135–157.

Leung, A. (2011). An epistemic model of task design in dynamic geometry environment. *ZDM— The International Journal on Mathematics Education, 43,* 325–336.

Leung, A., Baccaglini-Frank, A., & Mariotti, M. A. (2013). Discernment of invariants in dynamic geometry environments. *Educational Studies in Mathematics, 84,* 439–460.

Leung, A., & Bolite-Frant, J. (2015). Designing mathematics tasks: the role of tools. In A. Watson & M. Ohtani (Eds.), *Task design in mathematics education: The 22nd ICMI study* (pp. 191–225)., New ICMI study series Cham: Springer.

Leung, A., & Chan, Y. C. (2006). Exploring necessary and sufficient conditions in a dynamic geometry environment. *International Journal for Technology in Mathematics Education, 13* (1), 37–43.

Leung, A., & Lopez-Real, F. (2002). Theorem justification and acquisition in dynamic geometry: A case of proof by contradiction. *International Journal of Computers for Mathematics Learning, 7*(2), 145–165.

Lo, M. L., Pong, W. Y., & Chik, P. M. (Eds.). (2005). *For each and everyone: Catering for individual differences through learning studies.* Hong Kong: Hong Kong University Press.

Mariotti, M. A. (2002). Justifying and proving in the Cabri environment. *International Journal of Computers for Mathematical Learning, 6*(3), 257–281.

Mariotti, M. A., & Antonini, S. (2009). Breakdown and reconstruction of figural concepts in proofs by contradiction. In F.-L. Lin, F.-J. Hsieh, G. Hanna & M. de Villiers (Eds.), *Proceedings of the ICMI Study 19 Conference: Proof and Proving in Mathematics Education* (Vol. 2, pp. 82–87). Taiwan: National Taiwan Normal University.

Mariotti, M. A., & Maracci, M. (2012). Resources for the teacher from a semiotic mediation perspective. In G. Gueudet, B. Pepin, & L. Trouche (Eds.), *From text to 'Lived' resources—mathematics curriculum materials and teacher development* (pp. 59–75). New York: Springer.

Marton, F. (2015). *Necessary conditions of learning*. New York: Routledge.

Marton, F., & Booth, S. (1997). *Learning and awareness*. New Jersey: Lawrence Erlbaum.

Marton, F., & Tsui, A. B. M. (Eds.). (2004). *Classroom discourse and the space of learning*. Mahwah, NJ: Lawrence Erlbaum.

Trouche, L. (2004). Managing the complexity of human/machine interactions in computerized learning environments: Guiding students' command process through instrumental orchestrations. *International Journal of Computers for Mathematical Learning, 9*(3), 281–307.

Vérillon, P. (2000). Revisiting Piaget and Vygotsky: In search of a learning model for technology education. *The Journal of Technology Studies, 26*(1), 3–10.

Vérillon, P., & Rabardel, P. (1995). Cognition and artifacts: A contribution to the study of thought in relation to instrumented activity. *European Journal of Psychology of Education, 10*(1), 77–101.

Vygotsky, L. S (1978). *Mind in society: The development of higher psychological processes*. Cambridge: Harvard University Press. M. Cole, V. John-Steiner, S. Scribner & E. Souberman (Eds.).

Designing for Mathematical Applications and Modelling Tasks in Technology Rich Environments

Vince Geiger

Abstract Mathematical modelling and applications is a well-established field within mathematics education. Research in mathematical modelling and applications has maintained a focus on how to enhance students' capabilities in using mathematics learnt in school to solve problems identified in, or derived from, the real world. While significant progress has been made in understanding the processes that underpin the successful applications of mathematics in real world contexts, there has been limited research into how to design tasks that are authentic reflections of the role of digital technologies in solving problems situated in the work place or daily life. This chapter draws on data sourced from a research and development project that investigated the use of digital technologies in teaching and learning mathematical modelling and applications to identify principles of effective task design. The instantiation of these principles within classroom practice is illustrated through a classroom vignette. This chapter concludes with a reflection on the research needed to further develop understanding of the role of technology as an enabler of principles of design for mathematical modelling tasks.

Keywords Modelling · Mathematics · Technology · Design · Applications

1 Introduction

While significant progress has been made in understanding the processes that underpin the successful applications of mathematics in real world contexts, there has been limited research into how to design tasks that are authentic reflections of the role of digital technologies in solving problems situated in the work place or daily life (Geiger et al. 2010). This is despite the noteworthy progress of research that explores both the themes of mathematical modelling and applications and the use of digital tools to enhance mathematics learning.

V. Geiger (✉)
Australian Catholic University, Brisbane, Australia
e-mail: vince.geiger@acu.edu.au

Mathematical modelling and applications is a well-established field within mathematics education. Research in mathematical modelling and applications has maintained a focus on how to enhance students' capabilities in using mathematics learnt in school to solve problems identified in, or de-rived from, the real world as well as how the modelling process itself is played out while attempting to solve real world problems. A broadly accepted description of the act of modelling outlines a cyclic process that involves: the formulation of a mathematical representation of a real world situation (model); using mathematics in conjunction with the model to derive initial results; interpreting the resulting outcome in terms of the given situation to determine the validity of the model; and, if necessary, revising the model until it is determined to be effective (e.g., Blomhoj and Hojgaard Jensen 2003; Blum and Niss 1991). Simply put, the purpose of models is to interpret real world situations and/or make predictions about the future or past states of modelled systems (English et al. 2005). The need to build models, however, is motivated by a requirement to: measure some property of a system; decide between alternatives; allow one to replicate a system; predict the outcome of a system; explain the outcome of a system; and understand how to manipulate a system (Thompson and Yoon 2007). While there is now a large and still developing corpus of research related to mathematical modelling within educational contexts, to this point, studies have tended to coalesce around mathematical, cognitive, curricular, instructional, and teacher education perspectives (e.g., Cai et al. 2014).

Similarly, the body of knowledge related to the use of digital tools in mathematics classrooms has increased rapidly over the past two decades. Studies in this area, however, have tended to report on advantages to instruction in mathematical thinking and learning within content specific domains such as number (e.g., Kieran and Guzma'n 2005), geometry (e.g., Laborde et al. 2006), algebra and calculus (e.g., Ferrara et al. 2006) or social aspects of classroom practice such as collaborative investigative practice (e.g., Beatty and Geiger 2010).

The potential for digital tools to enhance the teaching and learning of modelling has been recognised, as is evident in this statement from Niss et al. (2007).

> Many technological devices are highly relevant for applications and modelling. They include calculators, computers, the Internet, and computational or graphical software as well as all kinds of instruments for measuring, for performing experiments etc. These devices provide not only increased computational power, but broaden the range of possibilities for approaches to teaching, learning and assessment (p. 24).

While there is a developing body of research that lends weight to this potential (e.g., Geiger et al. 2010; Villarreal et al. 2010), there is still much work to be done on how technology can be used in tandem with mathematical knowledge to work on problems that exist in the real world, as Zevenbergen (2004) observes:

> While such innovations [ICTs] have been useful in enhancing understandings of school mathematics, less is known about the transfer of such knowledge, skills and dispositions to the world beyond schools. Given the high tech world that students will enter once they leave schools, there needs to be recognition of the new demands of these changed workplaces (p. 99).

Zevenbergen's (2004) statement identifies a shortcoming of school mathematics instruction and implies there is a need to develop tasks and learning experiences where expectations of how real world problems are tackled and solved include the integrated use of digital tools. Others, such as Hoyles et al. (2010), have noted the need for the development of techno-mathematical literacies—new mathematics based competencies required by societies in which digital technologies are becoming ubiquitous.

The aim of this chapter is to explore one approach to the design and implementation of mathematical modelling tasks that integrate digital technologies. In doing so, the chapter will address the following research question—What are the principles of design for technology rich modelling and applications tasks that result in effective learning experiences for students?

The first section of this chapter will outline the theoretical framework that provides the background for this study, comprising of a review of the role of digital tools as mediators of mathematical learning and a discussion of general principles of task design. In the second section the research design and methods employed through the study are described. The third section will present one teacher's principles of task design and provide an example of how these were implemented via a classroom vignette. The final section will reflect on the effectiveness of the teacher's principles and compare these to the general principles of tasks design outlined in the theoretical framework.

2 Digital Tools as Mediators of Mathematical Learning

In developing principles of task design for technology integrated modelling and applications tasks, consideration must be given to the role of artifacts and instruments in mathematics teaching and learning. Verillon and Rabardel's (1995) iconic work on the distinction between an artifact and an instrument provides insight into the role of artifacts in mediating learning by distinguishing between an artifact, which includes both physical and sign tools that have no intrinsic meaning of their own, and an instrument in which an artifact is used in a meaningful way to work on a specific task. Different tasks make different demands on the user and their relationship with the artifact. The development of this relationship, and thus how the artifact is used, is known as instrumental genesis. Instrumental genesis is complex and involves, firstly, a process where the potentialities of the artifact for performing a specific task are recognised and the artifact is transformed into an instrument (instrumentalisation), and, secondly, a process that takes place within the user in order to use the instrument for a particular task (instrumentation) (Artigue 2002). Instrumentation generates schemas of instrumented action that are either original creations by individuals or pre-existing entities that are appropriated from others. An instrument, therefore, consists of the artifact and the user's associated schemas of instrumented action. Instrumental genesis is also a dynamic process between the instrument and the user, as the constraints and affordances of the artifact shape the user's conceptual development while at the same time the user's perception of the possibilities of the artifact during instrumentation can lead to the use of the artifact in ways that were not originally intended by the designers of a tool (Drijvers and Gravemeijer 2005).

Instrumental genesis has been used to explain how digital tools are transformed into instruments for learning through interaction with teachers and students (e.g., Artigue 2002). A teacher's activity in promoting a student's instrumental genesis is known as instrumental orchestration (Trouche 2005). This process recognises the social aspects of learning as it allows for the sharing of schemas as instrumented action that individuals have developed within a small group or whole class. A teacher can facilitate the appropriation of these schemas by other students by making the nature of these schemas explicit through orchestration of classroom interaction around the schemas through careful and selective questioning.

More recently, others have attempted to extend our understanding of an instrumental approach to the role of artifacts in mediating learning by recognising that the genesis of an artifact into an instrument takes place within highly interactive environments, such as school staff rooms or mathematics classrooms, where a number of artifacts are used simultaneously. Gueudet and Trouche (2009) extend the definition of artifact by introducing the term *resources* to encompass any artifact with the potential to promote semiotic mediation in the process of learning. Resources include entities such as computer applications, student worksheets or discussions with a colleague. A resource is appropriated and reshaped by a teacher, in a way that reflects their professional experience in relation to the use of resources, to form a schema of utilisation—a process parallel to the creation of a schema of instrumented action within instrumental genesis. The combination of the resource and the schema of utilisation is called a document. Documental genesis is an ongoing process in which utilisation schemas are reshaped as a teacher gains more experience through the use of a resource.

The idea that learning and problem solving are processes that require strategic deployment of a range of resources in an integrated fashion with the potential to transform tasks and learning environments is echoed in Kaput et al.'s (2007) perspective on the role of digital technologies in mathematics education. From their perspective "technologies and tools co-constitute both the material upon which they operate and the conditions, particularly social conditions, within which such operations occur" (p. 172). This means that digital technologies should be considered as essential infrastructure for mathematical problem solving in current and future societies.

3 General Principles for Task Design in Mathematics

As tasks are integral to many dimensions of mathematics learning, including mathematical content, processes, and modes of working, Burkhart and Swan (2013) argue for the importance of task design to improve mathematics instruction. For teachers, task selection, adaptation, and creation are intertwined with choices of pedagogies for realising opportunities that lie within specific tasks (Sullivan and Yang 2013). Evidence that coherent research and development approaches to task design are effective in improving teaching practice is provided by the long term success of programs such as Connected Mathematics (Lappan and Phillips 2009). At the same time, Schoenfeld (2009) argues for greater communication between designers and researchers as many designers do not make their design principles explicit, and so it is difficult for others, including teachers, to adopt effective approaches to task creation and adaptation. Thus, partnerships between teachers and researchers, where understandings of principles of task design and the effective integration of tasks with pedagogical approaches are explored, refined and documented, holds potential for improving teaching and learning practices in mathematics.

As most tasks are developed for implementation within specific curriculum and school contexts, the *fit to circumstance* of tasks with local conditions and constraints is a vital consideration for effective implementation (Kieran et al. 2013). Such circumstances include local curriculum specifications as well as other affordances, requirements or restrictions, for example, resources available within a particular school.

An appropriate level of *challenge* is important for students when engaging with tasks if real learning is to take place (Hiebert and Grouws 2007). Most guidelines for systemic improvement in learning outcomes stress the need for teachers to extend students' thinking, and to pose extended, realistic, and open-ended problems that challenge students (e.g., City et al. 2009). By posing challenging tasks, and adopting associated pedagogies, teachers provide opportunity for students to take risks, to justify their thinking, to make decisions, and to work with other students (Sullivan 2011). At the same time, students often resist engaging with challenging tasks and attempt to influence teachers to reduce the demands of an activity (Sullivan et al. 2013). Thus, for students to engage with the type of tasks that require the use of unfamiliar or developing capabilities, the completion of tasks must appear to be achievable, that is, tasks must be *challenging yet accessible*. In order for students to engage fully with tasks, however, activities must not only be accessible but also *transparent* in relation to their expected outcomes: that is, it is clear what is required of a student to achieve success with a task (Burkhart and Swan 2013).

As students need to take risks in order to extend their thinking, they must be provided with *opportunity to make decisions* (Geiger et al. 2014). Such opportunities also provide instances where students can exercise and develop their capacities to use mathematics critically. While closely linked to the notion of *challenge*, the opportunity to make decisions does not necessarily mean that highly complex or sophisticated mathematics is required to make judgments.

The articulation of carefully constructed principles for the design of a task does not guarantee the effectiveness of an activity as learning is also influenced by the choice of pedagogy. I have previously argued, in collaborations with other colleagues, that teachers must also adopt *investigative pedagogies* to fully realise the opportunities that such tasks afford (e.g., Goos et al. 2013). Such pedagogies must provide students with the opportunity to speculate, test ideas, and argue for or defend conjectures (Diezmann et al. 2001).

In order to be assured of the quality of a task, activities must also be developed, appraised, trialled, evaluated, and re-trialled in *iterative cycles of design and improvement* (Maass et al. 2013). Thus effective activities will take time to develop and require a commitment to reflective practice by teachers who aspire to be effective designers of instructional tasks.

4 A Technology-Rich, Modelling Task Oriented Research Project

This chapter reports on an aspect of a larger study that investigated the role of digital technologies in enhancing mathematical modelling teaching practice through a design research approach. The study was conducted with individual teachers working in secondary schools across two states within Australia. Six teachers were recruited from six schools; three from each of two different Australian states. Schools were drawn from across different educational systems (government and non-government) and were representative of a range of socio-economic characteristics. Teachers were invited into the project because of their reputations as effective teachers of mathematics, with particular skills in the use of digital tools in promoting students' learning. The project was managed by two university based researchers—one in each state. These researchers were primarily responsible for the conceptual development of the project and classroom data collection including lesson observations, teacher and student interviews, and collection of student samples. Teachers were primarily responsible for the development and implementation of technology demanding mathematical modelling tasks. Researchers played a vital role in providing feedback about the effectiveness of tasks trialled in teachers' classrooms. Together teachers and researchers developed principles of design for effective tasks based on their shared experiences while trialling tasks in individual mathematics classrooms.

The specific aspect of the study reported in this chapter is the work of one teacher and his students in a Year 11 (15–16 years of age) mathematics class. His curriculum context mandated the teaching, learning and assessment of mathematical modelling as a key objective of a state-wide syllabus (educational authorities are state based in Australia). Technology as a tool for teaching and learning mathematics was also prescribed in the Mathematics B program (incorporating the study of functions, calculus and statistics) in which his students were enrolled. Students had almost unrestricted access to digital technologies including: handheld digital devices with mathematical facilities such as data and function plotters and Computer Algebra Systems; computers with mathematically enabled applications; the internet; and electronic white boards.

Table 1 Research design and schedule

Time	Activity
Sept–Dec Year 1	Teacher workshops in each state: research team outline the aims of the project; offer prototype tasks; discussion of principles which underlie prototype tasks
Jan–April Year 2	Lesson observations; teacher and student interviews; collection of student work samples; feedback on effectiveness of trialled tasks in relation to modelling and the use of digital tools
April–June Year 2	Lesson observations; teacher and student interviews; collection of student work samples; feedback on effectiveness of trialled tasks in relation to modelling and the use of digital tools
July Year 2	Teacher workshops in each state: teachers share exemplars of digital tool and modelling tasks; discussion on principles which underlie teacher developed tasks; research team offer accounts of practice from classroom observations
Aug–Sept Year 2	Lesson observations; teacher and student interviews; collection of student work samples; feedback on effectiveness of trialled tasks in relation to modelling and the use of digital tools
Oct–Dec Year 2	Final project meeting and focus group interview in each state; teachers share exemplars of modelling and digital tool tasks; further discussion on principles that underlie teacher-developed tasks

The research design consisted of three components: (1) two whole day teacher professional learning meetings which took place at the beginning and middle of the project; (2) three classroom observations for each teacher; and (3) a focus group interview near the end of the project that involved all teachers. The scheduling and purpose of each of these activities is out-lined in Table 1. Further detail on the research methodology can be found in Geiger et al. (2010).

5 Principles of Task Design in Technology Demanding Modelling Tasks

The teacher whose work is the focus of this chapter demonstrated keen insight into his own design processes and how these developed through the duration of the project. A major feature of this teacher's approach to task design was the integration of digital technologies. Towards the end of the project, he identified what he believed to be the characteristics of technology integrated modelling tasks. These principles and associated descriptions are presented in Table 2.

The teacher also provided insight into the role of digital tools in relation to each principle of design. An outline of these in-sights along with supportive statements drawn from the inter-view data follows.

The use of digital tools is a mandatory element of the state-wide senior secondary mathematics syllabuses, and so the use of technology was a matter of *compliance*. Genuinely authentic problems are mathematically complex. The representational capabilities of digital tools allow students to accommodate this

Table 2 Characteristics of effective modelling tasks

Principles	Description
Syllabus compliance	The task must meet the requirements of the syllabus for content knowledge and the dimensions related to applications and technology
Authenticity and relevance	Tasks must be set in an authentic or life-related context. The task must be of interest to the teacher and be of potential interest to the student
Open-endedness	The mathematics necessary to solve the problem set up in the task should not be immediately apparent. The task must be open-ended in nature providing for opportunity for multiple solution pathways
Connectivity	Ideally the task must make links to different content areas within the syllabus
Accessibility	The task must provide opportunity for students to link to their previous learning. There should be provision for multiple entry and exit points. The task should allow for the introduction of scaffolding prompts or hints
Development	The task must provide challenge and so encourage students to go beyond what they presently know and can do through the modelling process. Students' engagement with the task should provide feedback to the teacher about the development of their understanding

complexity and thus provide access to *authentic* problems that otherwise might be considered beyond the scope of their capabilities.

> If we didn't have the CAS calculators we couldn't do half the stuff that we do. From my perspective it is the integration of the whole lot together. We have a set of data and we try and build a model from that. We do a scatter plot and we make decisions about the model. We build a model and make some sorts of predictions.

Digital tools also provide the means for students with gaps in their content knowledge to *access* challenging problem scenarios.

> Lower achievers may be struggling with differentiation or integration at that particular point in time...but they can still have access to the problem. My lower achieving kids can still engage in the problem and still make some meaningful contributions. If they don't get caught up in all that manipulation they can still be thoughtful about it.

The nature of *authentic open-ended* problems means there is no clear solution pathway and students need to evaluate options as they progress toward a solution. The teacher argued that digital tools offer facilities that are essential for exploring possible solution pathways. Technology also provides the means for connecting different types of mathematical knowledge, for example, data representations and functional relationships that modelled patterns in the data.

> Selecting authentic, open tasks to model generally implies the students will need to make use of technology. Even if the teacher has scaffolded the task to facilitate access to the context, there is a requirement that the task be sufficiently open for there to be multi-representations of the solution and perhaps different solutions.

The *authenticity* and *open-endedness* of a problem is enhanced if students are required to collect data relevant to a problem from an original source; a capacity provided by digital tools in his classroom.

There is often a need to collect data and then to determine whether a relationship exists within that data. Students may need to collect primary data, through the use of probes, or from a video that is then analysed using the technology or use secondary data collected from a newspaper, magazine, web site or some other source.

Used effectively, digital tools provide immediate feedback to students about their initial attempts to build models and solve problems thus progressing students' understanding of the underlying mathematics at the core of the task and hence their mathematical *development*.

Technology has a significant role to play in the provision of feedback to the student in the first instance, about the models they have built and how well they fit the context being investigated. In mathematical modelling it is important to look for consensus between the mathematics and the context, hence, it is necessary to consider the validity of the conclusions in terms of the context.

While a number of these principles are consistent with the principles of task design presented earlier in this chapter, there are also points of departure. The commonalities and differences between the teachers "home grown" principles and those developed from research literature in the field will be outlined in the commentary that accompanies the following illustrative example.

6 Exemplar Task and Commentary

Principles for the design of technology demanding modelling tasks are evident in the following description of a task developed and then implemented by the teacher in his Year 11 mathematics classroom—the Algal Bloom Problem outlined in Fig. 1. In developing this task, the teacher expected his students to build a mathematical model for these data by first creating a scatterplot using their CAS active calculator. The calculators were equipped with a computer algebra system, as well as data plotting and regression function capabilities among other facilities.

In previous lessons, students had gained experience with developing models by finding single functions that fit data from different situations drawn from real world contexts. Students had also been introduced to piece-wise functions but had not yet been asked to fit these to real-life data. For the Algal Bloom Problem, the data plot suggests a piecewise function (one part linear and one part power function) would be appropriate. The teacher had hoped that students would then use the plotting functions on their calculators to determine the general form of suitable functions and, in due course, develop an equation that best fit the data. In doing so, the teacher expected students to make use of a piece-wise function, which was covered in earlier work but had not been used to model real-life data via previous examples. Students were then asked to use the model they had created to respond to the question at the end of the task. Further, they were asked to list any assumptions they made in developing their model and to comment on any limitations they believed were inherent in the response they provided.

The CSIRO has been monitoring the rate at which Carbon Dioxide is produced in a section of the Darling River. Over a 20 day period they recorded the rate of CO2 production in the river. The averages of these measurements appear in the table below.

The CO2 concentration [CO2] of the water is of concern because an excessive difference between the [CO2] at night and the [CO2] used during the day through photosynthesis can result in algal blooms which then results in oxygen deprivation and death of the resulting animal population and sunlight deprivation leading to death of the plant life and the subsequent death of that section of the river.

From experience it is known that a difference of greater than 5% between the [CO2] of a water sample at night and the [CO2] during the day can signal an algal bloom is imminent.

Rate of CO2 Production versus time

Time in Hours	0	1	2	3	4	5	6	7	8	9
Rate of CO2 Production	0	-0.042	-0.044	-0.041	-0.039	-0.038	-0.035	-0.03	-0.026	-0.023

Time in Hours	10	11	12	13	14	15	16	17	18	19
Rate of CO2 Production	-0.02	-0.008	0	0.054	0.045	0.04	0.035	0.03	0.027	0.023

Time in Hours	20	21	22	23	24					
Rate of CO2 Production	0.02	0.015	0.012	0.005	0					

Is there cause for concern by the CSIRO researchers?
Identify any assumptions and the limitations of your mathematical model.

Fig. 1 Algal bloom problem

When observing the lesson in which this task was used, the researcher noticed that while every student was able to produce a plot of the data using their handhelds, few had drawn the conclusion that a piecewise function was necessary to model the data. Most students tried using a single function, generally by trying to generate a model for the data using the digital handhelds regression model facility—a facility that did not allow for the fitting of piece-wise functions. When their single functions were plotted on their screens with the original data points it was obvious that their various functions were a poor fit. In response to students surprise at their results, the teacher encouraged students to have a closer look at the nature of their data and explore a wider range of possibilities for fitting a model.

Sometime later, two students, working together near the researcher, attempted to fit a piecewise function to the data, and after performing fine adjustments to each part of their function were happy with the result. Their success prompted a subdued celebration by the two students which attracted the teacher's attention. After discussing their conjectured model with the teacher, students went on to complete the task. A short period of time after his discussion with these students, the teacher called for the attention of the whole class and asked them about their progress. The two students near the researcher volunteered and outlined their attempt. When they announced they had decided to make use of a piecewise function, sections of the class responded in different ways. A small number of students indicated agreement with the approach the pair of students were proposing even though the details of the functions other students had used were different. Most students, however, expressed exasperation that they had not noticed an obvious feature of the plotted data. These students then returned to the task and were able to develop a piecewise function that fitted the data for themselves. A small minority of students needed more direct assistance from the teacher and were then able to develop a model based on a piece-wise function by the end of the lesson. The lesson concluded when the teacher asked the students to do further work on their assumptions and limitations for homework.

7   Comparing Views on Task Design

Two views of task design have been presented in this chapter. The first, as a set of general principles drawn from the literature and the second as a set of principles specific to modelling tasks devised by a teacher of mathematics. The exemplar task discussed in the previous section satisfied the teacher's "home grown" principles of modelling task design as well as the general principles developed from the literature. The purpose for and use of digital tools in this task were also consistent with relevant elements of both sets of task design principles.

7.1   Parallels Between Two Perspectives on Task Design

The use of modelling tasks and digital tools is consistent with mandatory requirements of the relevant state curriculum authority and so observes both *syllabus compliance* and a *fit to circumstance* for the specific curriculum context. Further, it was a mandatory requirement of the relevant syllabus for technology to be incorporated into the teaching, learning, and assessment of mathematics.

Consistent with both sets of principles, the task is *open-ended* in that a variety of mathematical models are plausible and the use of different models will lead to different, but still valid, responses to the problem. The available digital tools are a crucial facilitating resource that provided the facility to trial a range of functions to fit a complex underlying pattern and offered immediate feedback on the appropriateness of a conjectured function allowing students to develop specific solutions from a wide range of possibilities.

Students found the task to be *accessible*, an aspect common to both sets of principles, as it linked to mathematical knowledge they had studied in previous classes and the teacher made use of progress made by other students to provide a prompt when many were experiencing difficulty. Digital tools were also important for this aspect of design as they provided the means for students to trial different functions against the data and receive immediate feedback providing an entry point for most students and so enhanced the accessibility of the problem.

As the task required students to make use of mathematical knowledge they had already studied in previous lessons within an unfamiliar context it provided opportunity for students with the *challenge* needed for the development of their mathematical knowledge and their capacity to apply this knowledge in real world contexts—parallel aspects of the two sets of principles. There is clear evidence in the example that the students were challenged, as their attempt to directly apply mathematics they had learned in a previous lesson, without considering the specific circumstances of the real life situation, proved to be unsuccessful. Digital tools acted as a catalyst for progressing their attempts to solve the problem by providing feedback which indicated students' first single function conjectures were not consistent with the data. Further, because the technology included the capacity to plot multiple functions and so explore possible solutions, students were more easily able to employ their knowledge of different functions in finding a fit that involved a piece-wise approach. Thus, while digital tools were not integral to the challenge aspect of the task, technology was a vital resource deployed by the students in order to meet the challenge inherent in the task.

An essential part of this teacher's practice was the *continual improvement* of tasks over successive teaching cycles (typically revisiting tasks on a yearly basis). This was the first time the teacher had trialled this task but noted the tendency of his students to apply mathematical knowledge learned in the most recent lessons without considering the specific features of the plotted data. He saw that the task had provoked the need for students to consider additional functions and change their approach (for further detail see Geiger et al. 2010). The teacher indicated he intended to explore the possibility of designing similar features into other tasks (for other examples of such tasks see the materials developed as part of the MAACAS project http://www.qamt.org/maacas-project).

As outlined above, there is an inseparable interplay between the task and digital tools for some aspects of design in a manner consistent with documental genesis (Gueudet and Trouche 2009). This study, however, extends the work of Gueudet and Trouche (2009) from the general work of teachers to the specific activity of designing technology enhanced modelling tasks.

7.2 Divergence Between Two Perspectives on Task Design

The teacher created the task by drawing on "home grown" principles for developing effective technology active modelling tasks. These were mainly consistent with general principles of task design derived from research literature but addressed additional features in order to accommodate the demands of modelling tasks.

In the exemplar task, a national scientific body monitored the blue-green algae in the various river systems because of the related consequences for aquatic wildlife. Thus, this task represents a situation set in a life-related context consistent with the aim of achieving *authenticity and relevance*. This is an extension of the general principles of task design and accommodates an aspect that is the essence of mathematical modelling—its connection to real world situations and circumstances.

Different types of mathematics were necessary to explore the data (data representation, different forms of function) and so, students were expected to make *connections* to different types of mathematical knowledge. This is another aspect of task design that is important to modelling because the act of applying mathematics to the real world often requires the deployment of a range of mathematical knowledge. This is not necessarily the case in other types of mathematical tasks as these can have a focus on developing specific mathematical knowledge. The aspect of connectivity is also more fully realised through the use of digital tools. In this case, the available technology provided the option of viewing different types of mathematical representations (e.g., scatterplots and function graphs) on the screen at the same time, so enhancing the connection between these types of mathematical knowledge.

8 The Role of Digital Tools in Modelling Task Design

In the exemplar described earlier, the successful deployment of both sets of principles in designing tasks was dependant on the intersection of the potentialities of the task and available digital tools for a number of aspects of design. In implementing the task, the teacher anticipated how students would interpret the potentials of the task for learning and of the digital tool to act as a resource.

8.1 Transformation of the Task, Learning and Teaching

The relationship between student, teacher, task and digital tool represents a documental genesis (Gueudet and Trouche 2009) as each element within this genesis transforms the other in some way. The task is transformed, from the perspective of the students when they realise the need to make use of a piece-wise rather than a single function in order to model the data presented in the problem. This transformation occurs as a result of an attempt by the students to use a single function and receiving feedback via the digital device that this was an inappropriate model. The use of the digital tool changes from that of a device that provided a specific solution for students once they had made a decision on the general form of the function to model the data into a tool used to explore the data and eventually find a model that fitted the data to their level of satisfaction. Students' learning is also transformed during this same process as they realise the purpose of the task and the digital tool was not to implement prior learning in an automated fashion but to apply their knowledge and understanding in an original way by taking into account unfamiliar features of the data. The teacher had to transform his approach to the lesson when students took a path he had not anticipated—attempting to fit a single function to the data. He changed his approach by revising his orchestration of the lesson by utilising new resources at his disposal, in this case deploying the insight of the two students who had solved the problem. When the two students informed their classmates that an approach based on a single function regression was not appropriate and that the data was best represented by a piece-wise function led to class members revising their attempts at a solution and allowed for the expansion of their repertoire of function fitting skills.

8.2 Digital Tools as Enablers of Task Design Principles

From the perspective of instrumental genesis, nearly all of the teacher's principles of design required the use of digital tools as enablers of the task. The principle of *authenticity* and *relevance* required students to recognise the potential of the available digital tools to assist them in exploring and solving the problem described in the task from both purely mathematical and real world contexts. There was a necessary duality about the schemas of instrumented action required to accommodate the purely mathematical and contextual demands of the task as students needed to recognise that the real world context demanded the development of a piecewise rather than single function to model the production of CO_2. Having decided that two functions were needed to model the data, a specific instrumentation of the digital tool was needed to find the most appropriate functions for each section of the piecewise function using a purely mathematical approach.

The *open-endedness* of the task placed students in a position where they were challenged to make choices among multiple potential solution pathways. Thus, students were required to make choices among existing schemas of instrumented action or to generate new schemas after recognising the potential of the digital tool for meeting the challenge defined by the task.

The principle of *connectivity* designed into this task required students to generate schemas of instrumented action that were inclusive of different types of mathematical content. The CAS active calculator students used while working with the task included the capacity to link statistical plots with the graphs of specific functions, and these functions could be developed using the regression facility of the calculator. Students needed to find ways of taking advantage of the capabilities when engaging with the demands of the task and pursuing a solution. This is a type of instrumental genesis in which the potential of an artifact is only realised through its instrumented action.

The task was designed to link the demands of the activity to students' previous learning as the separate functions required to build an appropriate piecewise function had been studied and applied to real world contexts in earlier classes although the use of multiple functions to model data had not been previously covered. Thus, the task was created to be *accessible* to students but, at the same time, required students to apply this previous learning in a more complex context one in which multiple functions were needed to model a phenomena rather than a single function—a genuine *challenge*. This meant that students' existing schemas of instrumented action required adaptation in order to accommodate a more complex scenario. By improvising and revising his approach to orchestrating students' learning the teacher promoted changes in students' schemas of instrumented action related to both the digital tool and also the task.

9 Conclusion

The episode included in this chapter demonstrates it is possible to design effective technology demanding modelling tasks, and so the approach offers direction for curriculum designers, teachers and teacher educators. Designing the modelling task itself appears to be largely consistent with general principles of mathematical task design although the teacher in this classroom vignette employed a number of additional principles specific to modelling. Further research is required into those elements of design for modelling tasks that differ from general principles of designing other mathematics tasks. The inclusion of digital tools did not emerge as a stand-alone element of the teacher's set of design principles; rather, technology acted as a vital enabler of a number of design principles. How digital tools can best enable the implementation of these aspects of design is another issue which requires further research. While the teacher had designed an engaging task based on his own principles, students took an approach that was not anticipated by their teacher. The teacher, however, was able to take advantage of students' original but inappropriate approaches, generating a dynamic learning environment where students' knowledge of using mathematics within real world contexts was transformed. This raises a challenge for teachers in how such triggers can be deliberately embedded in designed experiences in a way that provides space for the type of documental genesis described in this paper. This also indicates that further research is necessary to investigate how to take advantage of unanticipated events in a well-planned lesson.

References

Artigue, M. (2002). Learning mathematics in a CAS environment: The genesis of a reflection about instrumentation and the dialectics between technical and conceptual work. *International Journal of Computers for Mathematical Learning, 7*(3), 245–274.

Beatty, R., & Geiger, V. (2010). Technology, communication, and collaboration: Re-thinking communities of inquiry, learning and practice. In C. Hoyles & J.-B. Lagrange (Eds.), *Mathematics education and technology-rethinking the terrain* (pp. 251–284). New York: Springer.

Blomhoj, M., & Hojgarrd Jensen, T. (2003). Developing mathematical model-ling competence: Conceptual clarification and educational planning. *Teaching Mathematics and its Applications, 22*(3), 123–139.

Blum, W., & Niss, M. (1991). Applied mathematical problem solving, model-ling, applications, and links to other subjects: State, trends and issues in mathematics instruction. *Educational Studies in Mathematics, 22*(1), 37–68.

Burkhart, H., & Swan, M. (2013). Task design for systemic improvement: Principles and frameworks. In C. Margolinas (Ed.), *Task Design in Mathematics Education: The 22nd ICME Study Conference* (pp. 432–433). Oxford: ICME.

Cai, J., et al. (2014). Mathematical modeling in school education: Mathematical, cognitive, curricular, instructional, and teacher education perspectives. In P. Liljedahl, C. Nicol, S. Oesterle, & D. Allen (Eds.), *Proceedings of the Joint Meeting of PME 38 and PME-NA 36* (Vol. 1, pp. 145–172). Vancouver, Canada: PME.

City, E., Elmore, R., Fiarman, S., & Teitel, L. (2009). *Instructional rounds in education.* Cambridge, MA: Harvard Educational Press.

Diezmann, C., Watters, J., & English, L. (2001). Implementing mathematical investigations with young children. In J. Bobis, B. Perry, & M. Mitchelmore (Eds.), *Numeracy and Beyond: Proceedings of the 24th Annual Conference of the Mathematics Education Research Group of Australasia* (pp. 170–177). Sydney: MERGA.

Drijvers, P., & Gravemeijer, K. (2005). Computer algebra as an instrument: Examples of algebraic schemas. In D. Guin, K. Ruthven, & L. Trouche (Eds.), *The didactical challenge of symbolic calculators: Turning a computational device into a mathematical instrument* (pp. 163–196). New York: Springer.

English, L., Fox, J., & Watters, J. (2005). Problem posing and solving with mathematical modeling. *Teaching Children Mathematics, 12*(3), 156–163.

Ferrara, F., Pratt, D., & Robutta, O. (2006). The role and uses of technologies for the teaching of algebra and calculus. In A. Gutiérrez & P. Boero (Eds.), *Handbook of research on the psychology of mathematics education: Past, present and future* (pp. 237–273). Rotterdam: Sense Publishers.

Geiger, V., Faragher, R., & Goos, M. (2010). CAS-enabled technologies as 'agents provocateurs' in teaching and learning mathematical modelling in secondary school classrooms. *Mathematics Education Research Journal, 22*(2), 48–68.

Geiger, V., Goos, M., & Dole, S. (2014). Students' perspectives on their numeracy development across the learning areas. In Y. Li & G. Lappan (Eds.), *Mathematics curriculum in school education* (pp. 473–492). New York: Springer.

Goos, M., Geiger, V., & Dole, S. (2013). Designing rich numeracy tasks. In C. Margolinas (Ed.), *Task Design in Mathematics Education: The 22st ICME Study Conference* (pp. 589–598). Oxford: ICME.

Gueudet, G., & Trouche, L. (2009). Towards new documentation systems for mathematics teachers? *Educational Studies in Mathematics, 71*(3), 199–218.

Hiebert, J., & Grouws, D. A. (2007). The effects of classroom mathematics teaching on students' learning. In F. K. Lester (Ed.), *Second handbook of research on mathematics teaching and learning* (pp. 371–404). Charlotte, NC: National Council of Teachers of Mathematics.

Hoyles, C., Noss, R., Kent, P., & Bakker, A. (2010). *Improving mathematics at work: The need for technomathematical literacies.* London: Routledge.

Kaput, J., Hegedus, S., & Lesh, R. (2007). Technology becoming infrastructural in mathematics. In R. Lesh, E. Hamilton, & J. Kaput (Eds.), *Foundations for the future in mathematics education* (pp. 173–191). Mahwah, New Jersey: Lawrence Erlbaum Associate.

Kieran, C., & Guzma'n, J. (2005). Five steps to zero: Students developing elementary number theory concepts when using calculators. In W. Masalski & P. Elliott (Eds.), *Technology-supported mathematics learning environments* (pp. 35–50). Reston, VA: National Council of Teachers of Mathematics.

Kieran, C., Doorman, M., & Ohtani, M. (2013). Principles and frameworks for task design within and across communities. In C. Margolinas (Ed.), *Task Design in Mathematics Education: The 22st ICME Study Conference* (pp. 419–420). Oxford: ICME.

Laborde, C., Kynigos, C., Hollebrands, K., & Straesser, R. (2006). Teaching and learning geometry with technology. In A. Gutiérrez & P. Boero (Eds.), *Handbook of research on the psychology of mathematics education: Past, present and future* (pp. 275–304). Rotterdam: Sense Publishers.

Lappan, G., & Phillips, E. (2009). A designer speaks. *Educational Designer, 1*(3). Retrieved March 3, 2014 from http://www.educationaldesigner.org/ed/volume1/issue3/.

Maass, K., Garcia, J., Mousoulides, N., & Wake, G. (2013). Designing interdisciplinary tasks in an international design community. In C. Margolinas (Ed.), *Task Design in Mathematics Education: The 22st ICME Study Conference* (pp. 367–376). Oxford: ICME.

Niss, M., Blum, W., & Galbraith, P. (2007). Introduction. In W. Blum, P. Gal-braith, H. Henn, & M. Niss (Eds.), *Modelling and applications in mathematics education: The 14th ICMI study* (pp. 3–32). New York, NY: Springer.

Schoenfeld, A. H. (2009). Bridging the cultures of educational research and design. *Educational Designer, 1*(2). Retrieved March 3, 2014 from http://www.educationaldesigner.org/ed/volume1/issue2/article5/.

Sullivan, P. (2011). *Teaching mathematics: Using research-informed strategies. Australian Education Review, 59.* Camberwell, Victoria: Australian Council for Educational Research.

Sullivan, P., & Yang, Y. (2013). Features of task design informing teachers' decisions about goals and pedagogies. In C. Margolinas (Ed.), *Task Design in Mathematics Education: The 22st ICME Study Conference* (pp. 529–530). Oxford: ICME.

Sullivan, P., Clarke, D., & Clarke, B. (2013). *Teaching with tasks for effective mathematics learning.* New York: Springer.

Thompson, M., & Yoon, C. (2007). Why build a mathematical model? Taxonomy of situations that create the need for a model to be developed. In R. Lesh, E. Hamilton, & J. Kaput (Eds.), *Foundations for the future in mathematics education* (pp. 193–200). Mahwah, New Jersey: Lawrence Erlbaum Associate.

Trouche, L. (2005). Instrumental genesis, individual and social aspects. In D. Guin, K. Ruthven, & L. Trouche (Eds.), *The didactical challenge of symbolic calculators: Turning a computational device into a mathematical instrument* (pp. 197–230). New York: Springer.

Verillon, P., & Rabardel, P. (1995). Cognition and artifacts: A contribution to the study of thought in relation to instrumental activity. *European Journal of Psychology of Education, 10*, 77–103.

Villarreal, M., Esteley, C., & Mina, M. (2010). Modeling empowered by information and communication technologies. *ZDM, 42*(3), 405–419.

Zevenbergen, R. (2004). Technologizing numeracy: Intergenerational differences in working mathematically in new times. *Educational Studies in Mathematics, 56*(1), 97–117.

Designing Interactive Dynamic Technology Activities to Support the Development of Conceptual Understanding

Gail Burrill

Abstract Technology can make a difference in teaching and learning mathematics when it serves as a vehicle for learning and not just as a tool to crunch numbers and to draw graphs. This paper discusses a technology leveraged program to develop student understanding of core mathematical concepts. A sequence of applet-like dynamically linked documents allows students to take a meaningful mathematical action, immediately see the consequences, and then reflect on those consequences in content areas associated with the middle grades U.S. Common Core State Standards. The materials are based on the research literature about student learning, in particular enabling students to confront typical misconceptions, and designed to support carefully thought out mathematical progressions within and across the grades.

Keywords Conceptual understanding · Learning progressions · Interactive dynamic technology · Action consequence principle

1 Introduction

Researchers have investigated challenges in teaching and learning certain mathematical concepts such as fractions, ratios and proportions for years. Burrill and Dick (2008), in investigating student achievement on high stakes state assessments, identified core mathematical concepts in which students consistently underperformed. On international assessments, scores in the United States are usually below international averages. In addition, studies of U.S. texts reported that mathematics concepts addressed in mathematics textbooks are not well constructed, with presentations more mechanical than conceptual (Ginsburg and Leinwand 2009).

These concerns led to the development of the Common Core State Standards for Mathematics (CCSSM) (2010), which aims to improve mathematics education in

G. Burrill (✉)
Michigan State University, East Lansing, MI, USA
e-mail: burrill@msu.edu

© Springer International Publishing Switzerland 2017
A. Leung and A. Baccaglini-Frank (eds.), *Digital Technologies in Designing Mathematics Education Tasks*, Mathematics Education in the Digital Era 8,
DOI 10.1007/978-3-319-43423-0_15

the US by providing a focused and coherent set of standards to guide the teaching and learning of mathematics. The CCSSM emphasize the development of both conceptual understanding and procedural fluency. As mentioned above, prior emphasis in typical curricular materials was to a large degree on procedural fluency. Building Concepts was developed as a technology-based approach to developing mathematical understanding of core concepts that lead to computational proficiency in the mathematical strands outlined in the CCSSM.

2 Building Concepts

2.1 Learning Progressions

Almost all content strands in the CCSSM are supported by progressions documents (http://ime.math.arizona.edu/progressions/ 2011), narratives describing the learning progression of a topic across a number of grade levels, informed both by research on children's cognitive development and by the logical structure of mathematics. The progressions documents outline the important mathematical concepts in each content strand. These documents provide the framework for Building Concepts activities. The underlying premise is that static pictures or examples in the progression documents are made interactive in the Building Concepts activities.

Interactive dynamic technology is not new in mathematics education. Early work with SimCalc (Roschelle et al. 2000) used such technology to link real contexts with graphical representations of those contexts and provided opportunities and experiences for students to develop understanding of the mathematics of change and variation. Dynamic geometry software (Laborde 2001) allowed students to interact directly with objects, their shapes and measurements related to those shapes, looking for consequences that are invariant with respect to a certain shape. Computer algebra systems allowed students to make changes in variable values and parameters of functions and see immediate consequences (Heid 1995). Each of these projects involved "active learning" experiences, which laid the foundation for the "action consequence" principle that guides the development of the technology platform for the Building Concepts activities.

2.2 Action Consequence Principle

Many studies have pointed to the effectiveness of active learning where students are engaged in the process of learning by actively processing, applying, and discussing information in a variety of ways (Kilpatrick et al. 2001; National Research Council (NRC) 2012, 1999; Michael and Model 2003). The theories of Mezirow (1997),

Kolb's learning cycle model (1984), and the work of Zull (2002) on brain theory all suggest that people learn through the mechanism of participating in an immersive mathematics experience, reflecting on these experiences, and attempting similar strategies on their own. Mezirow introduced the notion of transformative learning as a change process that transforms frames of reference for the learner. Key elements in this process are an "activating event" (Cranton 2002) that contributes to a readiness to change (Taylor 2007). This is followed by critical reflection where the learner works through his understanding in light of the new experiences, considering the sources and underlying premises (Cranton 2002). The third element of this process is reflective discourse or dialogue in an environment that is accepting of diverse perspectives (Mezirow 2000). The final step is acting on the new perspective, central for the transformation to occur (Baumgartner 2001). Kolb's model of experiential learning (1984) is a cycle containing four parts: concrete experience, reflective observation, abstract conceptualization, and active experimentation; experimentation leads once again to concrete experience.

Dynamic interactive technology provides a virtual environment in which these kinds of learning opportunities can take place. Interactive dynamic technology goes beyond linking students to multiple representations—visual, symbolic, numeric and verbal—by providing them with visual representations they can directly manipulate and control (Roschelle et al. 2000; Sacristan et al. 2010). Interactive dynamic technology allows the learner to use technological tools to "explore and deepen understanding of concepts" (CCSSM). Too often mathematics learning technologies are used as a "servant", where the user employs the technology to create a graph, perform calculations or generate a table. Building Concepts represents a shift in the use of technology from "carrying out mathematical processes" to "learning mathematics" (Dick and Burrill 2009).

This perspective is supported by a number of studies that suggest the strategic use of technological tools can enhance the development of proficiencies such as problem solving and mathematical reasoning (Kastberg and Leatham 2005; Roschelle et al. 2010; Suh and Moyer 2007). Such technologies can help students transfer mental images of concepts to visual interactive representations that lead to a better and more robust understanding of the concept. Building Concepts activities were designed to embody this notion of active learning, employing an "action/consequence" principle, where the learner is to "deliberately take a mathematical action, observing the consequences, and reflecting on the mathematical implications of the consequences (Mathematics Education of Teachers II 2012, p. 34)". The software supports tasks that provide opportunities for the student to make mathematical choices and reflect on what happens because of those choices. The next section addresses the approach to content in Building Concepts and how it embodies the action consequence principle.

3   Building Conceptual Understanding

3.1   A Coherent Development of Concepts

The content in the K-8 CCSSM is designed to be focused and coherent within and across grades with an emphasis on conceptual understanding that lays the foundation for procedural fluency. Many traditional current materials in the U.S. covered a plethora of ideas in two textbook pages, giving students little opportunity to develop any one idea fully let alone make connections among ideas. Building Concepts is designed to thoughtfully consider the key ideas in building conceptual understanding of important mathematical concepts. Thus, the activities focus on fundamental concepts, typically one per activity, in a carefully developed sequence of explorations aligned with the progressions documents. For example, the progression for ratio and proportional relationships defines a ratio as a pair of non-negative quantities both of which are not 0, emphasizes equivalent ratios and suggests that pairs of quantities in equivalent ratios be recorded in a table. Figure 1 displays the screen from *What is a Ratio?*, the first activity in *Building Concepts*: *Ratios and Proportional Reasoning*, where the concept of ratio is introduced. Students see a physical representation of this pairing, two circles to three rectangles, and generate representations of equivalent ratios (action/consequence). They observe patterns in the rectangular array, noticing the "pairing" as each row is added to the representation and think about the numbers involved, initially additively—adding two blue circles and three green squares each time, but the multiplicative interpretation is also visible in the total number of circles and squares. The arrow keys at the top allow students to change the original ratio to verify their observations and conjectures with different numbers.

Figure 2, from *Building a Table of Ratios*, displays an original ratio, its physical representation and a table of the numbers that compose equivalent ratios. Now students are expected to reason about relationships among the numbers they see in

Fig. 1 Equivalent ratios

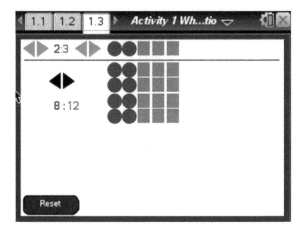

Fig. 2 Associating numbers and ratios

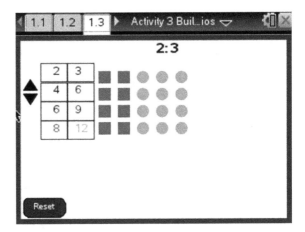

Fig. 3 Ratio table

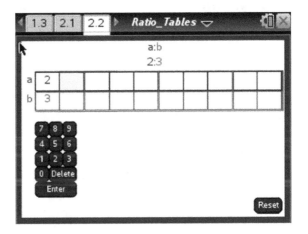

the table, as well as the physical pattern, and observe the multiplicative relationship between equivalent ratios. In *Ratio Tables* (Fig. 3), students move to the abstract, where the physical representation of squares and circles is absent but can be recalled as a basis for thinking about the ratios in the table. The next page in the file moves one step farther, allowing students to generate equivalent ratios in any order, building multiplicative understanding of equivalent ratios.

Another activity in *Ratios and Proportional Relationships* focuses on developing understanding of how to compare ratios and strategies for doing so. Figure 4 displays a problem posed in the progressions document about mixing cans of yellow and red paint. The activity, *Comparing Ratios*, allows students to associate visual representations of cans of paint with equivalent ratios displayed numerically in a table (Fig. 5). Students refer to earlier work with equivalent ratios to answer questions such as: Is a mixture of 2 red to 6 yellow a different shade than a mixture of 5 red and 15 yellow? In considering different approaches for comparing the two

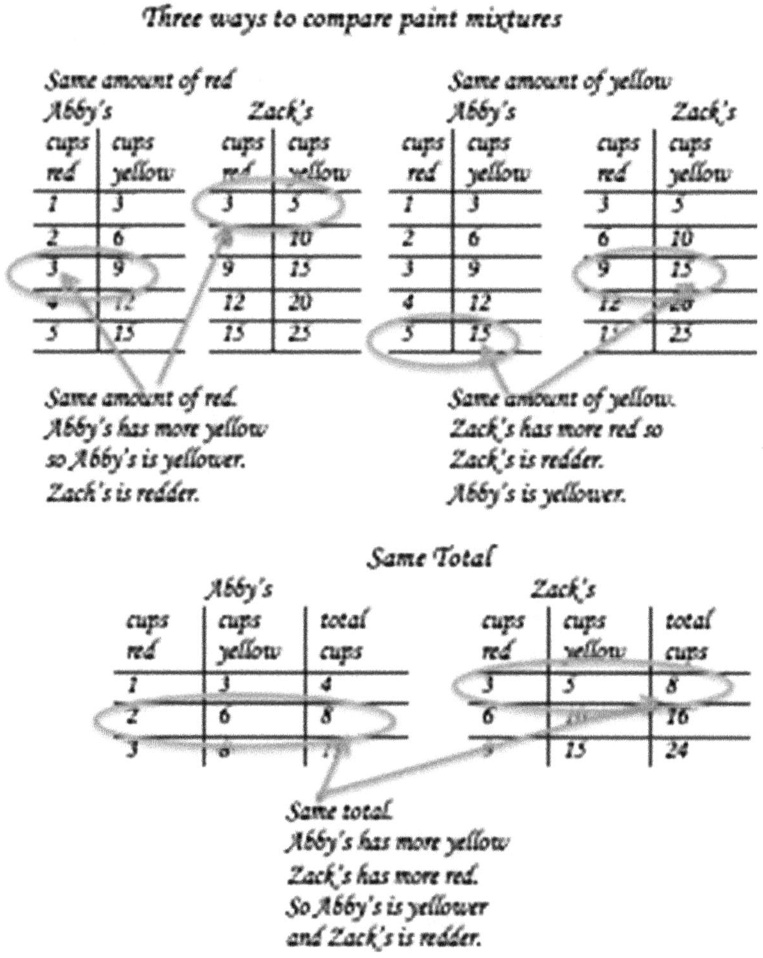

Fig. 4 Mixture problem

mixtures, students investigate whether any of the equivalent ratios can be useful in deciding which mixture would be more yellow.

When students select pairs of ratios with a common unit, such as 6 cans of red paint (Fig. 6), the "action/consequence" move produces a visual representation of the ratios that helps them make the comparison with respect to cans of yellow paint. They confront misconceptions such as pairing cans of red and yellow and counting the number of left over cans of yellow paint to determine the mixture that will have the most yellow as well as consider what other pairs of ratios might also be used to make the comparison.

Fig. 5 Visualizing ratios

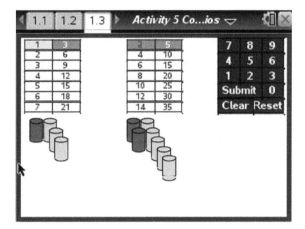

Fig. 6 Equivalent ratios

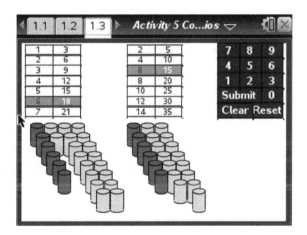

A third example from *Ratios and Proportional Relationships* illustrates how static diagrams in the progressions documents (Fig. 7) were made interactive. In Fig. 8, students repeatedly generate a horizontal and then vertical change associated with a collection of equivalent ratios, observe the corresponding table and consider the slope triangles and their relationship to each other and the line from the perspective of repeated addition. In Fig. 9, students enter values in the table to generate equivalent ratios by multiplication, and the resulting pair is graphed leading to the notion of scaling and similarity.

Because the activities within a content strand are based on the progressions for that content area, they are sequenced in a developmental order, beginning in middle grades and extending into high school. Figure 10 shows the progression of ratio concepts from the initial concept of ratio as pairings of quantities through a trajectory that leads to proportions to slope to functions and a parallel trajectory that leads to geometric ideas of scaling, similarity and trigonometric ratios. Similar

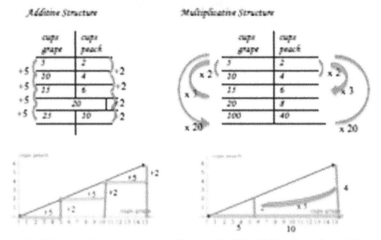

Showing structure in tables and graphs

In the tables, equivalent ratios are generated by repeated addition (left) and by scalar multiplication (right). Students might be asked to identify and explain correspondence between each table and the graph beneath it (MP7).

Fig. 7 Graphing ratios

Fig. 8 Additive structure

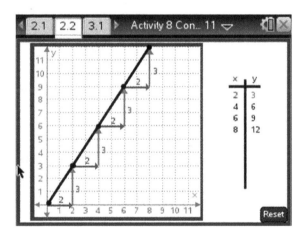

progression maps describe other content strands. While some of the activities can be used "out of sequence", the cumulative learning built into the complete set for a strand will not happen if the activities are used without regard to the progression. The activities can be associated with a grade level in the CCSSM but could be used at any grade level as long as the sequence of ideas is maintained.

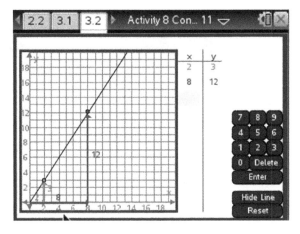

Fig. 9 Multiplicative structure

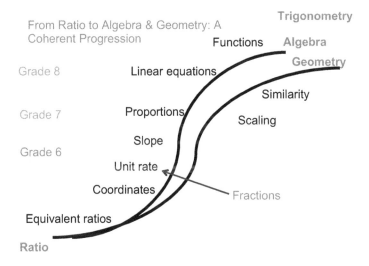

Fig. 10 Ratio learning progression

3.2 The Tasks

The tasks in each activity were constructed following the advice of Black and William (1998) with respect to formative assessment: "Tasks have to be justified in terms of the learning aims that they serve, and they can work well only if opportunities for pupils to communicate their evolving understanding are built into the planning (p. 143)." Thompson (2002) argued that the goal of a task is to have students participating in conversations that foster reflection on some mathematical "thing". Thus, the majority of tasks in the activities create opportunities to discuss

Fig. 11 Highlighting values

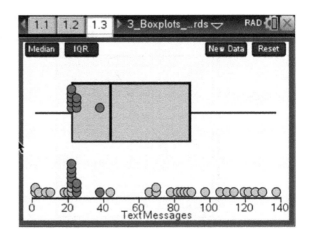

particular mathematical objects or ideas that need to be understood and to ensure that specific conceptual issues and misconceptions will arise for students as they engage in discussions.

Misconceptions: The tasks in the activities have been designed in light of the research related to student learning, challenges and misconceptions (e.g., Zehavi and Mann 2003). The well documented misconception that $(a+b)^2 = a^2 + b^2$ is deliberately addressed in the first activity, *What is an Exponent?*, in the Expressions and Equations strand, where students experiment with "distributing" exponents over all four operations, using the definition of exponents to examine expressions and, as is done in much of this CCSSM strand, making connections back to arithmetic to help their thinking. The misconception is confronted again in later activities in *Building Concepts: Expressions and Equations*.

A common misconception in the statistics and probability strand relates to box plots: the longer the section, the more data in that section. To build understanding of the connection between the data and a box plot, a dot plot "morphs" into the box plot, and students compare the number of data values in each section of the box plot (Fig. 11). Moving points in the dot plot immediately displays the effect on the corresponding box plot (Fig. 12), reinforcing the fact that medians and quartiles are summary measures based on counting.

Tough to teach/tough to learn concepts: Many students struggle with adding fractions, where they typically follow an algorithm they do not understand. The CCSS stress the number line as a representation for fractions and the unit fraction as a building block for developing operations with fractions. Figure 13 displays a screen from the activity on adding fractions with a common denominator, where students visibly see how addition is the concatenation of two fractions both multiples of the same unit fraction. They explicitly change the denominator of the fractions and observe the results, giving them a physical model for the algebraic formula, $a/b + c/b = (a + c)/b$. Students consider the number of unit fractions in each of the two fractions and justify why the sum of the two fractions is the total

Fig. 12 Moving points

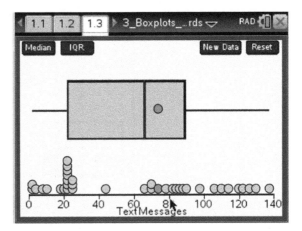

Fig. 13 Adding fractions

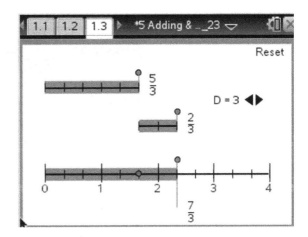

number of unit fractions. Reflecting on the process of adding fractions with unlike denominators in light of the visual representation of the sum of unit fractions, students recognize that to add they must find equivalent fractions based on a common unit fraction.

A second example of fragile conceptual understanding with respect to fractions is the fact that a fraction has meaning only when the unit related to the fraction is known. Figure 14 illustrates an activity in which students use geometric models to create equivalent fractions and compare their work with others to make sense of a "unit" using a visual model of equivalence.

In statistics, the conceptual transition from data represented in bar graphs to plotting data on a number line has long been problematic. One consequence is the fragile understanding of histograms, and another is the "make everything into a bar graph" approach to graphical representations. In the activity *Mean as Fair Share* students explore giving dogs "fair shares" of bags of dog food, first using a "take

Fig. 14 Different size units

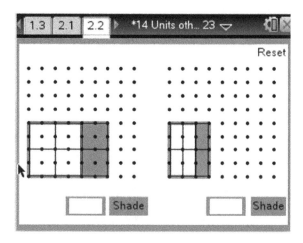

Fig. 15 Fair shares

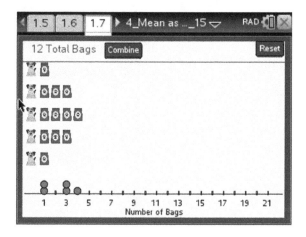

from the most and give to the least" strategy and then using a pooling strategy. At the end of the activity students return to the first strategy, but this time the display includes a number line (Fig. 15) where each dot represents a dog and its position on the number line indicates the number of bags of dog food assigned to that dog. Selecting a dot highlights the dog in the pictograph and vice versa. As students move the bags from dog to dog, the corresponding points move. When each dog has its "fair share", the points are stacked at the mean number of bags of dog food per dog. This lays the foundation for the next activity, which extends the definition of mean as fair share to mean as the balance point of a distribution of data.

Note that the nature of the activities indicates they are not intended to be used for "doing" mathematical procedures but rather provide a foundation for reasoning about the mathematics that can support the transition to procedural fluency. When students have a solid conceptual foundation, they can reason about the mathematics, are less susceptible to common errors, less prone to forgetting and are able to see connections and build relationships among ideas (NRC 1999).

3.3 Posing Questions

In addition to making sure that the tasks surface misconceptions and develop conceptual understanding of "tough to teach/tough to learn" concepts, the questions for each of the activities are created using some general guidelines below:

1. Activate prerequisite knowledge before it is used: e.g., Remember what the solution to an equation represents. How is the solution to the equation reflected in the picture on the screen? How do you know? (*Equations and Operations*)
2. Point out things to notice so students focus on what is important to observe; e.g., When you increase the value of the denominator of a unit fraction, how does the number of equal parts in the interval from 0 to 1 change? What happens to the length of those parts? (*What is a Fraction?*)
3. Ask for justifications and explanations; e.g., Make a conjecture about which data set will have the largest mean. Explain why you think your conjecture might be correct. Use the file to check your thinking (*Mean as Balance Point*).
4. Make connections to earlier tasks or to an immediately previous action taken by the student. (Questions should not come out of the blue.); e.g., Look at your answers for question 2 and see if you want to change them now that you have looked at the values when they are ordered (*Median and Interquartile Range*).
5. Include both positive and negative examples in developing understanding of definitions, theorems and rules; e.g., Which of the following seems like the best definition of an exponent? Explain your reasoning. An exponent a) is a multiplier; b) is a factor, c) tells how many times a number is used as a factor; d) tells you to multiply a number by another number (*What is an Exponent?*).
6. Have students consider the advantages/disadvantages of each approach when it is possible to carry out a task using multiple strategies; e.g., Petra claims you should always use a unit fraction or a unit rate for solving missing value ratio problems. Do you agree? Give an example to support your thinking? (*Double Number Line*)
7. Be explicit about possible misconceptions: e.g., Decide whether the following statements are true or false. Give an example to support your thinking.
   (a) Some equations have more than one solution. (b) Some equations do not have any solutions. (c) Some equations have an infinite number of solutions. (d) Some expressions always have even numbers as outputs (*What is an Equation?*).

Choosing good tasks, paying attention to cognitive demand and to student misconceptions, and asking the right questions are not the whole story. When a dynamic interactive platform is integral to the development of ideas, the platform must support both the mathematics and the user as a learner, i.e., careful attention must be paid to the design of the activities. The next section describes the principles used in designing Building Concepts interactive activities.

4 Design Principles for Building Concepts Activities

4.1 Mathematical Fidelity

To have mathematical fidelity, the software should be mathematically correct; for example, the boundary line for the graph of $y < 2x + 3$ should not be solid; a side of a triangle in the Euclidean plane should not be associated with a negative slope without reference to a coordinate system. To maintain mathematical fidelity, what students view onscreen should always be mathematically acceptable, i.e., two box plots on the same screen should refer to the same scale. Some technologies have serious flaws in their ability to be mathematical faithful (for example, round off error and limited precision can result in bizarre graphs in given situations). This suggests that the design of activities using the software should consider the context and the mathematical behaviours of objects on screen.

4.2 User Experience

To support the action/consequence principle, the user interface should eliminate obstacles that get in the way or distract the user from easily and immediately being able to attach meaning to both the action and the consequence. The design of the tool should pay attention to cognitive processes appropriate for students' reasoning and knowledge base. A decimal scale on the horizontal axis of a dot plot of data such as that in Fig. 16 (Statkey 2012), which might be appropriate for upper level students, would be conceptually difficult for younger students to interpret. They would typically struggle with why three of the dots are colored and what 0.025 on the right side of the screen represents. The aim should be to support mathematical thinking as opposed to finding results efficiently (the shortest way to a solution) or a "showy" illustration with little mathematical substance. Students should not be asked to spend time sorting out the actions on the screen but rather on making sense of the mathematics they can observe. (For example, in Fig. 17, dragging the point L changes measures on the screen, but the display is cluttered and does not help students see the connections between the sides, angles and proportions.)

Even the location of plots within a panel can make a difference in student understanding. Budgett and colleagues (2013) hypothesized that the vertical arrangement of the graphics panel within the dynamic visualization tool

Bootstrap Dotplot of Proportion ▾

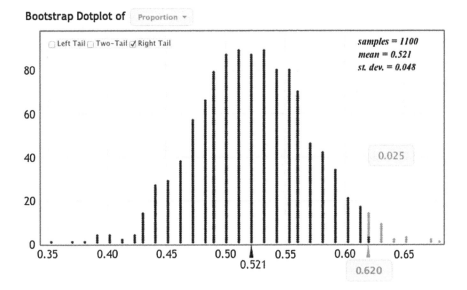

Fig. 16 Sampling proportions

Fig. 17 Similarity

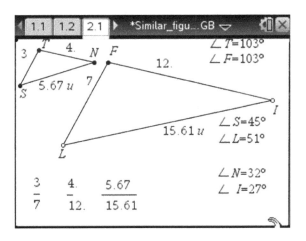

(http://www.stat.auckland.ac.nz/~wild/VIT/) used in their study of randomization in statistics made a difference in what students took from the activities.

Design principles used for creating websites can be useful in thinking about the user interface when designing interactive applets. Visual design guidelines advocated by the US Department of Health and Human Services (http://www.usability. gov/what-and-why/visual-design.html) include:

- Unity: everything on a page visually and conceptually belongs together; e.g., an image must relate to the text it is next to, for the overall message to make sense.
- Gestalt: users perceive the overall design as opposed to individual elements.
- Space: placement of objects reduces noise and increases readability. Simple designs are best.
- Hierarchy: difference in importance of items is conveyed using font sizes, colors, and placement on the page. Usually, items at the top are perceived as most important.
- Contrast: some items stand out because of differences in size, color, direction, and other characteristics.
- Consistency: continuity is maintained throughout a design where pieces work together over an interface. This simplifies learning the interface for the user.

Implicit in these principles is the notion of clarity, (Schwier and Misanchuk 1993) where the meaning of an image is readily apparent to the viewer and the message is reduced to the absolute essentials.

In Building Concepts, these guidelines from web design were adapted to ensure that the experience would maximize learning opportunities for students by creating interactive files that:

- Use simple but mathematically meaningful actions (examples: entering a value, changing a parameter by clicking on a directional arrow, dragging a point on a number line) (gestalt);
- Have visible cues for actions students can take and for the consequences students should be noticing or thinking about (space);
- Minimize use of text on screen (clarity);
- Use color only to make connections and enhance understanding (contrast);
- Locate changing quantities as close together as possible (proximity/unity);
- Display information in order of importance, in terms of position, font size (contrast);
- Use same core design features within and across the files (reset, representation of moveable dots, behaviour of arrow keys, etc.) (consistency).

Color is often misused in creating visual representations. If objects and text are colored gratuitously, the color can introduce unnecessary distractions rather than suggesting important connections. Figure 18 shows the color wheel (invented by Newton in 1666 when he transformed the bar of colors created by light passing through a prism into a segmented circle, where the size of segment differed according to wavelength and width in the spectrum) can help designers choose effective color combinations. To find a harmonious color scheme, use any two colors straight across from each other on the wheel, any three colors that are the vertices of an equilateral triangle or of an isosceles triangle or any four colors that are the vertices of a rectangle. Thus, blue and orange or purple, red-orange and yellow-green could be used to enhance visual images.

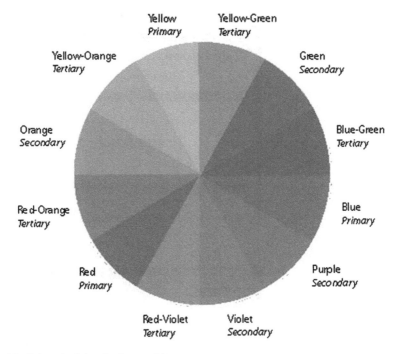

Fig. 18 Color wheel (sustland.umn.edu)

One facet of hierarchy or emphasis is sometimes not obvious; displaying information in order of importance has relevance for the location of buttons and elements that change. Eye tracking studies suggest that people scan computer screens in an "F" pattern, starting from the top and left of the screen. The right side of the screen is rarely seen. This suggests the design of interactive files should position important interactions or information at the top or left of the screen. http://shortiedesigns.com/2014/03/10-top-principles-effective-web-design/.

Figures 19 and 20 from *Building Concepts*: *Equations and Operations* illustrate the use of both color and emphasis. The additive change is colored green in both files (+10 and +4), a purplish pink color is used for the variable, and blue is used for the constant on the right. A violet color, complementary to the pinkish color, represents the multiplicative factor on Sect. 2.2. The arrow buttons and the important things to observe, the changing equation, are at the top. The cues signaling which objects are moveable are given by the handles on the line segments.

Designing technology interfaces should be attentive to user interface issues to fully exploit the action consequence principle, making both the action and consequences transparent and immediate. The next section describes TI Nspire software as a choice for the interactive dynamic documents.

Fig. 19 Equation $x + a = b$

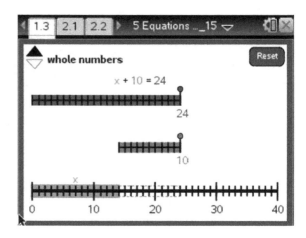

Fig. 20 Equation $cx = b$

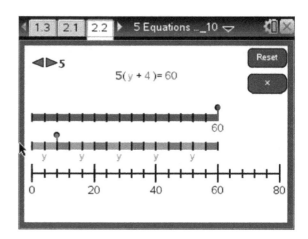

5 Use of TI Nspire Platform

The TI Nspire platform easily lends itself to the construction of the interactive documents, which are related to the applet-family concept (Dick and Burrill 2009). The documents are written in Lua and can be used on handhelds, computers or iPads. The developer has devised several "meta" programs, such as an interactive number line, buttons, and clickers that are used frequently in creating the files. Lua allows the creator to program behaviors using the infrastructure of the Nspire, but the end product restricts the user from interacting with any of the Nspire applications (spreadsheet, graphs, geometry, data collection). This has two advantages. First, the documents provide "safe" environments in which students can play with a mathematical idea in a variety of ways but where the opportunity to go astray is limited (Dick 2008). Second, the technology learning curve is short. The user needs only to know how to get the files on their device, find and open them, and turn pages. The interactivity is restricted to dragging, clicking or selecting an object, and entering numerical values.

Challenges to using the documents vary with the hardware platform. A user might experience some frustration due to lack of familiarity with the touchpad on the handheld device. To address this, when possible, the movements are enabled by using the arrows and tab keys on the handheld keyboard. In some instances, such as changing the factor in a multiplication problem, the user can select the handheld Menu and use the document specific options given there instead of moving the cursor over the number and making the change directly. Entering numerical values poses a problem on the iPad with its touchscreen interface. This was addressed by building a keypad into the document when it was necessary (See Fig. 3). Screen size, especially on the handheld, limits the use of multiple displays.

One challenge related to the computer software and displaying the documents on LCD projectors is the diffusion of color; projectors have various interfaces that change, mute or enhance certain colors in ways that vary from machine to machine. This makes testing the colors a time consuming task, and one that still may not produce effective results for some projectors.

Building Concepts is intended to serve each of the content strands in the CCSSM. The next section describes the activities in three of those strands.

6 Building Concepts Content Strands

6.1 Building Concepts: Fractions

Building Concepts: *Fractions* (2014) consists of a series of 15 interactive dynamic files designed to develop concepts related to fractions and operations with fractions. The development, based on the approach advocated by Wu (2011) and aligned with the CCSSM, uses number lines and area models to help students visualize a fraction as a number (Mack 1995) and develop the arithmetic operations and concepts related to the meaning of fraction, with a particular emphasis on equivalent fractions and their role in fraction operations. A strong emphasis is placed on the notion of a unit fraction and the role of unit in interpreting fraction relationships (Clark and Roche 2009; Lamon 1999). The file and questions are intended to support the transition from words to symbols (Sowder 1992), and enable students to recognize that fractions can be larger than 1, understand that whole numbers can be represented as fractions (Siegler and Pyke 2012), and recognize a larger denominator does not determine the larger fraction (Fazio et al. 2012).

6.2 Building Concepts: Ratios and Proportions

The 15 activities in *Building Concepts*: *Ratios and Proportions* (2015) develop ratio as pairings of quantities that vary together. Consistent with the CCSSM and countries such as Japan (Ministry of Education 2008), while a fraction such as a unit rate can be associated with a ratio, ratio as a concept is broader than fraction. Students engage in visual and interactive strategies (i.e., double number lines, ratio tables) for solving problems involving ratios and proportion to overcome the difficulty they typically have using algorithms (Lamon 2007; Singh 2000), where they often think any problem with three values and one unknown is a proportional relationship. The activities provide a deliberate and careful investigation into the difference between multiplicative and additive situations (Lamon 1999). A major focus is on equivalent ratios. Research suggests students can create equivalent ratios using simple numbers such as doubling and halving (Empson and Knudsen 2003) but have trouble with more complicated situations. The activities relate collections of equivalent ratios to ordered pairs in a coordinate grid, develop the notion of a slope triangle and the relation of slope to unit rates, introduce proportional relationships and connect them to graphs, and relate proportional reasoning to scale factors.

6.3 Building Concepts: Statistics and Probability

The activities in *Building Concepts*: *Statistics and Probability* (2016) are closely aligned with the CCSSM and also with the *Guidelines for Assessment and Instruction in Statistics Education* (Franklin et al. 2007), which describe the statistical process as consisting of four parts: formulating a question, collecting data, analyzing data and interpreting results. All of these are enacted in the presence of variability, a recurring theme in the statistics and probability progression. The activities begin with a focus on asking a statistical question and looking at distributions of life spans and maximum speed of animals. Measures of center and spread are introduced together, recognizing that either measure alone tells a very incomplete story about the distribution of the data. This helps students take both center and spread into account when reasoning about variation in a variety of situations (Shaughnessy et al. 1999). When appropriate, data points are moveable to call attention to features of the data and of the different plots. Probability is introduced through games, and a choice of simulation models such as coins and spinners allows students to simulate probability distributions and sampling distributions. The activities enable students to experience variability by comparing random samples, generating simulated distributions of sample statistics, and observing the effect of sample size on sampling distributions (Hodgson 1996; del Mas et al. 1999). The middle grade activities end with an investigation fitting models to data sets and examining the error in various models.

Each file is accompanied by supporting materials that include (1) a description of the mathematics that underlies the file; (2) a description of the file and how to use it; (3) possible mathematical objectives for student learning; (4) sample questions for student investigation; and (5) a set of typical assessment tasks.

7 Issues and Potential Pitfalls

7.1 Potential Pitfalls in Designing Activities

The platform affords a vast number of opportunities to enact the action/consequence principle by exploiting the dynamic linkages that can be created between virtually any two objects (where an object is a number, or an expression, or a graph, or a point, or a geometric figure, or a spreadsheet cell, or ...). Using this feature allows for the creation of mathematical scenarios or "microworlds" where a student can take an action on at least one of the objects and immediately see a change in the linked object(s). But it is also very easy to create a microworld that leaves the student as a passive observer where the "consequence" may be simply an animation triggered by pushing a button. Design decisions must be made as to what consequences are supplied by the device and which must be supplied by the student. For example, in a probability simulation, should the student or the device record the outcomes of tossing a coin until you have four heads? When should the process be automated with the number of successes being plotted for 500 repetitions of the simulation? The challenge is to design the interaction in ways that engage students in thinking about the mathematics and not just observing an outcome. Without careful guidance and questioning, this can too easily happen when students use a computer algebra system (CAS), where they turn over the mechanics to the device but are not engaged in reasoning about the process.

Another potential pitfall is to ensure that the focus of the activities is on developing conceptual understanding and not just "doing" the mathematics. Essential to the action/consequence principle is the notion that the action taken by the student is a purposeful choice that has mathematical meaning for the student. When the action is pushing a button and the consequence is the graph of a large data set, the action itself may not be perceived by the student as mathematically meaningful; the interaction between mathematical objects is missing, and the same results could have been achieved with simple graphing software. Such results, while obviously very useful, do not push students to reflect on connections to underlying concepts. In contrast, moving a point and observing no change in the interquartile range for a distribution of data provokes the opportunity to reflect on what an interquartile range is and how one is constructed. The challenge is to focus some of these output driven procedures in a more conceptual direction.

7.2 The Role of the Teacher

Technology alone will not make a difference in student learning. The teacher is the mediator of the interaction between the students, the technology and the learning (Drijvers 2012; Laborde 2001; Roschelle et al. 2010; Suh 2010). Research about effective use of interactive applets in learning statistical concepts suggests teachers should engage students in activities that not only help them confront their misconceptions but also provide them with feedback (del Mas et al. 1999). Allowing students to engage in unfettered "play" with interactive technology is appealing but by itself will not maximize learning opportunities; even a well-designed interactive activity is unlikely to be effective unless students' interaction with it is carefully structured by the teacher (Lane and Peres 2006). Managing classrooms to effectively use technology means involving students in discussing observations after an activity to focus on important observations, helping them become aware of missed observations, and engaging them in reflecting on how important observations are connected (Chance et al. 2007).

The teacher notes offer potential questions for the activities, suggestions for structuring lessons and for managing discussions in ways that support learning. But implementing the activities requires that teachers have confidence in their content knowledge and an understanding of what it means to teach, something not all school teachers in the U.S. are prepared to do.

7.3 Changes in Content

Perhaps the biggest challenge to the CCSSM and to Building Concepts is that "teachers prefer to teach as they were taught" (Cheek and Castle 1981; Kennedy 1991). The CCSSM advocates for coherent and consistent mathematical stories across the grades and not only organizes but presents mathematics from a different perspective. Unfortunately, many teachers work new ideas into their old curriculum and traditional practice rather than accepting an entirely new approach.

8 Conclusion

Very preliminary results from piloting seem promising. Initial results of a study using *Building Concepts: Fractions* (2014) with teachers in a preservice methods course for elementary teachers suggest that the activities made a difference for teachers' understanding of and ability to use fractions. Pre and posttest scores were compared for those who used the technology based activities with those who received instruction in use of concrete manipulatives, such as Cuisenaire rods and fraction strips. Evidence from a school test site suggests that students struggling with mathematical concepts outperformed other students on the state assessment after using *Building Concepts: Ratios and Proportional Reasoning* (2015). Other pilot sites are currently being established for the materials as they are being developed.

In Ben-Zvi and Friedland (1997) noted that technology for teaching and learning has evolved over the years, progressively allowing the work to shift to a higher cognitive level enabling a focus on planning and anticipating results rather than on carrying out procedures. Since then technology has provided powerful new ways to assist students in exploring and thinking about ideas, allowing them to focus on interpretation of results and understanding concepts rather than on computational mechanics. And technology continues to change and offers opportunity to rethink what and how we operate in our classrooms and how that is related to the world outside of the classrooms (Gould 2011). If we use technology to do what we have been doing, we will get the same results (Ehrmann 1995). This paper proposes a program based on an action consequence principle to add new thinking to new technology to enhance mathematics teaching and learning for all students.

Acknowledgments I wish to thank Thomas Dick and Wade Ellis, my collaborators on Building Concepts, Becky Byer, who develops all of the interactive dynamic files and Dan Ilaria, for his comments on the manuscript and support for the project.

References

Baumgartner, L.M. (2001). An update on transformational learning. In S.B. Merriam (Ed.), *New directions for adult and continuing education: No. 89. The new update on adult learning theory* (pp. 15–24). San Francisco: Jossey-Bass.

Ben-Zvi, D., & Friedlander, A. (1997). Statistical thinking in a technological environment. In J. B. Garfield & G. Burrill (Eds.), *Research on the role of technology in teaching and learning statistics* (pp. 45–55). Voorburg: International Statistical Institute.

Black, P., & Wiliam, D. (1998). Inside the black box: Raising standards through classroom assessment. *Phi Delta Kappan, 80*(2), 139–144.

Budgett, S., Pfannkuch, M., Regan, M., & Wild, C. (2013). Dynamic visualizations and the randomization test. *Technology Innovations in Statistics Education, 7*(2).

Building Concepts: Fractions (2014). Texas Instruments Education Technology. http://education.ti.com/en/us/home.

Building Concepts: Ratios and Proportional Relationships (2015). Texas Instruments Education Technology. http://education.ti.com/en/us/home.

Building Concepts: Statistics and Probability (2016). Texas Instruments Education Technology. http://education.ti.com/en/us/home.

Burrill, G., & Dick, T. (2008). *What state assessments tell us about student achievement in algebra*. Paper presented at National Council of Teachers of Mathematics 2008 Research Presession, Salt Lake City UT.

Chance, B., Ben-Zvi, D., Garfield, J., & Medina, E. (2007). The role of technology in improving student learning in statistics. *Technology Innovations in Statistics Education 1*, 1–26. Retrieved from http://eschlarship.org/uc/item/8sd2t4rr.

Cheek, N., & Castle, K. (1981). The effects of back-to-basics on mathematics education. *Contemporary Educational Psychology, 6*(3), 263–277.

Clarke, D. M., & Roche, A. (2009). Students' fraction comparison strategies as a window into robust understanding and possible pointers for instruction. *Educational Studies in Mathematics, 72*, 127–138.

Common Core State Standards (2010). *College and career standards for mathematics*. Council of Chief State School Officers (CCSSO) and National Governor's Association (NGA).

Cranton, P. (2002). Teaching for transformation. In J. M. Ross-Gordon (Ed.), *New directions for adult and continuing education: No. 93. Contemporary viewpoints on teaching adults effectively* (pp. 63–71). San Francisco: Jossey-Bas.

del Mas, R., Garfield, J., & Chance, B. (1999) A model of classroom research in action: Developing simulation activities to improve students' statistical reasoning. *Journal of Statistics Education, 7*(3), www.amstat.org/publications/jse/secure/v7n3/delmas.cfm.

Dick, T. (2008). *Tackling tough to learn/ tough to teach mathematics: A conceptual framework*. Unpublished paper prepared for Designing Professional Development Experiences Using Interactive Dynamic Technology.

Dick, T., & Burrill, G. (2009). *Shaping teacher attitudes toward technology from "tools for doing" to "tools for learning"*. Presentation at the Association of Mathematics Teacher Educators, Orlando, FL.

Drijvers, P. (2012). *Digital technology in mathematics education: Why it works (or doesn't)*. Paper presented for Technology Topic Study Group at the Twelfth International Congress on Mathematical Education, Seoul, Korea.

Ehrmann, S. C. (1995). Asking the right questions: What does research tell us about technology and higher learning? *Change, 27*, 20–27.

Empson, S., & Knudsen, J. (2003). Building on children's thinking to develop proportional reasoning. *Texas Mathematics Teacher, 2*, 16–21.

Fazio, L. K., Thompson, C. A., & Siegler, R. S. (2012, November). *Relations of symbolic and non-symbolic fraction and whole number magnitude representations to each other and to mathematics achievement*. Talk presented at the Annual Meeting of the Psychonomic Society, Minneapolis, MN.

Franklin, C., Kader, G., Mewborn, D., Moreno, J., Peck, R., Perry, M., et al. (2007). *Guidelines for assessment and instruction in statistics education (GAISE) report: A preK–12 curriculum framework*. Alexandria, VA: American Statistical Association.

Ginsburg, A., & Leinwand, S. (2009). *Informing grades 1–6 mathematics standards development: What can be learned from high performing Hong Kong, Korea and Singapore*. Washington DC: American Institutes for Research.

Gould, R. (2011). *Statistics and the modern student*. Department of statistics papers. Department of Statistics, University of California Los Angeles.

Heid, M. K. (1995). The interplay of mathematical understanding, facility with a computer algebra program, and the learning of mathematics. In *Proceedings of the 17th Annual Meeting of the North American Chapter of PME* (pp. 221–225). Columbus: Program Committee.

Hodgson, T. (1996). The effects of hands-on activities on students' understanding of selected statistical concepts. In E. Jakbowski, D. Watkins & H. Biske (Eds.), *Proceedings of the Eighteenth Annual Meeting of the North American Chapter of the International Group for the Psychology of Mathematics Education* (pp. 241–246). ERIC Clearing House for Science, Mathematics, and Environmental Education.

Japanese Ministry of Education (MoE) (2008). Elementary School Teaching Guide for the Japanese Course of Study: Mathematics.

Kastberg, S., & Leatham, K. (2005). Research on graphing calculators at the secondary level: Implications for mathematics teacher education. *Contemporary Issues in Technology and Teacher Education, 5*(1), 25–37.

Kennedy, M. M. (1991). Policy issues in teacher education. *Phi Delta Kappan, 72*, 658–665.

Kilpatrick, J., Swafford, J., & Findell, B. (Eds.). (2001). *Adding it up*. Washington DC: National Research Council, National Academy Press.

Kolb, D. (1984). *Experiential learning: Experience as the source of learning and development*. Englewood Cliffs: Prentice-Hall.

Laborde, C. (2001). Integration of technology in the design of geometry tasks with Cabri-geometry. *International Journal of Computers for Mathematical Learning, 6*, 283.

Lamon, S. (1999). *Teaching fractions and ratios for understanding: Essential content knowledge and instructional strategies for teachers*. Hillsdale: Erlbaum.

Lamon, S. (2007). Rational numbers and proportional reasoning: Toward a theoretical framework for research. In K. Lester Jr. (Ed.), *Second handbook of research on mathematics teaching and learning* (pp. 629–667). Charlotte: Information Age Publishing.

Lane, D. M., & Peres, S. C. (2006). Interactive simulations in the teaching of statistics: Promise and pitfalls. In A. Rossman and B. Chance (Eds.), *Proceedings of the Seventh International Conference on Teaching Statistics [CD-ROM]*. Voorburg: International Statistical Institute.

Mack, N. K. (1995). Critical ideas, informal knowledge, and understanding fractions. In J. T. Sowder & B. P. Schappelle (Eds.), *Providing a foundation for teaching mathematics in the middle grades* (pp. 67–84). Albany: SUNY Press.

Mathematics Education of Teachers II (2012). *Conference Board of the Mathematical Sciences*. Providence, Washington DC: American Mathematical Society, Mathematical Association of America.

Mezirow, J. (1997). Transformative learning: Theory to practice. In P. Cranton (Ed.), *New directions for adult and continuing education: No. 74*. Transformative learning in action: Insights from practice (pp. 5–12). San Francisco: Jossey-Bass.

Mezirow, J. (2000). Learning to think like an adult: Core concepts of transformation theory. In J. Mezirow & Associates (Eds.), *Learning as transformation: Critical perspectives on a theory in progress* (pp. 3–34). San Francisco: Jossey-Bass.

Michael, J., & Modell, H., 2003. *Active learning in secondary and college science classrooms: A working model of helping the learning to learn*. Mahwah: Erlbaum http://nces.ed.gov/nationsreportcard/itmrlsx/search.aspx?subject=mathematics.

National Research Council (1999). In J. D. Bransford, A. L. Brown & R. R. Cocking (Eds.), *How people learn: brain, mind, experience, and school*. Washington, DC: National Academy Press.

National Research Council (2012). In S. Singer, N. Nielsen & H. Schweingruber (Eds.), *Discipline-based education research: Understanding and improving learning in undergraduate science and engineering*. Washington, DC: The National Academies Press.

Progressions for the Common Core Standards in Mathematics (2011). Draft 3–5 Progression on Number and Operations—Fractions; Draft 6–8 Progression on Statistics and Probability; Draft 6–8 Progression on Expressions and Equations; Draft 6–7 Progression on Ratios and Proportional Relationships Common Core State Standards Writing Team. Retrieved January 15, 2015 from http://ime.math.arizona.edu/progressions/.

Roschelle, J. M., Pea, R. D., Hoadley, C. M., Gordin, D. N., & Means, B. M. (2000). Changing how and what children learn in school with computer-based technologies. *The Future of Children, 10*(2), 76–101.

Roschelle, J., Shechtman, N., Tatar, D., Hegedus, S., Hopkins, B., Empson, S., et al. (2010). Integration of technology, curriculum, and professional development for advancing middle school mathematics: Three large-scale studies. *American Educational Research Journal, 47*(4), 833–878.

Sacristan, A., Calder, N., Rojano, T., Santos-Trigo, M., Friedlander, A., & Meissner, H. (2010). The influence and shaping of digital technologies on the learning—and learning trajectories—of mathematical concepts. In C. Hoyles & J. Lagrange (Eds.), *Mathematics education and technology—rethinking the terrain: The 17th ICMI study* (pp. 179–226). New York: Springer.

Schwier, R. A., & Misanchuk, E. R. (1993). *Interactive multimedia instruction* (Chap. 9, pp. 155–192). Englewood Cliffs: Educational Technology Publications.

Shaughnessy, J. M., Watson, J., Moritz, J., & Reading, C. (1999). School mathematics students' acknowledgement of statistical variation. In C. Maher (Chair), *There's More to Life than Centers*. Presession Research Symposium, 77th Annual National Council of Teachers of Mathematics Conference, San Francisco, CA.

Siegler, R. S., & Pyke, A. A. (2012). Developmental and individual differences in understanding of fractions. *Developmental Psychology*. Advance online publication. doi:10.1037/a0031200.

Singh, P. (2000). Understanding the concepts of proportion and ratio constructed by two grade six students. *Educational Studies in Mathematics, 43*(3), 271–292.

Sowder, J. T. (1992). Estimation and number sense. In D. A. Grouws (Ed.), *Handbook of research on mathematics teaching and learning* (pp. 371–389). New York: Macmillan.

Statkey (2012). Lock, R., Lock, P., Lock, K., Lock, E., & Lock, D. Companion materials for Statistics: Unlocking the power of data. www.lock5stat.com/statkey/sampling_1_cat/sampling_1_cat.html.

Suh, J. M. (2010). Tech-knowledgy for diverse learners [Technology Focus Issue]. *Mathematics Teaching in the Middle School, 15*(8), 440–447.

Suh, J., & Moyer, P. S. (2007). Developing students' representational fluency using virtual and physical algebra balances. *Journal of Computers in Mathematics and Science Teaching, 26*(2), 155–173.

Taylor, E. W. (2007). An update of transformative learning theory: A critical review of the empirical research (1999–2005). *International Journal of Lifelong Education, 26*(2), 173–191. doi:10.1080/02601370701219475.

Thompson, P. (2002). Didactic objects and didactic models in radical constructivism. In K. Gravemeijer, R. Lehrer, B.v Oers, & L. Verschaffel (Eds.), *Symbolizing, modeling and tool use in mathematics education* (pp. 191–212). Dordrecht: Kluwer Academic.

Wu, H. (2011). *Understanding numbers in elementary school mathematics.* Washington DC: American Mathematical Society.

Zehavi, N., & Mann, G. (2003). Task design in a CAS environment: Introducing (In) equations. In J. Fey, A. Cuoco, C. Kieran, L. McMullin, & R. Zbiek (Eds.), *Computer algebra systems in secondary school mathematics education* (pp. 173–191). Reston: NCTM.

Zull, J. (2002). *The art of changing the brain: Enriching the practice of teaching by exploring the biology of learning.* Alexandria: Association for Supervision and Curriculum Development.

Tensions in the Design of Mathematical Technological Environments: Tools and Tasks for the Teaching of Linear Functions

Alison Clark-Wilson

Abstract The design of tasks for the exploration of mathematical concepts involving technology can take several starting points. In many cases the 'tool' is predefined as an existing mathematics application with an embedded set of design principles that shape the mathematical tasks that are possible. In other cases, the tool and tasks are designed through a more dynamic process whereby designers and educators engage in a discourse that influences the resulting tasks. The chapter will begin with a brief description of a longitudinal study, and its theoretical framework that resulted in a rubric to inform the design of tasks that privilege the exploration of mathematical variants and invariants (Clark-Wilson and Timotheus in *ICMI study 22 task design in mathematics education,* UK: Oxford, 2013; Clark-Wilson in How does a multi-representational mathematical ICT tool mediate teachers' mathematical and pedagogical knowledge concerning variance and invariance? 2010). This rubric is then used as a construct for the post-priori analysis of two tasks that introduced the concept of linear functions and that use different technologies. Conclusions will be drawn that highlight subtle tensions that relate to the mathematical knowledge at stake and to the design principles of the underlying technology and task.

Keywords Mathematics · Digital technology · Task design · Linear functions

1 Introduction

An important premise for the design of any task in mathematics education concerns the very nature of the mathematical knowledge that the task is intended to develop, which might encompass facts, skills, algorithms, relationships, notations etc. that are all situated within the particular mathematical culture. Alongside this, the diversity of the mathematical processes through which users engaged in the task

A. Clark-Wilson (✉)
UCL Knowledge Lab, University College London, London, UK
e-mail: a.clark-wilson@ucl.ac.uk

© Springer International Publishing Switzerland 2017
A. Leung and A. Baccaglini-Frank (eds.), *Digital Technologies in Designing Mathematics Education Tasks*, Mathematics Education in the Digital Era 8,
DOI 10.1007/978-3-319-43423-0_16

might construct their mathematical knowledge could require her to represent, visualise, conjecture, notate, estimate, reason, justify, generalise and so on. I am in strong agreement with Mason, Graham and Johnston-Wilder's premise that 'a lesson without the opportunity for learners to express a generality is not in fact a mathematics lesson' (Mason et al. 2005, p. 297). That is, the core purpose of the tasks that we offer to learners of mathematics is to expand their frame of mind through an ongoing process of validating or refuting mathematical knowledge. Consequently, the work described in this chapter has emanated from two projects in which tasks have been designed within technology-mediated environments to privilege learners' first-hand dynamic exploration of mathematical variants and invariants within English mathematics classroom settings (11–16 years).

2   Theoretical Framework

A longitudinal study that involved 15 English teachers of secondary school mathematics in the design, teaching and evaluation of 75 lesson activities resulted in a rubric for mathematical task design within dynamic multi-representational digital environments (Clark-Wilson 2010; Clark-Wilson and Timotheus 2013). In this study the teachers were designing tasks that required students to use the *TI-Nspire v1.8* handheld device or computer software (Texas Instruments 2007b), which at that time was a new digital environment for all concerned.

This research was framed within an activity-theoretic approach that interprets the Vygotskian notion of activity as a 'unit of analysis that included both the individual and his/her culturally defined environment' (Wertsch 1981). Verillon and Rabardel elaborated this earlier theory to develop the *instrumental approach* within technological environments (Verillon and Rabardel 1995). This construct has been further expanded by the mathematics education research community to include the notions: instrumentation; instrumentalisation; instrumental genesis; instrumental orchestration and documentational genesis. (Drijvers and Trouche 2008; Guin and Trouche 1999; Trouche 2004; Gueudet and Trouche 2009; Drijvers 2012; Haspekian 2014). These ideas concern the complex and interrelated processes of:

- Learning to use a new technology for purposeful mathematical activity;
- Designing tasks for students to initiate purposeful mathematical activity;
- Collating the various artifacts that comprise the 'document system' for the activity;
- Supporting students to learn to use technology for purposeful mathematical activity;
- Articulating the teacher's role in supporting the students to navigate their respective routes through the various artifacts that comprise the activity to include interaction with the technology.

It is important to comment that within the research contexts from which these notions have emanated, the chosen technologies fit Pierce and Stacey's description of 'mathematical analysis tools' (Pierce and Stacey 2008), which include technologies such as computer algebra software (CAS), dynamic geometry software (DGS), graphing software and spreadsheet software. The TI-Nspire technology used within my earlier research afforded a range of 'applications' that included: calculator; spreadsheet; dynamic geometry; function graphing; statistical calculation and graphing; built in commands i.e. *factor(n)*; and text editing. In all of these environments, the facility to save numeric outputs as variables supported the linking of variables within and between these different representations.

A second important theoretical construct of significance to the study was that of a multiple representational environment, which was postulated initially by Kaput (1986) in his vision for the way in which technology might support higher–level engagement with mathematics. In the intervening years, different genres of technologies have afforded opportunities to engage with mathematics dynamically by observing the simultaneous views of different representations, for example, the representations of a function, its graph and a table of its associated coordinate values. The development of 'dragging' an image through the interface of a mouse (or pen or finger) has afforded further forms of mathematical interaction.

As the study progressed, an element of the teachers' epistemological development was related to their realisation that expressing generality was a very important aspect of the tasks that they went on to design, although this was not necessarily realised at the time. Other elements of the teachers' professional learning concerned increasing attention to the way that the digital environment supported or hindered the expression of generality, the design of the associated supporting resources, and the teacher's role in mediating the associated classroom discourse. The evidence from the study suggested that the process of designing tasks that utilise such environments to privilege explorations of variance and invariance is a highly complex process, which requires teachers to carefully consider how variance and invariance might be manifested within any given mathematical topic. The relevance and importance of the initial example space and how this might be productively expanded to support learners towards the desired generalisation is a crucial aspect of task design. For example, the example space might need to be flexible enough to enable the students to explore and generate different example sets, which might be accomplished by dragging an on-screen object that drives a variant property.

The starting point for any classroom task is its initial design, and the following set of questions, generated as a result of this study, offer a research-informed approach to the design process:

- What is the generalisable property within the mathematics topic under investigation?
- How might this property manifest itself within the multi-representational technological environment—and which of these manifestations is at an accessible level for the students concerned?

- What forms of interaction with the multi-representational technology will reveal the desired manifestation?
- What labelling and referencing notations will support the articulation and communication of the generalisation that is being sought?
- What might the 'flow' of mathematical representations (with and without technology) look like as a means to illuminate and make sense of the generalisation?
- What forms of interaction between the students and teacher will support the generalisation to be more widely communicated?
- How might the original example space be expanded to incorporate broader related generalisations? (Clark-Wilson 2010, p. 242-3)

These questions will be used as a rubric later in this chapter.

Discussions during the ICMI Study Conference 22 on Task Design (Margolinas 2013) led Paul Drijvers to contribute a further question: *How do you know that this generalisation is true for all cases? (Can it be proved?)* However, these questions only become useful as one begins to consider the study of a particular mathematical topic in relation to the teaching context, that is the age, prior attainment and prevalent teaching and learning culture for the students for whom a task is being designed.

What follows are two examples of mathematical tasks that have been designed as early introductions to linear functions within lower secondary mathematics. The first example is a task designed by one of the participating teachers within the original research study that used *TI-Nspire* computer software (the teacher) and handheld technology (the teacher and students). The second task was designed to be accessed within a web browser for the more recent *Cornerstone Maths* project (Clark-Wilson et al. 2015b, a brief description of which is provided below). These examples are used both to provide a deeper discussion of the task design rubric and to highlight some of the tensions within the process of task design.

3   Task Examples: Introducing Linear Functions

When these tasks were designed, the English National Curriculum (Department for Children Schools and Families 2007) stipulated the following content knowledge related to linear functions for students aged 11–14 years[1]: *The study of mathematics should include linear equations, formulae, expressions and identities* (2007 p. 145), which was exemplified by the attainment target:

> They [the students] formulate and solve linear equations with whole-number coefficients. They represent mappings expressed algebraically, and use Cartesian coordinates for graphical representation interpreting general features (2007, p. 150).

---

[1]This was replaced by a new National Curriculum in 2013 (Department of Education 2013).

It is from this starting point that teachers make decisions about the tasks they design and adapt, which requires a consideration of the particular mathematical and pedagogic starting points alongside the finer mathematical progression of the stipulated content knowledge.

3.1 Task 1—Investigating Straight Lines

The task that follows was designed by an experienced teacher who was confident with a range of existing mathematical technologies and chose to use the TI-Nspire PC software with a group of 11–12 year olds to meet her mathematical learning objective 'To be able to discover the gradient and intercept and how they connect to the [linear] equation'. She displayed the task instructions as shown in Fig. 1 and informed the students to: 'work with a partner; be systematic; use lots of different pages to record your findings; and experiment with different layouts'.

The students, a homogenous[2] class of 30 boys and girls, worked in small groups of twos and threes around laptop computers in their regular mathematics classroom. During the one hour lesson, the teacher moved around the classroom, interacting with groups of students to support them to: get started on the task; overcome technological issues (how to input functions, how to split the page to enable them to record their learning notes alongside their graphs, etc.); and to question them about their choice of functions and provide motivational encouragement. The teacher did not choose to convene a whole-class discussion at any point during this particular lesson. Instead, the students posted their task conclusions to the school's virtual learning environment, which the teacher reviewed and responded to after the lesson. In the subsequent lesson, the students worked further on the task before each group presented their findings to the whole class.

The work of one pair of students (a boy and a girl), which is typical of the work produced by the class in terms of its content, layout, and the informal language within the learning notes, is shown below in Figs. 2, 3, 4 and 5 in the order in which they presented to the class.

In her detailed evaluation of the students' activity during the lesson, the teacher concluded the following:

> Previously they had plotted coordinates and joined them up to make a straight line. They were first of all quite amazed that they could just type in the equation and the line would appear automatically. They began to realise that changing the equation affected the graph in different ways, and that the number before the x affected it differently from changing the number added on.

---

[2]The students in most English state schools are organised into setted mathematics classes, according to their prior attainment.

Fig. 1 Task instructions as
displayed to the students

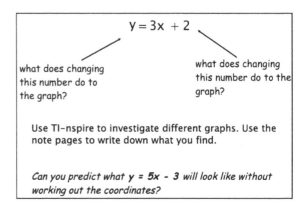

Fig. 2 Pupils'response:
Screen 1

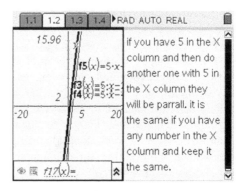

Fig. 3 Pupils'response:
Screen 2

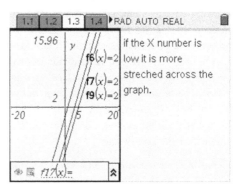

They first of all were very unsure about what to do and needed some prompting, especially on how to fix one variable and alter the other so they did not end up with loads of random looking lines on the page. Mostly it was just an idea of where to start and what equation to type in initially, and then once they had told me what they wanted to fix and what they wanted to change they were fine. Most students managed to reach the conclusion that as the number before the x gets bigger the line gets steeper, and that the number on the end moves the graph and you can make parallel lines. Hardly any had yet managed to generalise to look at fractions or negatives.

Fig. 4 Pupils'response:
Screen 3

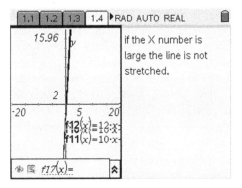

Fig. 5 Pupils'response:
Screen 4

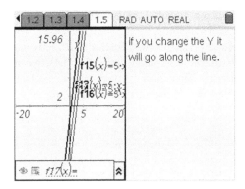

This task design is highly typical of tasks that introduce the gradient and intercept properties of linear functions using mathematical technologies, which have prevailed in English classrooms since the late 1980s.[3] Although the student use of technology to explore mathematical concepts is still under-reported in English secondary school practice (Office for Standards in Education 2008, 2012), research continues to report similar approaches (Ruthven and Hennessy 2003; Godwin and Sutherland 2004).

3.2 Task 2—Controlling Characters with Equations

The example that follows 'Controlling characters with equations' is a task from a sequence of tasks focused on linear functions—one of three curriculum units developed during the Cornerstone Maths project (2011–2014). Cornerstone Maths (CM) is a collaborative design research project involving colleagues at the UCL

---

[3]From graphing calculators and software packages such as Mouseplotter (BBC Micro), Coypu (Acorn/PC), Omnigraph (PC) and Autograph (PC/Mac/iPad).

Knowledge Lab, University College London and SRI International, USA that has the particular aim to widen student access to dynamic mathematical technology in lower secondary classrooms across England to support the teaching of 'hard to teach topics'. (For a fuller description of this project and its research outcomes, see (Clark-Wilson et al. 2015a; Hoyles et al. 2013). Central to its design is the 'curriculum activity system', which incorporates digital resources, pupil workbooks, teacher guides and teacher professional development (Vahey et al. 2013). The digital resources for each of the curriculum units have been developed in html5 to enable wider access by students through a web browser and so overcome the need for software to be installed and maintained on school computer networks, a known barrier to technology use in English mathematics classrooms. In each case a rapid prototyping methodology was adopted to the design of the web-based software by taking the desirable features of existing software that had already been shown to enhance students' mathematical learning. In the case of the CM curriculum unit on linear functions, its software antecedent was *SimCalc*, for which a body of research exists (Hegedus and Roschelle 2013; Kaput and Schorr 2008). The curriculum unit includes 14 separate tasks for students, not all of which require access to technology. This particular task has been selected as its learning objectives most closely align with those of the earlier example.

> Equations are a form of mathematical representation. Graphs and tables are other forms. Equations can be written based on tables or graphs. You can "translate" between graphs, tables and equations. Time, distance and speed are represented differently in these three representations. For equations of the form $y = mx$, in motion contexts, m is the speed of a moving object. (SRI International & Institute of Education 2013, p. iv).

Figure 6 shows the digital resource that accompanies the task. When the play button is activated, the character (Shakey the robot) moves along the horizontal number line, and Shakey's position and time are highlighted simultaneously on the position-time graph and within the table (using colour). In Fig. 6. the animation has been paused at $t = 3$ seconds.

In the task, the students adopt the role of a digital games designer. The task narrative informs them that they are learning the underlying mathematics to enable them to design interesting computer games for mobile devices. The pupils are asked to edit[4] the scenario in Fig. 6 to meet different mathematical constraints (i.e. to make 'Shakey' move slower and faster) and to record the resulting graph, table of values and equation in their workbooks. The process of editing the software, which has the effect of altering the starting position, speed and overall travel time, is accomplished in the following ways:

- The starting position of the character is varied by: dragging the character; dragging the point representing $t = 0$ on the position-time graph in a vertical

---

[4]The pupils are not given guidance on how to do this in the pupil workbook. Also, during their initial professional development teachers are discouraged from demonstrating the different ways to edit the software to pupils before pupils have had an opportunity to explore the editing functionality for themselves.

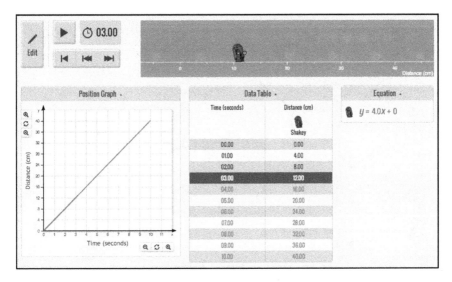

Fig. 6 The dynamic digital environment that accompanies the task 'Controlling characters with equations'

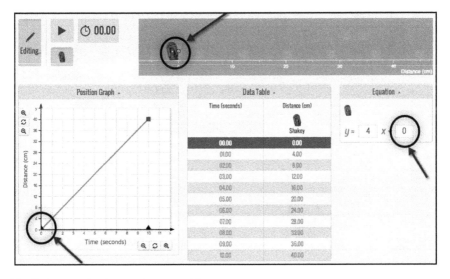

Fig. 7 Varying the character's start position

direction; and/or inputting a numeric value representing 'c' in the equation (Fig. 7).

• The gradient/speed is varied by: dragging the end-point of the line segment in a vertical direction and/or inputting a numeric value representing 'm' in the equation (Fig. 8).

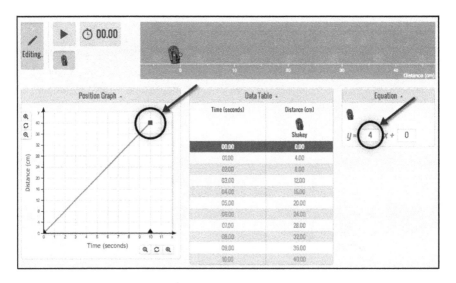

Fig. 8 Varying the speed/gradient

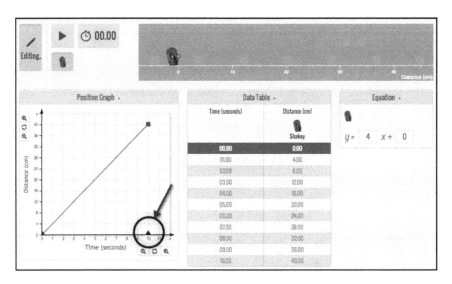

Fig. 9 Varying the travel time

- Dragging the position of the 'hot spot' on the x-axis in a horizontal direction varies the overall travel time (Fig. 9).

Due to the scale of the Cornerstone Maths project, over 180 teachers have taught all or some of the linear functions unit to approximately 6000 students. A scrutiny of the pupil workbooks of one particular gender mixed class of twenty-eight 12–13 year

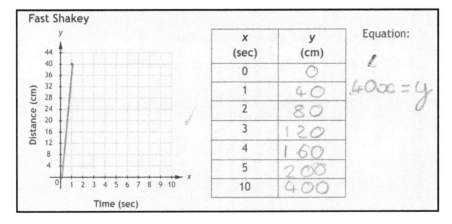

Fig. 10 One student's own graph of 'Fast Shakey'

olds revealed that all of the students were able to edit the graph and sketch the graphs to meet the given constraints (slower and faster). Furthermore, sixteen students gave a written description of the mathematical differences between the two scenarios that they had created, which used language such as 'steeper', 'more shallow', 'more gradient' to explain the differences between the slower and faster scenarios. There was also a great variety in the notations that pupils used to record the 'equation' and their interpretations of the decimal notation that the software displayed. For example, most students recorded the equation exactly as it was displayed, i.e. $y = 8.0x + 0$, whereas others recorded it as $y = 8x + 0$ or $y = 8x$. One student represented the equation in a way that was consistent with the table of values, recording the equation as $40x = y$ (see Fig. 10).

The diversity of the students' responses exemplifies the software tool's role as a *semiotic mediator* supporting the students' personal constructions of meaning related to linear functions and related notations (Bartolini Bussi and Mariotti 2008).

4   Post-priori Analysis

The task design rubric is now used to analyse the two tasks, paying attention to both the designer's perspective and the implications of this supported by the evidence of the students' responses to the tasks in the respective classrooms (Table 1).

Table 1 A post-priori analysis of the two tasks

Question	Task 1: Investigating straight line graphs	Task 2: Controlling characters with equations
What is the generalisable property within the mathematics topic under investigation?	Designers' intentions: There were two generalizable properties: The value of m defines the gradient/steepness of a linear function $y = mx + c$; and the value of c defines the position of the intercept on the y-axis In reality the students were required to choose which of these properties they would investigate first. They were also free to choose the type of numbers that they input for 'm' and 'c'. (i.e. positive/negative, integer/fraction/decimal)	Designers' intentions: For equations of the form $y = mx$, in motion contexts, m is the speed of a moving object
How might this property manifest itself within the multi-representational technological environment?—and which of these manifestations is at an accessible level for the students concerned?	The gradient property: The appearance of the 'steepness' of the line within the graph domain. *This is accessible to the students* The value of 'm' as displayed in the equation. *This was visible to the students, although as multiple lines were on the screen, students would need to remember the creation of each line to link it to its respective equation* The increase in y-value for a unit increase in x-value. *This is accessible to students through the Table view, however, in the lesson concerned, the students were not made aware of this functionality. Although the value of 'm' defines the gradient, it is not clear whether students were able to connect the value of 'm' in a numeric sense to the particular graph that they were looking at as the resolution of the screen did not allow for accurate interpretations* The intercept property	The real-time speed with which the character moves, the line segment is highlighted on the graph and the corresponding rows are highlighted in the table *Students' written responses suggest that that most students were able to make sense of these different representations* The value of 'm' as displayed in the equation. *This was visible to the students* The numeric increase in y-value for unitary increases in x-value as highlighted within the table of values. *This was visible to the students*

(continued)

Table 1 (continued)

Question	Task 1: Investigating straight line graphs	Task 2: Controlling characters with equations
	The position of the intercept on the y-axis. *This was accessible to students* The value of 'c' as displayed in the equation. *This was visible to the students* The y-value when x = 0, which can be observed in the Table view. *This functionality was not used by the students during the lesson*	
What forms of interaction with the multi-representational technology will reveal the desired manifestation?	Having decided whether to vary the value of m or c, students could vary these values by: Inputting the right hand side of equations in the form 'mx + c' (the left hand syntax is given automatically by the tool, i.e. fn(x) = where n increases by one to define each new function.) Dragging the position of the line using one of two 'hotspots. A rotate hotspot - to vary the gradient around the point (0, c) and a translate hotspot to vary the value of c, whilst maintaining the gradient. *In the lesson concerned, the students did not interact with the graphs in this way*	Editing the graph to vary the gradient/speed and overall travel time, as shown in Figs. 7 and 8 Editing the equation to vary the gradient/speed
What labelling and referencing notations will support the articulation and communication of the generalisation that is being sought?	Multiple functions were visible at the same time, each with its own reference, i.e. f3(x) = 2x + 3. This could result in a 'pile-up' of representations as seen in Figs. 2, 3, 4 and 5	The representations referred to a single animation of the character (Shakey). The initial animation represented the reference point to which the animations of 'Slow Shakey' and 'Fast Shakey' could be compared
What might the 'flow' of mathematical representations (with and without technology) look like as a means to illuminate and make sense of the generalisation?	Function input (using algebraic notation) Observation of resulting graph in graphics view Further input(s) of function(s) and observation/comparison of resulting graphs in graphics view	Playing of animation Observation of: the emergent trace of the line segment; the highlighted values in the table; and the overall appearance of the graph on the given axes

(continued)

Table 1 (continued)

Question	Task 1: Investigating straight line graphs	Task 2: Controlling characters with equations
	[Away from the technology] Justification of why a higher/lower value of m (or c) affects the graph in particular ways Reveal the Table view for particular equations to identify key features that relate to particular values of 'm' and 'c'	Varying the animation by editing one of the variables as described in Figs. 7, 8 and 9, which would lead to multiple 'flows' of representations, dependent on the focus of attention
What forms of interaction between the students and teacher will support the generalisation to be more widely communicated?	Discussion to ensure that students focus on varying either 'm' or 'c' in the first instance Discussion about the notation Discussion to highlight how particular equations generate particular lines and of their distinctive features. This would involve direct interaction with the software, including inputting equations and dragging lines to new positions Discussion to relate the distinctive features of the lines and equation to the distinctive features of the related function machine and table of values	Discussion to relate the distinctive features of the initial animation to the graph, table of values and equation. This would involve direct interaction with the software Discussion to highlight how the different hotspots on the graph affect the animation, graph, table of values and equation. This would involve direct interaction with the software to edit the graph and/or equation
How might the original example space be expanded to incorporate broader related generalisations?	The flexibility of the tool would enable the students to: • Reveal the table of values in order to make generalisations about the relationship between the function and its displayed values • Input other families of functions, such as quadratics and cubics • Explore how 'zooming' in and out of the graphing window affects the gradient both visually and numerically	The flexibility of the tool would enable the students to: • Edit the scenario to vary the start position of the character (i.e. to vary 'c') and to show backward motion, i.e. graphs of negative gradient • Explore how 'zooming' in and out of the graphing window affects the gradient both visually and numerically

5 Conclusions

The analysis of the two task examples, which had both been designed to introduce the concept of linear functions to lower secondary students in a dynamic technological environment reveals subtle tensions that relate to the mathematical knowledge that is being addressed by the task and aspects of the process of task design.

5.1 Mathematical Knowledge

It is clear that different aspects of mathematical knowledge concerning linear functions were being addressed by the two tasks, with the first task adopting a pure mathematical context whereas the second task involved a realistic motion context. However, both tasks sought to involve students in explorations of the variant and invariant properties of linear functions.

The analysis does indicate that the cognitive load for Task 1 is higher as it not only requires the students to begin by choosing which variable they will focus on but the task also relies on them making sense of:

- which line relates to which function;
- the particular notation adopted by the tool (i.e. $\mathbf{f17}(x) = 5 \cdot x + 2$);
- and the range of values of x that is automatically plotted.

Consequently, although the task enables students to be 'successful' in that they can notice the most obvious generalizations—that the value of 'm' controls the appearance of the graph and that greater values of 'm' result in steeper lines—the task did not provide opportunities for students to link this with other representations in the technology, in particular the table of values, which would have enabled a deeper justification.[5]

By contrast, even though Task 2 involved more representations on the screen that were dynamically linked, each animation generated an example for which the links between the representations had been made visually explicit. By looking at fewer linear functions in a greater depth, it is possible for students to recognize key features within each representation and, therefore be better placed to be able to see the connections between them. This presents a tension for the designer. Does she offer a task environment that gives a global view of the mathematical domain using multiply-linked representations and then 'zoom' in on particular features to reveal particular variant and invariant properties or does she offer a focused view and subsequently 'pan-out' to support the student to connect the variant and invariant properties within the dynamically connected representations?

---

[5]The teacher did begin the lesson by reminding the students that, in order to generate each graph, the computer used a 'function machine'—an idea and representation that was familiar to the students.

This highlights the complexity of the initial task design process in defining the mathematical domain that a task is intended to address, the nature of the initial example space and the intended user pathway through this space that incorporates different 'instrument utilization schema' (Verillon and Rabardel 1995). Increasingly, when designing tasks within dynamic mathematical environments, designers are including follow-on tasks away from the technology that support students to make more explicit links with the formal paper and pencil methods. For example, in the technology-mediated aspects of Task 2, which emphasizes the mathematical content of position-time graphs and the concept of speed, it was necessary to provide accompanying tasks away from the computer. These tasks required students to work flexibly from different mathematical starting points to develop a complete set of mathematical representations and support them to work fluently between these representations. For example, given some key values within the table of values, could they construct the related equation and graph?

5.2   Design Principles—Technology and Tasks

It is important to (re)state that Task 1 was designed by a teacher for use in her own classroom as part of her early experiences with a new software tool. This example has been selected here as it typifies a genre of tasks that have been prevalent within technology use in English classrooms. However, although prevalent, this task approach has not been widely used and, on reflection, the post-priori analysis provided by the task design rubric may offer some insight into why such tasks have not become embedded within localised schemes of work. The very open nature of the task coupled with the resulting display of the software may have been sufficient for students to draw a broad conclusion, but there may have been insufficient direction in the task design to draw students' direct attention to key features, that is to support them to 'notice' important aspects of the graph. Interestingly, the functionality is present in the software to support this further work, for example, to reveal the table of values. However, in the teacher's early lesson design, she was either unaware or chose not to use this representation within the task.

By comparison, Task 2 was designed by a team that involved software designers, researchers and teachers over several years, and the task included multiple dynamic representations of several particular functions. The analysis of Task 2 using the design rubric, supported by evidence of students' outcomes suggest that the cognitive load of Task 2 was manageable for the students. In some ways this could be seen as an example of *discrepancy potential*, as described by Leung and Bolite-Frant (2015), whereby the limitations of one tool might be complemented by the affordances of another. The more contained example space in Task 2 enabled students to be successful in their early work, but it may also have constrained some students from making other mathematical insights, for example exploring non-linear functions. This highlights a tension when designers choose whether designing a task in an existing mathematical technological environment or to create a completely new digital space that is wholly 'bespoke' for its intended mathematical purposes. Given the multitude of existing tools that might be suited to early explorations of linear functions (Graphing calculators, GeoGebra, Autograph, TI-Nspire, The Geometer's Sketchpad, SimCalc..), why create another environment?

The task design rubric includes an important consideration that seems critical to this early consideration in the design process, 'ascertaining the forms of interaction with the tool that reveal the desired variant/invariant properties'. This requires a deep knowledge of the tool's mathematical affordances and constraints. For example, if, as in Task 1, we choose to explore linear functions using TI-Nspire handhelds, there are many alternative tasks that could be designed to explore gradient and intercept properties. The software file could be pre-written with 'm' and 'c' predefined and the table of values visible. Students could have a more directed task in which they are instructed to change particular values (i.e. vary the value of 'm' by dragging an on-screen slider) to meet certain constraints and to observe particular features.

The resolution of this dilemma involves many considerations that include the need for the designer's deep understanding of the mathematical content appropriate to the students, its representations and connections alongside a level of familiarity with affordances and constraints of existing software tools. However, repeated research studies have shown over many years that, as it is a teacher's principle role to be a task designer, it is important that teachers have opportunities to work alongside more experienced colleagues, researchers and task designers to develop this aspect of their role (Noss et al. 1991; Clark-Wilson 2008; Artigue 1998).

5.3   Implications and Further Research

In concluding this chapter, it is important to highlight one aspect of the task design rubric for which there was insufficient data from the post-priori analysis of the two tasks to draw any substantial conclusions. This concerns the forms of interaction between teacher and students to support mathematical generalizations. These interactions might be evident in teachers' lesson designs (i.e. a 'lesson plan'), but can only be robustly researched through lesson observations and interviews. Within English teaching practices, it is most common for teachers to share teaching resources with each other and, in the case of digital lesson resources this is usually the software file and/or the task 'idea'. It is far less common for these resources to include the teacher's narrative to accompany how a task is introduced, developed and assessed. Hence the 'blank' page start with a digital tool adopted by the first example is a common one. It required little advanced preparation, that is, the software file did not need to be made available to students via the school network for the beginning of the lesson.

Other studies have revealed the subtleties of the teacher's role within technology-mediated lessons of this type as it demands a high level of teacher interaction, not just with the students but also involving the software tool itself (Aldon 2011; Clark-Wilson 2010). The teacher is required to have a depth of instrumentalisation with the software such that she can select particular cases, change and display key features in order to support the discourse such that generalizations can emerge, be formalised and ultimately proven.

The nature of teachers' 'mathematical pedagogic practices' whilst designing and teaching technology-mediated lessons is a research focus for a 3-year study in England, funded by the Nuffield Foundation[6] and co-directed by Celia Hoyles and myself. Set in the context of the Cornerstone Maths project, we have a adopted a lesson study approach to the design, implementation and evaluation of 'landmark activities' (Clark-Wilson et al. 2015) within each curriculum unit that aims to articulate teachers' practices.

Acknowledgments This chapter draws on research from two studies. The *TI-Nspire* evaluation study was funded by Texas Instruments and has been subsequently reported in Clark-Wilson (2008). *Cornerstone Maths* was generously funded by the Li Ka Shing Foundation as a multi-year collaborative project between London Knowledge Lab, UCL Institute of Education and SRI International, USA, and directed by Celia Hoyles, Richard Noss, Jeremy Roschelle and Phil Vahey.

References

Aldon, G. (2011). *Interactions didactiques dans la classe de mathématiques en environnement numérique: construction et mise à l'épreuve d'un cadre d'analyse exploitant la notion d'incident.* Thèse de doctorat, Université Lyon 1, Lyon.

Artigue, M. (1998). Teacher training as a key issue for the integration of computer technologies. In D. Tinsley & D. Johnson (Eds.), *Proceedings of the IFIP TC3/WG3.1 Working Conference on Secondary School Mathematics in the World of Communication Technology: Learning, Teaching, and the Curriculum: Information and Communications Technologies in School Mathematics* (Vol. 119, pp. 121–129). London: Chapman and Hall.

Bussi, M. G. B., & Mariotti, M. A. (2008). Semiotic mediation in the mathematics classroom: Artifacts and signs after a Vygotskian perspective. In L. English (Ed.), *Handbook of international research in mathematics education* (2nd ed., pp. 746–783). London: Routledge.

Clark-Wilson, A. (2008). *Evaluating TI-Nspire[TM] in secondary mathematics classrooms: research report.* Chichester, UK: University of Chichester.

Clark-Wilson, A. (2010). How does a multi-representational mathematical ICT tool mediate teachers' mathematical and pedagogical knowledge concerning variance and invariance? *Institute of Education, PhD thesis.*

Clark-Wilson, A., Hoyles, C. & Noss, R. (2015a). Conceptualising the scaling of mathematics teachers' professional development concerning technology. In J. Novotna (Ed.), *9th congress of european research on mathematics education, Prague, Czech Republic, 4th –8th February 2015.* Czech Republic: Charles University.

[6]More information can be found at: http://www.nuffieldfoundation.org/developing-teachers-mathematical-knowledge-using-digital-technology.

Clark-Wilson, A., Hoyles, C., Noss, R., Vahey, P., & Roschelle, J. (2015b). Scaling a technology-based innovation: Windows on the evolution of mathematics teachers' practices. *ZDM Mathematics Education, 47*(1), 79–92. doi:10.1007/s11858-014-0635-6.

Clark-Wilson, A. & Timotheus, J. (2013). Designing tasks within a multi-representational technological environment: An emerging rubric. In C. Margolinas (Ed.), *ICMI study 22 task design in mathematics education* (Vol. 1, pp. 47–54). UK: Oxford.

Department for Children Schools and Families (2007). National curriculum for mathematics. London, UK: Qualifications and Curriculum Agency.

Department of Education (2013). *The national curriculum in England: Key stages 3 and 4 framework document* London: Department of Education.

Drijvers, P. (2012). Teachers transforming resources into orchestrations. In G. Gueudet, B. Pepin, & L. Trouche (Eds.), *From text to lived resources: Mathematics curriculum material and teacher development*. Berlin: Springer.

Drijvers, P., & Trouche, L. (2008). From artifacts to instruments: A theoretical framework behind the orchestra metaphor. In G. Blume & K. Heid (Eds.), *Research on technology in the learning and teaching of mathematics: Syntheses, cases and perspectives* (Vol. 2, pp. 363–392)., Cases and perspectives Charlotte: National Council of Teachers of Mathematics/Information Age Publishing.

Godwin, S., & Sutherland, R. (2004). Whole-class technology for learning mathematics: The case of functions and graphs. *Education Communication and Information, 4*(1), 131–152.

Gueudet, G., & Trouche, L. (2009). Towards new documentation systems for mathematics teachers? *Educational Studies in Mathematics, 71*(3), 199–218.

Guin, D., & Trouche, L. (1999). The complex process of converting tools into mathematical instruments: The case of calculators. *International Journal of Computers for Mathematical Learning, 3*(3), 195–227.

Haspekian, M. (2014). Teachers' instrumental geneses when integrating spreadsheet software. In A. Clark-Wilson, O. Robutti, & N. Sinclair (Eds.), *The mathematics teacher in the digital era: an international perspective on technology focused professional development* (pp. 241–276). Dordrecht: Springer.

Hegedus, & Roschelle, J. (2013). *The SimCalc vision and contributions*. Netherlands: Springer.

Hoyles, C., Noss, R., Vahey, P., & Roschelle, J. (2013). Cornerstone Mathematics: Designing digital technology for teacher adaptation and scaling. *ZDM, 45*(7), 1057–1070.

Kaput, J. (1986). Information technology and mathematics: Opening new representational windows. *Journal of Mathematical Behavior, 5*(2), 187–207.

Kaput, J., & Schorr, R. (2008). Changing representational infrastructures changes most everything: The case of SimCalc, algebra and calculus. In G. Blume, & K. Heid (Eds.), *Research on technology in the learning and teaching of mathematics: Syntheses, cases and perspectives. Vol 2 Cases and perspectives* (Vol. 2, pp. 211–254). Charlotte: National Council of Teachers of Mathematics/Information Age Publishing.

Leung, A., & Bolite-Frant, J. (2015). Designing mathematics tasks: The role of tools. In Anne Watson & Minoru Ohtani (Eds.), *Task Design in Mathematics Education: The 22nd ICMI Study (New ICMI Study Series)* (pp. 191–225). New York: Springer.

Margolinas, C. (2013). *Proceedings of the ICMI Study Conference 22: Task design in mathematics education* (Vol. 1). UK: Oxford.

Mason, J., Graham, A., & Johnston-Wilder, S. (Eds.). (2005). *Developing thinking in algebra*. London: Sage Publications Ltd.

Noss, R., Sutherland, R., & Hoyles, C. (1991). Final Report of the Microworlds Project Vol. II: Teacher attitudes and interactions. London: Institute of Education.

Office for Standards in Education. (2008). *Mathematics: Understanding the score*. London: Department for Children, Schools and Families.

Office for Standards in Education. (2012). *Mathematics: Made to measure*. London: Department for Children, Schools and Families.

Pierce, R., & Stacey, K. (2008). Using pedagogical maps to show the opportunities afforded by CAS for improving the teaching of mathematics. *Australian Senior Mathematics Journal, 22* (1), 6–12.

Ruthven, K., & Hennessy, S. (2003). A teacher perspective on successful ICT use in secondary mathematics teaching. *Micromath, 19*(2), 20–24.

SRI International, C. f. T. i. L., & Institute of Education, U. o. L. (2013). *Teacher guide: Designing mobile games: A module on linear functions*. London: Institute of Education.

Texas Instruments (2007b). *TI-Nspire^{TM} Software Guide*. Dallas, TX: Texas Instruments.

Trouche, L. (2004). Managing the complexity of human/machine interactions in computerized learning environments: Guiding students' command process through instrumental orchestrations. *International Journal of Computers for Mathematical Learning, 9*, 281–307.

Vahey, P., Knudsen, J., Rafanan, K., & Lara-Meloy, T. (2013). Curricular activity systems supporting the use of dynamic representations to foster students' deep understanding of mathematics. In C. Mouza & N. Lavigne (Eds.), *Emerging technologies for the classroom: A learning sciences perspective* (pp. 15–30). New York: Springer.

Verillon, P., & Rabardel, P. (1995). Cognition and artefacts: A contribution to the study of thought in relation to instrumented activity. *European Journal of Psychology of Education, 10*(1), 77–102.

Wertsch, J. (1981). *The concept of activity in Soviet psychology*. New York: ME Sharpe.

Erratum to: What Can You Infer from This Example? Applications of Online, Rich-Media Tasks for Enhancing Pre-service Teachers' Knowledge of the Roles of Examples in Proving

Orly Buchbinder, Iris Zodik, Gila Ron and Alice L.J. Cook

Erratum to:
Chapter "What Can You Infer from This Example? Applications of Online, Rich-Media Tasks for Enhancing Pre-service Teachers' Knowledge of the Roles of Examples in Proving" in: A. Leung and A. Baccaglini-Frank (eds.), *Digital Technologies in Designing Mathematics Education Tasks*, Mathematics Education in the Digital Era 8, DOI 10.1007/978-3-319-43423-0_11

In the originally published version of the chapter, Figure 4 in Chapter "What Can You Infer from This Example? Applications of Online, Rich-Media Tasks for Enhancing Pre-service Teachers' Knowledge of the Roles of Examples in Proving" was portrait oriented and downsized, hence the text was virtually unreadable. The erratum of the book has been updated with the change.

The online version of the original chapter can be found under DOI 10.1007/978-3-319-43423-0_11

O. Buchbinder (✉)
University on New Hampshire, Durham, NH, USA
e-mail: orlybuchbinder@gmail.com

I. Zodik · G. Ron
Technion, Israel Institute of Technology, Haifa, Israel

G. Ron
Ohalo College, Katzrin, Israel

A.L.J. Cook
University of Maryland, College Park, MD, USA

© Springer International Publishing Switzerland 2017   E1
A. Leung and A. Baccaglini-Frank (eds.), *Digital Technologies in Designing Mathematics Education Tasks*, Mathematics Education in the Digital Era 8,
DOI 10.1007/978-3-319-43423-0_17

Task parts / Task characteristics	Part I: Examination of a given statement and determining its truth value	Part II: Examination of students' examples	Part III: Analysis of the classroom scenario and making suggestions for a class discussion	Part IV: Reflection and participation in a discussion forum	Post-task whole class discussion
Pedagogy of enactment	—	Decomposition and representation	Representation and approximation	—	—
Goals and Learning Opportunities — Content-oriented	Engagement with mathematical content and determine truth-value of the statement.	Opportunity to expand personal example space and change decision about the statement in light of new evidence.	Examine questions such as: What does it mean to contradict a universal statement? How many counterexamples can a statement have?	Participation in the community of learners. Opportunity to discuss and clarify content- and pedagogy-oriented ideas. Opportunity for collective reflection on the learning process in each part of the task and as a whole.	Opportunity to share, reflect on and enhance both personal and shared understanding of the status of examples in proving by exposure to the theoretical framework, and expanding the repertoire of the relevant pedagogical approaches.
Goals and Learning Opportunities — Pedagogy-oriented	—	Interpretation of students' thinking. Opportunity to envision oneself as a teacher facilitating a proof oriented task. Teacher's role is implicit.	Planning a whole-class discussion and support students' understanding of the status of examples in proving. Teacher's role is explicit.		
Individual / Group interaction:	Individual	Individual	Individual	Group	Group
Digital technology interaction: Direct / Indirect	Direct	Direct	Direct	Direct	Indirect (but referenced to the digital task)
Facilitation type: No MTE facilitation / With MTE facilitation	No MTE (Mathematics Teacher Educator) facilitation	No MTE (Mathematics Teacher Educator) facilitation	No MTE (Mathematics Teacher Educator) facilitation	No MTE (Mathematics Teacher Educator) facilitation	With MTE facilitation

Fig. 4 The framework for design of media-rich tasks for PSTs

Index

CPSIA information can be obtained
at www.ICGtesting.com
Printed in the USA
LVHW011658041118
595906LV00003B/40/P